Cultural Turn

University of the
West of England

BRISTOL

**BOLLAND
LIBRARY**

Please ensure that this book is returned by the end of
the loan period for which it is issued.

3 0. NOV 2000	2 4. MAY 2007
0 8. MAY 2001	1 3. NOV 2008
1 0. OCT 2001	
2 2. JAN 2002	
1 6. MAY 2002	
0 5. NOV. 2002	
1 6. OCT 2006	
13 Nov 06	
11 Dec 06	

Telephone Renewals: 0117 344 3757
Library Web Address: http://www.uwe.ac.uk/library/

Culture and Economy
after the
Cultural Turn

edited by
Larry Ray and Andrew Sayer

SAGE Publications
London • Thousand Oaks • New Delhi

First published 1999

SAGE Publications Ltd
6 Bonhill Street
London EC2A 4PU

SAGE Publications Inc.
2455 Teller Road
Thousand Oaks, California 91320

SAGE Publications India Pvt Ltd
32, M-Block Market
Greater Kailash – I
New Delhi 110 048

British Library Cataloguing in Publication data

A catalogue record for this book is available
from the British Library

ISBN 0 7619 5816 9
ISBN 0 7619 5817 7 (pbk)

Library of Congress catalog card record available

Typeset by Mayhew Typesetting, Rhayader, Powys
Printed and bound in Great Britain by Athenaeum Press,
Gateshead

Contents

Notes on contributors

Harriet Bradley is Senior Lecturer in the Department of Sociology, University of Bristol. Her research interests include gender, especially women's employment, social inequalities, trade unions and industrial relations. She is the author of *Gender and Power in the Workplace* (1998), *Fractured Identities* (1996) and *Men's Work, Women's Work* (1989).

Stephen Driver is a Senior Lecturer in Sociology and Social Policy at the Roehampton Institute, London, where he teaches government and politics. He is co-author with Luke Martell of *New Labour: Politics after Thatcherism* (1998). He has previously done research on the cultural industries and is currently working on the new media in Britain.

Mary Evans is a Professor in the Department of Sociology, University of Kent at Canterbury. Her books include *Missing Persons* (1999), *Introducing Contemporary Feminist Thought* (1997), *Simone de Beauvoir: A Feminist Mandarin* (1985) and *The Battle for Britain: Citizenship and Ideology in the Second World War* (1993), with David Morgan.

Steve Fenton is Head of Department of Sociology, Bristol University. He has written widely on ethnicity and is presently working on an ESRC project connecting health, ethnicity and socio-economic position; and, with Tariq Modood, on a study of ethnicity and staffs of higher education institutions.

Patricia Findlay is Senior Lecturer in Organisation Studies, Department of Business Studies, University of Edinburgh. Current research includes the area of organization theory generally, and specifically performance appraisal and employee response to organizational change.

Nancy Fraser is Henry A. and Louise Loeb Professor of Political Science and Philosophy in the New School of Social Research in New York. She has published widely on feminism and social and political theory. She is the author of *Unruly Practices* (1989) and *Justice Interruptus* (1997), a co-author of *Feminist Contentions: A Philosophical Exchange* (1995) with

Seyla Benhabib, Judith Butler and Drusilla Cornell, *Adding Insult to Injury: Social Justice and the Politics of Recognition* and *Redistribution or Regnition? A Philosophical Exchange* (2000) with Axel Honneth.

Russell Keat is Professor of Political Theory in the Department of Politics, University of Edinburgh. He co-edited *Enterprise Culture* (1992) with Nicholas Abercrombie, and *The Authority of the Consumer* (1994) with Nigel Whiteley and Nicholas Abercrombie. A collection of his essays on market boundaries and cultural goods is shortly to be published.

Luke Martell is Senior Lecturer in Sociology, University of Sussex. His interests lie in political sociology in relation to social democracy, socialism and the green movement. He is the author of *Ecology and Society* (1994) and co-author with Stephen Driver of *New Labour: Politics after Thatcherism* (1998).

John O'Neill is a Professor in the Department of Philosophy, Lancaster University. He works on political philosophy and theory, with special interest in environmental philosophy. He is author of *Worlds without Content* (1991), *Ecology, Policy and Politics* (1994) and *The Market: Ethics, Knowledge and Politics* (1998).

Larry Ray is a Professor in the Department of Sociology at the University of Kent at Canterbury. His recent publications include *Theorizing Classical Sociology* (1999), *Social Theory and the Crisis of State Socialism* (1996) and *Rethinking Critical Theory* (1993).

Andrew Sayer is Professor of Social Theory and Political Economy in the Department of Sociology, Lancaster University. He is author of *Method in Social Science* (1992), *The New Social Economy* (1992) with R.A. Walker, and *Radical Political Economy: A Critique* (1995) and *Realism and Social Science* (in press).

Bronislaw Szerszynski is Lecturer in Environment and Culture at the Centre for the Study of Environmental Change, Lancaster University. His research interests include risk and modernity, religious and philosophical aspects of environmentalism, social movements, lifestyles and the media. He is co-author with Scott Lash and Brian Wynne of *Risk, Environment and Modernity* (1996).

Paul Thompson is Professor of Organizational Analysis in the Department of Human Resource Management, University of Strathclyde. His research and publishing interests focus on organization theory, the labour process and workplace innovation. Recently published work includes *Workplaces of the Future* (1999), co-edited with Chris Warhurst and *Organisational Misbehaviour* (1999) with Stephen Ackroyd.

Nigel Thrift is a Professor and Head of the School of Geographical Sciences at the University of Bristol. His chief interests are social and cultural theory, new forms of capitalism, and the historical geography of time. Recent books include *Spatial Formations* (1995), *Mapping the Subject* (1995) co-edited with Steve Pile, *Money/Space* (1994) with Andrew Leyshon, and *Shopping, Place and Identity* (1998) with Daniel Miller, Peter Jackson, Beverley Holbrook and Mike Rowlands.

Acknowledgements

We would like to thank Lancaster University's Political Economy Group and the Institute for Cultural Research (formerly the Centre for the Study of Cultural Values), particularly Paul Heelas, for supporting this project and we also thank all the contributors to this volume.

Introduction

Larry Ray and Andrew Sayer

The cultural turn

One of the most striking features of social science at the end of twentieth century has been a growth of interest in culture and a turn away from economy. The cultural turn has been especially strong in radical social science and studies of history, including a turn towards discourse and away from materialism and the Marxist-influenced political economy which was so strong in the 1970s and early 1980s (Barrett, 1992). What was previously secondary, merely superstructural, is now primary, and notions of structure are regarded as suspect in many circles. Where previously language reflected material being, it is now treated as itself the 'house of being'. Where previously radicals were concerned with capitalism, they now talk of modernity and postmodernity. Postmodernism itself is overwhelmingly cultural in its concerns, with economics notable by its absence, political economy being presumably tainted by its association with materialism and grand narratives. Nevertheless there are many parallels between postmodernism and the more political-economic discourse of neoliberalism, such as their suspicion of grand narratives/ theories and affirmation of local knowledges, their resistance to paternalism and normative discourse (Sayer, 1995). However, the parallels are rarely acknowledged. Such is the dominance of concerns with discourse and difference that even to mention the categories of political economy is to appear hopelessly passé. Yet not even the strongest enthusiasts for cultural studies can deny the continued importance of economic matters, for they are obliged to acknowledge it in their lives even if they ignore it in their writing. As a famous slogan from Bill Clinton's first election campaign put it, the key issue was 'the economy, stupid!'. On the other hand, there are arguments that, despite such slogans, it has actually been the cultural dimension of politics which has been decisive of late.

In this book we present a number of responses to the changing relationship between culture and economy. The collection is motivated by curiosity about the reasons for the 'cultural turn' in much social science, and the corresponding decline of interest in (political) economy, plus the paradox of it happening at a time of widening economic divisions and increasing economic problems. It explores the dialectic of culture and economy from a range of standpoints and in relation to substantive topics, in particular concerning politics and workplace culture. It asks whether societies are changing in ways which involve a new relationship between culture and economy. In so doing it provides some insights regarding the connection or lack of connection between the cultural turn in academia and life outside. It also confronts a diverse range of concrete issues, thereby testing more general and abstract claims made about culture, economy and politics. Thus, for example, the question of whether there is a cultural turn in politics is answered in relation to post-communist transition, environmental politics, Britain's New Labour, and the politics of recognition. In engaging with these issues, we hope incidentally to throw new light on debates about post-modernism versus modernism. As the paradox of the turn away from economy and the persistence of economic forces and problems becomes evermore glaring and intolerable, the need for these issues to be addressed grows stronger.

There are many positive effects of the cultural turn – both in taking culture, discourse and subjectivity more seriously and in escaping from reductionist treatments of culture as mere reflection of material situation. Materialist analyses of culture, race and gender had difficulty addressing their discursive content in its own right and acknowledging its relative autonomy from material circumstances. Feminism combined a cultural turn with a psychoanalytic turn, in particular exploring the discourse, subjective experience and meanings associated with gender difference which earlier socialist feminism had inadequately addressed. Consumption has been rescued from the often dismissive and negative treatment it received at the hands of Marxists. Post-colonial literature has looked beyond economic imperialism to illuminate the pervasive effects of cultural imperialism in discourse and the social construction of identities. Where materialist treatments of race and gender could explain their economic effects and implications but not their sources, insofar as these lay in cultural and psychological processes, the cultural turn opened these up to scrutiny.

Why then, has there been a cultural turn? It could be construed as largely endogenous to academia – as simply a stage in the development of academic thought: but it would be surprising if it bore no relation to changes in society, culture and politics at large. In diverse recent works, including Lash and Urry's *Economies of Signs and Space* (1994) and Crook et al.'s *Postmodernization* (1994), it is claimed that contemporary societies have experienced a collapse of the boundaries between economy and culture. Crook et al. argue that culture is gaining the effectivity once ascribed to material relations. These ideas are part of a wider movement in the social sciences, resonating with concerns such as the aestheticization of everyday life and the shift from material to symbolic consumption. It links up too with a considerable amount of work on postmodernism. Such claims about 'culturalization' challenge classical formulations of the problem, which presupposed culture and economy as mutually interacting, but separate, institutional orders.

The cultural turn further coincides with the decline of socialism and the diversification of concerns of radical politics beyond economic questions of distribution to cultural questions of recognition (Fraser, 1995). Research into forms of domination and division that went beyond those deriving from capital and class was long overdue. In academic circles, the growth of feminism and research on ethnicity helped raise awareness of the dangers of class reductionism and of how the pursuit of equality could invoke a spurious universalism, which actually masked particularism and suppressed difference. However, outside academia, declining concern with equality has arguably less to do with postmodernism and more to do with the rise of neoliberalism and individualism, and the decline of the Keynesian welfare state. Politics has become more pluralist; yet, as Gregor McLennan (1995) observes, where radical social scientists previously used to dismiss pluralism by arguing that it dealt merely with appearances and failed to see the force of the underlying structures of capitalism, many have now turned pluralist themselves. This is apparent in their insistence on de-differentiation and the primacy of difference, even if they prefer not to acknowledge the similarities to the older pluralism and indeed to liberalism.

Yet the cultural turn is more puzzling in relation to the continuing prominence of economic matters in everyday life and mainstream politics – unless it is simply a sign of academic ghettoization, in which the social and ideological distance between the more abstruse postmodernist theory and popular discourse is huge. One interpretation of the paradox is that the new fronts on which radicals now work, together with postmodernism's textual radicalism, have allowed radical academics to maintain their radicalism, and indeed even to outdo the old New Left, without having to make any painful concessions to the ascendant New Right (Eagleton, 1995; Sayer, 1995). As we have already noted, the irony of this is that there are striking affinities as well as differences between postmodernism and liberalism, concealed by the contrast between the cultural character of the former and the overwhelmingly political and economic character of the latter.

In the case of feminism, it is not clear why the cultural turn should have been accompanied by such a marked decline in interest in economic aspects of gender. It is not explained by the fact that men dominate political economy, for that is what has to be explained, and in any case, 1970s socialist feminism did take economy seriously. Moreover, given that women suffer more than men from economic problems one might have expected larger numbers of women to have moved into the study of political economy. A relatively small number of feminist researchers continue to work on economy (e.g. Folbre, 1992; Nelson, 1996; Jackson and Pearson, 1998). But as Harriet Bradley and Steve Fenton note in this volume, they tend to have been absorbed into mainstream social studies and have not been seen as part of the vanguard of feminist theory, which is overwhelmingly cultural in focus.

In these and other cases, there are intriguing shifts in the relationships between culture and economy and in the approaches to them. In what follows we begin by discussing the basic terms of the debate, whether the culture–economy distinction is tenable, and what its political significance might be. We then review possible changes in the relationship between culture and economy in terms of the social and cultural embeddedness of economic activities, in consumption, in workplace culture and, at greater length, with regard to politics.

Defining 'culture' and 'economy'

There is little doubt that arguments about an increasingly close relationship between economy and culture can point to processes which, if not entirely new, are growing. Some authors have even argued that the distinction is no longer tenable (e.g. Hall, 1988; Jameson, 1990; Lash, 1990). In the discussions which preceded this volume, our attempts to define and distinguish culture and economy often met with scepticism, though no one offered an alternative way of making the distinction. Significantly, those who have expressed scepticism about the distinction are unable to stop referring to the cultural and the economic separately, which suggests that we actually still need it. We would argue that there are still crucial differences between culture and economy, and that it is politically as well as theoretically important to understand them. 'Culture' and 'economy' are not synonyms. If they were, we could interchange them without causing any problems – for example, 'Cultural Studies' courses could be renamed 'Economic Studies', and vice versa, and no one would be misled. Since they certainly *would* be misled, 'culture' and 'economy' must be different, and hence it ought to be possible to say what the difference is. Yet neither are they antonyms, and neither do they refer to separable 'spheres' of social life. Furthermore, since the basic terms have several meanings, there may be more than one culture–economy distinction. Our contributors have differing views on the distinction, but here we set out one version of it as an invitation or provocation to further debate.

As Raymond Williams famously demonstrated, 'culture' is formidably polysemic (Williams, 1958). The 'anthropological' definition of culture (used, at times by Williams himself) as a 'whole way of life', is too broad to succeed in distinguishing anything. If this is what culture is, then of course economy must already be included in it. Often, however, one finds that it isn't: the danger is that appealing to this definition allows authors to pass off what are actually selective accounts – ignoring economy – as if they were inclusive (Hall, 1997), thereby engaging in a kind of cultural or anthropological imperialism. Arguably, this is what has happened in the cultural turn. Attempts to drop the distinction merely allow culture to swamp economy, reducing the latter to a simplistic and highly questionable grand narrative about 'Fordism and post-Fordism', whose understanding, as Eagleton notes, requires less economic knowledge than is needed for reading the financial pages of the newspapers. Yet the narrower sense of culture noted by Williams as 'artistic and intellectual activities' now seems to carry connotations of high culture and needs broadening to include popular cultural activities of sport and entertainment, fashion and advertising. It is culture in this sense that is the primary focus of Russell Keat's contribution to this collection. In this respect, as Williams noted, there is some convergence towards the broader, anthropological definition of culture (Williams, 1977).

Common to all uses of 'culture' is a concern with practices and relationships to which meanings, symbols or representations are central: in short, 'signifying practices'. These patterns give meaning to, and orient social behaviour, within particular groups. Since any and every social act can be a signifying practice, culture is everywhere. However, this does not mean that culture is everything, that the only thing that goes on in society is signifying practice, or that the signifying aspects of practices and artefacts exhaust all we need know about them. Things also happen to people regardless of discourses or the level of meaning, and the effects of the formal economy are particularly important in this respect.

Although they are hardly ever constructed under egalitarian conditions, cultural phenomena must in some sense be shared, even if they are contested; they cannot simply be imposed. This is because the realm of meaning is at least immanently dialogical. As critical theorists have argued, even where there are attempts to impose meanings, the processes of communication cannot reduce wholly to monologic transmission, and the same must go for culture (Williams, 1958; Lash and Urry, 1994).

A crucial feature of many of the goals or goods associated with culture is that they are primarily internal (Sayer, 1997). For example, the elderly or a certain kind of music might be valued, but this respect or value is not accorded merely in order to achieve some external goal, but because the elderly or that kind of music are valued in themselves.[1] In saying that these values are intrinsic we do not mean that the objects are beautiful or good in themselves, independently of a subject or of discourse, for value is always relational. By intrinsic we merely mean non-instrumental. Although some things – such as a BMW – may sometimes be valued as a means to an end, often of distinguishing ourselves from others, they may also be valued for their own particular qualities. Sometimes their function as signifier of distinction may be conditional on their intrinsic qualities; the BMW would not be a source of prestige for its owner if it were unreliable and awful to drive.

Cultural norms and values regarding actions are, at least in part, judged as good or bad in themselves rather than purely in terms of their consequences. However, while stressing the normative, moral element within cultures, it is important not to idealize them, since some norms may actually be repressive. The intrinsic values of sexism and racism are cases in point. The relationship between culture and economy should therefore not be coded: culture (good), economy (bad).

By contrast, economic activities and processes involve a primarily instrumental orientation; they are ultimately a means to an end, satisfying external goals to do with provisioning. Economic work may of course be satisfying in itself as well as a means to an end, and while this is obviously desirable, the work itself is rarely more important than its product, be it material production or interpersonal work such as childcare. The needs which the economy provides for include not merely transhistorical physical needs but ones which are social, aesthetic and geohistorically-specific, such as beer-drinking or wearing jeans, and even the transhistorical or species-wide needs are always met in culturally specific ways. Economic activities are always culturally inflected or 'embedded' (Granovetter, 1985). There is no way in which they could be conducted independently of systems of meanings and norms. 'The economy' is as much a cultural site as any other part of society, such as the family, community or school, but while mainstream economists abstract from the cultural side, political economists and institutional economists have been increasingly willing to consider both.

The form of the union of the economic and the cultural is almost certainly changing but since there has always been some such union, despite their different logics, we are looking at a transhistorical, rather than a postmodern, phenomenon. However, this does not imply that the distinction between the economic and cultural is untenable. To speak of a unity does not preclude the possibility that culture and economy may follow separate logics of development. Following Weber's concept of differentiated value spheres, for example, Habermas offers a multi-dimensional theory of social change in which the economy and culture represent two different dimensions of social learning that are nonetheless dependent on one another (e.g. Habermas, 1979: 152ff; Ray, 1993: 38–46). The meaningful aspects of activities, artifacts and relationships, whose value is primarily internal, are combined in various ways with instrumental activities directed towards the external goal of reproduction of social life. But this combination does not undermine the distinction itself. Moreover, while all economic activities have a cultural dimension, the converse does not apply, for not all cultural activities are directed to provisioning – watching a television programme, for example, is not an economic activity. That such cultural activities do not escape economic implications (the television must be produced) doesn't make them in any meaningful sense economic. The relationship between culture and economy is therefore asymmetric. Counselling a friend who has problems and offering counselling services for money as a way of making a living are both cultural activities insofar as they involve meanings and representations, but only the second is economic too, for the first does not serve as a means of making a living. The existence of activities such as this which are simultaneously economic and cultural does not mean that the distinction is no longer valid, for it is primarily about logics and purposes of action rather than about different spheres of everyday life.[2]

This association of the cultural and the economic implies that it is wrong to think of the relation between them as simply external. A question like 'How has the economy been influenced by culture?' implies that there was first a pristine economy which somehow later fell under the influence of culture, when of course economic activities have always been culturally influenced.[3] It also ignores those economic activities which take place outside the formal economy, for example in households. Neoclassical economists tend to assume that 'culture' need only be invoked where motivations diverge from self-interest, but as the classical economists realized and historians have documented, the pursuit of self-interest and associated moral sentiments and social norms are themselves a cultural development associated with the rise of modernity and capitalism. On the other hand, this doesn't make the question meaningless, for if one is talking purely about the formal economy, then at least some cultural influences are indeed external to it. Nor does the fact that economies are always culturally inflected mean that there cannot be tensions rather than harmony between culture and economy. At times, the logic of one may dominate the other, as when cultural practices are subordinated to economic demands. Although it is common in such situations to talk of culture as being threatened, this does not mean that the domain of culture shrinks, merely that one kind of culture gives way to another one.

If we move to a more specific level to consider advanced economies, especially capitalism, then the relationship between economy and culture takes on another form. Here, the part of the economy we call the formal or money economy differentiates out from the lifeworld to become a major social system standing to a certain extent opposed to it and dominating it. The combination of unprecedented degrees of division of labour and knowledge with dependence of economic survival on competition for the spending of often distant and unknown others, and on the movements of 'market forces', makes the influence of individuals over their own life-chances more indirect and uncertain than ever before. This leads to the situation in which we speak more readily of the human problems of economic activities than the economic problems of humans. What matters is the product and price, and the abstract or formal rationality of exchange-value.[4]

Some authors point to recent developments in capitalism as evidence of a collapse of the culture–economy distinction. The rise of the service sector has been cited as indicating the emergence of a post-industrial society in which traditional material production is becoming secondary to a more strongly culturally inflected service economy. But it is not clear that much has changed here. First, the expansion of services is widely exaggerated since many of the activities classified as service production, such as catering, have a major element of manufacture (Sayer and Walker, 1992). True services involving interpersonal communication, provision of information or ambiance, such as teaching or counselling, do indeed involve stronger cultural elements than material production, and have a dialogical and performative character in which the 'consumer' as well as the producer affect the quality of the service. Moreover, in the case of the professions, the work has a normative character insofar as it involves evaluating the situations and behaviour of clients/patients/students and deciding what they need. Yet all these remain activities pursued for economic reward and subject to economic constraints. Further, alongside the expansion of non-material commodities in the form of service work proper, the wealth of material commodities continues to expand relentlessly, even though fewer people are involved in making them. Thus the air hostess's smile presupposes planes, in-flight meals, baggage handling systems, radar and airports and the hundreds of thousands of material components that go into them.

Another line of argument popular amongst cultural analysts takes up Baudrillard's emphasis of the growing importance of the 'sign value' of commodities, that is their symbolic significance as means by which lifestyles and identities can be constructed. While this aestheticization is probably increasing in consumer products, two things have to be remembered. First, sign value has certainly not replaced exchange value as the regulator of economic activity in capitalism – company accounts or bank balances are not assessed in sign value! Secondly, the majority of commodities in a modern economy are not consumer commodities but intermediate products like oil, computer chips or bearings, which do not need to be aestheticized, even if some of them do end up in consumer products.

A stronger argument for a fusion of culture and economy could be drawn from Bourdieu, who analyses culture as having an economic logic (1977; 1986). Bourdieu sees almost every act either in instrumental, indeed explicitly economic terms, or as barely conscious products of the habitus. In the former case the pursuit of honour or status, expressions of goodwill and especially gift-giving are seen as disguised strategies of exchange through which symbolic, social or cultural capital are accumulated. Both interpretations are indeed illuminating for a wide range of actions, both for pre-capitalist and capitalist societies, but not all actions are purely instrumental or subconscious; some – particularly actions in response to moral dilemmas – are done for their own sake, and on the basis of deliberation (Sayer, this volume).

So, in summary, we can agree with Stuart Hall that culture is not 'a decorative addendum to the "hard world" of production and things, the icing on the cake of the material world' and that 'through design, technology and styling, "aesthetics" has already penetrated the world of modern production'. But it doesn't follow from this that the distinction between the economic and cultural 'is now quite useless', as he once claimed (Hall, 1988), since, as we noted, such authors cannot avoid continuing to use it, which Hall now seems to acknowledge (Hall, 1997). Similarly we accept that 'the economy is increasingly culturally inflected and . . . culture is more and more economically inflected' (Lash and Urry, 1994: 64). But despite the inflections, economic and cultural logics remain different and often pull in opposite directions.

Evaluating economic influences upon cultures

We claimed earlier that the culture–economy distinction is not only theoretically important but matters politically. Why might this be? Here there is a striking divergence between modernist and postmodernist thinkers. Many of the former have seen culture and economy in a destructive (rather than creative) tension, and have been concerned about both the dominance of an economic logic oriented to accumulation in capitalism and industrialism and the abstraction or disembedding of economy within society. By contrast, postmodernists have had a much more sanguine view of the matter and regard the modernist critiques as infected by elitism and an implicit productionism (Ferguson and Golding, 1997).

Critical theorists have highlighted the dangers of the expansion of the sphere of instrumental reason at the expense of practical reason and the risk of devaluation of substantive values. As the range of commodities grows, 'the imperialism of instrumental reason threatens the immanently dialogical qualities of cultural values' (Lash and Urry, 1994: 83). Actions then become judged not according to substantive values but according to whether they are profitable. Individuals are positioned as consumers rather than citizens, moral and political issues are displaced by market decisions according to self-interest, and the public good is steadily corroded. Non-monetized versions of this distortion of values are possible too, where, to use Adam Smith's terms, love of display and praise is given priority over love of praiseworthy acts. As John O'Neill's chapter shows, the 'good life' is defined in terms of fame, appearance and riches (or cultural, symbolic and social capital, in Bourdieu's terms), rather than in terms of virtue (Smith, 1759). In Lash and Urry's terms, aesthetic, taste categories take the place of moral-practical values in the assessment of actions and ways of life (Lash and Urry, 1994: 133).

This last line of critique implies that celebrating – or even just uncritically reporting – the sign value of cultural practices, relations and products, forms of consumption, and lifestyles, or 'the stylization of life' as Bourdieu (1986) and Featherstone (1994) call it, is complicit in the very erosion of cultural values that capitalism and industrialism have brought about. If culture, as an object of study, is treated as no more than the stylization of life, then arguably this is worse, since it ignores the possibility of another side to culture more directly to do with social relations and virtue. For critical theorists and a long line of other philosophers and political economists, if this is actually happening in the modern world, then we are in trouble. While dominant conceptions of culture differ by country and discipline, it is no accident (as Marxists used to say) that this impoverished concept of culture is to be found in the most economically and politically liberal societies. Equally, it is no accident that in more social democratic societies, such as Scandinavia, where there is a stronger sense of the public or the common, a more anthropological and moral-political way of understanding culture, going beyond the stylization of life, is still strong.

On the other side, not only postmodernists but also many liberals argue that this kind of critique is elitist and dogmatic. It fails to recognize the 'civilizing effects' of market relations. It implies the dubious assumption that in the absence of capitalism's imperatives, benign cultural norms and forms would automatically prevail. It is one-sided and undialectical in allowing a concern with the status of many cultural activities and products as commodities and sources of profit to obscure the way in which material consumption can be creative and enabling. It is anti-liberal in implying that individuals do not know what is in their best interest, and it ignores the way markets allow people to pursue their own conceptions of the good life by buying and selling as they choose. It implies an elitist distinction between high and low culture and a right to pass judgement on the tastes of others. It dogmatically and ethnocentrically proclaims as universal and foundational, normative principles which are actually local, particular, and without any ultimate foundation. Its anti-consumerism reflects the elitism and asceticism of intellectuals, and derives from the fact that they have so much cultural capital that they do not need to seek prestige through consumption, or perhaps from their lack of awareness of just how much they consume themselves. Worse, and unforgivably, they are too unreflexive to realize that they are treating their own special interests as universal. On this view, the expansion and diversification of commodity production also contributes to the expansion of civil society and the diversification of social worlds in which ordinary people live, thereby expanding the positionalities and identities available to them, or at least to those with sufficient income (Hall, 1988).

Furthermore, both liberals and postmodernists might argue that far from devaluing cultural goods, markets for them may oblige cultural producers to raise their standards so as to survive against competitors. Critical theory and Marxism are biased against consumption, failing to appreciate that it can be active and creative, and hence a source of cultural innovation. The extraordinary explosion in the number of commodities noted in the first sentence of Marx's *Capital* signals an unprecedented unleashing of creativity, and not only on the producers' side. Just as cheap commodities break down 'all Chinese Walls', they break the isolation ('rural idiocy') of closed societies and bring about an ever-wider cosmopolitanism in which cultural cross-fertilization and enrichment can take place. They bring hitherto unknown or inaccessible goods within the reach of the pockets of the majority.[5] The resulting hybridization of culture replaces a world of non-relational diversity with one of interdependence and difference, and is to be celebrated. In the process, market forces provide the means by which people can develop new identities and cultural forms. Postmodernism's relativistic leanings can be realized in the neutrality of markets:

> capital has fallen in love with difference: advertising thrives on selling us things that will enhance our uniqueness and individuality. It's no longer about keeping up with the Joneses, it's about being different from them . . . cultural difference sells. This is the 'difference' of commodity relations, the particular experience of time and space produced by transnational capital. In the commodification of language and culture, objects and images are torn free of their original referents and their meanings become a spectacle open to almost infinite translation. Difference ceases to threaten, or to signify power relations. (Rutherford, 1990: 11)

While few would disagree that transnational capital has a disembedding effect on cultural objects and images, many would demur at this upbeat view of deracination and commodification, and of course one can point to the continued lack of differentiation of many of the most popular commodities. Others, including Stuart Hall (1990), who discusses identity and cultural diaspora in the same volume, would argue that difference can most definitely involve oppressive power relations, indeed this is what the politics of recognition is centrally about. Of course, these are just the briefest summaries of the arguments and there are clearly many possibilities for accepting and combining points from both sides, but sketching them in this manner should be sufficient to indicate something of the political and moral significance of the relationship between economy and culture.

Culture and economy: moral-political dimensions

One of the most striking political aspects of the relationship between culture and economy concerns the relationship between the politics of recognition and the politics of distribution. The former, concerning claims for recognition of the distinctive perspectives and values of ethnic, gender and sexual differences, have become particularly salient in recent times, sometimes overshadowing the politics of the distribution of resources. Our first contributor, Nancy Fraser, follows up her seminal earlier work on these matters (Fraser, 1995) with a discussion of their implications for normative questions of social justice. Proponents of the politics of recognition often neglect egalitarian redistribution or see it as falsely universalizing dominant groups' norms at the expense of other norms, such as those of male breadwinners or heterosexuals. On the other hand, proponents of the politics of redistribution often see identity politics as a diversion from the 'real' economic issues, and one which allows the powerless to be divided and ruled. Nancy Fraser rejects such either/or positions and argues that both kinds of politics cut across all social movements, be they centred on class, gender, ethnicity or sexuality. Approaching the politics of recognition via a Weberian concept of status groups, she develops an analysis of the intricate relationships between economic and cultural differences, and indeed between the concepts of economy and culture. This provides a basis for a 'bivalent theory of justice' which combines redistribution and recognition in a single comprehensive paradigm. Rather than seeing redistribution and recognition as referring to two substantive societal domains – economy and culture – a 'perspectival dualism' is proposed which treats them as two analytical perspectives that can be applied to any domain, exposing the complex imbrication of economy and culture. Thus egalitarian economic redistribution cannot be achieved without changing patterns of cultural value which code genders, ethnicities and sexualities hierarchically, and vice versa.

Central to the question of the moral-political significance of relationships between culture and economy is that of the nature and role of moral-political values themselves. Andrew Sayer argues that contemporary approaches to the study of both culture and economy are ill-equipped to grasp their significance. The tendency of the former to reduce culture to the stylization of life is complicit in the aestheticization of moral-political values, or the de-moralization of culture. The expulsion of consideration of questions of morality from political economy, reflecting the disembedding of the formal economy, weakens both its explanations and critiques of contemporary economic life. In both areas there is a tendency to ignore moral influences on social life, usually by interpreting them either as merely subjective and emotive or in instrumental, power-based terms, as in Bourdieu's 'strategies of distinction'. In order to counter these tendencies, a new version of the concept of moral economy is proposed in order to highlight the ways in which all economic activities – both formal and informal or domestic – are influenced by norms, including ethical principles. Who should work (paid or unpaid)?; who is our keeper and whose keeper are we? These are among the key questions to which these norms provide answers. While the norms regulate the political economy, they are always also adapted to it and to some degree compromised by it, indeed they may be partly a rationalization of the political economic order. Two aspects of the post-war moral economy are now changing – its strongly gendered character and its institutionalization in the welfare state. These are being destabilized from two directions – from changes in civil society, particularly involving the new 'life politics' and families, and by changes in the formal economy.

According to John O'Neill, questions of identity and recognition are not new but have a long history in classical political economy. However, what is different now is the denial of a series of normative distinctions which classical political economy used to make an important critique of market society. Moreover, whereas the cultural turn is associated with a turn away from political economy, it arguably endorses neoliberal values and is convergent with the latter's defence of markets, especially where identity depends on consumption and images, or vanity, as older theorists termed it, rather than on some independent good such as achievement. Whereas the older critique attacked the way in which markets encourage strategic behaviour and the cultivation of appearance and credibility and undermine any independent standards regarding what is worthy of praise or recognition, the cultural turn elides such distinctions and neutralizes the critique. The same goes for recent sociology of science. A further consequence of the divorce of concerns with cultural recognition from issues of economic distribution is the loss of the argument that equality in economic and social standing is a condition for proper appraisals of differences of worth.

Russell Keat develops a different and novel kind of critique of the commodification of culture in relation to markets and their limitation. While he accepts that markets should be allowed wherever they enhance human well-being, this will only happen if consumers are able to make good judgements about what will contribute to their well-being. Here, *non*-market institutions are required to enable people to make good judgements about the use-value of practices and hence about commodities related to them. Certain important cultural 'products' themselves explore the nature and possibilities of human well-being, helping us to evaluate different ways of life. By contrast, the instrumental character of assessments of this generated within markets through advertising are unreliable, increasingly producing a spurious culturalization of commodities: for example, implying that purchase of a certain product will bring us sociability and happiness.

Economy and culture: class and difference

The cultural turn from materialism to discourse (Barrett and Phillips, 1992) brought not only a change in approach but in primary objects of study. Approaches suitable for understanding economic systems are inappropriate for understanding discursive processes, and vice versa, with the result that each side either ignores or misunderstands those phenomena inaccessible to its approach. One of the contributory factors in the shift from economy to culture was the realization that most non-class social divisions could not be explained on the model of class. But the converse is also true: class cannot be understood in the terms appropriate for gender, ethnicity or sexuality. Whereas the class divisions of capitalism – in the sense of differences of income and wealth rather than 'subjective' class culture – have no *necessary* connection to ascribed or actual characteristics of particular groups, non-class divisions such as those of gender and ethnicity and sexualities obviously do. Class differences are hierarchical; they are not differences to be accepted or celebrated; they are not discursively produced and performative (Coole, 1996). Where consumers do not know who makes the commodities they buy, their decisions and the repercussions these have on the incomes of producers, cannot derive from culturally ascribed characteristics. In this respect, the formal economy is identity-blind. This 'indifference to persons', a function of the disembedding of modern economies, is a crucial, indeed defining feature of systems such as capitalism. This is so, even though in many other respects, such as employment, the systems are clearly gendered and differentiated according to ethnicity in their concrete form.

There may, however, be a contingent relation between non-class divisions and class in the above sense, where certain identifiable groups may be pressed into particular classes and occupations by virtue of their cultural characteristics. Such grounds are always spurious, for even if the ascribed characteristics of a particular group are favourable to the occupancy of particular class positions, there are usually others who would be able to take their places; economic systems may be embedded in ways which are responsive to cultural difference, for example, but they are not utterly dependent on this form of embedding.[6] For a while, some variants of Marxist feminism tried to argue that capitalism depended on unpaid female domestic work, but the reasons why it is overwhelmingly women rather than men who do this work have nothing to do with capitalism, and there is no reason why class and capital accumulation could not exist in a differently gendered or non-patriarchal society. Gender and ethnic divisions are not restricted to life outside the economic system but are found within it too, but it does not follow from this that the system of capital is dependent on them, even though competitive pressures may encourage their exploitation where they exist (Sayer, 1995). In the abstract, we can identify or isolate capitalism as a system whose survival is not dependent on gender, ethnic or other differences, but its concrete practices are usually gendered. A dual systems theory such as that developed by Walby (1986; 1997), which allows for conflicts as well as compatibilities between capitalism and patriarchy or other culturally ascribed divisions, is therefore appropriate.

It must be stressed again that these arguments about class concern its objective dimensions in terms of individuals' incomes and access to resources. Matters are different regarding the subjective experience of class, for this is always mediated by gender and ethnicity (Skeggs, 1997). While this is true, the danger of considering class exclusively at the level of subjective experience and discourse is that we may ignore the way in which the system of the formal economy shapes and differentiates actors' material circumstances without any necessary regard for their identities (though as we have noted it may contingently respond to them). The turn to culture and discourse illuminates the former, but occludes or misrepresents the latter.

While the logic of the formal economy does not require culturally-ascribed differences, it is a major error to suppose that all economic problems derive from within the formal economic system. A significant proportion of economic activity takes place outside it, particularly in the domestic economy, and many of the most serious economic problems are cultural in origin, deriving from the way in which individuals' economic activities and obligations are ascribed to them. Thus, one of the main causes of female poverty lies in cultural restrictions on the entry of women into the public sphere, especially the labour market. For example, certain widows and their children in India and Bangladesh are at risk from starvation even though such women are capable of going out and earning a wage, because patriarchal pressures prohibit them from leaving the home (Nussbaum and Glover, 1995). The gendered household division of labour is itself a consequence of signifying practices rather than system demands. The allocation of particular economic roles to men and women is a major feature of the constitution of gender. As Nancy Fraser puts it, political collectivities based on gender (and also ethnicity) are 'bivalent' in that they are concerned with both the economic politics of distribution and the cultural politics of recognition, and injustices with respect to the one are reinforced by injustices with respect to the other.

Whereas political economy largely neglected the cultural determinants of economic problems, the cultural turn has produced a neglect of the systemic origins of economic problems (although arguably it has not paid much attention to culturally determined economic problems either). The realization that gender differences have cultural–psychological determinants rather than economic determinants helps to explain why an economic (Marxist) feminist research gave way to a highly cultural feminism in the 1980s. Just as Marxism dismissed social divisions it could not assimilate to the model of class, so much of postmodernist cultural studies dismisses class difference as it cannot be assimilated to its models of difference. However, one-sided, either–or thinking is not inevitable, and as Harriet Bradley and Steve Fenton argue, it is possible to grasp the dialectic of these two forms of difference in order to understand concrete societies. As they observe, the recent history of sociological research on both gender and ethnicity is one of a shift from political economic standpoints which grossly underplayed identity and meaning to a focus on culture, identity and difference in which class, as Michele Barrett famously noted, is now 'non grata'. Bradley and Fenton argue for reconciliation and draw upon their own respective researches on gender and ethnicity to propose how it might be done in practice. Thus they illustrate the changing dialectic of culture and economy with respect to Quebec nationalism and French Canadian ethnicity and to Madonna's commodification of her sexuality. As they show, such a reconciliation has far-reaching implications for sociological theory and methodology.

'Economizing culture' or 'culturizing economy'?: capitalism and work culture

Even if the balance between culture and economy is changing, it is possible to understand the *direction* of this change in quite opposed ways. To begin with, there is the insight that money and markets have to be culturally embedded in various ways, an argument used now in opposition to neoclassical economics' 'under-socialized' conception of actors. Thus sociologists and political economists have emphasized how economic life is embedded in cultural forms. One example of this is the current interest in trust as a precondition for economic performance (e.g. Luhmann, 1979; Misztal, 1996). However, these arguments are not in themselves new. Adam Smith's theory of market behaviour presupposed the existence of internalized moral regulation. Durkheim's concern with the moral basis of contract is well known. More recently Parsons posited a process of multidimensional adaptive upgrading from material determination in which the symbol became crucial to social reproduction. Here social differentiation creates expanding social space mediated by differentiated cultural value spheres. Karl Polanyi argued that abstract instrumental exchanges are culturally embedded in normative and institutional frameworks, a process Weber described as *Vergesellschaftung* ('societalization'). Thus, although the relationship between culture and economy may have changed, traditional approaches, analysing the cultural preconditions for different forms of economic organization, may still be useful.

A novel and stronger claim here is that economic life is becoming 'culturalized' in a more fundamental sense. This is claimed in relation to work culture, which some firms attempt to mould, in order to improve company performance. Although this elevates the place of culture, it is clearly an attempt to instrumentalize culture for economic ends. In such cases, the tension noted earlier between cultural values which are largely intrinsic or non-instrumental and instrumental economic rationales is likely to be sharp. Motivating people in purely instrumental ways – 'do this and there will be a pay-off' – may sometimes be successful on its own, but arguably, external goals such as profit can be attained more effectively by harnessing cultural norms. To take an optimistic view, the more liberal economies may be suffering not from having overestimated the importance of market ends in economic success, but from having underestimated the possibilities of more dialogical forms of organization as means for meeting those ends. Sometimes the instrumentalization of values is completely transparent, as in exhortations to salespersons to believe in their products, but often the exhortations appeal to the intrinsic value of particular ways of working with others rather than to the economic consequences. Some instrumentalized cultures are constructed openly, as in 'designer work cultures' (Casey, 1995); others disguise the element of construction and appeal to existing values outside, as in the case of large Japanese companies adopting the rhetoric of family values (Eccleston, 1989). When practices influenced by moral and aesthetic values become means to ends which have nothing to do with the moral, the good or the beautiful, those qualities are arguably degraded or tainted to some degree. The conflict between integrity and personal or corporate gain and the respective rewards they are likely to receive invites cynicism and reaction. Nevertheless, it must be remembered that although new 'Human Resource Management' and the like are introduced for instrumental reasons, they may be better than what preceded them.

The source of many such projects consists in lessons from successful companies, often foreign ones, whose success seems to lie in 'soft' characteristics rather than straightforward technological or cost advantages. This has proved a source of rich pickings for management consultants, who have gone beyond the rhetoric of 'corporate culture' to promoting 'culture management', 'value-driven companies', 'Japanization' and 'designer work cultures' (Smith, 1996). At times, contemporary management science literature almost seems to suggest that economic success automatically flows from a healthy work culture – a view that would surprise many business people as well as social scientists. As Nigel Thrift argues here, capitalism seems to be going through its own cultural turn, evident particularly in the increasing attention attached by business to knowledge, especially within management discourse, as a means for coping with constant change and uncertainty. This extends beyond work culture to growing connections between academia and capitalism. As he puts it, 'the increasing commodification of knowledge has only pointed to the value of knowledge which can't be commodified, and especially to the value of knowledge that cannot be written down and packaged'. Although the emphasis on culture, knowledge and creativity invites the label 'soft capitalism', as Thrift notes it still has its hard material edge in terms of 'downsizing' of workforces, and super-exploitation of managers and key workers.

There is little doubt that the way in which workers and managers communicate and co-operate makes a difference to both the internal operations and external relations of companies, though of course it is not the only determinant of their success. However, as Paul Thompson and Patricia Findlay note here, there have always been work cultures – often of resistance – and they are not easily changed, so it is not clear how far 'culture management' and the like go beyond the level of rhetoric and actually 'change the people'. Reviewing theoretical and empirical literature relating to work culture, they argue that though speculation has run far ahead of empirical evidence, something is going on, albeit producing effects which are often different from those intended. Significantly, insofar as change programmes are successful, they tend to have more effect on workers' practice than on their values, usually because surveillance, sanctions and incentives back up exhortations at the level of values, so that 'behavioural compliance' may be a better description than cultural change.

Politics and culture

The complexities of the changing dialectic of culture and economy are further evident in politics, where one can find both examples of heightened concern for economic matters, albeit on an increasingly individualized basis, and elements of culturalization. As we have suggested, the cultural turn itself possibly reflects a shift from the 'politics of distribution' to a new 'politics of recognition' which is more cultural in character. The cultural turn in social science could be a reflection of this culturalization of politics, and the desertion of economy a consequence of the defeat of the Left's alternative economic agenda. No matter how important the economy remains, the scope for progressive change looks greater in more cultural directions where the politics of recognition are prominent.[7]

It is tempting to take the decline of trade union and class politics as an indication of the declining importance of economics in politics, but there are other forms of economic politics. Other kinds of economic division, between the employed and the unemployed, between men and women, home-owners and tenants, are becoming more prominent, and more individualistic concerns have grown. There is also the rise of new social movements, less narrowly economic in their focus. Gender politics includes but goes beyond economic matters. The consequent challenge to the traditional division between public/private has redrawn the map of political contestation, introducing new sites of politicization such as the kitchen and the bedroom. These point to a diversification of the concerns of both mainstream and radical politics, though the decline of a socialist agenda could also be taken as evidence of deradicalization. The loss of interest in economic issues parallels a decline of a particular kind of economic concern within politics – egalitarian redistribution – and its replacement by one of economic management.

These issues are not restricted to the developed post-welfare capitalist world. The fall of communism in eastern Europe could be interpreted as evidence of a more general crisis in materialist, redistributive and productivist politics in favour of a more fluid, carnivalesque celebration of expressivity. Larry Ray's chapter on the theatrical and ironic politics of 'Orange Alternative' in Poland during the 1980s explores the way in which the space created by the collapse of the political system allowed the appearance of new, experimental and highly cultural forms of street protest that evaded the conventional scripts of instrumental political action. However, his chapter concludes by suggesting that this episode was exceptional rather than indicative of a global cultural shift in the nature of political protest. The establishment of a post-communist government was accompanied by a 'normalization' of politics and re-differentiation of institutional orders as the theatricality of street politics gave way to more sombre modes of articulation. Two central issues are raised here. First, that the transgression of boundaries between the conventionally 'cultural' and 'political' is not in itself new but can be traced back at least to Renaissance comedy and the figure of Harlequin. Second, the transgression of boundaries may be politically potent but its very effectiveness is dependent on the continued existence of borders to be crossed.

Identity politics and instrumental economic goals have always been intertwined (e.g. in nationalist movements), but arguably the dominant tendency of post-war politics has actually been increasingly instrumental at the expense of older solidarities. Thus increasing privatization (in both senses of the word) has eroded the solidarities embodied in the welfare state. However, this does not mean that nothing other than a growth of individualism is happening, for there are also signs of a revival of ethical issues in politics and a political contestation around the particular kinds of lives people seek to live rather than merely about the growth of some unspecific notion of opportunity. Environmental issues, animal rights, and the politics of the body are all marked primarily by ethical rather than economic concerns. This theme is developed by Bronislaw Szerszynski's chapter on roads protests in which he argues that the recent upsurge in environmental protest has been dominated by expressive gestures (the use of bodies, costumes, theatrical devices and the carnivalesque) in preference to 'rational' political debate. Although roads protests are responses to economically driven developments, their motivations are not merely economically instrumental. Indeed, they exhibit a 'semiotic excess', an excess of meaning beyond narrow notions of political effectiveness, or indeed affirmation of identity. Where mainstream politics (arguably) offers rival prescriptions for economic prosperity which do not challenge existing social norms, the roads protests are concerned with substantive values. As such, the protests are not reducible to identity politics and the defence of difference, for they seek to change the wider society's values.

There may now be a cultural turn within mainstream politics too. In the early post-war period in Britain, there was a relative consensus regarding the moral basis of politics. Until the 1970s both major parties held similar views about redistribution. The very success of the welfare state meant that earlier battles over such values could be regarded as won. Radical politics was notable for its lack of interest in ethical questions, the gaining of power being seen as not only necessary but sufficient for resolving any such issues. Mainstream politics was mainly concerned with the means to the good life – economic organization – rather than the end itself.[8] Insofar as substantive values regarding the good life figured in political discourse, conservatism was the main interested party. This neglect of ethical issues was related to still strong class identities and a traditional gender order. Two aspects of this post-war order – its strongly gendered character and its institutionalization in the welfare state – are now being destabilized from two directions: from changes in civil society, particularly involving the new 'life politics', and by economic changes. Regarding the former, by the end of the post-war boom, several kinds of social changes began to upset the previous com-promise (e.g. changes in sexual behaviour, gender relations, marriage, multiculturalism). De-traditionalization means that traditional roles which people followed are being threatened as critical reflexivity about those roles and their hitherto hidden inequalities develops. While this process is as old as modernity, it is at long last profoundly affecting families in particular. Conservatism's response is of course to attempt to defend tradition – but particularly with regard to gender relations this amounts to trying to put the genie back into the bottle (Beck, 1992). At the same time economic changes were also destabilizing the post-war moral economy, putting state spending on welfare under increased pressure. National social settlements became a factor in economic com-petition, with norms of universal provision coming under increasing fire and a striking shift towards a 'workfare state'. With the 'flexibilization' of labour markets, economic insecurity has coincided with changes in the gender order. Neoliberalism – itself no friend of tradition – figured prominently in these changes, though the resulting widening of social divisions, rising crime rates and perceived decline in social responsibility have prompted many to look towards various forms of communitarian-ism for solutions.

Our final two chapters offer contrasting perspectives on such political changes. Mary Evans suggests that the Labour Party's overwhelming victory in the May 1997 UK General Election was attributable in part to a shift in cultural values, in particular those regarding gender, away from the order that underpinned conservatism. 'The Conservatives lost as overwhelmingly as they did', Evans argues, 'not just because voters wanted more money spent on education and health but because they could no longer identify with the understanding and experience with which the Conservative Party was associated', and this extended beyond

Conservative policies to their politicians' personal behaviour.[9] Although New Labour proved to be more in tune with changes in families, in sexual behaviour, and women's participation in paid work, new stresses arose among these tendencies, as has been particularly clear in relation to their policy on getting single mothers into paid work. Thus while there are signs of a feminization of politics, the changes have not been without their contradictions.

While for Mary Evans, cultural shifts have figured prominently in recent political changes in Britain, Stephen Driver and Luke Martell argue that New Labour's agenda is only superficially 'cultural' and that at its core are a set of economic strategies for coping with the post-Thatcher, post-welfare economy. With its references to the value of community and the need for people to recognize their responsibilities, New Labour rhetoric has emphasized an ethical agenda. However, Driver and Martell see Labour's shift away from egalitarianism as being more to do with embracing flexible labour markets than responding to difference as prioritizing *economic* inclusion. Insofar as New Labour involves a cultural politics, much of it is essentially conservative in favouring conformist rather than pluralist forms of community. Further, they argue that Labour's communitarianism is as much a *political* response to the New Right and social democracy as an instance of the culturalization of politics.

As ever, politics is richly ambiguous, and we leave it for readers to decide on their preferred interpretation.

Conclusion

This discussion has attempted to map out some of the issues addressed by the contributors to this volume. The paradox of a turn away from economy to culture at a time of continuing if not growing economic problems is becoming increasingly apparent. The silence on these matters cannot continue much longer, and a fresh examination of the relationships between culture and economy is required. The following chapters contribute to the resolution of this situation by presenting a variety of perspectives on these issues via a variety of concrete topics, and most generally by confronting rather than ignoring the ever-changing tensions between culture and economy. In the course of this debate we should try to separate the extent to which we are looking at a shift in academic style and fashion and the extent to which the social universe is itself changing. Both positions are prima facie tenable. One may feel that sociologists have an insatiable desire for novel perspectives and it is less that debates in the discipline get resolved but that people get bored with them. If this is the case, then perhaps the 'cultural turn' is an attempt to shift the focus from an overly materialist stance of the preceding decades towards a more 'culturalized' one. In the process perhaps we are forgetting how much the classical theoretical tradition itself had to say about the interpenetration of culture and economy, which was after all one of the main themes of many works, notably Durkheim's *Division of Labour* and Weber's *Protestant Ethic* study. On the other hand one may feel that the increasing complexity and speed of contemporary life, the increasing significance of images and symbols, along with the disappearance of familiar institutional markers, have generated new configurations of what we used to separate into 'cultural' and 'economic' categories. If this is so, then our received cognitive maps need reorienting in new and perhaps exciting directions. This collection attempts to bring together analyses of culture and economy informed by each of these approaches and, although the above discussion betrays the leanings of the editors towards a cautious evaluation of the cultural turn, our aim is to open the debate up in ways that will overcome narrowly defined camps and oppositions.

Notes

1 Although, as Bourdieu (1986) points out, it is possible that they may also be cultivated instrumentally, for other ends, such as distinction.

2 If this still seems fuzzy, it should be noted that fuzzy distinctions can be useful, such as that between night and day, or between the front of someone's head and the back.

3 This is the problem with the debate between culturalists and economic rationalists which has occurred particularly with reference to analyses of non-western economies. Thus there has been a debate about whether Japanese forms of economic organization are to be explained in cultural terms or in terms of economic rationality, as if economic behaviour could avoid being culturally inflected.

4 Many have followed Polanyi in arguing that this preoccupation with 'economizing' in terms of economical use of labour and resources is restricted to capitalism, and is absent in pre-capitalist societies where economy is indistinguishable from culture (Polanyi, 1957; 1993; see also Sahlins, 1973). However, more recently, it has become common to regard this as exaggerating the contrast with pre-capitalist societies by underestimating the social embeddedness of economic processes in industrial societies and the instrumentality of much behaviour and the need to use labour and other resources efficiently in pre-industrial ones (Bourdieu, 1977; Granovetter, 1985; Holton, 1993; Sayer, 1995).

5 Whether all such commodities are good is another matter, although not one which neoliberals or postmodernists would want to judge.

6 Some forms of embedding, particularly those to do with understanding and trust, are not merely contingent features of systems but necessary for their functioning.

7 Thatcherism also had a cultural side, albeit one shaped mainly by neoliberal economics, particularly 'enterprise culture' (Keat and Abercrombie, 1991; Heelas and Morris, 1992). More recently, 'New Labour' has taken a cultural turn, hoping to effect change by cultural as well as economic means (Demos, 1995), though of course this may merely be an acknowledgement of economic impotence.

8 This is not to deny that socialist theory in either Fabian or Marxist versions did show some concern with questions of ethics and the good.

9 The lateness of this response to trends which have been established for three decades could be attributable in part to the fact that, as Martin Jacques has remarked, the British have difficulty acknowledging just how radical they have become in the reorganization of their personal lives.

References

Barrett, M. (1992) 'Words and things: materialism and method in contemporary feminist analysis', in M. Barrett and A. Phillips (eds), *Destabilizing Theory*, Cambridge: Polity.

Barrett, M. and Phillips, A. (eds) (1992) *Destabilizing Theory*, Cambridge: Polity.

Beck, U. (1992) *Risk Society: Towards a New Modernity*, London: Sage.

Benhabib, S. (1992) *Situating the Self*, Cambridge: Polity.

Berggren, C. (1994) 'Japan as number two: competitive problems and the future of alliance capitalism after the burst of the bubble boom', *Work, Employment and Society*, 9 (1): 53–95.

Bourdieu, P. (1977) *Outline of a Theory of Practice*, Cambridge: Cambridge University Press.

Bourdieu, P. (1986) *Distinction: Towards a Social Critique of the Judgement of Taste*, London: Routledge.

Casey, C. (1995) *Work, Self and Society*, London: Routledge.

Coole, D. (1996) 'Is class a difference that makes a difference?', *Radical Philosophy*, 77: 17–25.

Crook, S., Pakulski, J. and Waters, M. (1992) *Postmodernization: Change in Advanced Societies*, London: Sage.

Demos (1995) 'Missionary government', *Demos Quarterly*, 7.

Eagleton, T. (1995) Review of Derrida 'Spectres of Marx', *Radical Philosophy*, 73: 35–7.

Eccleston, B. (1989) *State and Society in Post-war Japan*, Cambridge: Polity.

Etzioni, A. (1992) *The Spirit of Community*, New York: Crown Publishers.

Featherstone, M. (1994) 'City cultures and post-modern lifestyles', in A. Amin (ed.), *Post-Fordism*, Oxford: Blackwell, pp. 387–408.

Ferguson, M. and Golding, P. (1997) *Cultural Studies in Question*, London: Sage.

Folbre, N. (1992) *Who Pays for the Kids?*, London: Routledge.

Fraser, N. (1995) 'From redistribution to recognition? Dilemmas of a "post-socialist age"', *New Left Review*, 212: 68–93.

Giddens, A. (1994) *Beyond Left and Right*, Cambridge: Polity.

Granovetter, M. (1985) 'Economic action and social structure; the problem of embeddedness', *American Journal of Sociology*, 91 (3): 481–510.

Habermas, J. (1979) *Communication and the Evolution of Society*, Boston: Beacon Press.

Habermas, J. (1989) *The Theory of Communicative Action, Lifeworld and System: a Critique of Functionalist Reason, vol. 2*, Cambridge: Polity.

Hall, S. (1988) 'Brave New World', *Marxism Today*, October 24–29.

Hall, S. (1990) 'Culture, identity and diaspora', in J. Rutherford (ed.), *Identity: Community, Culture and Difference*, London: Lawrence and Wishart.

Hall, S. (1997) *Representations: Cultural Representations and Significatory Practices*, London: Sage.

Heelas, P. and Morris, P. (1992) *The Values of Enterprise Culture*, London: Routledge.

Hirshman, A.O. (1982) 'Rival interpretations of market society: civilizing, destructive or feeble?', *Journal of Economic Literature,* 20: 1463–84.

Holton, R. (1993) *Economy and Society,* London: Routledge.

Ignatieff, M. (1984) *The Needs of Strangers,* London: Vintage.

Jackson, C. and Pearson, R. (eds) (1998) *Feminist Visions of Development,* London: Routledge.

Jameson, F. (1990) *The Cultural Logic of Late Capitalism,* London: Verso.

Keat, R. and Abercrombie, N. (1991) *Enterprise Culture,* London: Routledge.

Keat, R., Whiteley, N. and Abercrombie, N. (1994) *The Authority of the Consumer,* London: Routledge.

Lash, S. (1990) *Postmodernist Sociology,* London: Routledge.

Lash, S. and Urry, J. (1994) *Economies of Signs and Space,* London: Sage.

Luhmann, N. (1979) *Trust and Power,* Chichester: John Wiley.

McLennan, G. (1995) *Pluralism,* Milton Keynes: Open University Press.

Mill, J.S. (1869/1975) 'The subjection of women', in *John Stuart Mill: Three Essays,* Introduced by R. Wollheim, Oxford: Oxford University Press.

Misztal, B. (1996) *Trust in Modern Societies,* Cambridge: Polity.

Nelson, J.A. (1996) *Feminism, Objectivity and Economics,* London: Routledge.

Nussbaum, M. and Glover, J. (eds) (1995) *Women, Culture and Development,* Oxford: Clarendon Press.

Polanyi, K. (1957) *The Great Transformation,* Boston: Beacon.

Polanyi, K. (1993) 'The economy as an instituted process', in M. Granovetter and R. Swedberg (eds), *The Sociology of Economic Life,* Boulder, CO: Westview Press, pp. 29–52.

Ray, L.J. (1993) *Rethinking Critical Theory – Emancipation in an Age of Global Social Movements,* London: Sage.

Rutherford, J. (1990) 'A place called home: identity and the cultural politics of difference', in J. Rutherford (ed.), *Identity: Community, Culture, Difference,* London: Lawrence and Wishart.

Sahlins, M. (1973) *Stone Age Economics,* London: Tavistock.

Sayer, A. (1995) *Radical Political Economy: a Critique,* Oxford: Blackwell.

Sayer, A. (1997) 'Contractualisation, work and the anxious classes', in J. Holmer and J.Ch. Karlsson (eds), *Work – Quo Vadis?: Rethinking the Question of Work,* Aldershot: Ashgate.

Sayer, A. and Walker, R.A. (1992) *The New Social Economy,* London: Routledge.

Skeggs, B. (1997) *Formations of Class and Gender,* London: Routledge.

Smith, A. (1759/1975) *The Theory of Moral Sentiments,* Indianapolis: Liberty Fund.

Smith, A. (1776/1976) *A Treatise on the Wealth of Nations,* ed. E. Cannan, Chicago, IL: University of Chicago Press.

Smith, V. (1996) 'Employee involvement, involved employees: participative work arrangements in a white-collar service occupation', *Social Problems,* 43: 166–79.

Walby, S. (1986) *Patriarchy at Work,* Oxford: Polity.

Walby, S. (1997) *Gender Transformations,* London: Routledge.

Williams, K. et al. (1994) *Cars: History, Analysis,* London: Berghahn.

Williams (1958) *Culture and Society,* Harmondsworth: Penguin.

Williams, R. (1997) *Marxism and Literature,* Oxford: Oxford University Press.

1

Social Justice in the Age of Identity Politics: Redistribution, Recognition, and Participation

Nancy Fraser

In today's world, claims for social justice seem increasingly to divide into two types. First, and most familiar, are redistributive claims, which seek a more just distribution of resources and goods. Examples include claims for redistribution from the North to the South, from the rich to the poor, and (not so long ago) from the owners to the workers. To be sure, the recent resurgence of free-market thinking has put proponents of egalitarian redistribution on the defensive. Nevertheless, egalitarian redistributive claims have supplied the paradigm case for most theorizing about social justice for the past 150 years.

Today, however, we increasingly encounter a second type of social-justice claim in the 'politics of recognition'. Here the goal, in its most plausible form, is a difference-friendly world, where assimilation to majority or dominant cultural norms is no longer the price of equal respect. Examples include claims for the recognition of the distinctive perspectives of ethnic, 'racial', and sexual minorities, as well as of gender difference. This type of claim has recently attracted the interest of political philosophers, moreover, some of whom are seeking to develop a new paradigm of justice that puts recognition at its centre.

In general, then, we are confronted with a new constellation. The discourse of social justice, once centred on distribution, is now increasingly divided between claims for redistribution, on the one hand, and claims for recognition, on the other. Increasingly, too, recognition claims tend to predominate. The demise of communism, the surge of free-market ideology, the rise of 'identity politics' in both its fundamentalist and progressive forms – all these developments have conspired to de-centre, if not to extinguish, claims for egalitarian redistribution.

In this new constellation, the two kinds of justice claims are often dissociated from one another – both practically and intellectually.

Within social movements such as feminism, for example, activist tendencies that look to redistribution as the remedy for male domination are increasingly dissociated from tendencies that look instead to recognition of gender difference. And the same is true of their counterparts in the US academy, where feminist social theorizing and feminist cultural theorizing maintain an uneasy arms-length co-existence. The feminist case exemplifies a more general tendency in the United States (and elsewhere) to decouple the cultural politics of difference from the social politics of equality.

In some cases, moreover, the dissociation has become a polarization. Some proponents of redistribution reject the politics of recognition outright, casting claims for the recognition of difference as 'false consciousness', a hindrance to the pursuit of social justice. Conversely, some proponents of recognition approve the relative eclipse of the politics of redistribution, construing the latter as an outmoded materialism, simultaneously blind to and complicit with many injustices. In such cases, we are effectively presented with what is constructed as an either/or choice: redistribution or recognition? class politics or identity politics? multiculturalism or social democracy?

These, I maintain, are false antitheses. It is my general thesis that justice today requires *both* redistribution *and* recognition. Neither alone is sufficient. As soon as one embraces this thesis, however, the question of how to combine them becomes paramount. I contend that the emancipatory aspects of the two paradigms need to be integrated in a single, comprehensive framework. Theoretically, the task is to devise a two-dimensional conception of justice that can accommodate both defensible claims for social equality and defensible claims for the recognition of difference. Practically, the task is to devise a programmatic political orientation that integrates the best of the politics of redistribution with the best of the politics of recognition.

My argument proceeds in four steps. In the first section below, I outline the key points of contrast between the two political paradigms, as they are presently understood. Then, in the second section, I problematize their current dissociation from one another by introducing a case of injustice that cannot be redressed by either one of them alone, but that requires their integration. Finally, I consider some normative philosophical questions (in the third section) and some social-theoretical questions (fourth section) that arise when we contemplate integrating redistribution and recognition in a single comprehensive framework.

Redistribution or recognition? anatomy of a false antithesis

I begin with some denotative definitions. The paradigm of redistribution, as I shall understand it, encompasses not only class-centred orientations, such as New Deal liberalism, social-democracy, and socialism, but also those forms of feminism and anti-racism that look to socio-economic transformation or reform as the remedy for gender and racial–ethnic injustice. Thus, it is broader than class politics in the conventional sense. The paradigm of recognition, in contrast, encompasses not only movements aiming to revalue unjustly-devalued identities – for example, cultural feminism, black cultural nationalism, and gay identity politics – but also deconstructive tendencies, such as queer politics, critical 'race' politics, and deconstructive feminism, which reject the 'essentialism' of traditional identity politics. Thus, it is broader than identity politics in the conventional sense.

With these definitions, I mean to contest one widespread misunderstanding of these matters. It is often assumed that the politics of redistribution means class politics, while the politics of recognition means 'identity politics', which in turn means the politics of sexuality, gender, and 'race'. This view is erroneous and misleading. For one thing, it treats recognition-oriented currents within the feminist, anti-heterosexist, and anti-racist movements as the whole story, rendering invisible alternative currents dedicated to righting gender-specific, 'race'-specific, and sex-specific forms of economic injustice that traditional class movements ignored. For another, it forecloses the recognition dimensions of class struggles. Finally, it reduces what is actually a plurality of different kinds of recognition claims (including universalist claims and deconstructive claims) to a single type, namely, claims for the affirmation of difference.

For all these reasons, the definitions I have proposed here are far preferable. They take account of the complexity of contemporary politics by treating redistribution and recognition as *dimensions of justice that can cut across all social movements.*

Understood in this way, the paradigm of redistribution and the paradigm of recognition can be contrasted in four key respects. First, the two paradigms assume different conceptions of injustice. The redistribution paradigm focuses on injustices it defines as socio-economic and presumes to be rooted in the political economy. Examples include exploitation, economic marginalization, and deprivation. The recognition paradigm, in contrast, targets injustices it understands as cultural, which it presumes to be rooted in social patterns of representation, interpretation, and communication. Examples include cultural domination, non-recognition, and disrespect.

Second, the two paradigms propose different sorts of remedies for injustice. In the redistribution paradigm, the remedy for injustice is political-economic restructuring. This might involve redistributing income, reorganizing the division of labour, or transforming other basic economic structures. (Although these various remedies differ importantly from one another, I mean to refer to the whole group of them by the generic term 'redistribution'.) In the paradigm of recognition, in contrast, the remedy for injustice is cultural or symbolic change. This could involve upwardly revaluing disrespected identities, positively valorizing cultural diversity, or the wholesale transformation of societal patterns of representation, interpretation, and communication in ways that would change everyone's social identity. (Although these remedies, too, differ importantly from one another, I refer once again to the whole group of them by the generic term 'recognition'.)

Third, the two paradigms assume different conceptions of the collectivities who suffer injustice. In the redistribution paradigm, the collective subjects of injustice are classes or class-like collectivities, which are defined economically by a distinctive relation to the market or the means of production. The classic case in the Marxian variant is the exploited working class, whose members must sell their labour power in order to receive the means of subsistence. But the conception can cover other cases as well. Also included are racialized groups of immigrants or ethnic minorities that can be economically defined, whether as a pool of low-paid menial labourers or as an 'underclass' largely excluded from regular waged work, deemed 'superfluous' and unworthy of exploitation. When the notion of the economy is broadened to encompass unwaged labour, moreover, women become visible as a collective subject of economic injustice, as the gender burdened with the lion's share of unwaged carework and consequently disadvantaged in employment and disempowered in relations with men. Also included, finally, are the complexly defined groupings that result when we theorize the political economy in terms of the intersection of class, 'race', and gender.

In the recognition paradigm, in contrast, the victims of injustice are more like Weberian status groups than Marxian classes. Defined not by the relations of production, but rather by the relations of recognition, they are distinguished by the lesser esteem, honour, and prestige they enjoy relative to other groups in society. The classic case in the Weberian paradigm is the low-status ethnic group, whom dominant patterns of cultural value mark as different and less worthy. But the conception can cover other cases as well. In the current constellation, it has been extended to gays and lesbians, who suffer pervasive effects of institutionalized stigma; to racialized groups, who are marked as different and lesser; and to women, who are trivialized, sexually objectified, and disrespected in myriad ways. It is also being extended, finally, to encompass the complexly defined groupings that result when we theorize the relations of recognition in terms of 'race', gender, and sexuality simultaneously as intersecting cultural codes.

It follows, and this is the fourth point, that the two approaches assume different understandings of group differences. The redistribution paradigm treats such differences as unjust differentials that should be abolished. The recognition paradigm, in contrast, treats differences either as cultural variations that should be celebrated or as discursively constructed hierarchical oppositions that should be deconstructed.

Increasingly, as I noted at the outset, redistribution and recognition are posed as mutually exclusive alternatives. Some proponents of the former, such as Richard Rorty (1998) and Todd Gitlin (1995), insist that identity politics is a counterproductive diversion from the real economic issues, one that balkanizes groups and rejects universalist moral norms. They claim, in effect, that 'it's the economy, stupid'. Conversely, some proponents of the politics of recognition, such as Charles Taylor (1994), insist that a difference-blind politics of redistribution can reinforce injustice by falsely universalizing dominant group norms, requiring subordinate groups to assimilate to them, and misrecognizing the latters' distinctiveness. They claim, in effect, that 'it's the culture, stupid'.

This, however, is a false antithesis.

Exploited classes, despised sexualities, and bivalent categories: a critique of justice truncated

To see why, imagine a conceptual spectrum of different kinds of social differentiations. At one extreme are differentiations that fit the paradigm of redistribution. At the other extreme are differentiations that fit the paradigm of recognition. In between are cases that prove difficult because they fit both paradigms of justice simultaneously.[1]

Consider, first, the redistribution end of the spectrum. At this end let us posit an ideal-typical social differentiation rooted in the economic structure, as opposed to the status order, of society. By definition, any structural injustices attaching to this differentiation will be traceable ultimately to the political economy. The root of the injustice, as well as its core, will be socio-economic maldistribution, while any attendant cultural injustices will derive ultimately from that economic root. At bottom, therefore, the remedy required to redress the injustice will be redistribution, as opposed to recognition.

An example that appears to approximate this ideal type is class differentiation, as understood in orthodox, economistic Marxism. In this conception, class is an artifact of an unjust political economy, which creates, and exploits, a proletariat. The core injustice is exploitation, an especially deep form of maldistribution in which the proletariat's own energies are turned against it, usurped to sustain a social system that disproportionately burdens it and benefits others. To be sure, its members also suffer serious cultural injustices, the 'hidden (and not so hidden) injuries of class' (Sennett and Cobb, 1973). But far from being rooted directly in an autonomously unjust status order, these derive from the political economy, as ideologies of class inferiority proliferate to justify exploitation. The remedy for the injustice, consequently, is redistribution, not recognition. The last thing the proletariat needs is recognition of its difference. On the contrary, the only way to remedy the injustice is to restructure the political economy in such a way as to put the proletariat out of business as a distinctive group.

Now consider the other end of the conceptual spectrum. At this end let us posit an ideal-typical social differentiation that fits the paradigm of recognition. A differentiation of this type is rooted in the status order, as opposed to the economic structure, of society. Thus, any structural injustices implicated here will be traceable ultimately to the reigning patterns of cultural value. The root of the injustice, as well as its core, will be cultural misrecognition, while any attendant economic injustices will derive ultimately from that root. The remedy required to redress the injustice will be recognition, as opposed to redistribution.

An example that appears to approximate this ideal type is sexual differentiation, understood through the prism of the Weberian conception of status. In this conception, the social differentiation between heterosexuals and homosexuals is not grounded in the political economy, as homosexuals are distributed throughout the entire class structure of capitalist society, occupy no distinctive position in the division of labour, and do not constitute an exploited class. The differentiation is rooted, rather, in the status order of society, as cultural patterns of meaning and value constitute heterosexuality as natural and normative, while simultaneously constituting homosexuality as perverse and despised. When such heteronormative meanings are pervasively institutionalized, for example, in law, state policy, social practices, and interaction, gays and lesbians become a *despised sexuality*. As a result, they suffer sexually specific forms of *status subordination*, including shaming and assault, exclusion from the rights and privileges of marriage and parenthood, curbs on their rights of expression and association, and denial of full legal rights and equal protections. These harms are injustices of misrecognition. To be sure, gays and lesbians also suffer serious economic injustices: they can be summarily dismissed from civilian employment and military service, are denied a broad range of family-based social-welfare benefits, and face major tax and inheritance liabilities. But far from being rooted directly in the economic structure of society, these injustices derive instead from the status order, as the institutionalization of heterosexist norms produces a category of despised persons who incur economic disadvantages as a byproduct. The remedy for the injustice, accordingly, is recognition, not redistribution. Overcoming homophobia and heterosexism requires changing the sexual status order, dismantling the cultural value patterns (as well as their legal and practical expressions) that deny equal respect to gays and lesbians. Change these relations of recognition, and the maldistribution will disappear.

Matters are thus fairly straightforward at the two extremes of our conceptual spectrum. When we deal with groups that approach the ideal type of the exploited working class, we face distributive injustices requiring redistributive remedies. What is needed is a politics of redistribution. When we deal with groups that approach the ideal type of the despised sexuality, in contrast, we face injustices of misrecognition. What is needed *here* is a politics of recognition.

Matters become murkier, however, once we move away from these extremes. When we posit a type of social differentiation located in the middle of the conceptual spectrum, we encounter a hybrid form that combines features of the exploited class with features of the despised sexuality. I call such differentiations 'bivalent'. Rooted at once in the economic structure and the status order of society, they may entrench injustices that are traceable to both political economy and culture simultaneously. Bivalently oppressed groups, accordingly, suffer both maldistribution and misrecognition *in forms where neither of these injustices is an indirect effect of the other, but where both are primary and co-original*. In their case, neither the politics of redistribution alone nor the politics of recognition alone will suffice. Bivalently oppressed groups need both.

Gender, I contend, is a bivalent social differentiation. Neither simply a class, nor simply a status group, it is a hybrid category with roots in both culture and political economy. From the economic perspective, gender structures the fundamental division between paid 'productive' labour and unpaid 'reproductive' and domestic labour, as well as the divisions within paid labour between higher-paid, male-dominated, manufacturing, and professional occupations and lower-paid, female-dominated, 'pink collar', and domestic service occupations. The result is an economic structure that generates gender-specific modes of exploitation, economic marginalization, and deprivation. Here, gender appears as a class-like differentiation. And gender injustice appears as a species of maldistribution that cries out for redistributive redress.

From the perspective of the status order, however, gender encompasses elements that are more like sexuality than class and that bring it squarely within the problematic of recognition. Gender codes pervasive patterns of cultural interpretation and evaluation, which are central to the status order as a whole. As a result, not just women, but all low-status groups, risk being feminized and thereby demeaned. Thus, a major feature of gender injustice is androcentrism: a pattern of culture value that privileges traits associated with masculinity, while pervasively devaluing things coded as 'feminine' – paradigmatically, but not only, women. Institutionalized in law, state policies, social practices, and interaction, this value pattern saddles women with gender-specific forms of *status subordination*, including sexual assault and domestic violence; trivializing, objectifying, and demeaning stereotypical depictions in the media; harassment and disparagement in everyday life; and denial of full legal rights and equal protections. These harms are injustices of recognition. They cannot be remedied by redistribution alone but require additional independent remedies of recognition.

Gender, in sum, is a 'bivalent' social differentiation. It encompasses a class-like aspect that brings it within the ambit of redistribution, while also including a status aspect that brings it simultaneously within the ambit of recognition. Redressing gender injustice, therefore, requires changing both the economic structure and the status order of society.

The bivalent character of gender wreaks havoc on the idea of an either/or choice between the paradigm of redistribution and the paradigm of recognition. That construction assumes that the collective subjects of injustice are either classes or status groups, but not both; that the injustice they suffer is either maldistribution or misrecognition, but not both; that the group differences at issue are either unjust differentials or unjustly devalued cultural variations, but not both; that the remedy for injustice is either redistribution or recognition, but not both.

Gender, we can now see, explodes this whole series of false antitheses. Here we have a category that is a compound of both status and class, that implicates injustices of both maldistribution and misrecognition, whose distinctiveness is compounded of both economic differentials and culturally constructed distinctions. Gender injustice can only be remedied, therefore, by an approach that encompasses both a politics of redistribution and a politics of recognition.

Gender, moreover, is not unusual in this regard. 'Race', too, is a bivalent social differentiation, a compound of status and class. Rooted simultaneously in the economic structure and the status order of capitalist society, racism's injustices include both maldistribution and misrecognition. Yet neither dimension of racism is wholly an indirect effect of the other. Thus, overcoming racism requires both redistribution and recognition. Neither alone will suffice.

Class, too, is probably best understood as bivalent for practical purposes. To be sure, the ultimate cause of class injustice is the economic structure of capitalist society.[2] But the resulting harms include misrecognition as well as maldistribution (Thompson, 1963). And cultural harms that originated as byproducts of economic structure may have since developed a life of their own. Left unattended, moreover, class misrecognition may impede the capacity to mobilize against maldistribution. Thus, a politics of class recognition may be needed to get a politics of redistribution off the ground.[3]

Sexuality, too, is for practical purposes bivalent. To be sure, the ultimate cause of heterosexist injustice is the heteronormative value pattern that is institutionalized in the status order of contemporary society.[4] But the resulting harms include maldistribution as well as misrecognition. And economic harms that originate as byproducts of the status order have an undeniable weight of their own. Left unattended, moreover, they may impede the capacity to mobilize against misrecognition. Thus, a politics of sexual redistribution may be needed to get a politics of recognition off the ground.

For practical purposes, then, virtually all real-world axes of oppression are bivalent. Virtually all implicate both maldistribution and misrecognition in forms where each of those injustices has some independent weight, whatever its ultimate roots. To be sure, not all axes of oppression are bivalent in the same way, nor to the same degree. Some axes of oppression, such as class, tilt more heavily toward the distribution end of the spectrum; others, such as sexuality, incline more to the recognition end; while still others, such as gender and 'race', cluster closer to the centre. Nevertheless, in virtually every case, the harms at issue comprise both maldistribution and misrecognition in forms where neither of those injustices can be redressed entirely indirectly but where each requires some practical attention. As a practical matter, therefore, overcoming injustice in virtually every case requires both redistribution and recognition.

The need for this sort of two-pronged approach becomes more pressing, moreover, as soon as we cease considering such axes of injustice singly and begin instead to consider them together as mutually intersecting. After all, gender, 'race', sexuality, and class are not neatly cordoned off from one another. Rather, all these axes of injustice intersect one another in ways that affect everyone's interests and identities. Thus, anyone who is both gay and working-class will need both redistribution and recognition. Seen this way, moreover, virtually every individual who suffers injustice needs to integrate those two kinds of claims. And so, furthermore, will anyone who cares about social justice, regardless of their own personal social location.

In general, then, one should roundly reject the construction of redistribution and recognition as mutually exclusive alternatives. The goal should be, rather, to develop an integrated approach that can encompass, and harmonize, both dimensions of social justice.

Normative-philosophical issues: for a two-dimensional theory of justice

Integrating redistribution and recognition in a single comprehensive paradigm is no simple matter, however. To contemplate such a project is to be plunged immediately into deep and difficult problems spanning several major fields of inquiry. In moral philosophy, for example, the task is to devise an overarching conception of justice that can accommodate both defensible claims for social equality and defensible claims for the recognition of difference. In social theory, by contrast, the task is to devise an account of our contemporary social formation that can accommodate not only the differentiation of class from status, economy from culture, but also their mutual imbrication. In political theory, meanwhile, the task is to envision a set of institutional arrangements and associated policy reforms that can remedy both maldistribution and misrecognition, while minimizing the mutual interferences likely to arise when the two sorts of redress are sought simultaneously. In practical politics, finally, the task is to foster democratic engagement across current divides in order to build a broad-based programmatic orientation that integrates the best of the politics of redistribution with the best of the politics of recognition.

This, of course, is far too much to take on here. In the present section, I limit myself to some of the moral-theoretical dimensions of this project. (In the next, I turn to some issues in social theory.) I shall consider three normative philosophical questions that arise when we contemplate integrating redistribution and recognition in a single comprehensive account of social justice: First, is recognition really a matter of justice, or is it a matter of self-realization? Second, do distributive justice and recognition constitute two distinct, *sui generis*, normative paradigms, or can either of them be subsumed within the other? And third, does justice require the recognition of what is distinctive about individuals or groups, or is recognition of our common humanity sufficient? (I defer to a later occasion discussion of a fourth crucial question: how can we distinguish justified from unjustified claims for recognition?)

On the first question, two major theorists, Charles Taylor and Axel Honneth, understand recognition as a matter of self-realization. Unlike them, however, I propose to treat it as an issue of justice. Thus, one should not answer the question 'what's wrong with misrecognition?' by reference to a thick theory of the good, as Taylor (1994) does. Nor should one follow Honneth (1995) and appeal to a 'formal conception of ethical life' premised on an account of the 'intersubjective conditions' for an 'undistorted practical relation-to-self'. One should say, rather, that it is unjust that some individuals and groups are denied the status of full partners in social interaction simply as a consequence of institutionalized patterns of cultural value in whose construction they have not equally participated and which disparage their distinctive characteristics or the distinctive characteristics assigned to them.

This account offers several advantages. First, it permits one to justify claims for recognition as morally binding under modern conditions of value pluralism.[5] Under these conditions, there is no single conception of self-realization or the good that is universally shared, nor any that can be established as authoritative. Thus, any attempt to justify claims for recognition that appeals to an account of self-realization or the good must necessarily be sectarian. No approach of this sort can establish such claims as normatively binding on those who do not share the theorist's conception of ethical value.

Unlike such approaches, I propose an account that is deontological and non-sectarian. Embracing the modern view that it is up to individuals and groups to define for themselves what counts as a good life and to devise for themselves an approach to pursuing it, within limits that ensure a like liberty for others, it appeals to a conception of justice that can be accepted by people with divergent conceptions of the good. What makes misrecognition morally wrong, on my view, is that it denies some individuals and groups the possibility of participating on a par with others in social interaction. The norm of *participatory parity* invoked here is non-sectarian in the required sense. It can justify claims for recognition as normatively binding on all who agree to abide by fair terms of interaction under conditions of value pluralism.

Treating recognition as a matter of justice has a second advantage as well. It conceives misrecognition as *status subordination* whose locus is social relations, not individual psychology. To be misrecognized, on this view, is not simply to be thought ill of, looked down on, or devalued in others' conscious attitudes or mental beliefs. It is rather to be denied the status of a full partner in social interaction and prevented from participating as a peer in social life as a consequence of *institutionalized* patterns of cultural value that constitute one as comparatively unworthy of respect or esteem. When such patterns of disrespect and disesteem are institutionalized, they impede parity of participation, just as surely as do distributive inequities.

Eschewing psychologization, then, the justice approach escapes difficulties that plague rival approaches. When misrecognition is identified with internal distortions in the structure of self-consciousness of the oppressed, it is but a short step to blaming the victim, as one seems to add insult to injury. Conversely, when misrecognition is equated with prejudice in the minds of the oppressors, overcoming it seems to require policing their beliefs, an approach that is authoritarian. On the justice view, in contrast, misrecognition is a matter of externally manifest and publicly verifiable impediments to some people's standing as full members of society. And such arrangements are morally indefensible whether or not they distort the subjectivity of the oppressed.

Finally, the justice account of recognition avoids the view that everyone has an equal right to social esteem. That view is patently untenable, of course, because it renders meaningless the notion of esteem. Yet it seems to follow from at least one prominent account of recognition in terms of the self-realization.[6] The account of recognition proposed here, in contrast, entails no such *reductio ad absurdum*. What it *does* entail is that everyone has an equal right to pursue social esteem under fair conditions of equal opportunity. And such conditions do not obtain when, for example, institutionalized patterns of interpretation pervasively downgrade femininity, 'non-whiteness', homosexuality, and everything culturally associated with them. When that is the case, women and/or people of colour and/or gays and lesbians face obstacles in the quest for esteem that are not encountered by others. And everyone, including straight white men, faces further obstacles if they opt to pursue projects and cultivate traits that are culturally coded as feminine, homosexual, or 'non-white'.

For all these reasons, recognition is better viewed as a matter of justice than as a matter of self-realization. But what follows for the theory of justice?

Does it follow, turning now to the second question, that distribution and recognition constitute two distinct, *sui generis* conceptions of justice? Or can either of them be reduced to the other? The question of reduction must be considered from two different sides. From one side, the issue is whether standard theories of distributive justice can adequately subsume problems of recognition. In my view, the answer is no. To be sure, many distributive theorists appreciate the importance of status over and above the allocation of resources and seek to accommodate it in their accounts.[7] But the results are not wholly satisfactory. Most such theorists assume a reductive economistic-cum-legalistic view of status, supposing that a just distribution of resources and rights is sufficient to preclude mis-recognition. In fact, however, as we saw, not all misrecognition is a byproduct of maldistribution, nor of maldistribution plus legal dis-crimination. Witness the case of the African-American Wall Street banker who cannot get a taxi to pick him up. To handle such cases, a theory of justice must reach beyond the distribution of rights and goods to examine patterns of cultural value. It must consider whether institu-tionalized patterns of interpretation and valuation impede parity of participation in social life.[8]

What, then, of the other side of the question? Can existing theories of recognition adequately subsume problems of distribution? Here, too, I contend the answer is no. To be sure, some theorists of recognition appreciate the importance of economic equality and seek to accom-modate it in their accounts.[9] But once again the results are not wholly satisfactory. Such theorists tend to assume a reductive culturalist view of distribution. Supposing that economic inequalities are rooted in a cultural order that privileges some kinds of labour over others, they assume that changing that cultural order is sufficient to preclude mal-distribution (Honneth, 1995). In fact, however, as we saw, and as I shall argue more extensively later, not all maldistribution is a byproduct of misrecognition. Witness the case of the skilled white male industrial worker who becomes unemployed due to a factory closing as a result of a speculative corporate merger. In that case, the injustice of maldis-tribution has little to do with misrecognition. It is rather a consequence of imperatives intrinsic to an order of specialized economic relations whose raison d'être is the accumulation of profits. To handle such cases, a theory of justice must reach beyond cultural value patterns to examine the structure of capitalism. It must consider whether economic mech-anisms that are relatively decoupled from cultural value patterns and that operate in a relatively impersonal way can impede parity of parti-cipation in social life.

In general then, neither distribution theorists nor recognition theor-ists have so far succeeded in adequately subsuming the concerns of the other.[10] Thus, instead of endorsing either one of their paradigms to the exclusion of the other, I propose to develop what I shall call a two-dimensional conception of justice. Such a conception treats distribution and recognition as distinct perspectives on, and dimensions of, justice. Without reducing either one of them to the other, it encompasses both dimensions within a broader, overarching framework.

The normative core of my conception, which I have mentioned several times, is the notion of *parity of participation*.[11] According to this norm, justice requires social arrangements that permit all (adult) members of society to interact with one another as peers. For participatory parity to be possible, I claim, it is necessary but not sufficient to establish standard forms of formal legal equality. Over and above that requirement, at least two additional conditions must be satisfied.[12] First, the distribution of material resources must be such as to ensure participants' independence and 'voice'. This I call the 'objective' precondition of participatory parity. It precludes forms and levels of material inequality and economic dependence that impede parity of participation. Precluded, therefore, are social arrangements that institutionalize deprivation, exploitation, and gross disparities in wealth, income, and leisure time, thereby denying some people the means and opportunities to interact with others as peers.[13]

In contrast, the second additional condition for participatory parity I call 'intersubjective'. It requires that institutionalized cultural patterns of interpretation and evaluation express equal respect for all participants and ensure equal opportunity for achieving social esteem. This condition precludes cultural patterns that systematically depreciate some categories of people and the qualities associated with them. Precluded, therefore, are institutionalized value schemata that deny some people the status of full partners in interaction – whether by burdening them with excessive ascribed 'difference' from others or by failing to acknowledge their distinctiveness.

Both the objective precondition and the intersubjective precondition are necessary for participatory parity. Neither alone is sufficient. The objective condition brings into focus concerns traditionally associated with the theory of distributive justice, especially concerns pertaining to the economic structure of society and to economically defined class differentials. The intersubjective precondition brings into focus concerns recently highlighted in the philosophy of recognition, especially concerns pertaining to the status order of society and to culturally defined hierarchies of status. Thus, a two-dimensional conception of justice oriented to the norm of participatory parity encompasses both redistribution and recognition, without reducing either one to the other.

This brings us to the third question: does justice require the recognition of what is distinctive about individuals or groups, over and above the recognition of our common humanity? Here it is important to note that participatory parity is a universalist norm in two senses. First, it encompasses all (adult) partners to interaction. And second, it presupposes the equal moral worth of human beings. But moral universalism in these senses still leaves open the question whether recognition of individual or group distinctiveness could be required by justice as one element among others of the intersubjective condition for participatory parity.

This question cannot be answered, I contend, by an *a priori* account of the kinds of recognition that everyone always needs. It needs rather to be approached in the spirit of pragmatism as informed by the insights of a critical social theory. From this perspective, recognition is a remedy for injustice, not a generic human need. Thus, the form(s) of recognition justice requires in any given case depend(s) on the form(s) of *mis*recognition to be redressed. In cases where misrecognition involves denying the common humanity of some participants, the remedy is universalist recognition. Where, in contrast, misrecognition involves denying some participants' distinctiveness, the remedy could be recognition of difference.[14] In every case, the remedy should be tailored to the harm.

This pragmatist approach overcomes the liabilities of two other views that are mirror opposites and hence equally decontextualized. First, it avoids the view, espoused by some distributive theorists, that justice requires limiting public recognition to those capacities all humans share. That approach dogmatically forecloses recognition of what distinguishes people from one another, without considering whether the latter might be needed in some cases to overcome obstacles to participatory parity. Second, the pragmatist approach avoids the opposite view, also decontextualized, that everyone always needs their distinctiveness recognized (Taylor, 1994; Honneth, 1995). Favoured by recognition theorists, this anthropological view cannot explain why it is that not all, but only some, social differences generate claims for recognition, nor why only some of those that do, but not others, are morally justified. More specifically, it cannot explain why dominant groups, such as men and heterosexuals, usually shun recognition of their (gender and sexual) distinctiveness, claiming not specificity but universality. By contrast, the approach proposed here sees claims for the recognition of difference pragmatically and contextually – as remedial responses to specific harms. Putting questions of justice at the centre, it appreciates that the recognition needs of subordinate groups differ from those of dominant groups; and that only those claims that promote participatory parity are morally justified.

For the pragmatist, accordingly, everything depends on precisely what currently misrecognized people need in order to be able to participate as peers in social life. And there is no reason to assume that all of them need the same thing in every context. In some cases, they may need to be unburdened of excessive ascribed or constructed distinctiveness. In other cases, they may need to have hitherto underacknowledged distinctiveness taken into account. In still other cases, they may need to shift the focus onto dominant or advantaged groups, outing the latter's distinctiveness, which has been falsely parading as universality. Alternatively, they may need to deconstruct the very terms in which attributed differences are currently elaborated. Finally, they may need all of the above, or several of the above, in combination with one another and in combination with redistribution. Which people need which kind(s) of recognition in which contexts depends on the nature of the obstacles they face with regard to participatory parity. That, however, cannot be determined by abstract philosophical argument. It can only be determined with the aid of a critical social theory, a theory that is normatively oriented, empirically informed, and guided by the practical intent of overcoming injustice.

Social-theoretical issues: an argument for 'perspectival dualism'

This brings us to the social-theoretical issues that arise when we try to encompass redistribution and recognition in a single framework. Here, the principal task is to theorize the relations between class and status, and between maldistribution and misrecognition, in contemporary society. An adequate approach must allow for the full complexity of these relations. It must account *both for the differentiation of class and status and for the causal interactions between them*. It must accommodate, as well, *both the mutual irreducibility of maldistribution and misrecognition and their practical entwinement with one another*. Such an account must, moreover, be historical. Sensitive to shifts in social structure and political culture, it must identify the distinctive dynamics and conflict tendencies of the present conjuncture. Attentive both to national specificities and to transnational forces and frames, it must explain why today's grammar of social conflict takes the form that it does: why, that is, struggles for recognition have recently become so salient; why egalitarian redistribution struggles, hitherto central to social life, have lately receded to the margins; and why, finally, the two kinds of claims for social justice have become decoupled and antagonistically counterposed.[15]

First, however, some conceptual clarifications. The terms class and status, as I use them here, denote socially entrenched orders of domination. To say that a society has a class structure, accordingly, is to say that it institutionalizes mechanisms of distribution that systematically deny some of its members the means and opportunities they need in order to participate on a par with others in social life. To say, likewise, that a society has a status hierarchy is to say that it institutionalizes patterns of cultural value that pervasively deny some of its members the recognition they need in order to be full, participating partners in interaction. The existence of either a class structure or a status hierarchy constitutes an obstacle to parity of participation and thus an injustice.

In what follows, then, I assume an internal conceptual relation between class and status, on the one hand, and domination and injustice, on the other. I do not, however, present a full theory of class or status. Deferring that task to another occasion, I assume only that both orders of domination emerged historically with developments in social organization, as did the conceptual distinction between them and the possibility of their mutual divergence. I assume, too, that a society's class structure becomes distinguishable from its status order only when its mechanisms of economic distribution become differentiated from social arenas in which institutionalized patterns of cultural value regulate interaction in a relatively direct and unmediated way. Thus, only with the emergence of a specialized order of economic relations can the question arise, whether the society's class structure diverges from its status hierarchy or whether, alternatively, they coincide. Only then, likewise, can the question become politically salient whether the status hierarchy and/or the class structure are unjust.

What follows from this approach for our understanding of the categories, economy and culture? Both of these terms, as I use them here, denote social processes and social relations.[16] Both, moreover, must be grasped historically. As I just noted, specifically economic processes and relations became differentiated from unmediatedly value-regulated processes and relations only with historical shifts in the structure of societies. Only with the rise of capitalism did highly autonomous economic institutions emerge, making possible the modern ideas of 'the economic' and 'the cultural', as well as the distinction between them.[17] To be sure, these ideas can be applied retrospectively to precapitalist societies – provided one situates one's usage historically and explicitly notes the anachronism. But this only serves to underline the key point: far from being ontological or anthropological, economy and culture are *historically emergent categories of social theory*. What counts as economic and as cultural depends on the type of society in question. So, as well, does the relation between the economic and the cultural.

An analogous point holds for maldistribution and misrecognition. It is not the case that the former denotes a species of material harm and the latter one of immaterial injury. On the contrary, status injuries can be just as material as distributive injustices – witness gay-bashing, gang rape, and genocide.[18] Far from being ontological, this distinction, too, is historical. Distribution and recognition correspond to historically specific social-structural differentiations, paradigmatically those associated with modern capitalism. *Historically emergent normative categories*, they became distinguishable dimensions of justice only with the differentiation of class from status and of the economic from the cultural. Only, in other words, with the relative uncoupling of specialized economic mechanisms of distribution from broader patterns of cultural value did the distinction between maldistribution and misrecognition become thinkable. And only then could the question of the relation between them arise. To be sure, these categories too can be applied retrospectively, provided one is sufficiently self-aware. But the point, once again, is to historicize. The relations between maldistribution and misrecognition vary according to the social formation under consideration. It remains an empirical question in any given case whether and to what extent they coincide.

In every case, the level of differentiation is crucial. In some societies, conceivable or actual, economy and culture are not institutionally differentiated. Consider, for example, an ideal-typical pre-state society of the sort described in the classical anthropological literature, while bracketing the question of ethnographic accuracy.[19] In such a society, the master idiom of social relations is kinship. Kinship organizes not only marriage and sexual relations, but also the labour process and the distribution of goods; relations of authority, reciprocity, and obligation; and symbolic hierarchies of status and prestige. Of course, it could well be the case that such a society has never existed in pure form. Still, we can imagine a world in which neither distinctively economic institutions nor distinctively cultural institutions exist. A single order of social relations secures (what *we* would call) both the economic integration and the cultural integration of the society. Class structure and status order are accordingly fused. Because kinship constitutes the overarching principle of distribution, kinship status dictates class position. In the absence of any quasi-autonomous economic institutions, status injuries translate immediately into (what *we* would consider to be) distributive injustices. Misrecognition directly entails maldistribution.

This ideal-type of a fully kin-governed society represents an extreme case of non-differentiation, one in which cultural patterns of value dictate the order of economic domination. It is usefully contrasted with the opposite extreme of a fully marketized society, in which economic structure dictates cultural value. In such a society, the master determining instance is the market. Markets organize not only the labour process and the distribution of goods, but also marriage and sexual relations; political relations of authority, reciprocity, and obligation; and symbolic hierarchies of status and prestige. Granted, such a society has never existed, and it is doubtful that one ever could.[20] For heuristic purposes, however, we can imagine a world in which a single order of social relations secures not only the economic integration but also the cultural integration of society. Here, too, as in the fully kin-governed society, class structure and status order are effectively fused. But the determinations run in the opposite direction. Because the market constitutes the sole and all-pervasive mechanism of valuation, market position dictates social status. In the absence of any quasi-autonomous cultural value patterns, distributive injustices translate immediately into status injuries. Maldistribution directly entails misrecognition.

As mirror-opposites of each other, these two imagined societies share a common feature: the absence of any meaningful differentiation of the economy from the larger culture.[21] In both of them, accordingly, (what *we* would call) class and status map perfectly onto each other. So, as well, do (what *we* would call) maldistribution and misrecognition, which convert fully and without remainder into one another. As a result, one can understand both these societies reasonably well by attending exclusively to a single dimension of social life. For the fully kin-governed society, one can read off the economic dimension of domination directly from the cultural; one can infer class directly from status and mal-distribution directly from misrecognition. For the fully marketized society, conversely, one can read off the cultural dimension of domination directly from the economic; one can infer status directly from class, and misrecognition directly from maldistribution. For understanding the forms of domination proper to the fully kin-governed society, therefore, culturalism is a perfectly appropriate social theory.[22] If, in contrast, one is seeking to understand the fully marketized society, one could hardly improve on economism.[23]

When we turn to other types of societies, however, such simple and elegant approaches no longer suffice. They are patently inappropriate for the actually existing capitalist society that we currently inhabit and seek to understand. In this society, a specialized set of economic institutions has been differentiated from the larger social field. The paradigm institutions are markets, which operate by instrumentalizing the cultural value patterns that regulate some other orders of social relations in a fairly direct and unmediated way. Filtering meanings and values through an individual-interest-maximizing grid, markets decontextualize and rework cultural patterns. As the latter are pressed into the service of an individualizing logic, they are disembedded, instrumentalized, and resignified. The result is a specialized zone in which cultural values, though neither simply suspended nor wholly dissolved, do not regulate social interaction in a direct and unmediated way. Rather, they impact it indirectly, through the mediation of the 'cash nexus'.

Markets have always existed, of course, but their scope, autonomy, and influence attained a qualitatively new level with the development of modern capitalism. In capitalist society, these value-instrumentalizing institutions directly organize a significant portion of the labour process (the waged portion), the distribution of most products and goods (commodities), and the investment of most social surplus (profit). They do not, however, *directly* organize marriage, sexuality, and the family; relations of political authority and legal obligation; and symbolic hierarchies of status and prestige. Rather, each of these social orders retains distinctive institutional forms and normative orientations; each also remains connected to, and informed by, the general culture; some of them, finally, are regulated by institutionalized patterns of cultural value in a relatively direct and unmediated way.

Thus, in capitalist society, relations between economy and culture are complex. Neither devoid of culture, nor directly subordinated to it, capitalist markets stand in a highly mediated relation to institutionalized patterns of cultural value. They work through the latter, while also *working over* them, sometimes helping to transform them in the process. Thoroughly permeated by significations and norms, yet possessed of a logic of their own, capitalist economic institutions are neither wholly constrained by, nor fully in control of, value patterns.

To be sure, capitalist market processes heavily influence non-market relations. But their influence is indirect. In principle and, to a lesser degree, in practice, non-marketized arenas have some autonomy vis-à-vis the market, as well as vis-à-vis one another. It remains an empirical question exactly how far in each case market influence actually penetrates – and a normative question how far it should. The reverse is, by contrast, fairly clear: in capitalist societies, market processes generally have considerable autonomy vis-à-vis politics, although the precise extent varies according to the regime. In its Western European heyday, Keynesian social democracy sought with some success to use 'politics to tame markets' within state borders. In the current climate of post-Keynesian, neoliberal, globalizing capitalism, the market's scope, autonomy, and influence is sharply increasing.

The key point here is that capitalist society is structurally differentiated. The institutionalization of specialized economic relations permits the partial uncoupling of economic distribution from structures of prestige. As markets instrumentalize value patterns that remain constitutive for non-marketized relations, a gap arises between status and class. The class structure ceases perfectly to mirror the status order, even as each of them influences the other. Because the market does not constitute the sole and all-pervasive mechanism of valuation, market position does not dictate social status. Partially market-resistant cultural value patterns prevent distributive injustices from converting fully and without remainder into status injuries. Maldistribution does not directly entail misrecognition, although it may well contribute to the latter. Conversely, because no single status principle such as kinship constitutes the sole and all-pervasive principle of distribution, status does not dictate class position. Relatively autonomous economic institutions prevent status injuries from converting fully and without remainder into distributive injustices. Misrecognition does not directly entail maldistribution, although it, too, may contribute to the latter.

In capitalist society, accordingly, class and status do not perfectly mirror each other, their interaction and mutual influence notwithstanding. Nor, likewise, do maldistribution and misrecognition convert fully and without remainder into one another, despite interaction and even entwinement. As a result, one cannot understand this society by attending exclusively to a single dimension of social life. One cannot read off the economic dimension of domination directly from the cultural, nor the cultural directly from the economic. Likewise, one cannot infer class directly from status, nor status directly from class. Finally, one cannot deduce maldistribution directly from misrecognition, nor misrecognition directly from maldistribution. It follows that neither culturalism nor economism suffices for understanding capitalist society. Instead, one needs an approach that can accommodate differentiation, divergence, and interaction at every level.

What sort of social theory can handle this task? What approach can theorize both the differentiation of status from class and the causal interactions between them? What kind of theory can accommodate the complex relations between maldistribution and misrecognition in contemporary society, grasping at once their conceptual irreducibility, empirical divergence, and practical entwinement? And what approach can do all this *without reinforcing the current dissociation of the politics of recognition from the politics of redistribution*? If neither economism nor culturalism is up to the task, what alternative approaches are possible?

Two possibilities present themselves, both of them species of dualism.[24] The first approach I call 'substantive dualism'. It treats redistribution and recognition as two different 'spheres of justice', pertaining to two different societal domains. The former pertains to the economic domain of society, the relations of production. The latter pertains to the cultural domain, the relations of recognition. When we consider economic matters, such as the structure of labour markets, we should assume the standpoint of distributive justice, attending to the impact of economic structures and institutions on the relative economic position of social actors. When, in contrast, we consider cultural matters, such as the representation of female sexuality on MTV, we should assume the standpoint of recognition, attending to the impact of institutionalized patterns of interpretation and value on the status and relative standing of social actors.

Substantive dualism may be preferable to economism and culturalism, but it is nevertheless inadequate – both conceptually and politically. Conceptually, it erects a dichotomy that opposes economy to culture and treats them as two separate spheres. It thereby mistakes the differentiations of capitalist society for institutional divisions that are impermeable and sharply bounded. In fact, these differentiations mark orders of social relations that can overlap one another institutionally and are more or less permeable in different regimes. As just noted, the economy is not a culture-free zone, but a culture-instrumentalizing and -resignifying one. Thus, what presents itself as 'the economy' is always already permeated with cultural interpretations and norms – witness the distinctions between 'working' and 'caregiving', 'men's jobs' and 'women's jobs', which are so fundamental to historical capitalism. In these cases, gender meanings and norms have been appropriated from the larger culture and bent to capitalist purposes, with major consequences for both distribution and recognition. Likewise, what presents itself as 'the cultural sphere' is deeply permeated by 'the bottom line' – witness global mass entertainment, the art market, and transnational advertising, all fundamental to contemporary culture. Once again, the consequences are significant for both distribution and recognition. *Contra* substantive dualism, then, nominally economic matters usually affect not only the economic position but also the status and identities of social actors. Likewise, nominally cultural matters affect not only status but also economic position. In neither case, therefore, are we dealing with separate spheres.[25]

Practically, moreover, substantive dualism fails to challenge the current dissociation of cultural politics from social politics. On the contrary, it reinforces that dissociation. Casting the economy and the culture as impermeable, sharply bounded separate spheres, it assigns the politics of redistribution to the former and the politics of recognition to the latter. The result is effectively to constitute two separate political tasks requiring two separate political struggles. Decoupling cultural injustices from economic injustices, cultural struggles from social struggles, it reproduces the very dissociation we are seeking to overcome. Substantive dualism is not a solution to, but a symptom of, our problem. It reflects, but does not critically interrogate, the institutional differentiations of modern capitalism.

A genuinely critical perspective, in contrast, cannot take the appearance of separate spheres at face value. Rather, it must probe beneath appearances to reveal the hidden connections between distribution and recognition. It must make visible, and *criticizable*, both the cultural subtexts of nominally economic processes and the economic subtexts of nominally cultural practices. Treating *every* practice as simultaneously economic and cultural, albeit not necessarily in equal proportions, it must assess each of them from two different perspectives. It must assume both the standpoint of distribution and the standpoint of recognition, without reducing either one of these perspectives to the other.

Such an approach I call 'perspectival dualism'. Here redistribution and recognition do not correspond to two substantive societal domains, economy and culture. Rather, they constitute two analytical perspectives that can be assumed with respect to any domain. These perspectives can be deployed critically, moreover, against the ideological grain. One can use the recognition perspective to identify the cultural dimensions of what are usually viewed as redistributive economic policies. By focusing on the production and circulation of interpretations and norms in welfare programmes, for example, one can assess the effects of institutionalized maldistribution on the identities and social status of single mothers.[26] Conversely, one can use the redistribution perspective to bring into focus the economic dimensions of what are usually viewed as issues of recognition. By focusing on the high 'transaction costs' of living in the closet, for example, one can assess the effects of heterosexist misrecognition on the economic position of gays and lesbians.[27] With perspectival dualism, then, one can assess the justice of any social practice, regardless of where it is institutionally located, from either or both of two analytically distinct normative vantage points, asking: Does the practice in question work to ensure both the objective and intersubjective conditions of participatory parity? Or does it, rather, undermine them?

The advantages of this approach should be clear. Unlike economism and culturalism, perspectival dualism permits us to consider both distribution and recognition, without reducing either one of them to the other. Unlike substantive dualism, moreover, it does not reinforce their dissociation. Because it avoids dichotomizing economy and culture, it allows us to grasp their imbrication and the crossover effects of each. And because, finally, it avoids reducing classes to statuses or vice versa, it permits us to examine the causal interactions between those two orders of domination. Understood perspectivally, then, the distinction between redistribution and recognition does not simply reproduce the ideological dissociations of our time. Rather, it provides an indispensable conceptual tool for interrogating, working through, and eventually overcoming those dissociations.

Perspectival dualism offers another advantage as well. Of all the approaches considered here, it alone allows us to conceptualize some practical difficulties that can arise in the course of political struggles for redistribution and recognition. Conceiving the economic and the cultural as differentiated but interpenetrating social orders, perspectival dualism appreciates that neither claims for redistribution nor claims for recognition can be contained within a separate sphere. On the contrary, they impinge on one another in ways that may give rise to unintended effects.

Consider, first, that redistribution impinges on recognition. Virtually any claim for redistribution will have some recognition effects, whether intended or unintended. Proposals to redistribute income through social welfare, for example, have an irreducible expressive dimension;[28] they convey interpretations of the meaning and value of different activities, for example, 'childrearing' versus 'wage-earning', while also constituting and ranking different subject positions, for example 'welfare mothers' versus 'tax payers' (Fraser, 1993). Thus, redistributive claims invariably affect the status and social identities of social actors. These effects must be thematized and scrutinized, lest one end up fuelling misrecognition in the course of remedying maldistribution.

The classic example, once again, is 'welfare'. Means-tested benefits aimed specifically at the poor are the most directly redistributive form of social welfare. Yet such benefits tend to stigmatize recipients, casting them as deviants and scroungers and invidiously distinguishing them from 'wage-earners' and 'tax-payers' who 'pay their own way'. Welfare programmes of this type 'target' the poor – not only for material aid but also for public hostility. The end result is often to add the insult of misrecognition to the injury of deprivation. Redistributive policies have misrecognition effects when background patterns of cultural value skew the meaning of economic reforms, when, for example, a pervasive cultural devaluation of female caregiving inflects Aid to Families with Dependent Children as 'getting something for nothing'.[29] In this context, welfare reform cannot succeed unless it is joined with struggles for

cultural change aimed at revaluing caregiving and the feminine associations that code it.[30] In short, no redistribution without recognition.

Consider, next, the converse dynamic, whereby recognition impinges
on distribution. Virtually any claim for recognition will have some distributive effects, whether intended or unintended. Proposals to redress
androcentric evaluative patterns, for example, have economic implications, which work sometimes to the detriment of the intended
beneficiaries. For example, campaigns to suppress prostitution and
pornography for the sake of enhancing women's status may have negative effects on the economic position of sex workers, while no-fault
divorce reforms, which appeared to dovetail with feminist efforts to
enhance women's status, may have had at least short-term negative
effects on the economic position of some divorced women, although their
extent has apparently been exaggerated and is currently in dispute
(Weitzman, 1985). Thus, recognition claims can affect economic position,
above and beyond their effects on status. These effects, too, must be
scrutinized, lest one end up fuelling maldistribution in the course of
trying to remedy misrecognition. Recognition claims, moreover, are liable
to the charge of being 'merely symbolic'.[31] When pursued in contexts
marked by gross disparities in economic position, reforms aimed at
recognizing distinctiveness tend to devolve into empty gestures; like the
sort of recognition that would put women on a pedestal, they mock,
rather than redress, serious harms. In such contexts, recognition reforms
cannot succeed unless they are joined with struggles for redistribution. In
short, no recognition without redistribution.

The need, in all cases, is to think integratively, as in the example of
comparable worth. Here a claim to redistribute income between men
and women is expressly integrated with a claim to change gender-
coded patterns of cultural value. The underlying premise is that gender
injustices of distribution and recognition are so complexly intertwined
that neither can be redressed entirely independently of the other. Thus,
efforts to reduce the gender wage gap cannot fully succeed if, remaining
wholly 'economic', they fail to challenge the gender meanings that code
low-paying service occupations as 'women's work', largely devoid of
intelligence and skill. Likewise, efforts to revalue female-coded traits
such as interpersonal sensitivity and nurturance cannot succeed if,
remaining wholly 'cultural', they fail to challenge the structural economic conditions that connect those traits with dependency and power-
lessness. Only an approach that redresses the cultural devaluation of the
'feminine' precisely *within* the economy (and elsewhere) can deliver
serious redistribution and genuine recognition.

Conclusion

Let me conclude by recapitulating my overall argument. I have argued
that to pose an either/or choice between the politics of redistribution and

the politics of recognition is to posit a false antithesis. On the contrary, justice today requires both. Thus, I have argued for a comprehensive framework that encompasses both redistribution and recognition so as to challenge injustice on both fronts.

I then examined two sets of issues that arise once we contemplate devising such a framework. On the plane of moral theory, I argued for a single, two-dimensional conception of justice that encompasses both redistribution and recognition, without reducing either one of them to the other. And I proposed the notion of *parity of participation* as its normative core. On the plane of social theory, I argued for a *perspectival dualism* of redistribution and recognition. This approach alone, I contended, can accommodate both the differentiation of class from status in capitalist society and also their causal interaction. And it alone can alert us to potential practical tensions between claims for redistribution and claims for recognition.

Perspectival dualism in social theory complements participatory parity in moral theory. Taken together, these two notions constitute a portion of the conceptual resources one needs to begin answering what I take to be the key political question of our day: How can we develop a coherent programmatic perspective that integrates redistribution and recognition? How can we develop a framework that integrates what remains cogent and unsurpassable in the socialist vision with what is defensible and compelling in the apparently 'postsocialist' vision of multiculturalism?

If we fail to ask this question, if we cling instead to false antitheses and misleading either/or dichotomies, we will miss the chance to envision social arrangements that can redress both economic and cultural injustices. Only by looking to integrative approaches that unite redistribution and recognition can we meet the requirements of justice for all.

Notes

Portions of this chapter are adapted and excerpted from my Tanner Lecture on Human Values, delivered at Stanford University, 30 April to 2 May, 1996. The text of the Lecture appears in *The Tanner Lectures on Human Values*, volume 9, ed. Grethe B. Peterson (The University of Utah Press, 1998: 1–67). I am grateful to the Tanner Foundation for Human Values for permission to adapt and reprint this material. I thank Elizabeth Anderson and Axel Honneth for their thoughtful responses to the Tanner Lecture, and Rainer Forst, Theodore Koditschek, Eli Zaretsky, and especially Erik Olin Wright for helpful comments on earlier drafts.

1 The following discussion revises a subsection of my essay, 'From redistribution to recognition?' (Fraser, 1995: 68–93), reprinted in Fraser (1997a).

2 It is true that pre-existing status distinctions, for example, between lords and commoners, shaped the emergence of the capitalist system. Nevertheless, it was only the creation of a differentiated economic order with a relatively autonomous life of its own that gave rise to the distinction between capitalists and workers.

3 I am grateful to Erik Olin Wright (personal communication, 1997) for several of the formulations in this paragraph.

4 In capitalist society, the regulation of sexuality is relatively decoupled from the economic structure, which comprises an order of economic relations that is differentiated from kinship and oriented to the expansion of surplus value. In the current 'post-Fordist' phase of capitalism, moreover, sexuality increasingly finds its locus in the relatively new, late-modern sphere of 'personal life', where intimate relations that can no longer be identified with the family are lived as disconnected from the imperatives of production and reproduction. Today, accordingly, the heteronormative regulation of sexuality is increasingly removed from, and not necessarily functional for, the capitalist economic order. As a result, the economic harms of heterosexism do not derive in any straightforward way from the economic structure. They are rooted, rather, in the heterosexist status order, which is increasingly out of phase with the economy. For a fuller argument, see Fraser (1997c). For the counter-argument, see Butler (1997).

5 I am grateful to Rainer Forst for help in formulating this point.

6 On Axel Honneth's account, social esteem is among the 'intersubjective conditions for undistorted identity formation', which morality is supposed to protect. It follows that everyone is morally entitled to social esteem. See Honneth (1995).

7 John Rawls, for example, at times conceives 'primary goods' such as income and jobs as 'social bases of self-respect', while also speaking of self-respect itself as an especially important primary good whose distribution is a matter of justice. Ronald Dworkin, likewise, defends the idea of 'equality of resources' as the distributive expression of the 'equal moral worth of persons'. Amartya Sen, finally, considers both a 'sense of self' and the capacity 'to appear in public without shame' as relevant to the 'capability to function', hence as falling within the scope of an account of justice that enjoins the equal distribution of basic capabilities. See Rawls (1971: §67 and §82; 1993: 82, 181 and 318ff), Dworkin (1981), and Sen (1985).

8 The outstanding exception of a theorist who has sought to encompass issues of culture within a distributive framework is Will Kymlicka. Kymlicka proposes to treat access to an 'intact cultural structure' as a primary good to be fairly distributed. This approach was tailored for multinational polities, such as the Canadian, as opposed to polyethnic polities, such as the United States. It becomes problematic, however, in cases where mobilized claimants for recognition do not divide neatly (or even not so neatly) into groups with distinct and relatively bounded cultures. It also has difficulty dealing with cases in which claims for recognition do not take the form of demands for (some level of) sovereignty but aim rather at parity of participation within a polity that is crosscut by multiple, intersecting lines of difference and inequality. For the argument that an intact cultural structure is a primary good, see Kymlicka (1989). For the distinction between multinational and polyethnic politics, see Kymlicka (1996).

9 See especially Honneth (1995).

10 To be sure, this could conceivably change. Nothing I have said rules out *a priori* that someone could successfully extend the distributive paradigm to encompass issues of culture. Nor that someone could successfully extend the recognition paradigm to encompass the structure of capitalism, although that seems more unlikely to me. In either case, it will be necessary to meet several essential requirements simultaneously: first, one must avoid hypostatizing culture and cultural differences; second, one must respect the need for non-sectarian, deontological moral justification under modern conditions of value pluralism; third, one must allow for the differentiated character of capitalist society, in which status and class can diverge; fourth, one must avoid overly

unitarian or Durkheimian views of cultural integration that posit a single pattern of cultural values that is shared by all and that pervades all institutions and social practices. Each of these issues is discussed in my contribution to Fraser and Honneth (2000).

11 Since I coined this phrase in 1995, the term 'parity' has come to play a central role in feminist politics in France. There, it signifies the demand that women occupy a full 50 per cent of seats in parliament and other representative bodies. 'Parity' in France, accordingly, means strict numerical gender equality in political representation. For me, in contrast, 'parity' means the condition of being a *peer*, of being on a *par* with others, of standing on an equal footing. I leave the question open exactly to what degree or level of equality is necessary to ensure such parity. In my formulation, moreover, the moral requirement is that members of society be ensured the *possibility* of parity, if and when they choose to participate in a given activity or interaction. There is no requirement that everyone actually participate in any such activity.

12 I say '*at least* two additional conditions must be satisfied' in order to allow for the possibility of more than two. I have in mind specifically a possible third class of obstacles to participatory parity that could be called 'political', as opposed to economic or cultural. Such obstacles would include decision-making procedures that systematically marginalize some people even in the absence of maldistribution and misrecognition: for example, single-district winner-take-all electoral rules that deny voice to quasi-permanent minorities. (For an insightful account of this example, see Guinier (1994).) The possibility of a third class of 'political' obstacles to participatory parity adds a further Weberian twist to my use of the class/status distinction. Weber's own distinction was tripartite not bipartite: 'class, status, and party'. I do not develop it here, however. Here I confine myself to maldistribution and misrecognition, while leaving the analysis of 'political' obstacles to participatory parity character for another occasion.

13 It is an open question how much economic inequality is consistent with parity of participation. Some such inequality is inevitable and unobjectionable. But there is a threshold at which resource disparities become so gross as to impede participatory parity. Where exactly that threshold lies is a matter for further investigation.

14 I say the remedy *could* be recognition of difference, not that it must be. Elsewhere I discuss alternative remedies for the sort of misrecognition that involves denying distinctiveness. See my contribution to Fraser and Honneth (2000).

15 In this brief essay, I lack the space to consider these questions of contemporary historical sociology. See, however, my contributions in Fraser and Honneth (2000).

16 As I use it, the distinction between economy and culture is social-theoretical, not ontological or metaphysical. Thus, I do not treat the economic as an extra-discursive realm of brute materiality any more than I treat the cultural as an immaterial realm of disembodied ideality. For a reading of my work that mistakes economy and culture for ontological categories, see Butler (1997). For a critique of this misinterpretation, see Fraser (1997c).

17 This is not to deny the prior existence of other, premodern understandings of 'economy', such as Aristotle's.

18 To be sure, misrecognition harms are rooted in cultural patterns of interpretation and evaluation. But this does not mean, contra Judith Butler (1997), that they are 'merely cultural'. On the contrary, the norms, significations, and constructions of personhood that impede women, racialized peoples, and/ or gays and lesbians from parity of participation in social life are materially instantiated – in institutions and social practices, in social action and embodied habitus, and in ideological state apparatuses. Far from occupying some wispy,

ethereal realm, they are material in their existence and effects. For a rejoinder to Butler see Fraser (1997c).

19 For example, Marcel Mauss, *The Gift*, and Claude Lévi-Strauss, *The Elementary Structures of Kinship*.

20 For an argument against the possibility of a fully marketized society, see Polanyi (1957).

21 It is conceivable that our hypothetical fully marketized society could contain formal institutional differentiations, including, for example, a legal system, a political system, and a family structure. But these differentiations would not be meaningful. *Ex hypothesi*, institutions and arenas that were extra-market *de jure* would be *de facto* market-governed.

22 By culturalism, I mean a monistic social theory that holds that political economy is reducible to culture and that class is reducible to status. As I read him, Axel Honneth subscribes to such a theory. See Honneth (1995).

23 By economism, I mean a monistic social theory that holds that culture is reducible to political economy and that status is reducible to class. Karl Marx is often (mis)read as subscribing to such a theory.

24 In what follows, I leave aside a third possibility, which I call 'deconstructive anti-dualism'. Rejecting the economy/culture distinction as 'dichotomizing', this approach seeks to deconstruct it altogether. The claim is that culture and economy are so deeply interconnected that it doesn't make sense to distinguish them. A related claim is that contemporary capitalist society is so monolithically systematic that a struggle against one aspect of it necessarily threatens the whole; hence, it is illegitimate, unnecessary, and counterproductive to distinguish maldistribution from misrecognition. In my view, deconstructive anti-dualism is deeply misguided. For one thing, simply to stipulate that all injustices, and all claims to remedy them, are simultaneously economic and cultural, evacuates the actually existing divergence of status from class. For another, treating capitalism as a monolithic system of perfectly interlocking oppressions evacuates its actual complexity and differentiation. For two rather different versions of deconstructive anti-dualism, see Young (1997) and Butler (1997). For detailed rebuttals, see Fraser (1997b; 1997c).

25 For more detailed criticism of an influential example of substantive dualism, see 'What's critical about critical theory? The case of Habermas and gender' in Fraser (1989).

26 See 'Women, welfare, and the politics of need interpretation' and 'Struggle over needs', both in Fraser (1989); also, Fraser and Gordon (1994), reprinted in Fraser (1997a).

27 Jeffrey Escoffier has discussed these issues insightfully in 'The political economy of the closet: toward an economic history of gay and lesbian life before Stonewall', in Escoffier (1998: 65–78).

28 This formulation was suggested to me by Elizabeth Anderson in her comments on my Tanner Lecture, presented at Stanford University, 30 April to 2 May 1996.

29 Aid to Families with Dependent Children (AFDC) is the major means-tested welfare programme in the United States. Claimed overwhelmingly by solo-mother families living below the poverty line, AFDC became a lightning rod for racist and sexist anti-welfare sentiments in the 1990s. In 1997, it was 'reformed' in such a way as to eliminate the federal entitlement that had guaranteed (some, inadequate) income support to the poor.

30 This formulation, too, was suggested to me by Elizabeth Anderson's comments on my Tanner Lecture, presented at Stanford University, 30 April to 2 May 1996.

31 I am grateful to Steven Lukes for insisting on this point in conversation.

References

Butler, J. (1997) 'Merely cultural', *Social Text*, 52/53: 265–77.

Dworkin, R. (1981) 'What is equality? Part 2: Equality of resources', *Philosophy and Public Affairs*, 10 (4): 283–345.

Escoffier, J. (1998) *American Homo: Community and Perversity*, Berkeley: University of California Press.

Fraser, N. (1989) *Unruly Practices: Power, Discourse and Gender in Contemporary Social Theory*, Minneapolis: University of Minnesota Press.

Fraser, N. (1993) 'Clintonism, welfare and the antisocial wage: the emergence of a neoliberal political imaginary', *Rethinking Marxism*, 6 (1): 9–23.

Fraser, N. (1995) 'From redistribution to recognition? Dilemmas of justice in a "postsocialist" age', *New Left Review*, 212: 68–93.

Fraser, N. (1997a) *Justice Interruptus: Critical Reflections on the 'Postsocialist' Condition*, London: Routledge.

Fraser, N. (1997b) 'A rejoinder to Iris Young', *New Left Review*, 223: 126–9.

Fraser, N. (1997c) 'Heterosexism, misrecognition and capitalism: a response to Judith Butler', *Social Text*, 52/53: 278–89.

Fraser, N. and Gordon, L. (1994) 'A genealogy of "dependency": tracing a keyword of the US welfare state', *Signs*, 19 (2): 309–36.

Fraser, N. and Honneth, A. (2000) *Redistribution or Recognition? A Political–Philosophical Exchange*, London: Verso.

Gitlin, T. (1995) *The Twilight of Common Dreams: Why America is Wracked by Culture Wars*, New York: Metropolitan Books.

Guinier, L. (1994) *The Tyranny of the Majority*, New York: The Free Press.

Honneth, A. (1995) *The Struggle for Recognition: the Moral Grammar of Social Conflicts*, trans J. Anderson, Cambridge: Polity.

Kymlicka, W. (1989) *Liberalism, Community and Culture*, Oxford: Oxford University Press.

Kymlicka, W. (1996) 'Three forms of group-differentiated citizenship in Canada', in S. Benhabib (ed.), *Democracy and Difference*, Princeton, NJ: Princeton University Press.

Polanyi, K. (1957) *The Great Transformation*, Boston: Beacon.

Rawls, J. (1971) *A Theory of Justice*, Cambridge, MA: Harvard University Press.

Rawls, J. (1993) *Political Liberalism*, New York: Columbia University Press.

Rorty, R. (1998) *Achieving Our Country: Leftist Thought in Twentieth-Century America*, Cambridge, MA: Harvard University Press.

Sen, A. (1985) *Commodities and Capabilities*, Amsterdam: North-Holland.

Sennett, R. and Cobb, J. (1973) *The Hidden Injuries of Class*, New York: Knopf.

Taylor, C. (1994) 'The politics of recognition', in A. Gutmann (ed.), *Multiculturalism: Examining the Politics of Recognition*, Princeton, NJ: Princeton University Press.

Thompson, E.P. (1963) *The Making of the English Working Class*, New York: Random House.

Weitzman, L. (1985) *The Divorce Resolution: the Unexpected Social Consequences for Women and Children in America*, New York: The Free Press.

Young, I.M. (1997) 'Unruly categories: a critique of Nancy Fraser's dual systems theory', *New Left Review*, 222: 147–60.

2

Valuing Culture and Economy

Andrew Sayer

We live in a highly economized culture, one that has accommodated to division of labour, class, commodification and instrumental rationality to a considerable degree. A long tradition of social theory has been concerned with precisely this. In different ways, thinkers such as Habermas, Polanyi, Weber, Marx, Smith, and as far back as Aristotle have argued that this economization has detrimental effects on culture, including the moral fabric of societies. Such theory arguably presents too narrow a view of modernity, as the dominant focus on capitalism and the public sphere overlooks important other aspects of contemporary society. In the last thirty years forms of oppression and degradation relating to gender, race, sexuality and cultural imperialism, which were largely ignored by the older critical theory, have been exposed. At the same time, this more recent work either ignores or offers a more positive view of the targets of the older theory. Especially with the cultural turn, it provides a more favourable view of features of modernity such as commodification and the aestheticization of politics which the previous generation attacked – to such an extent in some cases that it might be regarded as complicit in those tendencies. In particular, the treatment of culture as 'the stylization of life' in recent cultural studies is arguably complicit in the aestheticization of moral-political issues or the de-moralization of culture.

Early political economy was bound up with moral and political philosophy, as in the work of authors such as Smith and Mill. The divorce of these two areas of interest reflects the disembedding of economy brought by the rise of capitalism. Economic, political and bureaucratic systems became detached from the lifeworld and then began to colonize it, products began to dominate producers, and people became increasingly dependent on the workings of an economic system which, far more than any preceding economy, had a logic and momentum of its own. To paraphrase Habermas, the development of capitalism turned questions of validity into questions of behaviour (Habermas,

1979: 6), and this is what has happened to many of the fundamental questions of political economy. As people lost control over their economic lives, the competitive laws of global economy tended to reduce the purchase of normative standpoints on political economy, correspondingly making philosophical discourse on ethics appear irrelevant (Bauman, 1995: 211). Instead of considering our economic responsibilities towards others, we inquire into the workings of the system and actors' behaviour within it, and where we can find a niche in it. From a contemporary academic observer's perspective, this might look merely like a shift from normative to positive theory. However, that distinction itself is partly a product of the changes in economy and society at issue. Like economic behaviour itself, the study of economics has become devalued in the sense that moral values have been expelled from consideration.[1] Conversely, values and norms have been de-rationalized so that they become mere subjective, emotional dispositions, lying beyond the scope of reason. Thus the (attempted) normative–positive split reflected a real subjectivization and de-rationalization of values on the one hand and the devaluation and expulsion of moral questions from matters of the running of economies on the other.

This devaluation of political economy is ironic because today *'political'* economy – as distinct from economics – tends to see itself as radical and critical of capitalism. In consequence, political economy has come to reflect its enemy and tends to underestimate the extent to which economies are influenced by and have implications for moral-political values. Thus on the one hand, the focus of some recent cultural studies on the stylization of life disables any critical intent, while on the other, the reduction of economy to system and the exclusion of its normative regulation has a similar effect.

Much of the debate over the cultural turn and postmodernism amounts to an argument about whether they represent the end of a critical stance towards contemporary society or a new kind of radical critique. At the same time, in many societies, we are witnessing both a decline of old moral-political principles regarding poverty, equality and fairness, and what amounts to a new moralization of issues formerly accepted without much question, for example concerning gender roles, sexuality and environment. The decline of the former values is of course highly congenial to the political right, the latter not, though right-wing liberals should in principle have no objection to much of the latter. These developments also reflect the rise of the (cultural) politics of recognition relative to the (economic) politics of distribution. To understand and assess this uneven development, we need to look at both culture and economy and to take values – especially those to do with morality – seriously.

I wish to argue that any adequate understanding of culture and economy and the relationship between them requires a recognition of the extent to which they contain and are shaped by norms and values, including moral-political values. Treating such values as either merely conventional in character or as disguises for instrumental interests weakens explanation and undermines critique. In particular, any study of culture or economy which overlooks or evades the moral dimension or transmutes it into something else, such as aesthetic judgement, power-play or instrumentality, is bound to lack any consistent critical purchase on its object, indeed it is more likely to mystify.

It is not currently fashionable in either cultural or political economic studies to pay great attention to norms and values, particularly those concerning moral issues. In areas influenced by post-structuralism and postmodernism, 'ethical disidentification' (Connor, 1993) has been widespread. This refers to the refusal of 'normativity', the concealment or repression of normative standpoints in research, and the suspicion of accounts of social life which acknowledge norms, particularly morality, as anything other than camouflaged power. It is associated with a predominantly relativist mood which discourages both prescription and taking seriously the prescriptions of others regarding the good and how to live. In political economy, relativism is less common, but interest in norms in economic life is limited and normative discussion of justice tends to be left to philosophy. In politics itself, interest in morality and responsibilities tends to be dominated by the right and is regarded with suspicion on the left. In view of these circumstances, it will be necessary to begin with a discussion of how values can best be understood. I shall then examine three main themes regarding morality under modernity – de-traditionalization, instrumentalization, and the aestheticization of moral-political values – with particular reference to cultural studies. By way of illustration I shall refer to Pierre Bourdieu's economic analysis of culture. Then, turning to political economy, I discuss the influence of moral values on economic activity and introduce a new version of the concept of moral economy. I also argue for a revival of normative theory in assessing economic matters.

Culture and values

Even though a good deal of social action involves little conscious deliberation, social life always also involves judgement, whether it concerns the use-value of objects or skills, aesthetic qualities, or moral-political issues regarding good and bad ways of living, forms of social organization, and ways of acting towards others. Of course, values and norms, as more settled judgements, show significant cultural variation and indeed are a central feature of culture in the broad, anthropological sense. Values range from those regarding matters which have only minor implications for others (for example tastes in music) and there-fore give rise to little serious dispute,[2] through to those which have great consequences for others (including non-humans), such as those regarding rights to work, medical ethics, and environment, and hence whose disputation is serious.

At one level this is elementary, but how we interpret values is critical. Many are non-instrumental; what they value is seen as good or bad in itself rather than in terms of being a means to some other end. Thus education might be valued not merely as useful for getting a job, but as good in itself. As we shall see, the distinction between instrumental and non-instrumental action and how they should be evaluated is fundamental to critiques of modernity and interpretations of the relationship between culture and economy.

In saying that things are valued in themselves I don't mean to suggest that the thing valued could be good or bad independently of anyone valuing them, as if, say, a mountain could be intrinsically beautiful regardless of the existence of anyone to value it. Values are essentially relational, involving both subject and object. Equally this implies that values – or at least most values – cannot be understood as purely subjective, conventional, and arbitrary, that is as having nothing to do with the qualities of the valued object or practice. To treat values as relational is to acknowledge both that the object has particular qualities and that there are different ways that these can be understood and valued in different societies, so that they can be contested. Where there is contestation, it implies there is something that the disputants are addressing in common, even though it cannot be addressed outside some framework or other.

Two common *non*-relational and hence problematic views of values and value-judgement are those of subjectivism and conventionalism/ relativism. Values are not reducible to subjective, individual preferences as in rational choice theory but are intersubjective and supra-individual (Williams, 1972). Conventionalist or relativist approaches accept the latter point but treat values as arbitrary conventions. In an ironic parallel with positivism, they treat values as beyond rational evaluation, as if they were 'science-free' (Bhaskar, 1979; Matteo, 1996). Both individualism and conventionalism resonate with the tendency of markets to individualize action, and to prioritize questions of what will meet others' preferences – and hence what will sell – over questions of what is right or good. In other words, while relativist positions on values might appear radical, they are actually very congenial to capitalism.

Even if social scientists do not adopt such views explicitly, the common wish to avoid making judgements of the values of those whom they study, for fear of ethnocentrism or related kinds of bias, coupled with the absence of normative theory in much of social science, pushes them in the same direction.[3] For example, in studying a struggle of anti-racists against a racist society, advocates of this value-neutrality would have to abstain from evaluating the explanations and justifications offered by each side for their behaviour. However, whether the lay explanations are correct makes a difference to what happens. If the causes of, say, different living standards of different ethnic groups are not those assumed by racists, then the social scientist's explanation of those differences must say so and diverge from – *and hence be critical of* – the racists. Whether actors' beliefs are valid is an important fact about them which often has consequences for what happens. There may also be structures, such as those of patriarchy, which tend to reproduce the misunderstandings which are in the interest of dominant groups. Therefore, as the basic rationale of critical social science argues, we may have to be critical of practices and the ideas behind them in order to explain them and their effects (Fay, 1975; Bhaskar, 1979; Collier, 1994).

Non-relativists consider that there is some connection between conceptions of the good and human flourishing; thus the normative judgement that a starving person should be given food is grounded in a conception of what their needs really are. Although needs are always interpreted via particular cultural conventions, some needs are transcultural. Likewise the normative judgement that at some level human beings are of equal worth is grounded in an understanding of what human beings are like and what their needs are (see Doyal and Gough, 1991; Nussbaum, 1992).

While this non-relativist standpoint is undoubtedly difficult to defend, particularly where it goes beyond basic needs like that for food, the relativist option, with its neutral 'god's-eye view', is, on closer inspection, worse. Not only does relativism render resistance and struggle arbitrary, that is, lacking any defensible justification, but it also generates contradictions, including a theory–practice inconsistency on the part of the observer. A consistent conventionalist/relativist would be torn between reporting or at least implying that there was no justification for anti-racists' struggle (for there are no grounds for any values beyond mere convention) and saying that it was as justified as any other (which would also mean including racist actions). Moreover, moral scepticism or agnosticism involves denying what most of our actions presuppose:

> *Moral judgment is what we 'always already' exercise in virtue of being immersed in a network of human relationships that constitute our life together.* Whereas there can be reasonable debate about whether or not to exercise juridical, military, therapeutic, aesthetic or even political judgment, in the case of moral judgment this option is not there. The domain of the moral is so deeply enmeshed with those interactions that constitute our lifeworld that to withdraw from moral judgment is tantamount to ceasing to interact, to talk and act in the human community. (Benhabib, 1992: 125–6, emphasis in original. See also Habermas, 1990)

Of course in contemplative mode we may temporarily suspend certain moral judgements, but we cannot *act* in the social world without making some such judgements. Everyday conversation and action includes and presupposes claims to validity – based on grounds that force us into yes or no positions:

> Thus, built into the structure of action oriented to reaching understanding is an element of unconditionality. And it is this unconditional element that makes the validity that we claim for our views different from the mere de facto acceptance of habitual practices. From the perspective of first persons, what we consider justified is not a function of custom but a question of justification or grounding. [Even, we might add, if it turns out to be a mistaken justification.] (Habermas, 1990: 19)[4]

Social scientists are guilty of contradiction if they unreflexively project their professional third person or observer's stance onto those whom they study or indeed onto their own lives.

Although not all critical social scientists acknowledge that their work has normative, especially moral, standpoints, this is a condition of their work being critical (Young, 1990; Sayer, 1997b). Using terms such as 'oppression', 'domination', 'racism' 'exploitation', etc., implies normative evaluation. If we ask what is wrong with any of these, we expect rational defences of the judgements and not answers which merely appeal to convention, to 'what we do round here'. Although 'morality' tends to be regarded with suspicion in progressive movements such as feminism, their critiques are in the strongest sense moral, in that they concern how people treat one another. Certainly, moral norms and rhetoric can serve to camouflage domination, but any studies which regard *all* moral discourse and actions in this way deny themselves any basis for criticizing the phenomena they study.

A second mistake is to see morality as nothing more than a disguised form of instrumental, opportunistic, self-interested action, typically involving attempts to win praise or other rewards. This view, associated with Mandeville and Hobbes, was countered by Adam Smith, who pointed out that a diagnostic characteristic of morality is that actions are taken to be good or bad regardless of whether those responsible for them receive praise or condemnation (Smith, 1759: 113 ff.; O'Neill, this volume). Of course this is not to say that the appearance of moral concern cannot be used disingenuously to conceal other motives, but that does not mean all action is of this kind.[5]

While it is possible in theory to abstract out the moral from the instrumental and the conscious from the habitual, in practice behaviour is often shaped by mixed motives and influences. If we do consciously decide on a course of action, it is often both because we feel it is the right thing to do in itself and because it happens to have beneficial consequences for us. Thus within organizations people may be friendly to one another both because they feel that is the proper way to behave towards others and because it will make it easier to get things done if they do so. One does not necessarily cancel out the other; the presence on some occasions of instrumental motives does not mean that there are not also moral considerations of what is right and good in itself. Cynical views of the world are not necessarily more correct for being cynical.

Turning to judgements of taste and utility, here again we find that to refuse to acknowledge that any such judgements might be valid generates problems for both explanation and critique. Recent cultural studies has rejected hierarchical distinctions between high and popular culture. One way of responding to elitist derogation of the latter is to adopt a relativist/conventionalist standpoint in which values regarding consumption and taste have nothing to do with the qualities of their objects or referents and nothing can be deemed better than anything else. Ironically this has the effect of disqualifying actors' own appeals to such qualities as reasons for liking things, as if what they liked was purely a matter of arbitrary convention and peer group pressure. The relativist view therefore actually demeans those it is intended to support. In fact non-relativist conceptions of value need not be elitist – they can as easily work in favour of popular culture as against. Moreover, a non-relativist view is needed to avoid flipping from elitism of high culture to a sycophantic view of popular culture on the other.

It is one thing to challenge an existing hierarchy of values as unjustified, but quite another to suppose that no hierarchy of values could ever be justified, for valuation is precisely about discriminating between better and worse, and as we noted above, value judgement is unavoidable. Unless we acknowledge this, the phenomena of social distinction and symbolic struggle – envy, disdain – are unintelligible, for they appear to be only accidentally connected to particular beliefs, practices and artefacts, never connected to them for good reason. Capitalism gives those with sufficient money plenty of scope not only to indulge their vanity through conspicuous consumption but to acquire goods which are genuinely superior to others. The rich are not necessarily fools: if big houses were no better than damp shacks, no-one would envy them for owning big houses. By the same token the poor are not fools for envying them, though there is a crucial difference between envying and admiring. While academics who fear the charges of foundationalism and elitism may hesitate to endorse any hierarchy of values, those whom they study (and academics themselves when marking essays or off-duty) know very well that some things are better than others and that such distinctions are not merely arbitrary just because they are not absolute.

One of the most important contributions of cultural studies has been in analysing how judgements of taste are related to the social position of actors and associated with struggles for distinction. Here I want to comment on some aspects of Pierre Bourdieu's work and his economic analysis of culture. Such an approach is particularly relevant in this context, for we have distinguished culture from economy partly in terms of a contrast between the former's dialogical nature and concern with non-instrumental values and the latter's instrumental character (see Introduction). For Bourdieu, social action is determined primarily by deeply sedimented dispositions and semiconscious instrumental action. Through his concepts of cultural, social and symbolic capital, he shows how social practice involves hidden struggles for benefits in the form of goodwill and status which can be drawn upon to their possessors' advantage. While under certain conditions these forms of capital may be converted to economic capital (and back), they can also function somewhat independently of money and wealth. It should be noted that Bourdieu applies this theory to pre-capitalist societies as much as capitalist ones (e.g. Bourdieu, 1977); it is not a specific response to the economized culture of capitalism.[6] Now an economic view of culture is bound to be an instrumental one, and, as such, I wish to argue that it is one-sided and misleading, even for a highly instrumentalized society such as our own.

In his major work, *Distinction*, subtitled 'a social critique of the judgement of taste', Bourdieu argues via his concept of habitus that our judgements are overwhelmingly shaped by the dispositions that we develop through our particular socialization and through our situations within, and trajectories through, the social field (Bourdieu, 1986). Hence what we imagine is a matter of disinterested judgement of taste on purely aesthetic values is actually strongly constrained and enabled by our particular habitus; thus we try to make a virtue of necessity, refusing what we are refused and choosing what is effectively chosen for us. In addition to this, Bourdieu sees taste in instrumental terms, involving strategies of distinction, albeit – in somewhat oxymoronic fashion – unconscious ones (Alexander, 1995). Thus the tastes of the petit bourgeois reflect a constant struggle to distinguish themselves from those above and below, and the whole social field as a whole is characterized by struggles to define and obtain the various kinds of capital and to convert them into the most advantageous form.

Impressive though *Distinction* is, it tends to sociologize values as matters capable of rational assessment out of existence and to render all action and judgement as instrumental, albeit in a semi- or un-conscious form. It rejects explanations of taste in terms of what actors think is good in itself rather than merely conventional for, and consistent with, their position within the social field, and moral-political motives are either ignored or treated as mere convention-following and/or as disguised strategies of distinction. Thus someone who is not acquisitive on the grounds that he or she considers that excessive acquisitiveness is morally wrong, is treated as either rationalizing their inability to afford to be acquisitive or as sufficiently well-endowed with cultural capital to be able to win distinction without engaging in conspicuous consumption. This may be correct of course, but a total, *a priori* refusal of the assumption that actors' normative reasoning is not reducible wholly to these sociological and instrumental aspects is untenable. Thus if we take a particular genre, such as opera, we do indeed find that its acolytes have a distinctive position in the social field. However, we cannot explain the valuations of such people of particular practices within the genre without reference to non-social qualities (see also Frith, 1989; McGuigan, 1996). There may be good reasons to do with habitus why art dealers are more likely than builders to appreciate opera, but this does not explain why they would prefer to hear it sung by Pavarotti rather than me. Furthermore, while Bourdieu insists that his own tastes are what one would expect of someone with his background, he does not of course explain his methodological preferences in this way, but rather by reasoning in terms of their intrinsic value. Equally the reason why I and many others appreciate his work is not merely because of our habitus or because we are involved in unconscious strategies of distinction – trying to ingratiate ourselves with academic colleagues – but rather because his work is exceptionally good, and we would be able to *argue* the case. Here we have an instance of the inconsistency noted earlier between many social scientists' third-person accounts which refuse or ignore reasoned judgement by actors and their first-person accounts of their own actions.[7] Moreover, while Bourdieu certainly demonstrates the social correlates of judgements of taste, he does not adequately explain why doing so should amount to a critique, for if judgements of taste can only be disguises for struggles over social distinction, then there is nothing that is being repressed or lost which we could regret. Bourdieu's *Distinction* produces a universal deflation of actors' normative claims, presenting them as no more than emanations and rationalizations of their habitus, and as unconscious strategies for the defence and achievement of status, a status which has no defensible grounding. The struggles of the social field are apparently merely for power, not (also) over what is good or right or just or worthy of distinction.

Bourdieu's concept of capital needs to be qualified, for as it stands, it fails to distinguish between investments in goods – such as education, culture, social relations – from the point of view of their use-value as it were, and investments from the point of view of their exchange-value, that is, in terms of what advantages (or disadvantages) they bring in the struggles of the social field. In relation to all Bourdieu's forms of capital – cultural, educational, linguistic, social and symbolic – this distinction is vital from both an explanatory and a critical point of view. Thus I may 'value' some people as friends, appreciating their sense of humour, intelligence, sensitivity, loyalty or whatever, but if I value them as social contacts, able to 'open doors' for me and bring me monetary and non-monetary rewards, then they become social capital for me.[8] Getting an education, enjoying music, making friends may contingently give one educational, cultural and social capital, but to treat the former as the same as the latter is a disastrous mistake.

The use-value/exchange-value distinction as developed by Aristotle, and later Marx, is crucial (Meikle, 1995). Marx insisted on distinguishing capital from mere machines, materials or buildings. The latter have use-value, but only become capital when they are acquired in order to command the labour or tribute of others and to earn exchange-value. In equivalent fashion we might insist on a difference between 'investments' – say in education – made for their own sake (for example, learning German) and investments made in order to enhance the possessor's social standing (educational capital). Of course, the use-value of education includes an instrumental dimension – enabling one to communicate with people who speak a different language, or whatever – as well as a possible intrinsic interest, but this is different from instrumentalization in order to gain social advantage vis-à-vis others, and a separate issue from any unintended effects it may have in terms of cultural and social capital. One would expect this distinction to be elided in a highly commodified society, given that peoples' livelihoods depend on exchange-value: but while the use-value/exchange-value distinction is elided in liberal economics, one would not expect this to be the case in a critical analysis of a highly commodified culture. In being overly critical of actors' ability to make judgements of use-value, in the broad sense in which I have used it, Bourdieu's analysis ironically becomes uncritical.

Social action is not wholly reducible to the effects of habitus and disguised battles for status over taste; it also involves judgements regarding the moral worth of particular actions or ways of life. It is apparent from his comments in interview regarding his politics that Bourdieu sees the unmasking of such strategies as an important political task (Bourdieu and Wacquant, 1992), which it is. But by excluding moral issues, he ironically and presumably inadvertently contributes to the aestheticization and instrumentalization of practice in contemporary capitalist society.

Morality and modernity

I now want to consider some key themes in the relationship between morality and modernity, first mainly from the side of culture, then from the side of economy. In recent years there have been divergent tendencies in relation to morality and modernity: on the one hand there has been an evident rise in interest in moral and political philosophy, which owes much to the rise of new social movements and their related critical social sciences (e.g. Young, 1990; Benhabib, 1992) as well as critical theory (e.g. Habermas, 1990); on the other hand, in more postmodern quarters, 'ethical disidentification' (Connor, 1993) has been dominant.

De-traditionalization

The relationship between modernity and morality is double-edged. The usual story is that the upheavals, rationalization and disenchantment of modernity have changed the nature of social relations from conventional and moral to contractual. What had previously been social relations in which how one ought to behave was dictated by the particular obligations traditionally attaching to the position into which one was born, gave way to contractual relations or at least relations subject to reflection and deliberation on the part of individuals.[9] On the other hand, the freeing of people from such pre-modern ties, coupled with the bringing of more and more aspects of life under critical scrutiny, obliges them to develop their own 'post-conventional' or 'post-traditional' norms. Once normative value judgements had been severed from binding social relations they became the subject of choices exercised by sovereign liberal subjects (McMylor, 1994). This can been seen negatively in terms of a 'de-moralization' of society and a slide into an anarchy of choice or preference in which individuals simply choose the conception of the good that suits them. Alternatively, and more positively, actors are freed to make judgements according to principles rather than tradition. At the same time, their liberation can be seen as coming at the price of taking on a moral burden not experienced by their predecessors, precisely because they become responsible for determining what is moral (Wolfe, 1989; Poole, 1991).[10] With 'de-traditionalization', existing, conventional social relations and actions are critically evaluated. Even where this does not result in change, and traditions are retained, they are so on the basis of comparison with alternatives rather than merely being accepted without question (Beck, 1992; Beck and Beck-Gernsheim, 1995).

Early moral and political philosophers such as those of the Scottish Enlightenment were much exercised by the challenge posed by this burden and attempted to formulate a rational science of morality. In such work there is no clear distinction between positive and normative theory. Subsequently, such ambitions were largely abandoned and moral and political philosophy became separated off from positive social science, reflecting the growth of liberal hostility to prescriptions of the good and the associated rise of a division between ethics (private) and politics (public).

Instrumentality vs intrinsic values

Another concern of commentators on modernity has been the enlargement of the scope of instrumental action at the expense of action based on intrinsic values. In what MacIntyre terms 'practices', such as sports or academic disciplines, the standards governing action are internal, both regulating and being regulated by the practitioners (MacIntyre, 1981; Keat, 1994). But if practices or their products are then commodified, they become subject to external judgement, including that of outsiders who may have little or no understanding of the practice. More importantly, money, rather than internal goods, comes to regulate the activity. Thus, if we commodify degree courses, we increasingly teach what will sell rather than what we think is worth teaching in itself. In Habermas's terms, system – in particular the self-regulating economy – comes to colonize the lifeworld. Strategic action in response to external commands and signals (especially price signals) increasingly overrides the practical reason (including deliberation over moral-political issues) supposedly characteristic of the lifeworld. In Marxian terms, our activities become controlled by economic forces operating behind our backs, rather than under our control.

Within organizations, instrumentalization attempts to take advantage of what otherwise would be considered largely intrinsic virtues, such as diligence, creativity and the ability to communicate, by using them to achieve external goals. In so doing, instrumental rationalization is often assumed to 'drain' human activities and relationships of their normative significance (Poole, 1991: 85). The loss of normative significance results both from the narrowing of the range of tasks in which each is involved and from the lengthening of the chain between producer and consumer. But division of labour also brings important benefits, such as allowing some people to become full-time specialist scientists, musicians or sportsmen and women, and hence in a position to advance their specialism beyond that possible without this division of labour. Once these become ways of earning a living they may become subject to the influence of those who fund them – tax payers and consumers – and whose goals may be external to those of the producers, though since it is to such others that the producers owe their living, this hardly seems unreasonable.[11]

All these considerations are hugely important for any critique of modernity, but there are important qualifications to make to them.

Firstly, these arguments involve a kind of philosophical and sociological reductionism and *a priorism*; having reduced concrete objects such as economies, organizations or communities to abstract principles or ideal types, such as those of 'practical reason', 'the market', or 'bureaucracy', it is then assumed that concrete behaviour can be adequately described by them. Take, for example, Bauman's bleak view of bureaucracy, based on an ideal type of this form of organization (Bauman, 1995). While instrumental rationalization is undoubtedly prominent in such organizations, there are also likely to be countervailing forces, as when workers reverse the instrumentalization and take advantage of the scope for sociability afforded by belonging to a large organization and put this before meeting its external goals (though of course they have to disguise this sufficiently to avoid being sacked). This, after all, is an important attraction of having a job aside from its being a source of income. Similarly, inferences about behaviour in market societies based purely on abstract principles of 'the market' (as in Poole, 1991 and McMylor, 1994) involve two kinds of reduction – firstly from society to markets, as if the former consisted only of markets, and secondly through the assumption that when one is *in* a market situation, one is governed by market forces alone. Against this it must be remembered that there are always other things going on both outside and within markets and bureaucracies. The effect of these reductionist characterizations of modernity is not neutral: they inevitably produce understandings whose negativity jars with the real or apparent acceptability of contemporary society to many of its members.

Secondly, although capitalism encourages and indeed requires an instrumental approach to activity on the part of producers, for final consumers the point of buying commodities is primarily for their use-value, though they may also in some cases function instrumentally as means towards the end of winning approval or envy of others, or in Bourdieu's terms, as capital.

Thirdly, as Nancy Fraser points out in her critique of Habermas, the distinction between system and lifeworld can only be aligned with a distinction between economy and state on the one side and family or community on the other at the cost of gross mystification. Capitalism does not exhaust the economy, for households are also involved in material as well as symbolic reproduction and hence have an economic dimension, while relations within markets and capitalist organizations also have a moral-cultural dimension. Although instrumental action is more strongly represented in the formal capitalist economy than outside, it is not absent in domestic situations (Fraser, 1991). Families (and communities) are never solely structured by norms, and even to the extent that they are, they are rarely arrived at democratically; the home is also a site in which exploitation, instrumentality, violence and power are common. Moreover, insofar as lifeworld still influences the state and the formal economy, patriarchal power remains significant there too. One of the most beneficial effects of the cultural turn has been an increased awareness of oppression in the lifeworld, and hence a realization of the dangers of reducing modernity to capitalism. Oppression in the capitalist economy is mainly system-related and to do with distribution; in Giddens's terms, it is based on allocative power through the control of the means of production, rather than on symbolic or authoritative power (Giddens, 1979). The converse is true for patriarchy and racism, though of course they structure social relations within the formal capitalist economy as well as in the household economy, and the inequalities they generate are routinely taken advantage of by capitalist interests, whether in the super-exploitation of oppressed groups or the conversion of symbolic capital into economic capital.

Fourthly, there is a further fundamental flaw in the critique of instrumentality. Quite simply, instrumental action should not be seen as necessarily inferior to action based on non-instrumental values, for the former may be directed towards good ends while the latter may be bad. When reading about morality, virtue and conceptions of the good, it is easy to forget that racists, snobs, mysogynists and homophobes all have certain intrinsic values. Hence aspects of life governed by such norms are not necessarily better than those dominated by instrumental rationality.[12] If the domestic sphere is treated as a prime case of social integration, Habermas's critique comes too close to treating it as 'a haven-in-a-heartless-world'. Although the formal economy is dominated by instrumental reason and the family less so, many people may find relationships in the organizations where they are employed more satisfactory than those at home. For many women, entering the labour market – commodifying their labour power – freed them from worse circumstances in the home. This is a contemporary equivalent of the liberation of people from traditional conventional power relations by market forces noted in theories of the transition from feudalism to capitalism.[13] Moreover, it has long been argued that markets can have a 'civilizing influence' where they oblige actors to put profit before prejudice in decisions of who to employ and who to sell to (Hirschman, 1982; Sayer, 1995).[14]

These points are not advanced in order to reject the critique of instrumentalization but rather to qualify it. Critiques of instrumentalization and markets such as Habermas's are impressive in their sweep but they do not enable us to read off and judge the concrete quality of life in capitalist societies. We need to be rigorously ambivalent about this aspect of modernity. However, turning to recent cultural studies, we find a different kind of slant on capitalism and (post)modernity, one which highlights a more positive face, while often forgetting what is worth retaining in the older critiques. The most striking differences are perhaps the validation of popular culture and the celebration of the creative possibilities for constructing identities through consumption of commodities and discursive strategies. This could be seen as merely bending the stick to counter the implicitly negative view of consumption of commodities in traditional critical theory and to flush out any elitism from critiques of the commodification of practices, but there is a great danger of simply forgetting what is valid in the critique of instrumentality and commodification.

Aesthetics versus morality

A third concern of critiques of modernity focuses on the dangers of moral judgement giving way to aesthetic considerations. Morality matters in a way which aesthetics does not. While we might argue with someone about what is beautiful, failure to reach agreement is not as serious as in an argument about how we should treat one another; indeed in the case of aesthetics we might enjoy difference. Failing to persuade someone of the quality of a painting is less serious than failing to persuade them not to be racist.

The problem is that this ranking of moral-political values and aesthetic values is often reversed, as when politicians or employees are judged on their looks rather than their policies or ability. For producers of consumer products and services, success depends on the aesthetic and affective qualities of their product as well as on any functional adequacy they may have. Recent cultural studies have emphasized how consumption is increasingly serving as a means of identity construction. Although consumption may be active and creative rather than passive, it is hard to resist the conclusion that often this means that appearance becomes more important than how people behave towards others. This aestheticization goes beyond the direct effects of purchasing commodities. Pervasive media images also provide a prism through which a great number of objects and events can be classified. As regards pop culture, Lash and Urry argue:

> The negative consequences of this are that the ubiquity and centrality of such popular culture objects to youth lifestyle can swamp the moral-practical categories available to young people. And entities and events which would otherwise be classified and judged by moral-political universals are judged instead through these aesthetic, taste categories. (1994: 133)

Thus moral-political aspects of culture become reduced to matters of taste, and politics is directed towards the cultivation of style and the nurturing of an individualized, subjective, 'feelgood factor'. This kind of 'devaluation' is entirely in line with what one would expect of a deeply commodified culture.

Theories of culture which conceive it in terms of the stylization of life (e.g. Featherstone, 1994), and ignore the moral-political dimension, could be said to be complicit in this tendency for aesthetic judgements to take the place of moral ones.[15] The aestheticization of politics may on occasion be impressive and have progressive intentions and effects,[16] but it can of course be used for any purpose, fair or foul. It can lead to groups being celebrated or dismissed on the grounds of presentation rather than the content of their views. A cultural studies which ignores the moral-political content of culture and considers only aesthetics therefore hardly deserves to be called critical.

Valuing economy: moral economy

So far I have been critical mainly of cultural studies' approach to values, but political economy's disregard of (non-economic) values is equally problematic. Even though radical political economy rejects neoclassical economics' assumption that economic behaviour is overwhelmingly self-interested, it generally fails to probe the moral-political sentiments that might actually or potentially motivate it. To be sure, there has been much written of late on how economic relationships presuppose trust (Misztal, 1996), but trust is quite compatible with purely self-interested action. Beyond this, economic activities have in varying degrees a moral dimension. Both in order to examine this, and to subject economic activities – formal and informal – to normative scrutiny, I now want to propose that it would be helpful to revive and adapt the concept of 'moral economy' for understanding both culture and economy and the relation between them.

Pre-capitalist economies are sometimes termed moral economies in order to register the extent to which their economic processes were normatively regulated, in contrast to contemporary capitalism, where, as we have seen, system supposedly colonizes lifeworld. Yet even though we are increasingly subject to economic forces over which we have no control, economies are still regulated or at least influenced by such norms. This is the most politically significant way in which economy is culturally inflected.

The moral economy embodies norms regarding the responsibilities and rights of individuals and institutions with respect to others and regarding the nature and qualities of goods, services and environment. These norms shape both the formal and informal, including household, economies. While the norms may be considered part of a moral order, they are invariably influenced by networks of power and considerations of cost;[17] indeed many such norms are compromised by, or are rationalizations of, the effects of economic power. The story of capitalism and modernity is often told as one of the replacement of moral economy by a political economy, in which the fate of actors comes to depend on the outcomes of anonymous contending market forces, the positioning of people as consumers turns moral judgements concerning the social good into matters of private preference, and their fortunes become heavily dependent on luck, as even market advocates such as Hayek, acknowledge. Polanyi's critique of the commodification of labour-power, recently taken up by authors such as Will Hutton and Maurice Glasman, is directed at a major instance of this de-moralization (Polanyi, 1957; Hutton, 1995; Glasman, 1995).

However, there is a danger of exaggerating the extent to which these changes have been at the expense of the influence of moral norms (e.g. Poole, 1991; McMylor, 1994), especially if we overlook the way in which markets and other economic institutions are socially embedded, and if we ignore families, communities and other non-market relations and organizations (Wolfe, 1989). Particularly in the latter but even in the formal economy, the influence of moral norms is still significant (Storper and Salais, 1996). As Etzioni has argued in his 'I/we paradigm', even in market situations, both as buyers and sellers, we tend to have to balance desire and self-interest with moral commitments, although the incentives of the former may be more powerful than the latter (Etzioni, 1988).

What is ethical and unethical is of course contentious. While we may refer to the moral economy in a neutral, descriptive way, we may actually judge it negatively as unethical. I therefore don't want to give an unqualified endorsement to the moral economy as it stands. For those who are oppressed by it, markets – especially the labour market – may offer an escape, as we saw in the case of married women. Consequently practices, like market exchange, which corrode the moral economy are not necessarily bad. In any case, as Smith anticipated, and Hayek later argued, where there is an advanced social division of labour with millions of producers and consumers spread across large parts of the world, producers cannot know what others want independently of feedback from markets.

For our society the fundamental questions of moral economy might include the following.

- Whose keeper are we? Who is our keeper? – What are our responsibilities towards children, the elderly, the disabled and infirm, to distant others and future generations, and to the environment?
- What standards of care and provision should we expect to receive, give and fund? – What goods should be provided?
- How should we discharge our responsibilities to others? – through paying taxes to fund transfer payments? through direct unpaid labour? by paying others to do the work?
- How should these responsibilities be allocated between men and women, between parents and non-parents, between different age-groups, between people of different incomes and wealth?
- What standard of living should people expect? Should there be limits on pay and income from capital?
- To what extent should people be reliant on wages/salaries for their income? (How far should income be subject to the 'stark utopia' of the 'self-adjusting' market (Polanyi, 1957)?)
- What things should not be commodified?

Of course, in a sense many of these are academic questions, for in practice the arrangements to which they refer depend heavily on the working of the economic system and on convention and power (in the lifeworld as well as systems) rather than being decided normatively in any considered manner. However, from a normative point of view – and any critical social science presupposes such a standpoint – they are crucial to any assessment of economy in the broad sense. As we have seen, modernity is associated with the rise of post-conventional morality, in which people are burdened with moral decisions which are no longer solved for them by religion and custom. If this is the case, it would be odd to write off moral economy as a thing of the past.

The moral economy as it currently exists is clearly strongly gendered, both in terms of the nature of many of the norms themselves and the expectations regarding who is expected to meet them; in its gendered form it is therefore a major target of feminism, which, in effect, exposes its immoral side. In this area, de-traditionalization still has a long way to go. The most important example of the persistence of traditional morality in modern society concerns conceptions of the responsibilities of mothers, and also, complementing this, the view of many men that their responsibilities to their partners and children consist largely of being bread-winner, and perhaps gendered role model. From a normative point of view, a minimum condition for a truly 'moral' economy would be the overthrow of gendering of responsibilities for the provision of parental and other care. This would involve not only an equalization with regard to what women and men do but a re-evaluation of the responsibilities themselves. However, while this would amount to a re-moralization of economy, de-traditionalization does not automatically follow this course, and indeed it could lead to widespread refusals of moral responsibilities.[18]

A key component of the moral economy is the welfare state, though some authors regard its bureaucratization of responsibilities as reducing individuals' sense of moral obligations (e.g. Ignatieff, 1985; Wolfe, 1989). Both through its expenditure and its own employment generation, the welfare state influences the economy and structure of households, and the life-courses of individuals within it (Esping-Andersen, 1999). Conversely, changing conventions and norms regarding gender and families put new demands on the welfare state. During the long post-war boom, forms of welfare which supported traditional family arrangements and ways of life needed little defence in ethical terms because their provision had been routinized and bureaucratized and hence removed from conscious individual responsibility, and there were few dissenting voices anyway. The moral economy of the idealized family was of course *im*moral and oppressive. With the combination of the break-up of those traditions, the welfare state's support for them comes under question. The crisis of the welfare state is therefore not only a fiscal one, exacerbated by globalization and the related squeeze on public sectors and national social settlements, but a consequence of the disarray of the moral economy, which has thrown many of the above normative questions wide open (Mitchell and Goody, 1997).

Talk of responsibilities has recently come to be associated with conservative forms of communitarianism (e.g. Etzioni, 1994), and hence not surprisingly is regarded with deep suspicion on the left. However, to treat all responsibilities as oppressive and unjustified is to lapse into an anti-social, adolescent or puerile anarchism: the problem is not responsibilities *per se*, but their definition and allocation. In a post-traditional moral economy, it should be possible to negotiate these matters democratically, rather than simply hoping to duck them. Often, the left's suspicion of morality talk as the disguise of the powerful tends to lead it to opt for liberal responses to moral-political dilemmas (i.e. ones which individualize decisions regarding the good) rather than develop better alternative moral norms.

The point of a focus on moral economy is to bring out what is so easily overlooked, that economies are strongly influenced by moral norms and that changing such norms is fundamental to any alternative organization of economy. This is not reducible to the bland point that economic processes are socially embedded or indeed that they pre-suppose trust, for it identifies a crucial aspect of that embedding on which trust depends. To develop a critical political economy, we need to appreciate the scope of the often repressed normative questions regarding moral economy.

Conclusions

My intention in entitling this chapter 'valuing culture and economy' was not to prioritize one over the other (for which is more important depends on what one is trying to explain) but to put values back into both. Equally I don't wish to prioritize the politics of distribution over the politics of recognition. Rather I have argued that if we are to understand culture or economy or the relationship between them, we need to acknowledge the role of values concerning the nature of the good as fundamental to culture and to the regulation of capitalist and household economies. Unless this is done, social theory will tend to absorb rather than critically expose the tendency for values to be relativized and subjectivized with the development of liberal market societies.

De-traditionalization, instrumentalization and the aestheticization of politics and recognition are all to be expected in a capitalist society. Whether they are progressive or regressive depends on the values in question and what happens to them. In principle, de-traditionalization seems progressive but it may of course merely lead to more indivi-dualistic and selfish behaviour. Instrumentalization may drain or appear to drain activities of their intrinsic value, but this does not mean that it is always retrograde, for the values being weakened may be reactionary. Although it is important for critical social science to identify hidden instrumental strategies and power relations behind apparently innocent and disinterested action, to characterize all behaviour in this fashion suppresses recognition of any possible emancipatory alternatives. The aestheticization of politics may be used by progressive or reactionary movements. It may draw attention to hitherto ignored groups and causes, but it can also distract attention from what the causes are about, and disqualify those whose image does not fit. Instrumentalization and aestheticization are not unrelated to capitalist society, they are encour-aged by competition for sales and political support. Similarly, under-standing economies – household as well as capitalist – depends on acknowledging the nature and extent of their moral regulation, and a critical approach requires us to evaluate such norms. In the absence of this, even radicals may note specific problems such as exploitation, while taking the wider moral economy for granted. For these reasons, and as a parting thought, we might consider reviving – albeit in a new mode – the link that existed in the eighteenth and nineteenth centuries between the normative discourse of moral and political philosophy and the discourse of political economy.

Notes

1 This devaluation is partly a consequence of a more literal devaluation – in the prices of necessities. As these become lower and the provision of such goods becomes more reliable, their significance in how people make their living reduces and correspondingly they lose their moral-political significance. Thus the bread riots which were the focus of Thompson's essay on moral economy could only be repeated in situations where this staple accounted for most of people's expenditure (Thompson, 1971).

2 This is not to deny the importance of tastes in the struggles of the social field in terms of their ascribed class and status associations, but reaching agreement on them is not so important as in the case of moral-political values, indeed in aesthetic matters difference and dissensus may be preferred to consensus.

3 One might distinguish between a selective suspension of values, in which the researcher has a definite value standpoint on the practices under study but brackets it out as irrelevant to their explanation, and a thoroughgoing relativist position in which the researcher believes it to be impossible to adjudicate between different value positions including her own, in life in general. However, I shall argue that neither type is tenable.

4 For both Habermas and Aristotelians our basic moral intuitions stem from something deeper and more universal than contingent features of our local tradition – in the case of Habermas from the normative presuppositions of social interaction in any society, for Aristotelians from our nature as social beings.

5 A further common misunderstanding of morality involves reducing it to altruistic (or self-sacrificing) behaviour in contrast to self-interested behaviour, it being assumed that behaviour must be one or the other. It fails to note that many kinds of motivation are neither egoistic nor altruistic in the sense of self-sacrificing but involve pursuing goods which are considered to be common (O'Neill, 1992). Of course, those who hold individualist social ontologies and subjectivist–emotivist theories of value have difficulty acknowledging the common, the public, as 'we'.

6 As Alexander notes, for Bourdieu, 'even the most traditional peasant plays the game of life like the stock market' (1995: 150).

7 This is ironic, for Bourdieu is particularly emphatic about the dangers of researchers projecting features of their own standpoint onto those whom they study. Thus he argues that the prominence given to rationally motivated action in social scientific analysis is an instance of this unaware projection. While this is often correct, the problem here is that Bourdieu goes to the opposite extreme, and refuses to acknowledge in the behaviour of others that which his own behaviour presupposes (Alexander, 1995). See also Craib (1997) for a more general critique of this kind of inconsistency in 'social constructionism'.

8 In this case, it is significant that the intentional instrumentalization of the good (friendship) also undermines it.

9 An exclusive emphasis on the 'contractual' nature of social relations in modernity is too economistic, missing the continuation of moral commitments. It also tends to conceal power by making social relations appear to be consensual/freely agreed upon.

10 The necessity of moral deliberation as a result of not having ready-make answers to moral questions might be a late modern characteristic, though I very much doubt that it was totally absent in pre-modern societies. Even in a society with strict expectations of behaviour attached to roles, there must have been moral dilemmas which required deliberation, moral reasoning.

11 Note that this is not uniquely tied to commodification – the same effects occurred under centrally planned economies.

12 One of the virtues of Smith's work is that he is able, in appropriate circumstances, to defend both non-instrumental and instrumental action.

13 This is also important for understanding the middle classes' – particularly men's – acquiescence to capitalism and their role as willing slaves in it: it is not merely a function of income.

14 This is of course double-edged; an unprejudiced employer might be driven by competition to take advantage of oppressed groups as cheap sources of labour.

15 Like capitalism and its economic theory – neoclassical economics – the study of the stylization of life tends to lead to a focus mainly on the relationship between people and things. A virtue of theories of work or management culture is that it puts relations between people first.

16 See Szerszynski, this volume.

17 In Bourdieu's work on peasant societies, the moral economy of gifts and obligations is seen as a collectively misrecognized instrumental order of exchange. While this avoids romanticized views of moral economies, it also goes too far in instrumentalizing norms as geared to reciprocity or exchange. A diagnostic feature of moral responsibilities or commitments is that they are followed even where there is no prospect of reward or recognition, as in the case of care for young children or the terminally ill (Bourdieu, 1977).

18 For example, whether increasing rates of marital break-up will lead to fathers disowning responsibilities for children or to a change in those responsibilities is a moot point (Mitchell and Goody, 1997). See also Barbara Ehrenreich's analysis of men's 'flight from commitment' (Ehrenreich, 1983).

References

Alexander, J.C. (1995) *Fin de Siècle Social Theory*, London: Verso.

Bauman, Z. (1995) *Life in Fragments*, Oxford: Blackwell.

Beck, U. (1992) *Risk Society*, London: Sage.

Beck, U. and Beck-Gernsheim, E. (1995) *The Normal Chaos of Love*, Cambridge: Polity.

Beck, U. and Beck-Gernsheim, E. (1996) 'Individualization and "precarious freedoms"', in S. Lash, P. Heelas and P. Morris (eds), *Detraditionalization*, Oxford: Blackwell, pp. 23–48.

Benhabib, S. (1992) *Situating the Self*, Cambridge: Polity.

Bhaskar, R. (1979) *The Possibility of Naturalism*, Hassocks: Harvester.

Bourdieu, P. (1977) *Outline of a Theory of Practice*, Oxford: Oxford University Press.

Bourdieu, P. (1986) *Distinction: a Social Critique of the Judgement of Taste*, London: Routledge.

Bourdieu, P. and Wacquant, L.J.D. (1992) *An Invitation to Reflexive Sociology*, Chicago: University of Chicago Press.

Collier, A. (1994) *Critical Realism*, London: Verso.

Connor, S. (1993) 'The necessity of value', in J. Squires (ed.), *Principled Positions*, London; Lawrence and Wishart, pp. 31–49.

Craib, I. (1997) 'Social constructionism as a social psychosis', *Sociology*, 31 (1): 1–18.

Doyal, L. and Gough, I. (1991) *A Theory of Human Need*, London: Macmillan.

Ehrenreich, B. (1983) *The Hearts of Men*, London: Pluto.

Esping-Andersen, (1999) *Social Foundations of Postindustrial Economies*, Oxford: Oxford University Press.

Etzioni, A. (1988) *The Moral Dimension*, New York: The Free Press.

Etzioni, A. (1994) *The Spirit of Community*, New York: Crown.

Fay, B. (1975) *Social Theory and Political Practice*, London: Allen and Unwin.

Featherstone, M. (1994) 'City cultures and postmodern lifestyles', in A. Amin (ed.), *Post-Fordism: a Reader*, Oxford: Blackwell, pp. 387–408.

Ferguson, M. and Golding, P. (1997) *Cultural Studies in Question*, London: Sage.

Fraser, N. (1991) 'The case of Habermas and gender', reprinted in (1994) *The Polity Reader in Social Theory*, Cambridge: Polity, pp. 201–12.

Fraser, N. (1995) 'From redistribution to recognition? Dilemmas of a "post-socialist age"', *New Left Review*, 212: 68–93.

Frith, S. (1989) 'Towards an aesthetic of popular music', in R. Leppert and S. McClary (eds), *Music and Society: the Politics of Composition, Performance and Reception*, Cambridge: Cambridge University Press, pp. 133–50.

Giddens, A. (1979) *Central Problems of Social Theory*, London: Macmillan.

Glasman, M. (1995) 'The great deformation: Polanyi, Poland and the terrors of planned spontaneity', *New Left Review*, 205: 59–86.

Habermas, J. (1979) *Communication and the Evolution of Society*, Boston: Beacon Press.

Habermas, J. (1990) *Moral Consciousness and Communication*, Cambridge: Polity.

Hirschman, A.O. (1982) 'Rival interpretations of market society: civilizing, destructive or feeble?', *Journal of Economic Literature*, 20: 1463–84.

Hutton, W. (1995) *The State We're In*, London: Fontana.

Ignatieff, M. (1985) *The Needs of Strangers*, London: Chatto and Windus.

Keat, R. (1994) 'Scepticism, authority and the market', in R. Keat, N. Whiteley and N. Abercrombie (eds), *The Authority of the Consumer*, London: Routledge.

Lash, S. and Urry, J. (1994) *Economies of Signs and Space*, London: Sage.

McGuigan, J. (1996) *Culture and the Public Sphere*, London: Routledge.

MacIntyre, A. (1981) *After Virtue: a Study in Moral Theory*, London: Duckworth.

McMylor, P. (1994) *Alasdair MacIntyre: Critic of Modernity*, London: Routledge.

Matteo, A.M. (1996) 'In defense of moral realism', *Telos*, 106: 64–76.

Meikle, S. (1995) *Aristotle's Economic Thought*, Oxford: Clarendon Press.

Misztal, B. (1996) *Trust in Modern Societies*, Cambridge: Polity.

Mitchell, J. and Goody, J. (1997) 'Feminism, fatherhood and the family in Britain', in A. Oakley and J. Mitchell (eds), *Who's Afraid of Feminism?* London: Hamish Hamilton, pp. 200–23.

Nussbaum, M.C. (1992) 'Human functioning and social justice: in defence of Aristotelian essentialism', *Political Theory*, 20 (2): 202–46.

O'Neill, J. (1992) 'Altruism, egoism, and the market', *Philosophical Forum*, XXIII (4): 278–88.

O'Neill, J. (1997) 'The political economy of identity: identity, authority and equality', Lancaster University.

Polanyi, K. (1957) *The Great Transformation: the Political and Economic Origin of our Times*, Boston: Beacon Press.

Poole, R. (1991) *Morality and Modernity*, London: Routledge.

Sayer, A. (1995) *Radical Political Economy: a Critique*, Oxford: Blackwell.

Sayer, A. (1997a) 'The dialectic of culture and economy', in R. Lee and J. Wills (eds), *Geographies of Economy*, London: Arnold.

Sayer, A. (1997b) 'Critical realism and the limits to critical social science', *Journal for the Theory of Social Behaviour*, 27 (4): 101–16.

Sayer, A. and Storper, M. (1997) 'Ethics unbound: for a normative turn in social theory', *Environment and Planning D: Society and Space*, 15: 1–18.

Simmel, G. (1978) *The Philosophy of Money*, London: Routledge.

Smith, A. (1984) [1759] *The Theory of Moral Sentiments*, Indianapolis: Liberty Fund.

Storper, M. and Salais, R. (1996) *Worlds of Production: the Action Frameworks of the Economy*, Cambridge, MA: Harvard University Press.

Thompson, E.P. (1971) 'The moral economy of the English crowd in the eighteenth century', in his *Customs in Common*, London: Merlin.

Williams, B. (1972) *Morality*, Cambridge: Cambridge University Press.

Williams, R. (1958) *Culture and Society*, Harmondsworth: Penguin.

Williams, R. (1977) *Marxism and Literature*, Oxford: Oxford University Press.

Wolfe, A. (1989) *Whose Keeper? Social Science and Moral Obligation*, Berkeley, CA: University of California Press.

Young, I. (1990) *Justice and the Politics of Difference*, Princeton, NJ: Princeton University Press.

3

Economy, Equality and Recognition

John O'Neill

The cultural turn in social theory has manifested itself both in a shift away from political economy towards a politics of identity, recognition and voice in the cultural sphere and in a shift within political economy away from traditional issues of power, property and distribution towards a treatment of the economy itself as a cultural sphere of consumption. This cultural turn is often presented as a new departure in social theory. That presentation displays a common amnesia in social theory about its own past. As I shall show, questions concerning recognition and identity and of the 'sign value' as against the 'use-value' of commodities have a long history in political economy. The cultural turn has involved a rediscovery of older issues in classical political economy. What is distinctive about more recent discussions of these issues is the denial of a series of normative distinctions that underlay the classical discussions. The consequence has been a disarming of a certain form of critique of market society and indeed the opposite – a generalization of specifically market modes of recognition to incorporate all spheres. One result has been a remarkable convergence in the work of social theory in its postmodern and constructivist modes with neoliberal criticisms of non-market spheres of association. This is most notable in the case of the sociology of knowledge, in which scientific institutions are modelled on markets in recognition. A second result has been a divorce of issues of recognition and identity from those of distribution. Arguments about recognition in classical political economy were at the heart of socialist arguments for equality in economic power and wealth.

My purpose in this chapter is both to rescue classical discussions of recognition and to defend the distinctions they employ. The first section outlines the classical distinctions. The second section examines the ways in which these have been discarded in recent discussion of recognition. The final section defends the classical position: much in the recent cultural turn, despite the radical postures it adopts and the undoubted intentions of its proponents, is inimical to criticism of the existing economic and social order. I point to the ways in which the classical discussions of recognition were redeployed in socialist theory in arguments for equality.

Recognition and commercial society

The recent cultural turn in social theory is in many ways an unrecognized return to older cultural themes in political economy. In particular the issues of recognition and identity on which much recent theory has focused were at the heart of classical political economy. Consider, for example, the claim that we live in a postmodern condition characterized, in part, as a world in which 'the very memory of use-value is effaced' in which the 'original consumers' appetite for a world [is] transformed into sheer images of itself' (Jameson, 1991: 18). Hence it is a condition in which identity 'is constituted theatrically through role play and image construction. While the locus of modern identity revolved around one's occupation, one's function in the public sphere (or family), postmodern identity revolves around leisure, centred on looks, images and consumption' (Kellner, 1992: 153). The claim that commodities are bought not for their use-value, but for symbolic consumption is a variation of claims defended by the earliest theorists of commercial society. Hence Smith's account of the motivations that drive commercial society:

> For to what purpose is all the toil and bustle of this world? what is the end of avarice and ambition, of the pursuit of wealth and power, and preeminence? Is it to supply the necessities of nature? The wages of the meanest labourer can supply them. . . . From whence, then, arises that emulation which runs through all the different ranks of men, and what are the advantages which we propose by that great purpose of human life which we call bettering our condition? To be observed, to be attended to, to be taken notice of with sympathy, complacency and approbation, are all the advantages which we can propose to derive from it. It is vanity, not the ease, or the pleasure, which interests us. But vanity is always founded upon the belief of our being the object of attention and approbation. The rich man glories in his riches, because he feels that they draw upon him the attention of the world. (Smith, 1982a: I.iii.2.1, p. 50)[1]

For Smith, this pandering to concern for appearance is at one and the same time the source of the improvement of land, industry and the arts – the invisible hand makes its appearance in Smith's economic writings in this context (Smith, 1982a: IV.1.10–11; 1981: I.xi.c.7) – and of the corruption of the moral character (Smith, 1982a: I.iii.3).

The claim that commercial society is a source of corruption relies upon the contrast between appearance of worth and the real worth of character. Central to the moral theory of Smith's *The Theory of Moral Sentiments* is the distinction between 'the love of praiseworthiness' and 'the love of praise'. To desire to be praiseworthy is to desire those characteristics for which praise is owed: 'to be that thing which, though it should be praised by nobody, is, however, the natural and proper object' (Smith, 1982a: III.2.1). The desire for praise itself is properly parasitic on the desire for praiseworthiness: it is a good where it confirms our worth and it can only do so where we believe that those who proffer praise are themselves competent to do so: 'Their praise necessarily confirms our own self-approbation. Their praise necessarily strengthens our sense of our own praiseworthiness. In this case, so far is the love of praise-worthiness from being derived altogether from that of praise: that the love of praise seems, at least in a great measure, to be derived from that of praiseworthiness' (Smith, 1982a: III.2.3). Vanity is defined as the love of praise for its own sake, divorced from this relationship to the charac-teristics that deserve praise: 'To be pleased with groundless applause is a proof of the most superficial levity and weakness. It is what is properly called vanity' (Smith, 1982a: III.2.4). Vanity is recognition for its own sake, divorced from independent worth. The corrupting influence of commercial society lies in part in the confusion of different forms of recognition.

> The disposition to admire, and almost to worship, the rich and powerful, and to despise, or at least, to neglect persons of poor and mean condition, though necessary to establish and to maintain the distinction of ranks and order of society, is, at the same time, the great and most universal cause of corruption of our moral sentiments. That wealth and greatness are often regarded with the respect and admiration which are due only to wisdom and virtue; and that the contempt, of which vice and folly are the only proper objects, is often most unjustly bestowed upon poverty and weakness. (Smith, 1982a: I.iii.3.1)

Smith's themes concerning the corrupting influence of commerce run through early discussion of commercial society. Consider Rousseau's claim that the commercial society is a sphere of deception: 'To be and to appear to be, became two things entirely different; and from this dis-tinction arose imposing ostentation, deceitful guile, and all the vices which attend them' (Smith, 1982b: 252). The translation of Rousseau here is that of Smith (for a more recent translation see Rousseau, 1984: 119), and the distinction between being and appearance that lies at the heart of Smith's account of commercial society owes something to Rousseau. The distinction is also to be found in the political economy of Hume. Hume, like Smith and unlike Rousseau, displays ambivalence about the role of that concern for appearance in commercial society. While he defends commercial society as a condition of material and cultural development, in his more Stoical moments he is like Smith critical of the concern for appearance as against the development of character: hence, for example, his criticism of the sacrifice of 'the invaluable enjoyment of a character, with themselves at least, for the acquisition of worthless toys and gewgaws' (Hume, 1975: 232).

These eighteenth century accounts of the confusion of different forms of recognition play on classical themes that were central to Stoicism and go back at least as far as Aristotle's rejoinder to those who desire for honour, rather than virtue, as a final good:

> [T]heir aim in pursuing honour is seemingly to convince themselves that they are good; at any rate, they seek to be honoured by intelligent people, among people who know them, and for virtue. It is clear, then, that in the view of active people at least, virtue is superior [to honour]. (Aristotle, 1985: i, ch. 5)

Recognition is a good insofar as it involves the confirmation by others who are believed to be competent to judge the goods which an individual has achieved. Recognition is parasitic on objective worth.

The classical themes of Aristotle are also reworked in Hegel. Hegel's account of the need for mutual recognition in his discussion of the master–slave relation plays on the Aristotelian point that recognition counts only from beings whom we recognize to have a worth. The master's desire for recognition from the slave is self-defeating because it is not from a being he recognizes as having worth (Hegel, 1977). The self-defeating nature of the desire has a good Aristotelian foundation. It is self-defeating in virtue of the fact that recognition is parasitic on other goods. Recognition is required to confirm my self-worth as a being with powers of rationality and the capacities to stand above and shape particular desires. It is only from beings that I recognize as themselves having such powers and capacities that recognition counts. It is because recognition of worth is demanded, not being noticed *per se*, that one-sided recognition will not do.

The theme is taken up in Hegel's account of civil society. Corporations, associations of skill in which individuals are organized according to trade and profession, are a necessary component of civil society because they answer a need for recognition of worth that market exchange cannot provide. Corporations offer a sphere of recognition that maintains a link between recognition and the possession of a set of competencies one has in a practice. Recognition is situated within a community of skills. As a member of the corporation, a person's capability is 'a *recognized* fact': his membership of the corporation is 'evidence of his skill . . . that he is somebody' (Hegel, 1967: para. 253). Hegel contrasts to the member of civil society who is a member of no association of skill: '[H]is isolation reduces his business to mere self-seeking. . . . Consequently, he has to try to gain recognition for himself by giving external proofs of success in his business, and to these proofs no limits can be set' (Hegel, 1967: para. 253A).

Hegel's distinction between the two modes of recognition raises two important features of recognition that is not tied to some independent good, but which is concerned solely with appearance. First it is a competitive good in a possessive 'self-seeking' sense, not one that can be a good held in common in a community. Second, it is a good the pursuit of which is a never-ending struggle of the Hobbesian kind: there are no limits in its pursuit. The two features are related. Good appearance divorced from any independent good is a pure positional good: there is no standard available other than one's comparative standing to others. Recognition of worth in contrast is not a pure positional good. It is something one can have in virtue of meeting standards that are independent of one's comparative standing. One can be a competent boat builder, carpenter, philosopher, or whatever and be recognized by others as competent, as a person with skills and achievements of a particular standard that gives one a standing within a community of art or skill. At the same time one can recognize other individuals as achieving excellences within a practice without this being of necessity competitive. One can admire the achievements of others. Moreover, their achievements extend the practice and in this sense benefit the whole community (MacIntyre, 1985: 190–1). They are not a threat to the self-respect or self-esteem of others since their performance is measured against independent standards of competence. Those who assume that self-esteem is a purely positional good confuse it with vanity.[2] That worth is not a pure positional good also places limits on its pursuit that do not exist for the pursuit of appearance as an end in itself. For any practice the achievement of a certain level of performance is just that; an achievement recognized by standards independent of the mere fact of recognition itself. With appearance as an end in itself this is not so. Each attempts to stand above the crowd to be noticed, and since all strain upwards, none is satisfied. All desire to stand higher (Hirsch, 1977). As Hegel has it, there are no limits to the external proofs of success.

Recognition and economy after the cultural turn

The focus on the significance of recognition and identity in market economies is not new: it is a variation on an old theme. What is new is the way that these observations have been disarmed of the critical implications they previously had even among commercial society's defenders. The reason lies in the denial in recent social theory of the normative distinctions upon which these criticisms were built: between appearance and real worth; and between the desire for recognition for its own sake and the desire for recognition to confirm worth.

The denial of the distinctions is central to a number of recent neo-liberal defences of the market order, for example those found in public choice theory. However, possibly the most notable recent example is Fukuyama's account of modern liberal society as the culmination of the desire for recognition, *thumos*. In its realization of universal mutual and equal recognition, *isothymia*, the struggle for recognition that moves history has been completed. Hence the claim that in modern liberal market societies we have arrived at the end of history. Fukuyama's diagnosis of modern societies' remaining problems is Nietzschean – that of the last man who arrives at the end of history. The last man lacks the aristocratic impulse to excel: the desire for glory is defeated by the pursuit of material acquisition. The unresolved 'contradiction' of liberal democracy lies in the fact that the attempt to replace *megalothymia* with rational consumption cannot succeed: human beings will not accept that condition. They will reject the status of being last men: 'they will rebel at the idea of being undifferentiated members of a universal and homogeneous state' (Fukuyama, 1992: 314).

While Fukuyama claims to give an Hegelian account of recognition, unlike Hegel he assumes that *thumos*, the desire for recognition, is an end in itself. Individuals desire recognition for recognition's sake. Given this account, *megalothymia*, the desire to be recognized as superior, itself takes the form of simple recognition for its own sake. Hence Fukuyama introduces his account of the desire thus:

> [T]here is no reason to think that all people will evaluate themselves as the *equals* of other people. Rather, they may seek to be recognized as *superior* to other people, possibly on the basis of true inner worth, but more likely out of an inflated and vain estimate of themselves. The desire to be recognized as superior to other people we will henceforth label with a new word with ancient Greek roots, *megalothymia*. *Megalothymia* can be manifest both in the tyrant who invades and enslaves a neighbouring people so that they recognize his authority, as well as in the concert pianist who wants to be recognized as the foremost interpreter of Beethoven. Its opposite is *isothymia*, the desire to recognized as the equal of other people. *Megalothymia* and *isothymia* together constitute the two manifestations of the desire for recognition around which the historical transition to modernity can be understood. (Fukuyama, 1992: 182)

The desire of the pianist for recognition of her talents is treated in exactly the same way as the desire of the tyrant for recognition: both manifest the same desire in different spheres – the desire for recognition as such. What for Hegel or Smith would have been distinct – the love of praiseworthiness and the love of praise – in Fukuyama's account become identical – since the love of praise alone is what moves the individual.

Fukuyama's account of recognition rooted in self-obsession exhibits a peculiar market model of the desire for recognition that is common in recent writings on recognition among writers of different political persuasions. The market model is illustrated well, for example, in the account of recognition offered by Walzer in *Spheres of Justice*. Walzer also treats the quest for recognition as a separate sphere detached from others, which, once the differential status of pre-modern society disappears, takes its modern form of self-obsessed individuals who compete for admiration as an end in itself:

Since he has no fixed rank, since no one knows where he belongs, he must establish his own worth, and he can do that only by winning the recognition of his fellows. Each of his fellows is trying to do the same thing. . . . The competitors speculate on the market, intrigue against near rivals, and bargain for power, spend money, display goods, give gifts, spread gossip, stage performances – all for the sake of recognition. And having done all this, they do it all again, reading their daily gains and losses in the eyes of their fellows, like a stockbroker in his morning paper. (Walzer, 1983: 253)

What Walzer describes here is a struggle for recognition that takes place entirely at the level of appearances, in which there is no distance between recognition for looking good and for being good. Individuals do not seek recognition to confirm their independent worth: their worth is their appearance.[3] And appearance is something that is vied over by competitors in a market. The idea of independent worth disappears.

This market model of recognition permeates postmodern and constructivist writing in social psychology and sociology. It is particularly evident in the rhetorical turn in much of this work. Consider for example its use in the deflationary social constructionist accounts of science. Woolgar and Latour for example present scientific activity as a competition in professional credibility:

Scientists are investors in credibility. The result is a creation of a *market*. Information now has value because . . . it allows other investigators to produce information which facilitates the return of invested capital. There is a *demand* from investors for information which may increase the power of their own inscription devices, and there is a *supply* of information from other investors. The forces of supply and demand create the *value* of the commodity. (Woolgar and Latour, 1979: 206, emphasis in the original)

Not only the problems that scientists work on but what counts as 'good work' and what in the end becomes scientific knowledge is determined by the market in credibility, by investment in recognition by others in the community. The intent of the model is deflationary. The notion of standards of worth independent of appearance, of scientific truth and valid argument disappears.[4] All that is left is the outcome of a market competition over appearance. Science is described in the image of a commercial society in which worth is merely a matter of appearance.

The result is, in effect, a public choice model of the scientific community. The starting point of public choice theory is the claim that the assumptions made by economists about the nature of the economic agent in the market place are universal in the scope of their application. There is no reason to assume that what is true of actors in the market ceases to be true when they enter non-market situations. If it is true that individuals act as rational self-interested agents in the marketplace, 'the inference should be that they will also act similarly in other and nonmarket behavioral settings' (Buchanan, 1972: 22). The scope of the economic theory thus understood is quite general. In principle the theory applies in any social setting – not just to politics, but also to any other association, including that of science. Actors are understood as utility-maximizing agents who act in competition with each other in the pursuit of the satisfaction of their preferences. While its authors are critical of the language of interests, the model of science offered by Latour and Woolgar offers a public choice model of science characterized in terms of a market in credibility, with scientists as investors and the eventual value of the theory being determined by supply and demand. All behaviour is treated as strategic, all appeals to norms of reason are rhetorical stratagems to achieve different ends. What counts as 'true' is determined by the outcome of processes not different in kind to standard market forces. The deflationary purpose of the model parallels that of the public choice approach to politics. Hence as Hands notes: '[T]he economics of science is an inquiry that *should* come easy for economists. . . . For years economists have undermined and delegitimized the self-righteousness of politicians – "you are not acting in the societal or national interest, but your own self-interest" – now the argument can be applied to scientists' (Hands, 1994: 97). It is in the sociology of scientific knowledge that one finds public choice theory consistently applied. The plausibility of the model of science, like the public choice theory of politics, depends on the rhetoric of Hobbesian realism. The social world is presented as a battle between power-seeking agents, a presentation which must be 'true' since it describes the worst of all possible worlds.

The account of science as commerce and the identification of worth with successful appearance is a return, sometimes self-conscious, to the sophist view that all argument is rhetoric understood as the art of effective persuasion (O'Neill, 1998b). All communication is strategic action. The return of this view is of particular significance to the criticisms of market society outlined in the last section. As I noted above, those criticisms have their roots in classical philosophy. Within that tradition one central source of the distinction between real and apparent qualities is to be found in the criticism of the sophists as market actors who make money from appearance. The criticisms of sophism that are offered by Plato and Aristotle turn upon the distinction between the appearance of knowledge and its reality: 'the art of the sophist is the semblance of wisdom without the reality, and the art of the sophist is one who makes money from apparent but unreal wisdom' (Aristotle, 1928: I). The response of the sophist, ancient and modern, is to deny the distinction that lies at the basis of the criticism, that there is a distinction between apparent and real knowledge: knowledge is apparent knowledge that happens to be successful. It is a matter of who has power.

For all the undoubted radical intentions of many of its proponents, there is clearly something problematic about these recent moves in social theory, for they appear to disarm social criticisms. At a general level, if any appeal to a norm is simply a stratagem to enforce power, then there is no stance from which to criticize power. It is unclear how any emancipatory project is possible without some distinction between different forms of persuasions – those that appeal to standards of worth that are independent of power and those that do not. At a more specific level, the theories universalize a model of market society in a way that undermines the possibility of critique of the market order.

Recognition, character and equality

What are the sources of the recent denials of the classical distinctions between apparent and real worth and between recognition for its own sake and recognition for the sake of confirmation of worth? One source is the widespread acceptance of a form of constructivism according to which the self is simply a bundle of self-presentations. There is no unified self behind that bundle. Hence the distinction between what a person is and how they appear disappears. What one is, just is a matter of how one appears in different contexts. The view is underpinned by appeals to the 'death of the subject' that invoke a standard set of criticisms of the self as described by Descartes or Kant. However, whatever the power of these arguments against Descartes and Kant, such criticisms simply miss the central distinctions that underlie the classical criticisms of commercial society. These do not invoke 'the self' or 'the subject' in the form of a Cartesian cogito or Kantian transcendental ego. Rather the central critical concept is the classical virtue-based concept of 'character'. One specifies particular persons as embodied individuals who have an identity in the sense of having a character – a set of settled dispositions born of habituation and commitments to lasting projects and relationships. Indeed a feature of Cartesian and Kantian views of the self is that they portray the self as characterless in this sense – the self is defined in abstraction from such specific dispositions.

The classical argument runs that the market separates character in the sense of real dispositions, skills, and relationships an individual has, and defines social identity in terms of appearances purchased through the acquisition of commodities. A central difference between an identity given by the appearances and an identity founded upon character is that the former is ephemeral in a way that the latter is not. Dispositions of character, skills to be exercised in work and other practical activity, capacities of judgement both theoretical and practical take time and commitment to develop and time to fall into disuse. The virtues and vices that make up a character are not subject to immediate decisions and choices: they are gained and lost through habituation. If my social identity is merely a set of appearances then it is an identity that to a large extent I can acquire and cast off as I choose. Who one is is no longer a matter of projects and one's individual capacities to realize

them, more a question of appearances and the capacity one has to buy them. Appearances are alterable in a way that capacities, dispositions and skills, whose development requires time and commitments, are not.

The effect of the denial of distinction of character and appearance is the loss of critical perspectives on market society and the consequent convergence of a postmodern leftism with neoliberal defences of the market. It issues in a celebration of the market's disruption of the conditions for the development of character that had been at the centre of the classical critique. Thus much of what the postmodernist celebrates is the market's unsettling of the condition which makes possible an identity in the sense of character. Hence the characterless figure loved by the postmodernist, who plays with his identity, who takes pleasure in the different identities offered in the marketplace, who loves the arcade and the different images and appearances that can be bought there, who loves the new and the ephemeral.[5] The figure it celebrates is a recent version of the heroic romantic image of the autonomous self-creator who in fact is no self at all (O'Neill, 1998a: chs 6 and 7).

A second source of the denial of classical distinctions lies in a radical value subjectivism which denies there are standards of worth independent of the assignment of value by others. What is notable again is the convergence one finds between postmodern and social constructivists on the one hand and neoliberals on the other. Consider for example the criticism of educational autonomy in the humanities from market boundaries that is offered by a public choice theorist like James Buchanan. To the defence of the arts in terms of its cultivating 'higher qualities', Buchanan responds thus:

'The making of higher-quality men' – this familiar high-sounding objective has an appealing and persuasive ring. But we sense the emptiness once we think at all critically about definitions of quality. Who is to judge? By whose criteria are qualities to be determined? (Buchanan, 1979: 265)

For Buchanan, the appeals are empty because there are no standards of the good other than those offered by individual preference. Individuals have their 'own standards of evaluation', their own preferences, and it is the job of the universities to answer to them. Buchanan's argument here is based upon a value-subjectivism in ethical and aesthetic matters which is standard in both neoclassical and Austrian economics. Since values here are a matter of preference they should be left to consumer preference. Liberal economic theorists like Buchanan traditionally keep spheres in which the norms of reason hold sway as protected domains in which consumer sovereignty has no place. As we noted in the last section, the limited sphere of protection for the sciences has come under fire from the recent sceptical moves about science that inform postmodern and social constructionist accounts of scientific knowledge: the main impact of recent science studies has been to raise a sceptical challenge to the whole notion of independent norms of reason in science. In the cruder versions scientific truth itself is brought into the realm of preference – truth is merely a matter of preference in belief.

What both the neoliberals on the right and the postmoderns on the left play upon here is an egalitarianism about judgements of worth which is taken to require relativism about norms. Where they differ is in the scope of Buchanan's questions about 'definitions of quality': Who is to judge? By whose criteria are qualities to be determined? For the sceptic about science, it is not just the 'culturally cultivated' who are acting in an authoritarian fashion when they impose their standards on all. So also are the 'scientifically cultivated' when they impose their own particular knowledges on others and silence other voices, the voices of those who have 'local knowledge'. The authority of science is undermined by scepticism about the cognitive norms of science. There are no independent norms to either culture or knowledge. Hence both represent a form of power that lacks justification. Thus, in recent postmodern leftism, especially that influenced by Foucault, all epistemological norms in medicine, science and other disciplines, are understood as social norms through which power is enforced. The upshot is a still more radical defence of the sphere in which individual preference cannot be challenged. Hence the degree to which social constructionists have appealed to market models of science of the kind noted in the last section. Hence also again the odd alliance in defence of the market and consumer culture between the new right and the postmodern left.

There is a partial truth in the egalitarianism of both postmoderns and neoliberals. The appeal to standards of worth can often be a means by which social distinctions and power are enforced. Praise or honour from those 'whose judgement counts' is sometimes simply a veiled form of snobbery: it is simply a question of getting a particular positional good, not of confirmation of one's independent worth. These aristocratic prejudices run through many classical discussions of worth – most notably in the work of Aristotle himself. However, it would be false to conclude thereby that all appeals to such standards are mere exercises in social distinction and power. Indeed, unless such standards of worth are allowed, what is defensible in recent postmodern and social constructionist critiques of science – for example the defence of local knowledge against expert knowledge is lost. Scientism, the view that only science can give knowledge, and the corresponding denial of local and practical knowledge, is a proper object of criticism. But this requires putting a proper value on such local knowledge, of giving it its proper epistemological authority where it is due. The problem with the generalized scepticism that is exhibited in recent sociology of science is that by denying the possibility of *any* epistemological standards of worth it undermines the possibility of defending local knowledge against scientistic appeals to expert authority: each has to be treated symmetrically. The result is a relativistic neutrality that is robbed of critical power.

More generally, the undoubted truth that distinctions in worth are ways in which power and status can be defined and enforced is open to an egalitarian reversal: equality of social standing is a condition for proper distinctions of worth. Thus within the socialist tradition the classical claims about recognition were linked to arguments about property and distribution. Thus, Marx in his early work is the heir to themes in Hegel and classical political economy about the divorce of appearance and character in commercial society. Alienation involves in part a separation of appearance and real character. Typical are his arguments in the section on money in the 1844 manuscripts: 'The properties of money are my, the possessor's, properties and essential powers. Therefore what I *am* and what I *can do* is by no means determined by my individuality' (Marx, 1974: 377). The market separates character in the sense of real dispositions, skills, and relationships an individual has, from the social identity I have defined through the marketable goods I can buy. Whereas in commercial society, any quality can be exchanged for any other, in communism a person's virtues can only be those he actually has:

> If we assume *man* to be *man*, and his relation to the world to be a human one, then love can only be exchanged for love, trust for trust, and so on. . . . Each of your relations to man – and to nature – must be a *particular expression* corresponding to the object of your will, of your *real individual* life. (Marx, 1974: 379)

The argument for equality is that one's way through life is to be determined by the qualities of character one actually possesses, with all the misfortune and failure this entails, and not by ersatz powers that money is able to buy.

This argument from recognition to equality is one that runs through socialist thought. A central problem of recognition is taken to be distributional: of allocating social and economic power such that they no longer determine judgements of worth. Social equality is a condition for proper judgements of real worth. The move is contained in the following argument from Tawney:

> Progress depends, indeed, on a willingness on the part of the mass of mankind – and we all, in nine-tenths of our nature, belong to the mass – to recognize genuine superiority, and to submit themselves to its influence. But the condition of recognizing genuine superiority is a contempt for unfounded pretensions to it. Where the treasure is, there will the heart be also, and, if men are to respect each other for what they are, they must cease to respect each other for what they own. (Tawney, 1964: 87)

Tawney, like Marx, calls upon the distinction between 'respect . . . for what people are' and 'respect . . . for what they own'. Equality in economic and social standing is a condition for respect and recognition of worth.

This position relies upon a distinction between concepts of 'standing' and the concepts of 'virtue'[6] and correspondingly between equality in the social, economic and political standings of individuals and groups on the one hand and equality in the appraisal of the worth of character, judgements, goods, and achievements on the other. By 'standing' here I mean roughly the social, political and economic position, class or status a person has within a community: freeman and slave, lord and serf, citizen and non-citizen and so on. By 'virtues' I mean the excellences that individuals have and display where these are understood in their widest sense to include not only excellences in moral character – kindness, courage, good judgement, humility and so on – but also excellences in practices – of the scientist, artist, teacher, athlete, parent and so on. To make these distinctions is not to deny that there is not a complex set of relationships between the two sets of concepts. In traditional societies, the standing of a person is often in part constituted by a set of virtues peculiar to it: hence, for example, the traditional distinctions in the virtues demanded of women as wife and mother and those demanded of men as husbands, fathers and citizens. Likewise, it is possible to have a standing in a particular community, for example in an occupational association, in virtue of meeting some set of skills in a trade. However, to describe the relationships between standing and virtues is not to conflate them.

Conflation is, however, common. Fukuyama's account of the move to modern society as a transition to *isothymia* from *megalothymia* confuses these two sets of concepts. The passage from pre-modern to modern societies, understood as a move from 'status' to 'contract', has involved a shift in the standing of agents: from a system of differentiated political, social and moral standing defined by roles, each with its distinct bundles of virtues, rights and obligations, to undifferentiated standings defined in terms of rights and duties that an individual has under some general description – as 'citizen' or 'person'. Individuals are in this sense understood, formally at least, to be members of a community of equal standing. The liberal social and political order is defined by the existence of a class of rights that are held by individuals as persons whatever their particular qualities – to vote, to enter associations, to enter into contracts and so on. The struggle for such rights is, as Fukuyama claims, in part a struggle for recognition. Hence, where they are won, as they were recently by the majority of the population in South Africa, their significance is more than instrumental. They have value in virtue of granting to individuals recognition that they are someone. They are recognized as having standing that is equal to that of others. Much of the traditional socialist and feminist criticism of liberalism has concerned issues of standing – of the restricted domains in which the community of equal standing exists and the formal nature of that equality. While in the realm of politics and market exchange individuals related to each other as members of single-status communities, as citizen or contracting agents, in the sphere of production and the domestic sphere they meet as superordinate and subordinate, as capitalist and wage worker, as husband and wife. And in politics and market exchange, formal equality in standing exists alongside substantive inequality of powers. With respect to standing, the struggle for recognition has not ceased. Its boundaries have shifted.

What, however, is presupposed by such debates is a claim that the recent emphasis on 'difference' has obscured. The objective of a community of equal standing has its basis in the humanist thought that whatever the differences that might exist in achievements and virtues, human beings share certain universal powers which deserve to be recognized: by powers here I refer both to active powers, in particular the primary powers to develop skills and capacities, including powers of theoretical and practical reason and the capacity to shape one's own life, and what the scholastics called passive powers, to feel pain and pleasure, to suffer humiliation and the like. Acceptance of the existence of such powers is quite compatible with difference. For example, the forms in which humiliation can take are diverse and differ across gender, culture, and class. However, the capacity to feel humiliation is a universal one, and to meet other humans and to not be aware of that possibility of humiliation is to fail to recognize them as subjects to whom respect is owed.

Equality in standing is a condition for proper appraisal of the differences in worth. Both the implicit distinction and the relation between them deserve restatement. They do so just because the failure to recognize them lies at the basis of much of what is wrong in recent neoliberal and postmodern thought. Both assume that respect for difference entails a refusal to make distinctions of worth.[7] An egalitarianism about worth replaces that about standing. However, the consequent relativism about judgements of worth has resulted in a divorce of questions of recognition from those of distribution in social, political and economic standing. The cultural turn away from problems of economic power and inequality is in part the result of a misplaced egalitarianism about distinctions of worth. The consequence of the divorce is the failure to address still-pressing concerns about inequality in economic, social and political standing across class, gender, age and ethnicity.

Notes

1 It is worth noting here to pre-empt misunderstandings, that the appreciation of the aesthetic qualities of objects – the love of beauty – is distinct from vanity – the love of praise. However, there is clearly a complex set of relations

between the two. For Smith's observations on these, see Smith (1982a: III.2.18–19, IV and V).

2 For a notable instance of the confusion of self-esteem with vanity see Nozick (1974: ch. 8); for admirable criticism see Skillen (1977).

3 Walzer does not miss this point entirely. See his discussion of the distinction between self-respect and self-esteem. For a discussion of Walzer which has been influential on my thoughts here see Keat (1997).

4 My criticisms here are aimed not at the sociology of science as such, but at the constructivist versions outlined here. The Edinburgh school in particular does not deny the distinctions I have drawn here. Thus Barnes and Bloor are more careful: 'Our equivalence postulate is that all beliefs are on par with one another with respect to the causes of their credibility. It is not that all beliefs are equally true or false, but that regardless of truth and falsity the fact of their credibility is to be seen as equally problematic' (Barnes and Bloor, 1982).

5 The loss of critical intent is evident in the shift from situationism to postmodernism. Situationism represented a strong statement of the classical complaint against commercial society. The claim went that in the society of the spectacle everything becomes a matter of appearance. Postmodernism accepts the claim but denies the critical contrast, upon which situationism relied, between the appearance and the real condition of individual lives.

6 The distinctions I employ here owe a great deal to Vlastos (1962). I use 'standing' here where he employs the concept of 'worth', and 'virtue' where he uses the concept of 'merit'. The term 'worth' is I think unhelpful here, since it is used in the appraisal of the virtues of persons and their products: for example, 'there is little aesthetic worth in this picture'. The concept of 'merit' also brings with it a certain unwelcome baggage: in political theory it invokes particular theories of justice.

7 The conflation of the two forms of equal recognition often arises in discussions of multiculturalism. See Taylor (1992: 61–73) for criticisms of the failure to keep different forms of recognition apart.

References

Aristotle (1928) *De Sophisticis Elenchis*, I, trans. W. Pickard-Cambridge, London: Oxford University Press.

Aristotle (1985) *Nicomachean Ethics*, trans. T. Irwin, Indianapolis: Hackett.

Barnes, S.B. and Bloor, D. (1982) 'Relativism, rationalism and the sociology of knowledge', in M. Hollis (ed.), *Rationality and Relativism*, Oxford: Blackwell.

Buchanan, J. (1972) 'Towards analysis of closed behavioural systems', in J. Buchanan and R. Tollison (eds), *Theory of Public Choice*, Ann Arbor: University of Michigan Press.

Buchanan, J. (1979) 'Public finance and academic freedom', in *What Should Economists Do?*, Indianapolis: Liberty Press.

Fukuyama, F. (1992) *The End of History and the Last Man*, London: Hamish Hamilton.

Hands, D.W. (1994) 'The sociology of scientific knowledge', in R. Backhouse (ed.), *New Directions in Economic Methodology*, London: Routledge, pp. 75–106.

Hegel, G. (1967) *Philosophy of Right*, trans. T. Knox, Oxford: Oxford University Press.

Hegel, G. (1977) *Phenemonology of Spirit*, trans. A. Miller, Oxford: Oxford University Press.

Hirsch, F. (1977) *Social Limits to Growth*, London: Routledge and Kegan Paul.

Hume, D. (1975) *Enquiries Concerning Human Understanding and Concerning the Principles of Morals*, Oxford: Oxford University Press.

Jameson, F. (1991) *Postmodernism, of the Cultural Logic of Late Capitalism*, London: Verso.

Keat, R. (1997) 'Colonisation by the market: Walzer on recognition', *Journal of Political Philosophy*, 5: 95–7.

Kellner, D. (1992) 'Popular culture and the construction of postmodern identities', in S. Lash and J. Friedman (eds), *Modernity and Identity*, Oxford: Blackwell.

MacIntyre, A. (1985) *After Virtue*, 2nd edn, London: Duckworth.

Marx, K. (1974) *Economic and Philosophical Manuscripts*, ed. Colletti, *Early Writings*, Harmondsworth: Penguin.

Nozick, R. (1974) *Anarchy, State and Utopia*, Oxford: Blackwell.

O'Neill, J. (1998a) *The Market: Ethics, Knowledge and Politics*, London: Routledge.

O'Neill, J. (1998b) 'Rhetoric, science and philosophy', *Philosophy of Social Sciences*, 28: 205–25.

Rousseau, J. (1984) *A Discourse on Inequality*, trans. M. Cranston, Harmondsworth: Penguin.

Skillen, A. (1977) *Ruling Illusions*, Hassocks: Harvester.

Smith, A. (1981) *An Inquiry into the Nature and Causes of the Wealth of Nations*, Indianapolis: Liberty Press.

Smith, A. (1982a) *The Theory of Moral Sentiments*, Indianapolis: Liberty Press.

Smith, A. (1982b) *Essays on Philosophical Subjects*, Indianapolis: Liberty Press.

Tawney, R. (1964) *Equality*, London: Unwin.

Taylor, C. (1992) *Multiculturalism and 'The Politics of Recognition'*, Princeton, NJ: Princeton University Press.

Vlastos, G. (1962) 'Justice and equality', in R. Brandt (ed.), *Social Justice*, Englewood Cliffs, NJ: Prentice-Hall.

Walzer, M. (1983) *Spheres of Justice*, Oxford: Blackwell.

Woolgar, S. and Latour, B. (1979) *Laboratory Life: the Construction of Scientific Facts*, London: Sage.

4

Market Boundaries and the Commodification of Culture

Russell Keat

Justifying limitations on the market[1]

Both in Britain and elsewhere over the past twenty years, governments have implemented radical programmes of institutional change imposing market or quasi-market principles and forms of organization into a wide range of social institutions and practices which had previously operated in quite different ways. I have in mind here not so much the privatization of publicly owned industries, but the commercially modelled reconstruction of local government, educational and health-care institutions, and also, especially, of broadcasting, the various arts, academic research and so on. It is with the possible grounds for opposing the marketization of these 'cultural' institutions and practices, and hence more generally for resisting the 'commodification of culture', that I shall mainly be concerned in this chapter.[2]

In making a case against the commodification of culture it will not, I believe, prove helpful to rely on general critiques of commodification of the kind to be found in the socialist tradition, and hence to argue that since the market is an undesirable institution in any possible area of application, its further spread or expansion must always be resisted – that if something is bad, the more of it the worse. For the socialist case against the market *tout court* faces a major, and as yet unresolved, problem. It depends on the claim that there is some alternative form of economic organization which preserves what is best about the market, eliminates its specific ills, and does not generate additional and more serious ills of its own. But it is highly doubtful whether any such alternative has yet been constructed, either in practice or in theory.[3]

Instead, I suggest, it will be more fruitful to approach this issue by thinking of it in terms of 'market boundaries', of possible reasons either for excluding certain social institutions and practices from the market or for supporting their operation outwith the market, yet without thereby rejecting its overall merits as a way of organizing economic production. Such reasons must refer to the specific character of the institutions and practices concerned, and show why it is that their being subject to the logic of commodity production would be inappropriate, damaging etc. It may then be possible to justify their 'protection' from the market through various forms of intervention by the state.

In broad terms, the idea that the market has its place, but should not be permitted to exceed its proper sphere, is a quite obvious and familiar one. It is connected both to the insights of everyday wisdom – 'there are things that money can't buy' (and are at least as important as those that it can) – and to various influential theorizations of modernity, such as Hegel's differentiation of society into the family, civil society (including a market economy) and the state, with the activities in each sphere being conducted on the basis of distinctive kinds of social relationships, institutional structures and ethical norms which would be inappropriate and destructive were they to operate outside their proper domain.

Indeed, most theorists who extol the virtues of the market at least implicitly assume that what they are supporting are organizational principles for a specific domain, and not for 'society as a whole'. Admittedly, some of the arguments they deploy to support the market may turn out to be inconsistent with this assumption: they have so general a character that they would seem to imply that every sphere of society should be organized on this basis. For example, if the price-mechanism is such a brilliant device for transmitting information about individuals' preferences, why shouldn't we allow political offices and votes to be bought and sold in a thoroughgoing 'political' market – and likewise for marriage and friendship markets as well?

However, what is problematic about the marketization of cultural institutions is not easily assimilable to what would be objectionable about the marketization of the political and familial or personal domains. For instance, the sale and purchase of political offices would clearly be at odds with the underlying principles of liberal democracy, and would rightly be seen as 'corruption'. But nothing analogous to this could plausibly be said in making a case against the commodification of cultural goods.[4] Likewise, the buying and selling of 'friendship services' would be objectionable because it would undermine the essential nature of friendship as a specific kind of relationship between people.[5] But the same could not be argued in the case of theatre tickets or books about political theory.

Further, whereas the sale and purchase of political and personal goods is something one might reasonably wish to prohibit or try to prevent happening altogether, the same is not true in the case of cultural goods. The question is not whether it is desirable for these to be produced as commodities at all, but whether there should *also* be some major provision of these outwith the market, combined in at least many cases – such as the media – with the regulation of their production within it. Thus the political programme of marketization which I noted at the outset has consisted in the removal of such regulation, the reduction of state funding for non-commercial provision and, perhaps most significantly, the attempt to make such funding conditional on the cultural institutions concerned adopting organizational structures which are modelled upon, and intended to ensure that they operate 'as if in fact they were', commercial enterprises.

But on what grounds might this commodification of culture be resisted? If one 'listens' to what is said by those who oppose these changes, one will often hear claims of the following kinds: that the market-oriented reforms of the BBC will lead to a decline in programme quality and misdirected audience-chasing; that the deregulation of commercial broadcasting will reduce the proper coverage and analysis of political issues; that the attribution of consumer-status to university students will undermine the academic integrity of degrees; that the commerically modelled funding requirements placed on subsidized theatre and dance companies will inhibit artistic innovation and the production of challenging work; that transforming museums into part of the leisure industry will put at risk the proper purpose of their collections – and so on.

Thus the basic concern here is that various kinds of cultural goods, to which considerable value is attributed, are likely to be 'lost' and displaced by others of lesser value. But why should this be so? For surely, it could be argued, the value of cultural products, like that of any others, resides in their contribution to human well-being, in the benefits they make possible for those who 'consume' them, and it is precisely the ability of the market to generate such benefical products that justifies its overall use as the means of organizing economic production. So why should it fail to achieve this in the case of cultural goods, but not of others – bearing in mind that what is being opposed here is not any and every use of the market, but only its exclusive and unregulated application in the specific case of cultural institutions and production?

Furthermore, this objection might continue, a crucial feature of the market is that it is left to consumers to judge what will contribute to their own well-being, and hence the value of the different products available to them – 'expressing' these judgements through their willingness to pay. So it would seem that the critics of cultural commodification are simply unwilling to allow this. Instead, they take it upon themselves to assess the value of cultural goods, refusing to trust the judgements made by consumers; by doing so they lay themselves open to the charges of elitism, paternalism and the like.

But I think there is a way of 'turning the tables' here. If the chief virtue of the market is its ability to generate goods which enhance people's well-being – which may be termed the 'classical' justification for the market – and if it does so by ensuring that consumer judgements about the value of these goods hold sway in decisions about what is produced, then it is clearly important also to ensure that these judgements are made as well as they can be. But suppose it could be shown that this is itself dependent on the availability to consumers making these judgements of *cultural* goods, and that there are strong reasons for doubting that the market alone will secure their adequate provision? One would then be able to justify the *non*-market provision of cultural goods on the grounds that this is required if the market is to achieve 'its own objective', at least in 'classical' terms, i.e. to contribute to human well-being through the production of consumer goods.[6]

This is what I shall try to show in what follows, and I shall also defend this case for non-commodified culture against the accusations of elitism noted above. I shall begin, in the next section, by arguing that the significance that should be given to (improving) consumer *judgements* in market economies is obscured by their neo-classical representation as *preferences*. In the third section I shall look at various ways in which the ability to make these judgements is dependent both on the engagement by consumers in various social practices and on the availability of cultural goods. I conclude, in the fourth section, by arguing that the market cannot be relied upon adequately to provide these cultural goods.

Even if this argument is successful, however, it may well seem unappealing to critics of cultural commodification: to support non-market cultural institutions on the grounds that they will improve the market's performance seems like arguing for the importance of trust by showing that it reduces the costs of economic production, rather than by demonstrating its role in social relationships which are intrinsically valuable. But the overall position which I will defend has several additional features which may serve to remove this apparent weakness. In particular, I will argue that what it is about cultural goods which enables them to enhance the effectiveness of the market, namely their thematization of the nature and sources of human well-being, *also* enables us to recognize the *limitations* of the market as a source of such well-being, and hence the need to retain a wide range of social relationships and activities which are both conducted outwith the market and characterized by the absence of market mentalities. Further, one of the key reasons for the support of non-market cultural institutions will turn out to be their critical role in challenging the self-promotion of the market through advertising and related forms of 'cultural' production which, I shall suggest, can generally be relied upon to *mis*represent the relationship between consumer goods and human well-being.

Judgements vs preferences; well-being vs efficiency

Let us assume that the primary reason for people's purchasing consumer products is their belief that these will contribute to their own well-being. Of course, this assumption is not altogether correct, since consumers may also apply ethical or political considerations in making their purchases, and since goods are often purchased for the joint use and benefit of the purchaser and others, or as gifts. But these complications can be put aside.

What I have just called a 'belief' might also be termed a 'judgement': the consumer's decision to purchase some item is based on a judgement about its expected benefit to them. Correspondingly, the decision made to purchase one such item rather than another is based on a comparative judgement about their respective merits, defined in these terms. (Again, I shall simplify by ignoring differences of price, and hence of the differential impact of one purchase as against another on the consumer's budget.)

This benefit, I shall take it, is what is normally referred to as the product's 'use-value'. From the standpoint of the consumer, this is what matters about the product; from the standpoint of the producer in a market system, it is not, since the producer is concerned only with the product's 'exchange-value', and hence with the profitability or otherwise of its being produced (at a certain cost) and sold (at a certain price). But according to classical defenders of the market, the great virtue of this system is that it operates in such a way that, generally speaking, the attempt to maximize profits or exchange-values on the part of producers turns out also to maximize use-values for consumers.

By contrast, it is claimed, attempts to construct an economic system in which producers aim to maximize consumers' use-values will be much less successful. This is partly because one cannot rely on producers actually being governed by this unselfish aim, but also because even if they were, they would usually be less well-placed, or less competent, than consumers to make the necessary judgements of use-value, i.e. of the contribution their products would make to the latter's well-being. This, it is claimed, is because each individual is 'the best judge of their own well-being', i.e. a better judge of this than is anyone else. It is the fact that this is so, and that production decisions in a market system are so responsive to consumers' judgements, expressed through their willingness-to-pay, that accounts for the market's success as a system for generating human goods.

Although it is possible to challenge the 'best judge' thesis, I shall not do so here.[7] Instead I want to point out that this thesis does not entail that every individual is, as it were, 'always already' the best judge of their own well-being that they could be. For even if it is true that each person is better than anyone else at judging (what will contribute to) their own well-being, it may also be true that their ability to make these judgements may itself be better or worse. That is, it is possible for individuals to improve their ability to make such judgements; the ability may be less well developed in some people than in others, or at some times in someone's life than at others; the extent and subtlety of its development may depend on various conditions and circumstances, and so on.

What this implies is that although the market may be superior to other systems in its goods-generative capacities, it may itself do better or worse in this respect depending on the extent to which people are able, as consumers, to make correspondingly better or worse judgements about how the purchase of various products will contribute to their well-being. So any particular market economy with consumers who are good at making these judgements will be more successful, in its own (classical) terms, than one where this is not the case. To maximize the advantages stemming from the market, one must maximize the judgement-capacities of consumers.

What I have said so far should seem obvious enough, yet with some partial exceptions noted later (see the last section, on the commodification of cultural goods, below) it is largely ignored in standard accounts of the market provided by neoclassical theorists. For in neoclassical economics the vocabulary of 'judgement' and 'well-being' which I have employed is replaced by that of 'preferences' and their 'satisfaction', with the consequent exclusion of significant questions about the market's ability to generate human goods. This can be seen by considering briefly the neoclassical understanding of *efficiency*, which is taken to be the chief criterion by which the merits of different economic systems, and/or of specific instantiations of these at any one time, are to be judged.[8]

Utilizing the concept of Pareto-optimality to avoid what are seen as insuperable problems of interpersonal welfare comparisons, the allocation of productive resources in an economic system is said to be *efficient* when there is no other allocation which would make at least one person better-off without anyone else being made worse-off. Further, and crucially, someone's being 'better-off' is interpreted as their *preferring* the consequences for them of one such allocation of resources over another, with this preference itself being expressed by their willingness-to-pay, i.e. in the choices they make, or would make, as consumers. Subject to various 'ideal' conditions obtaining, which I shall consider later, market systems can then be demonstrated, by deductive argumentation, to be efficient.

What is problematic about this conception of efficiency – at least when viewed as a criterion by which the contribution of economic systems to human well-being is determined – is the weakness of its interpretation of well-being simply as the satisfaction of expressed (consumer) preferences, whatever grounds they may happen to rely upon.[9] As implied in my initial remarks in this section, one typically thinks of a person's preferences for certain consumer goods as based on the judgements they make about the likely contribution of these to their own well-being. It is because they make these judgements that they have, and act upon, these preferences; they prefer these goods because they judge them to *be* such. Correspondingly, the extent to which consumers succeed in improving their well-being through such purchases depends upon how well-supported these judgements actually are.

But these points get lost in the neoclassical account, a loss marked by the displacement of the vocabulary of judgement and well-being by that of preferences and their satisfaction. The effect of this is seriously to weaken the normative significance of what it is that the market can be *demonstrated* to achieve, namely efficiency, since for all one knows, the preferences satisfied by an efficient allocation of productive resources may be quite arbitrary or ill-considered ones that lack much basis in sound judgement. So whilst it may be true that, other things being equal, an efficient economic system is better than an inefficient one, the extent to which an efficient system enhances the well-being of consumers remains undetermined on the neoclassical account.[10]

It is important, however, not to overstate this objection to the neoclassical conception of efficiency. In particular, it may be tempting to think that, because the demonstrable efficiency of a market system is something that may, for all one knows, have relatively little value, there is no good reason to expect any actual market economy to contribute significantly to human well-being. But this would clearly be a mistake. For although the neoclassical *proof* of market efficiency does not by itself establish very much, it might perfectly well be the case that *actual* market economies achieve a good deal more than they can be proved to do. This would be so if, in fact, the consumer preferences satisfied by an efficient allocation of productive resources were supported by well-grounded judgements on their part.

So if one is to assess the extent to which market systems are in practice likely to fulfil their 'classical promise' of generating goods which contribute to human well-being, there are at least two crucial questions which need to be answered. (i) First, what kinds of conditions are required if the preferences of consumers are to be based on sound, well-informed and considered judgements – what is it that will enhance their ability to make such judgements? (ii) Second, having arrived at an answer to (i), what confidence can one have that the market can itself be relied upon generally to provide these conditions to a sufficient or maximal degree?

In the next two sections I shall argue, in response to (i), that amongst these judgement-enhancing conditions are both the discriminative abilities developed through the various social activities in which the use-value of consumer products is realized, and the existence of cultural goods which provide resources for critical reflection on the nature and possibilities of human well-being; and in response to (ii), that there are good reasons for doubting the ability of the market to ensure the adequate provision of these goods – and indeed for expecting its unbounded operation to put them at considerable risk. If these arguments succeed, one will have strong grounds for securing these conditions through *non*market means, and hence for opposing 'the commodification of culture'.

Cultural goods and the social bases of consumer judgements

One can begin by noting that the use-value of consumer goods is typically realized not through their purchase or acquisition as such, but through their further deployment by their purchasers so as to achieve certain purposes which they value. Consumer goods are not 'final' goods, but 'intermediate' ones: their value to the purchaser, their potential contribution to the consumer's well-being, depends both on the extent to which they enable these purposes to be achieved, and on the value of those purposes' achievement. So for consumers to make sound judgements about the use-value of consumer goods, they must be able to judge both the 'fitness for purpose' of these goods and the value of those purposes for their own well-being. The better they are at making these judgements, the greater their prospects of enhancing their overall well-being through consumption.[11]

In some cases, both types of judgement are of a relatively simple kind, namely for those consumer products whose main purpose is to enable 'necessary' tasks to be performed in effective, time-saving and minimally unpleasant ways. The home has to be cleaned, one's clothes have to be washed, one has to get to one's place of work, and so on: these are 'necessary' tasks in the sense not merely that they must be performed if other things to which value is attributed are to be pursued, but also that – typically – they are not themselves seen as valuable, and are indeed often experienced as unpleasant, irksome, mere drudgery and the like. The performance of these tasks makes it possible to engage in other activities seen as contributing positively to one's well-being, but these tasks themselves are not: the less time they take, and the less unpleasantly they can be performed, the better.

Correspondingly, the 'fitness for purpose' judgements made about such consumer products require only access to, and the ability to understand, relatively straightforward empirical information – about the performance, cost and so on of the vacuum-cleaner, washing-machine or car – together with basic introspective capacities enabling one to discern how much boredom, noise, tiredness, etc. is involved or avoided in their use. Further, there is little if any need to engage directly in the second kind of judgement, since the value of the purpose achieved through the use of these goods is essentially that of 'making space' for the pursuit of other, positively valued aims of a more or less unspecified nature. Provided there is reason to believe there is *something* worth doing in the space created by the deployment of these goods, there is no need to engage in any further reflection about its specific character and value in judging whether, and how far, these 'convenience' goods are indeed convenient.

In many other cases, however, judgement of the use-value of consumer products requires far more than this. One can see this, first, by considering those whose value is realized through their employment in 'productive' activities, i.e. in making other things to which positive value is more directly attributed: for example, the foodstuffs purchased to cook meals, the paint bought to decorate a room, the fabric purchased to make clothes, etc. In such cases the judgements made about fitness of purpose depend on corresponding judgements about the things they are used to make or produce. What count as good ingredients depend on what is judged to be a tasty etc. meal; good paint, on a well-decorated room; good fabrics on attractive clothing, and so on.

Judgements such as these may often require significant powers of discrimination, the ability to understand and apply the criteria associated with the kind of product concerned. These powers are acquired partly through experience, and partly also through access to various kinds of actual and virtual 'communities': those who cook, decorate, sew, etc. will often consult others who do likewise (especially those who are more experienced, skilful, etc. than themselves), and also food-columns, home-decorating magazines, fashion-pages and so on, thereby learning not only about the techniques of doing these things and 'what to buy', but also about the criteria by which the outcome of their efforts may be judged. So the soundness of the judgements they make about the fitness for purpose of the products they may purchase depends not only on their access to information about the relevant characteristics of the items concerned, but also on their ability to understand and apply the criteria by reference to which the merits of the 'final' products are to be judged. For it is these criteria which determine what count as the *relevant* characteristics of the items concerned.

Similar points about the potential complexity of fitness-for-purpose judgements emerge if one considers a further important category of consumer goods, those deployed in the conduct of various activities engaged in 'for their own sake', rather than as a means of generating some further, distinct product or outcome. So, for example, one may purchase boots to go climbing, an electronic keyboard to play music, binoculars to observe wildlife, a boat to go sailing, a brush to paint water-colours, and so on. In a broad sense of the term, these consumer goods may be conceived as 'equipment', whose purpose is to enable one to engage successfully and enjoyably in activities experienced as intrinsically satisfying.

Whether those who engage in such activities choose to do so alone or with others, the activities themselves are nonetheless essentially *social*, in that each is constituted as the specific kind of activity it is through the existence of an established and generally recognized set of norms and criteria by reference to which the performance of the activity is conducted and evaluated.[12] Thus learning to perform these activities is not only a matter of acquiring various technical skills and abilities, but also of coming to understand and apply both the criteria which serve to define what counts as a competent etc. performance, and the ethical rules and etiquette governing appropriate conduct. It is only through the acquisition of such capacities – which typically require what is, in effect, a period of 'apprenticeship' – that the potential benefits of engaging in these activities can be realized.

Correspondingly, the ability of those concerned to judge the equipment they may purchase and deploy in these activities is likewise dependent on their knowledge and understanding of the activity concerned, or at least on their willingness to seek the advice of those whose expertise they recognize. Thus the relevance of empirical information about the respective characteristics of different possible purchases is determined by the criteria by reference to which the activity itself is conducted and judged; the judgements made about fitness for purpose depend on complex discriminative capacities based on people's experience and understanding of the socially established criteria governing the activity concerned. The greater the extent and depth of their understanding and experience, the better-grounded are the judgements made by consumers, and the more the products they purchase will contribute to their well-being.

However, as I noted at the beginning of this section, the judgements made by consumers must take account not only of the fitness for purpose of the products concerned, but also of the value of such purposes being achieved for their own well-being. Yet there is no reason to expect that the criteria internal to the kinds of social practices I have been describing can also provide an adequate basis for this second, equally important element in consumer judgements. I shall illustrate this point through the kinds of 'own-sake' activities or practices just described, though what I have to say has a wider application.

Those who engage in the practice of sailing will typically be able to appreciate – and hence also to enjoy – all those things which count as competent, good or even excellent instances of the activity, and likewise all the attributes of 'a good sailor', whether displayed by themselves or by others. The same will be true of painting, mountain-climbing, music and so on. But their ability to make judgements of this kind does not ensure that they will also be able to answer the following kinds of questions: what is the good *of* sailing, or of painting, climbing, playing music, etc.? Yet these are the questions they need to answer if they are to judge whether engagement in these activities is valuable, worthy of the time (and money) they might spend on them, and so on.

It seems implausible to believe that these social practices possess the conceptual resources necessary to answer such questions about their own value: for example, the criteria which enable mountain-climbers to judge what counts as 'a challenging ascent well performed' do not tell us why it is worth making such ascents in the first place. Correspondingly, whilst the criteria internal to these practices provide the basis for judging the fitness for purpose of potential equipment purchases, they do not likewise enable consumers to judge the value of the activities which such purchases equip them to engage in.

Nor is it a matter simply of judging the value of each of these considered separately. For although each consumption decision made by an individual may be made primarily on the basis of specific judgements about the item concerned and what its purchase makes possible, the aggregative effect of these decisions is to give a particular character to the life being led by that individual. So ideally at least, each such decision should be made in the context of some overall conception of the kind of life the individual concerned 'wishes' to pursue, and hence, inter alia, of the relative priorities to be attributed to different areas of their life, to the different purposes they may value. Clearly, the criteria internal to the social activities through which these purposes are pursued cannot themselves provide the basis for making such 'overall' evaluations in an informed and considered way.

What is needed, then, is the ability to make judgements both about the value of particular purposes, and about how these contribute to the overall value of one's life, from some perspective other than, and external to, those embedded in the various social practices through which one's life is largely led.[13] It is here, I suggest, that the potential significance of *cultural* goods can be seen. For it is a characteristic feature of at least many cultural goods that, directly or indirectly, they address and explore the nature and possibilities of human well-being itself.

I have in mind here not so much the abstract, theoretical practices of academic philosophy and the like – though doubtless they may have some value – but the more concrete and engaging representations of the various ways in which human life may be conducted, the nuanced depictions of social relationships and individual characters, which are to be found in novels, films, plays, TV drama, soap operas and many other cultural 'products'. What is crucial about these cultural goods is that they enable us vicariously to extend our own range of experience, freeing us from the limitations imposed by the contingencies of our own existence, and thereby provide us with some understanding of the possibilities, dangers and attractions of lives we have not (yet) led, and some means of reflection on those which we already have. A certain critical 'distance' is thereby made available, but in a way that relies mainly on things being 'shown' rather than 'said'.

Thus cultural goods of this kind should not be conceived, as they often are in discussions about the commodification of culture, simply as 'one set of goods amongst others'. Rather, they should be seen as *meta-goods*, i.e. as goods whose nature consists at least partly in addressing questions about the nature of human goods and their potential contribution to human well-being. Relatedly, it would be a mistake to think of such cultural goods exclusively or primarily in aesthetic terms. No doubt their aesthetic qualities play some part in their appreciation and enjoyment by those who 'consume' them – by their 'audiences'. But at least in many cases their significance resides to a considerable extent in providing a means by which those audiences can reflect on other goods, and hence make better judgements about their value for them.

These 'other' goods include those that may be purchased through the market, and hence the various further activities, experiences and practices which these make possible. But cultural goods *also* enable us to reflect on the extent to which any amount or kind of consumption can contribute to our overall well-being, and hence what part the pursuit of this should play in our lives. We may thereby learn, not merely through our own experience, that much of what is most valuable to us is largely independent of the benefits that consumption can confer, or may even be threatened by too great an attention to these: that the things that matter most to us are simply not attainable in this way.[14] Thus cultural goods are a resource which not only improves our ability to make judgements about consumer goods, and the contribution these can make to our well-being; they also enable us to judge the value to be attributed to consumption by comparison with the many other sources of human well-being. They can thereby enhance both the benefits available through the market and our ability to keep these in a proper perspective.

Against the commodification of cultural goods

I have argued so far that the ability of the market to contribute to human well-being is dependent on that of consumers to make sound judgements about the extent to which the goods they may purchase will do this in their own case, and that this latter ability is itself dependent, inter alia, on their access to cultural 'meta-goods'. I turn now to the second of the two questions posed earlier: namely whether the market can itself be relied upon to provide the conditions for its own success; more specifically, in light of the preceding discussion, to generate sufficient cultural goods of this kind. I shall argue that the market cannot be relied upon to do so, and that there are good grounds for expecting it not to.

To see why this is so, one can usefully start from the neoclassical recognition of the possibility of 'market failures', i.e. the failure of actual market economies to achieve efficiency (in the sense of Pareto-optimality).[15] The possibility of such failures arises from the fact that although it can be demonstrated that, under certain specifiable conditions, a market system will be efficient, there is no guarantee that all these conditions will in practice obtain. These conditions serve to define an 'ideal' market; amongst them are the absence both of external costs and benefits and of public goods, and the presence of perfect competition, including perfect 'information'. Any failure of such conditions to obtain implies that the market will fail to be efficient. Since in the 'real' world such failures may often occur, it may then be necessary for non-market procedures to be employed – including those involving intervention by the state – if efficiency is to be achieved.

This neoclassical conception of market failures has sometimes been used to construct justifications for government subsidies for the arts, by claiming that these can properly be regarded as 'public goods' and hence as items which will be underproduced by the market alone. There are, however, notorious difficulties facing such attempts, and I shall not pursue them here.[16] Instead, I suggest it will prove more illuminating to focus on another of the conditions just noted for ideal markets, that of 'perfect information'.

Neoclassical theorists typically conceive of such information in straightforwardly empirical terms. For producers, it will include such things as knowledge of the costs involved in producing different goods, etc.; for consumers, knowledge of the different products available, their relevant characteristics and respective prices, etc. I have already argued, implicitly, that this conception of information is too narrow and simplistic. But putting aside this issue for the moment, the important point which emerges from this neoclassical perspective is that although the efficiency of actual markets is dependent on the presence of such information, so that they will perform suboptimally to the extent that it is absent or defective, there is nothing about the nature of the market as an economic system which ensures its adequate provision.

This is so, 'despite' the fact that the kind of information concerned is itself quite capable of being produced and purchased as a market-commodity. The problem is not that information cannot be commodified, but that there is no guarantee that whatever information is thus produced will be adequate or suitable for the purpose of achieving overall efficiency.[17] Indeed, in any unregulated market there will strong pressures towards the production of *mis*information by producers about their own products, and considerable difficulties for consumers in assessing the trustworthiness of any such 'information' they encounter. There is thus a strong prima facie case for the support of non-market information sources and/or for the regulation of commercial ones.

A parallel case, I suggest, can be made for the support of non-market *cultural* institutions, and/or for the regulation of their commercial counterparts. To establish this parallel one must accept that the judgements made by consumers require not only 'empirical information' but a reflectively grounded understanding of their own well-being, and that (at least certain kinds of) cultural institutions and their products can provide a significant resource for their achieving this. I have already argued for these claims in the preceding section. One can then apply to this much extended conception of 'information' the same arguments about market failure that neoclassical theorists apply to their narrower conception. But the implications are a good deal more radical: they point not only to the need for publications such as *Which?* magazine, or for consumer protection legislation concerning dangerous products etc., but also for such things as publicly funded broadcasting which produces humanly truthful soap opera, and the regulation of its commercial counterparts to ensure that serious attention is given to matters of ethical, political and cultural concern.

Now it might be objected that, even if this parallel with standard neoclassical arguments about market failures is correct, this is not enough to establish more than a prima facie case for such non-market provision. The most that has been shown is that there is no *guarantee* that the (unaided and unregulated) market will generate adequate information or cultural products. But this does not entail that, as a matter of fact, it will always or typically fail to do so: to show that this is so requires additional arguments. Furthermore, to do this in the case of cultural products and the availability of adequate resources for reflection on human goods is presumably more difficult than in the case of neoclassical 'information'. For instance, it is relatively easy to determine whether, for example, consumers have access to relevant health data about food. But it is less easy to know whether they have sufficient access to cultural resources which enable them to reflect on the vice of gluttony.

There are, nonetheless, a number of reasons for expecting the market to 'under-produce' cultural goods of the requisite character. I shall consider two in particular. The first is based on the specific character of the cultural goods at issue here. As I argued in the previous section, what is distinctive about these goods is that they are themselves concerned with the nature of human well-being, and hence function as a means by which people can evaluate and reflect upon the contribution that may be made to this by, inter alia, their possible purchases as consumers and the overall pattern of life made possible by these. Such cultural meta-goods enable people to make 'strong evaluations' of their current desires and preferences, etc. They may thus be said typically to possess *transformative*, as distinct from *demand* value: i.e. their value consists, at least in part, in providing the means by which an existing set of preferences or desires may be transformed, through critical reflection, into more considered ones – rather than in directly satisfying those preferences, which is the characteristic of goods possessing only 'demand' value.[18]

It can then be argued that the producers of cultural goods with transformative value can be expected to fare worse than those producing goods with demand-value in the competitive processes of an unregulated market system. TV 'ratings wars' provide plentiful examples confirming this theoretically based expectation: programmes which have been carefully constructed to provide audiences with 'just what they (happen to) want' are likely to force out those which, precisely because of their potentially transformative value, present something to their audiences which may challenge those preferences. Correspondingly, the producers of cultural goods with transformative value need to secure some degree of 'free space' in which they can act without immediate threat from their demand-value competitors, and without being wholly constrained by – and fixated upon – their potential audiences' existing preferences. Without such partial insulation, goods with transformative value will be 'under-produced', to the long-term disadvantage of consumers in terms of the well-being they may achieve through the market.[19]

Now it might be objected to this that if people want goods with transformative value enough, they will pay for them, and it will be profitable to produce them; but if they do not, there is no justification for supporting their provision through non-market or market-regulated means, since this would be unacceptably paternalistic, elitist, undemocratic, etc. But this objection relies on an unduly simplistic view of people's motivations and values, and the different contexts in which these may be expressed and acted upon. One can see the error here through the following, partly hypothetical example.

Suppose that, as the result of an (unregulated) ratings war between TV channels, substantial news and current affairs programmes are forced out of peak viewing time. Despite this being the outcome of a competitive market process based on people's actual preferences, expressed through their willingness to pay/watch, these same people might perfectly well vote in favour of some form of regulation which required such programmes to be shown. This would be because, in their role as citizens, they recognized that programmes of this kind play an essential part in maintaining the 'health' of the democratic system to which they are politically committed. They are therefore quite prepared to use the regulatory powers of the state to achieve this objective, and hence to prevent what they judge to be the damaging effects of an unregulated market which responds only to their expressed preferences as consumers. There is, I would suggest, no inconsistency on their part here; nor anything undemocratic or elitist about the decision they make.[20]

But there is also a second, quite different reason for doubting the likelihood of exclusively commodified cultural production providing an adequate 'supply' of appropriate cultural goods. This is based on the fact that an increasing proportion of such production nowadays consists, not in producing cultural commodities such as films, books and radio programmes directly for sale, but in constructing the cultural means through which the sale of *other* commodities can be achieved – i.e. through advertising and related forms of 'promotion'. What we find here is the deployment of cultural products concerned with the representation of various kinds of human well-being – happy families, challenging deeds, exciting encounters, proud achievements, etc. – to persuade people to purchase some other commodity supposedly connected with these.[21]

But the very fact that the aim of such promotional cultural production is to sell something other than itself should surely make us sceptical about its likely value, whether as a means for exploring the possibilities of human well-being or as a credible account of the relationship between the commodity being promoted and the good that is promised. We have no more reason to trust the integrity or truthfulness of these representations of the human good than we have for trusting the claims of the tobacco industry about the effects of smoking on people's health. Admittedly one cannot, in the case of claims about human goods, appeal to the results of independently conducted 'scientific' research to assess the extent to which such suspicions are justified, as one can, in principle at least, in the case of smoking and health. There is nonetheless a sufficient parallel between the two kinds of case to justify support for some analogously 'independent' sources of cultural reflection about the nature and sources of human well-being which are less likely to be corrupted by the strategic logic of promotional 'culture'.[22]

Further, there are reasonable grounds for believing that cultural production aimed at the selling of commodities other than themselves tends to exaggerate and misrepresent the extent and nature of the contribution to human well-being that can be achieved through the purchase – and 'use' – of consumer goods. It is true, for example, that having a drink with one's friends is a pleasant and satisfying experience, and that without the drink it may be a little less so. But it is not true that the availability of any particular such drink is crucial to the success of the occasion; nor that merely by purchasing a drink one will find oneself in the company of others with whom a relationship of friendship exists. Likewise, although going for a walk in the country is aided by having a suitable pair of boots, the capacity for enjoying this activity is neither consequent upon their purchase nor especially easy to develop if one's life is unduly influenced by the desire to acquire such things.

Yet everything one is 'told' and 'shown' through the promotional culture of consumption conspires to weaken one's grasp of such facts. For even in those areas of one's life where the availability and use of commodities plays an important part, it is typically also the case that their contribution to human well-being depends upon relationships, attitudes, motivations, etc. which are quite at odds with those required or fostered by the market itself. As I argued earlier, consumer goods are 'intermediate', not 'final' goods. Their value is realized not *within* the market, but *outside* it, through an array of social activities whose character is antithetical to that of market-governed transactions.

But the non-market character of these activities is increasingly put at risk by the self-promotional culture of the market, which encourages us both to see the value of such activities as residing in the opportunities they provide for the deployment of consumer goods, rather than the reverse, and also to adopt, in our conduct of these activities, the attitudes and motivations which belong to the market domain. Yet our relationships with friends will not flourish if conducted on the model of economic exchange; our enjoyment of making a home will be damaged by treating it as an investment; our ability to appreciate the skills and performance of others will be soured by an exclusive concern with our own advancement; and so on.[23]

Of course, the market is by no means incapable of generating cultural products which themselves challenge the potentially damaging effects of its own operation. But the fact that such considerable resources are now devoted to the self-promotion of the market surely strengthens the case already made for the provision of other resources to support cultural institutions of a non-market character, and hence to secure the conditions for more reflective and critical, less demand-driven and compromised, cultural goods.[24] By supporting such provision – by resisting both the commodification of culture and the spurious culturalization of commodities – one will be able to enhance both the extent to which the market *can* contribute to human well-being and one's appreciation of the limits of that contribution. To rely on the market alone to achieve such aims would be wishful thinking.

Notes

1 This section of the chapter is a much condensed version of material presented in greater detail in Keat (1996).

2 Along with the politically driven expansion of the market domain noted here, there has also been an 'intensification' of the logic of commodity production in areas such as publishing, commercial broadcasting, etc.; the argument I shall present would apply also to these developments.

3 This is not to deny that there is any alternative to the specific form of the market termed 'capitalism'; it is quite possible, at least in principle, to replace capitalism's distinctive modes of ownership and control of the means of production by those proposed in 'market socialist' theories (see e.g. Miller, 1990). However, the adoption of market socialism in place of the capitalist market economy leaves unresolved the question with which I am concerned, which is why I have stated it as a question about the expansion of the *market* and not of *capitalism*.

4 Of course, there may be principles of distributive justice which would require the free provision of such goods, but this is a different issue.

5 For this kind of argument about friendship, see Anderson (1990); for a more general defence of the idea of 'separate spheres', see Walzer (1983), and the critical response to this in Waldron (1995).

6 This classical defence of the market is not the only one available, though I believe it is the most plausible. There is also the 'liberal' defence, according to which what is desirable about the market is that it guarantees individual liberty, relying as it does on contractual exchanges between free and equal parties. For the liberal, the material outcomes of the market are irrelevant, as such; all that matters is the liberty-preserving character of the transactions which generate them. Classical justifications of the market are consistent with intervention by the state, wherever the market can be shown to fail in achieving its objective; liberals typically oppose such intervention. See Keat (1996) for further discussion of these differences, and Keat (1999) for an argument that liberals are mistaken in such opposition. The position taken in the present chapter is, I believe, consistent with those forms of liberalism, such as Mill's, which both value individual autonomy and recognize that this is a socially contingent achievement rather than a pre-established fact of human nature.

7 Notice that even if the 'best judge' thesis were not correct, there would be a standard anti-paternalist objection to allowing others to make such judgements

instead. Thus both classical and liberal defenders of the market (see note 6 above) tend to support the idea of consumer sovereignty, albeit for different reasons.

8 I shall put aside here, as do neoclassical theorists, considerations of justice or equity. For a useful account of efficiency and the conditions for ideal markets – including the possibilities for 'market failure', which I discuss in the last section of the chapter, see Buchanan (1985); for a standard 'textbook' account, see Sloman (1991: ch. 10).

9 The neoclassical account of the market has rightly been criticized for failing to recognize its inherently *dynamic* character, but I do not think this failing is relevant here – nor that the Austrian School's alternative to neoclassical theory, which does address this crucial feature of the market, brings any improvement on those aspects of neoclassical theory I criticize here. For a sophisticated critical assessment of both neoclassical and Austrian conceptions of economic well-being, see O'Neill (1998: chs 3 and 4). I have discussed neoclassical approaches to environmental decisions in Keat (1997b).

10 This objection does not assume the existence of some objective, authoritative definition of human well-being, by reference to which the preferences of consumers and the beneficial effects of their potential purchases are to be evaluated. As will be seen in the following section, it requires only that consumers may make better or worse judgements of what will contribute to their own well-being, with the evaluations of these judgements being made in terms which they themselves would willingly accept. The neoclassical position cannot therefore be defended by appeal to the supposed 'subjectivity' of conceptions of the human good, nor to the value of individual autonomy.

11 The following discussion of different kinds of consumer products is strongly influenced by Scitovsky (1986, especially ch. 14), including both his distinction between what he calls 'defensive' and 'creative' products and his more general thesis that consumer well-being depends on consumer 'education'.

12 In what follows I draw heavily on MacIntyre's account of social *practices*, in MacIntyre (1981: ch. 14), though the examples are mine, as is the use of this account to make claims about consumer goods; see Keat (1990) for a discussion of practices in relation to issues about consumer sovereignty. What I say is also influenced by Joseph Raz's account of 'social forms', in Raz (1986: ch. 12), including his remarks about the significance of fiction and drama to our understanding of the goods made possible through these.

13 For MacIntyre, the answer to this problem is provided partly by an Aristotelian conception of the human *telos*, of the overall purpose of human life. Although I have some sympathy with this, I do not rely on it in what follows; cf. note 10 above.

14 See Lane (1991), especially Part VII, for an exhaustive discussion of the empirical evidence supporting the view that consumption is far from being the main source of well-being, and of how and why people often fail to recognize this. To his suggestion in Part VIII that it is the responsibility of social scientists to help correct this error I would add 'and also that of (other) producers of cultural goods'.

15 See note 8 above for references.

16 See e.g. the discussions in Peacock (1976) and Dworkin (1985); for corresponding debates about education, see Bridges and McLaughlin (1994).

17 That markets cannot be relied upon to generate information of a suitable kind is partly just an instance of a more general point, that their outcomes are always indeterminate with respect to *any* specified objective. This is why it is normally unwise to 'leave things to the market' if there is any specific aim one wants to achieve. So, for example, war-time economies typically require a high degree of state intervention and planning, to ensure that the requisite supplies of

armaments will be produced. But the 'information' case is not simply an instance of this general point, since here what the market fails to ensure is something necessary for its own effective functioning. In this respect it is closer to cases such as trust, etc. More generally, the dependence of the market on non-market institutions and social relationships has been a recurrent theme of 'conservative' thought which, unlike both liberalism and socialism, provides considerable conceptual resources for thinking about the question of market boundaries. In the case of cultural institutions, however, conservative approaches have typically been marred by elitist defences of 'high culture' which I have attempted to avoid in the overall argument presented here.

18 I take the distinction between transformative and demand-value from Norton (1987: chs 2 and 10); he argues that the environment has transformative value, but I think it would have been better for him to claim this for cultural goods, which inter alia enable us to reflect upon the value of the environment. On 'strong evaluations' see Taylor (1990).

19 Of course, the effect of such cultural goods may also be to encourage people to give less attention to consumption-dependent well-being, and more to other areas of their lives; but there is no reason why this should worry anyone who justifies the market on classical grounds. In Keat (1990) and (1994) I have tried to show in more detail why it is undesirable for cultural institutions to be directly subject to consumer preferences.

20 On the contrast between the standpoints of citizen and consumer, see Sagoff (1988). The example I have used here is more obviously concerned with the need for non-market institutions if democratic politics is to flourish than with their contribution to reflective judgements about the good of consumption, etc. However, the example is relevant to the latter case also if one accepts, as one should, that political decisions are themselves dependent on collective judgements about the human good: see Keat (1996) and (1999) for an argument to this effect.

21 On the idea of 'promotional culture' see Wernick (1991), though my use of this phrase here is much looser than his. Some theorists of consumer culture would argue that I have mischaracterized what is going on here, preferring to see this as indicating the increasing significance of 'sign-value' over 'use-value': instead of consumers being persuaded of the use-value of various commodities through the attribution of certain 'meanings' to these, it is 'the meanings themselves' that are being bought and sold. I find this pretty unconvincing, but cannot pursue the matter here. See Slater (1997) for an illuminating account of different theories of consumer culture.

22 The point here is not that one should be sceptical about the market's ability to generate goods with genuine use-values, simply because they are being produced for some *other* purpose, i.e. to generate exchange-values or profits. This form of doubt would make one worry whether those who purchased the services of advertising companies could expect to get good advertising copy from them – and this is not the point at issue here.

23 What is implied by these remarks is the need to avoid the various social practices which take place outwith the market, and through which the use-value of consumer goods is often realized, being 'colonized' by social meanings derived from the market itself. I have discussed one example of such colonization and its damaging effects in Keat (1997a). It is in these terms, I suggest, that one can best understand Habermas's account of the 'colonization of the lifeworld', including his view of the lifeworld as the basis for consumer use-values: see Habermas (1987: Part VIII).

24 As I have tried to suggest throughout, 'critical reflection' is neither an abstract theoretical process nor something which relies solely on generic intellectual capacities; it takes place through engagement with cultural practices which often possess a concrete rather than abstract character.

References

Anderson, E. (1990) 'The ethical limitations of the market', *Economics and Philosophy*, 6: 179–205.

Bridges, D. and McLaughlin, T. (eds) (1994) *Education and the Market Place*, Brighton: Falmer.

Buchanan, A. (1985) *Ethics, Efficiency and the Market*, Oxford: Oxford University Press.

Dworkin, R. (1985) 'Can a liberal state support art?', *A Matter of Principle*, Oxford: Oxford University Press, pp. 221–33.

Habermas, J. (1987) *The Theory of Communicative Action*, vol. 2, trans. T. McCarthy, Cambridge: Polity.

Keat, R. (1990) 'Consumer sovereignty and the integrity of practices', in R. Keat and N. Abercrombie (eds), *Enterprise Culture*, London: Routledge, pp. 216–30.

Keat, R. (1994) 'Scepticism, authority and the market', in R. Keat, N. Whiteley and N. Abercrombie (eds), *The Authority of the Consumer*, London: Routledge, pp. 23–42.

Keat, R. (1996) 'Delivering the goods: socialism, liberalism and the market', *New Waverley Papers*, 96.9, Edinburgh: Department of Politics, University of Edinburgh.

Keat, R. (1997a) 'Colonisation by the market: Walzer on recognition', *Journal of Political Philosophy*, 5: 93–107.

Keat, R. (1997b) 'Values and preferences in neo-classical environmental economics', in J. Foster (ed.), *Valuing Nature*, London: Routledge.

Keat, R. (1999) 'Market boundaries and human goods', in J. Haldane (ed.), *Philosophy and Public Affairs*, Cambridge: Cambridge University Press.

Lane, R.E. (1991) *The Market Experience*, Cambridge: Cambridge University Press.

MacIntyre, A. (1981) *After Virtue*, London: Duckworth.

Miller, D. (1990) *Market, State and Community*, Oxford: Oxford University Press.

Norton, B. (1987) *Why Preserve Species Variety?*, Princeton, NJ: Princeton University Press.

O'Neill, J. (1998) *The Market: Ethics, Knowledge and Politics*, London: Routledge.

Peacock, A. (1976) 'Welfare economics and public subsidies to the arts', in M. Blaug (ed.), *The Economics of the Arts*, Oxford: Martin Robertson, pp. 70–86.

Raz, J. (1986) *The Morality of Freedom*, Oxford: Oxford University Press.

Sagoff, M. (1988) *The Economy of the Earth*, Cambridge: Cambridge University Press.

Scitovsky, T. (1986) *Human Desire and Economic Satisfaction*, London: Harvester Wheatsheaf.

Sen, A. (1977) 'Rational fools: a critique of the behavioural foundations of economic theory', *Philosophy and Public Affairs*, 6: 317–44.

Slater, D. (1997) *Consumer Culture and Modernity*, Cambridge: Polity.

Sloman, J. (1991) *Economics*, Hemel Hempstead: Harvester Wheatsheaf.

Taylor, C. (1990) *Sources of the Self*, Cambridge: Cambridge University Press.

Waldron, J. (1995) 'Money and complex equality', in D. Miller and M. Walzer (eds), *Pluralism, Justice and Equality*, Oxford: Oxford University Press, pp. 144–70.

Walzer, M. (1983) *Spheres of Justice*, Oxford: Martin Robertson.

Wernick, A. (1991) *Promotional Culture*, London: Sage.

5

Reconciling Culture and Economy: Ways Forward in the Analysis of Ethnicity and Gender

Harriet Bradley and Steve Fenton

The years to come will witness a tendency for researchers to combine the insights of feminist post-structuralism regarding the importance of culture and discourse to the constitution of gender, with more 'old-fashioned' attention to 'the material'. Such work may well contribute to a reconceptualization of the meaning of 'the material'. (Roseneil, 1995: 200)

In this chapter we consider the implications of the 'cultural turn' within sociology, and the consequent unease about how to deal with economic issues, in relation to work in the fields of ethnicity and gender. Like Roseneil, we are suggesting the need for a rapprochement between newer work dealing with cultural identities and discourses of difference and the more long-standing traditions in the sociology of 'race' and gender which focused on inequalities and material disadvantage. Our argument throughout is that it is desirable to utilize the insights which have been provided by the newer cultural analyses, while at the same time retaining aspects of previous materially-based accounts which are still of crucial importance. In a way, we are suggesting a need for a fusion of the politics of recognition and of redistribution as discussed in Nancy Fraser's important paper (1995).

We use examples from our own specialisms to demonstrate the benefits of achieving a reconciliation between cultural and economic analysis. We look at the impact of the 'cultural turn' on each area in turn, highlighting the move from a 'race relations' model through a class and racism problematic to a concern with ethnic identities (Fenton, 1996), and the similar 'paradigm switch' in gender analysis as described by Barrett and Phillips (1992). We then offer examples which demonstrate the fruitfulness of the newer approaches, first in the study of ethnicity and then of gender, but we also suggest that all ethnic and gendered phenomena must be located in an economic context. Finally we set out a programme of 'reconcilement' for sociological research, stressing particularly the need for bringing together qualitative and quantitative forms of methodology in the exploration of the interweaving of culture and economy in ethnic and gender differentiation. First, however, we give some brief attention to the ways in which the relation between culture and economy has previously been conceptualized. We should stress, however, that this account is inevitably schematic: we point to major trends, but obviously these gloss over subtleties and nuances which we have no space to deal with here.

Culture and economy: the sociological tradition

A long-standing preoccupation in sociology with the relation between economic and cultural phenomena can be traced back at least as far as Weber's attempt to marry analysis of social and economic organization and study of meaningful interaction. Weber's solution to the problem of handling these two aspects of the study of social life was a kind of methodological dualism; 'erklaren' and 'verstehen' would become two principles for sociological analysis which demanded separate approaches and techniques. It may be argued that a dualism of this kind has marked all subsequent major theoretical engagements with the economy and culture relation: there has been a tendency, exemplified for example in the work of Parsons or of Althusser, to discern separate 'spheres' or levels of analysis, with their own distinct principles or logics of operation. How to link these discrete levels or spheres has been a problem for sociology throughout the twentieth century.

Perhaps because of this problem, there has also been a tendency to splitting, so that either the economic or the cultural becomes the predominant preoccupation. Within British sociology, it is possible to characterize two phases of sociological thinking in recent decades, the first of which could be said to be 'socio-economic' in its phrasing and the second broadly 'cultural'. While many cases of non-fit could be cited, it remains the case that arguments about the economy and social structure dominated much British sociology in the 1960s and 1970s; arguments about culture, or a cultural re-phrasing of a wide range of sociological topics, have come to centre-stage in the later 1980s and the 1990s.

The first period could be exemplified by well known works by Westergaard, Beynon, Goldthorpe, Lockwood and many others. The central questions often appeared to be 'what were the directions taken by modern capitalist economies?' and 'what were the consequences of this for social and political consciousness?' The informing theories might be Weberian or Marxian. Dissatisfaction with the incomplete theoretical answers provided to these questions seemed to crystallize at the moment that postmodern and post-structuralist approaches were providing a major challenge to all forms of structural theory, while at the same time the growing body of work on gender and ethnicity as a source of inequality and of social identification threw into doubt the monolinear accounts of capitalism typical of 1960s and 1970s sociology and pointed to the plural nature of social and political relationships.

During the period under review, it could be argued that the prevailing theoretical approaches threw up three characteristic answers to the issue of the relation between the economy and culture. We should emphasize here that we make this comment in relation to the *theoretical* claims of sociologists: good *empirical* sociological studies have often dealt with both economic and cultural phenomena, whatever theoretical framework they allegedly espoused.

1. Classical economistic Marxism offered an account which reduced culture to an epiphenomenon, ultimately determined by the material base. While this kind of economic absolutism was an extreme position, rather than one which informed the writings of many practising Marxists, it is true that for many working in the tradition the issue of culture simply seemed uninteresting and irrelevant in comparison to analysis of the study of the operation of modes of production; and discussion of culture was often reduced to 'ideologiekritik'.

2. An important critique of this position arose within Marxism itself, in the form of cultural Marxism, as practised by Williams, Thompson and Hall among others, who drew particularly on the thinking of Antonio Gramsci. In this tradition culture was seen as an important aspect of social life and a crucial topic of study in its own right; typically it was accorded a status of 'relative autonomy' from the material base. Without doubt, this school of thought produced many rich and rewarding accounts of social relationships. Nevertheless, this still involved a deterministic and restricted approach to thinking about culture whereby it was characteristically analysed *in relation* to class structure and the social hegemony of economically dominant groups. In other words, culture, although it was awarded determinant status, was itself always viewed in terms of its relation to capitalism.

3. In its challenge to Marxism, postmodernist and post-structuralist thinking produced a contradictory vision in which culture is detached from its link to the economy and production. Instead it is conceived as a free-floating, autonomous sphere, characteristically seen as more central to social life than economic concerns. Thus, *study of production as a source of consciousness* is replaced by *study of culture and consumption as sources of identities*. In the more extreme post-structuralist versions, culture itself is reduced, de-socialized, to become no more than a free play of texts, representations or discourses. The dependence of these on any substratum of social institutions or relationships is at the least seen as problematic and contingent, at the most completely denied, as in the work of Baudrillard.

As the above shows, there have been two major ways in which the economy/culture dualism has characteristically been addressed. One is to posit a relation of dependence in which one of the couplet is secondary to the other. Within Marxism, it has been economic relationships that dominate culture; but it is at least theoretically possible to invert the relationship. In some contemporary accounts of the development of consumer capitalism it is hinted that culture may be becoming the driver of the economy (Jameson, 1991; Featherstone, 1991; Lash and Urry, 1994). The other position is simply to treat the two as distinct and focus on one or the other as of primary importance: thus, the recent trend in social science has been to study primarily culture and discourse, leaving economic aspects aside (for example, see Handler, 1988; Donald and Rattansi, 1992; Pringle and Watson, 1992). Thus, Rattansi suggests that a postmodern 'framing' will conceptualize ethnicity in terms of 'a cultural politics of representation' (1995: 257).

Currently, this seems to be the popular option. We have suggested elsewhere (Bradley, 1996) that postmodernists, because of their distrust of structural forms of analysis, feel uneasy about dealing with material issues: discussion of class, for example, seems to breach postmodern epistemological principles, and some postmodernists have proclaimed the death of class as either accomplished or imminent (Pakulski and Waters, 1996), a theme also echoed in the work of those who prefer to identify themselves as 'reflexive modernists' but equally stress the rise of pluralism and individualism (Giddens, 1991; Beck, 1992); indeed Waters (1997) actually argues that if sociology is to survive it needs to abandon class as a central concept. Barrett notes that 'social class is definitely non grata as a topic' in contemporary feminism (1992: 216). But rather than suggesting that the current intellectual dominance in sociology of postmodernist and post-structuralist theory has pushed the analysis of the economic aside, it is more accurate to posit a growing separation in some areas of sociology between the study of the economic and cultural aspects of social life. This is certainly the case in contemporary feminism. In Crompton and Le Feuvre's words:

> There is a vast gulf between feminist debates on psychoanalysis, discourse theory, cultural production . . . and the frameworks of political economy and industrial sociology within which most studies of work are situated. (Crompton and Le Feuvre, 1992: 98)

Our concern is to explore how this gulf may be bridged and to do this in the context of our own work in the areas of ethnicity and gender: it is to these areas that we now turn.

From 'race relations' to ethnicity

In the field of ethnicity, or 'race relations' as it was then usually called, the same preoccupations predominated in the 1960s and 1970s as those by which we have characterized British sociology in general. John Rex made some of the most telling contributions in setting out the nature of the articulation of what was referred to as 'race and class', suggesting that the key to the understanding of 'race' lay in explaining the nature of this articulation,[1] particularly in its colonial and post-colonial context (Rex, 1970, 1973, 1986; Rex and Tomlinson, 1979). In a rather extended and not very productive series of debates, a distinction was made between Marxist and Weberian conceptions of class structure as the proper setting for an understanding of racial formations. Miles and Phizacklea in particular emphasized that what was once seen as a problem of 'race relations' should be seen as a problem of racism and migrant labour, thereby inserting the question of race into the place where it belonged – into the political economy of capitalism and crisis. Migrant labour suited the needs of capitalism in the super-exploitation of labour and was the source of social, material and political divisions within the working class. The recurrent economic crises characteristic of late capitalism in turn provoked crises of political legitimacy to which the mobilization of racism was viewed as a response (Miles, 1982; Miles and Phizacklea, 1984).

The posing of migrant labour as the key context within which racialization occurred permitted socio-economic arguments, allied to arguments about the state, to dominate discussion of 'race' and ethnicity. To rectify the omissions of a race-blind economic sociology, a central concern was the place of ethnically defined migrant labour groups in the social and economic structure and the corresponding forms of political consciousness which they might develop. Would black and white unite and fight? With respect to the argument that capitalism racialized migrant labour (Miles) or that a racially discriminatory post-colonial society subordinated a class-situated racial minority whilst fostering white racism (Rex), the evidence of the persistence of ethnically structured disadvantage in the succession of reports on minorities in Britain (such as those produced by Political and Economic Planning in 1968 and the Policy Studies Institute in 1984), as well as the evidence of their own research, supported both positions equally, as did the evidence of discriminatory or racist attitudes among whites.

By the late 1980s and early 1990s some important pieces of evidence, as well as significant shifts in sociological attention, led to a redrawing of the outlines of debate. The racialization argument came up against the stubborn refusal of large parts of the South Asian population to identify simply as 'black', and Britain's Caribbean-origin and South Asian minorities neither hardened into a black underclass, nor identified unambiguously with white class allies. Later evidence of social mobility (Modood et al., 1997), particularly in some South Asian populations, began to take the ground away from the picture of a uniformly super-exploited race-class. Over a decade or so Tariq Modood (1992), Roger Ballard (1992), Vaughan Robinson (1990), Paul Iganski and Geoff Payne

(1996) among others began to persuade a sceptical sociological fraternity that many South Asians were emerging as a new middle class. At the same time research uncovered much more subtle and complex processes of social and political identification than previous characterizations had led anyone to expect (Modood, 1992). Islam had become an important focal point of politico-cultural battle, especially in the wake of the Rushdie affair, making Britain appear more like France in this respect; this corresponded with the global emergence of Islam as a cultural phrasing of human struggle. At least as importantly, young British-born South Asian women began to redefine their roles within their families and to speak out about them, while the Muslims among them turned their abilities towards re-forming Islamic culture and identity itself. Although the 1980s continued to witness irruptions of conflict in the inner cities, and the Conservative party in the elections of the period continued to seek advantage from an anti-immigrant/refugee stance, combined with law and order posturing, there emerged nothing like the racialized politics which the prophets of the late 1960s and 1970s had predicted. In the 1997 election an ethnicized and nationalist construction of politics in Conservative ranks focused less on 'immigrants' and 'race' and more on the unity of the United Kingdom and the threat to British or English integrity posed by the European Union. This nationalist appeal, reviving anti-French (Colley, 1992) and anti-German xenophobia, resoundingly failed.

In the current phase of debates there can be little doubt that a major shift away from 'race relations' to study of ethnicity and its cultural aspects has occurred, mirroring the general shift within sociology. In the 1970s and 1980s two of the leading concerns were with (1) 'race and class', in which the key questions about ethnicity were all tied to a programme of class analysis and (2) the political economy of racism, in which racialized forms of consciousness were seen as products of or diversions from forms of class consciousness (for a discussion see Anthias and Yuval-Davis, 1993); those who were interested in 'ethnicity' as a topic and its wider cultural import were portrayed as exoticists who diverted attention from the hard facts of class and racism.

But subsequently, over the last decade, journal articles with titles invoking class, state, and political economy have been almost supplanted by books and articles which signal their intent by the insistent reference to culture, identity and difference. We have seen the reappearance of an argument that once would have been seen as the very height of social psychological reductionism (that us/them oppositions are endemic in social structures), albeit de-psychologized and presented as 'the construction of the Other' in cultural and political discourses.

In many instances these studies are not only an indication that the same questions are being addressed with new conceptual tools but also that a new set of questions is being posed. 'How do the sons and daughters of migrant groups find their place in British society?' is less an issue of class and structural change and more an issue of culture and identity. Moreover, in all this there has been a de-objectification of the term 'group' whether signalled by 'race', racial(ized) group or ethnic group. The term 'race' was the first casualty, in line with the gradual acknowledgement that one of the greatest errors of earlier formulations was a barely hidden presupposition that 'races', albeit restated as *socially defined*, were real groups in society. Similarly, the more recent the writing the greater the likelihood that prior conceptualizations of ethnic groups are seen as having been bedevilled by a false concreteness. The emphasis has come to be quite different. Ethnicity is socially and culturally formulated, it is shifting and circumstantial in such a way as practically to invalidate the term 'ethnic group' altogether. If ethnic characteristics are socio-culturally defined, ever in motion, and variable in their social relevance, then the focus shifts to an examination of the processes by which ethnicity takes shape. These processes are seen as expressed through discourses, through the 'invention' of traditions and through the mobilization of cultural insignia for political ends. The term discourse has become a central point of reference, seemingly replacing an earlier stress on material structures. In some cases (notably Anthias and Yuval-Davis, 1993) there is an attempt to address an older set of questions about inequalities and power, with a newer set of tools: ethnicity, discourse, boundary and gender; while Rattansi and Westwood (1994) and Hall (1992) among others have made some bold strokes in attempting to situate questions of ethnicity and racism in a postmodern frame.

But what may appear as a radical disjuncture between an older political economy frame and a contemporary cultural frame may be more open to some reconciliations than is immediately apparent. We offer two reasons for thinking that this reconciliation is possible: the first may be termed the 'politicization of ethnicity' and the second 'the culturizing of racism'. It was once commonplace (see Anthias and Yuval-Davis, 1993) to see a concern with 'ethnicity' as, on the one hand a condescending and exoticized concern with culture and on the other a neglect of the material facts of race–class oppression and racist ideology. If this charge was ever justified,[2] the current uses of the concept of ethnicity make it unsustainable now. This is because, in seeing ethnicity not only as a matter of 'groups' but also as a matter of negotiation and of the mobilization of cultural insignia, the concept is deployed within a political framework. Even private cultural negotiations – for example of gender and kin relationships – are treated as broadly political in their consequences. The consequence is to re-emphasize[3] ethnicity as a dimension of political representation and of individual and collective action. In turn, this confirms the situating of ethnicity within a 'material' framework of economy and polity, whilst retaining within the concept the centrality of the concept of culture. In this way the recent reworkings of the concept of ethnicity may open the way for a reconsideration of the way culture and economy are integrated.

The second trend we have termed the culturizing of racism (see Fenton, 1999). By this we mean the very considerable broadening of the concept of racism to incorporate themes of cultural difference, of essentializing of peoples, of hierarchies of culture, as well as prior themes of scientific racism and ideologies of separation and superordination. This is represented, for example, in the later writing of Miles (1993) and also in Rattansi and Westwood (1994), in which a focus on nation-state ideologies within Western Europe is conceptualized as the setting for the devaluing of minorities. Similarly the arguments of Wieviorka present a more textured and cultural view of the nature of racisms, as well as describing the historical settings of variant forms of racism in ways which correspond to an interest in the 'material', the political and the economic. He suggests four settings, all related directly or indirectly to the nature of modernity, which prompt the emergence of racisms. 'In the first instance [it is] the companion of modernity triumphant . . . crushing different identities . . . inferior "races" are seen as obstacles to the process of expansion . . . or destined to be exploited in the name of their supposed inferiority.' The second instance is linked to downward mobility and social exclusion, a form of racism linked to the 'poor white' mentality. The third instance is where modernity is resisted and thus social groups which appear to be the 'bearers' of modernity are despised and stigmatized, as in the case of Jews and Asian minorities 'who are perceived as being particularly economically active'. The fourth instance he describes as 'anti-modernist positions' but which are not directed against groups who 'represent' modernity (Wieviorka, 1994: 174–5). In many respects these racisms are described in terms of both political power and class exploitation *and* of culture and modernity.

We shall further explore the interconnectedness of economic and cultural aspects in situations involving ethnicity later in this chapter; but first we turn to changes in the study of gender.

The cultural and linguistic turn in feminism

Equally dramatic shifts have occurred in feminism, although in this case they do not as yet promote the reconciliation of cultural and economic analysis which we have just identified in the case of ethnicity. The initial work that sprang from the second-wave feminist movement in the 1970s took as its starting point the material disadvantages faced by women and explored the sexual division of labour in its various aspects. Work inequalities, the gendering of technology, the domestic division of labour, reproduction, childbirth and family relations, male violence, the exclusion of women from politics and the public sphere were key research topics. Although the radical feminist perspective had also put on the agenda issues of sexuality, cultural representation and subjectivity, these tended to take a secondary place and were often discussed, as within Marxism, as aspects of ideology rather than meaning.[4] This was particularly the case in Britain (as opposed, perhaps, to France or America) because the various brands of Marxist feminism were more influential than the radical, liberal or psychoanalytic approaches, in tandem with the position of Marxism in British sociology in the late 1960s and 1970s as the dominant form of radical critique. The work of people like McIntosh (1979), Barrett (1980), Oakley (1981), Cockburn (1983), even Walby (1986), set the tone here. It is significant that for some while 'dual systems theory' in its various forms became the favoured theoretical framework within British feminist sociology, with its attempt to integrate some variant of a Marxian analysis of mode of production with an account of patriarchy as a complementary social system.

However, as Barrett and Phillips note, since the mid-1980s there has occurred what they see as amounting to an 'almost paradigmatic shift' (1992: 6), which has culminated in the ascendancy of what they call '1990s feminism'. This is much less concerned with material factors but with ' sexuality, subjectivity and textuality' (Barrett, 1992: 214); as Barrett says, there has been a shift of interest away from social structure to 'processes of symbolization and representation . . . questions of culture, sexuality or political agency' (p. 204). Many influences brought about this change:

1. The collapse of communism and subsequent questioning of Marxism, which ousted Marxist feminism from its central position.
2. The rise of postmodernism, with its stress on culture, allied to the growing influence of cultural studies as flagship for academic radicalism during this period.
3. An increasing interest within literary studies in psychoanalytic theories, especially of the post-Freudian and Lacanian variety.
4. The internal critique within feminism initiated by non-white feminists, which had grown steadily through the 1980s and which pointed to experiential diversity among women and the subsequent need to deconstruct the notion of 'women' as a category.
5. This latter concern fed into the post-structuralist and deconstructionist tendency which was becoming dominant at the more abstract theoretical level. Here the crucial influences were Foucault and Derrida, whose work has led to a preoccupation with language, with a critique of binary categories and with the analysis of discourses of gender, now seen not to reflect but to construct the experience of masculinity and femininity.

All this amounts, then, to both a cultural turn and a linguistic turn in the analysis of gender. In 1990s feminism, to use Chaney's words, 'categories of gender are held to be cultural categories' (1994: 33) whereas the project of Marxist feminists had been to establish gender as a fundamental economic category, parallel to class. The consequences of such a shift are multiple, but a few major effects can be listed here. First, it can be claimed that cultural studies, along with literature, psycho-analysis and especially philosophy, now hold the polar disciplinary position within feminism, rather than sociology (Barrett, 1992); this has tended to push feminist sociology, too, towards a greater concern with culture. Thus key heroines of the new 'postfeminisms' (Brooks, 1997) include de Lauretis (1984), Riley (1988), Butler (1990), Flax (1990), Haraway (1991), Benhabib (1992), and Mohanty (1995). Secondly, the shift of analysis has moved away from the sexual division of labour to the study of cultural productions (both mainstream and those of women themselves) often viewed as 'texts', of masculine and feminine subjec-tivities and identifications, of the body (considered to be 'discursively constructed'), of sexuality in all its various manifestations, and of lin-guistic practices and discourses (for example, Jacobus et al., 1990; Butler, 1993; Segal, 1994). Thirdly, favoured methods involve the ana-lysis of texts (broadly defined) and narratives, of discursive materials, rather than the collection of statistical data or use of social surveys (Scott, 1988; Sawicki, 1991; Schwichtenberg, 1993). If one is being rather critical of all this, one can also say that this has meant a kind of turning inward of the feminist gaze, a focus on individual subjectivities and meanings and the discourses in which they are embedded, on the per-sonal as opposed to the political. In the impatient phrase of one young feminist:

> Feminists still seem to be too bogged down in what goes on in women's wardrobes to worry about what goes on in their workplaces . . . too intent on their brash new weddings to listen to old fears about poverty and violence. And in the end the only ones who get hurt by these omissions are women. (Natasha Walter, *The Guardian*, 17 October 1996)

The end result, then, is the marginalizing of economic aspects of gender as a current feminist interest and, especially, diminishing atten-tion given to the relation of gender to class (though, rather curiously, ethnicity is a central topic of concern, perhaps because it is primarily read in terms of identification). Of course, work on topics such as gender segregation, domestic labour or violence has not ceased. One tendency has been a retreat into the mainstream, where a gender analysis has been integrated into the sociological study of labour markets or of strati-fication (as well as being pursued within geography, social policy or labour economics). There are individual feminists who have continued to research these issues, for example recent work by Glucksmann (1995) and Walby (1997). Another sign of the times is some alteration in the way old issues are being studied. Recently, for example, study of gender at work has been reoriented towards the topic of sexuality in the workplace or the symbolism surrounding work (e.g. Pringle, 1989; Adkins, 1995;

Gherardi, 1995) while childbirth may be discussed in terms of disciplinary regimes as described by Foucault (Sawicki, 1991).

This latter work may be seen as beginning to develop the reconciliation between the older materialist frameworks and the newer cultural approaches which we have discerned in the study of ethnicity. But this begs the question of how exactly we bring economic issues back into the picture? Should we graft a cultural analysis on to an economic one or vice versa? Should we consider a return to some of the basic premises of a Marxist feminist analysis, as Anna Pollert (1996) has recently proposed, concerning ourselves once more with the everyday experience of economic oppression within the workplace or home? In the field of ethnicity should we switch away from our concern with the complexity of cultural identifications and pay more attention to the way in which the racialization of particular groups is integral to the development of a globalizing capitalist economy?

The way forward: integrating the cultural and recovering the economic

As we stated at the commencement of this chapter, our own view is that an analysis of both cultural and economic factors, of meaning *and* materiality, is necessary if we are to gain a complete understanding of social phenomena such as gender or ethnic differences. The newer cultural approaches have led us to more subtle understandings of the nature of ethnic and gender relations in all their complexities, and such insights should not be abandoned; yet economic factors remain crucial in social life and they should not be neglected either. We have suggested that some tendencies in the study of ethnicity hint at the way cultural, political and economic considerations may be drawn together; while by contrast in recent feminist work cultural and economic analyses seem to have drifted apart.

In the final analysis it may be that the dualistic material/cultural distinction is problematic, and that formalistic debates about the distinction may be as fruitless as the equally protracted debates in sociology about the relationship between structure and agency. The relationship between culture and economy, we posit, can not be deduced from abstract principles, but can only be elucidated in specific contexts.

In this section of the chapter we illustrate this by means of examples, drawn from each field, which we use to unpack the cultural and material aspects of ethnic and gendered phenomena and show the way these intertwine in particular contexts. These examples are used to underpin the case for a broad based theoretical and methodological prospectus, with which we conclude the chapter. This is a prospectus which does not neglect the insights connected with the cultural turn but equally accepts that we cannot afford to ignore material constraints of a political and economic nature. These are conventionally described as 'structural': we cannot discard them simply because they are associated with discredited grand narratives or 'system-direction' theories (theories which imply an evolutionary pattern in the development of the system as a whole) as represented by Marxism, theories of modernization and development, or the 'convergence thesis' of Clark Kerr. Our immediate concern here, though, is to illustrate how 'material' and 'symbolic' emphases in socio-logical analysis should be complementary and not exclusive.

Politicizing culture: Quebecois ethno-nationalism

To illustrate these points in the field of ethnicity and nationalism we shall look generally at the case of Quebec nationalism and French Canadian ethnicity and particularly at a justly celebrated account of the production of culture in Quebec, Richard Handler's *Nationalism and the Politics of Culture in Quebec* (1988). The force of our argument is two-fold: one, that textured cultural analysis – exemplified by Handler – is both instructive and necessary and two, that a (conventionally defined) material and structural account, understated or neglected by Handler, should form part of a full sociological theorization.

The emphasis in Handler's book is almost exclusively on the social production of culture and the construction of a nation (Quebec); indeed, he mounts a radical attack on any structural conceptualization of classes. In earlier traditions an emphasis on class and on state power has been central to theories of nationalism (see Porter, 1965; Teeple, 1972; Clement, 1975). Quebec as the inheritor of the French tradition in Canada – having been defeated by British forces in 1760 – has a majority of French speakers (82 per cent), who are nonetheless a minority (30 per cent) within Canada. Quebec had seen itself as a disadvantaged region and some French Canadians saw themselves as a discriminated-against and exploited class (Vallieres, 1971), but in recent years the emphasis in the nationalist movement has been much more on cultural survival – the Francophone minority in a sea of Anglo-American culture – and less on economic disadvantage (see Reitz and Breton, 1994). Handler's research illustrates the way in which anthropological and textual studies of the production of culture are essential to the understanding of nationalism; but it equally clearly does not make a convincing case for neglecting class structures, economic tendencies or macro-political change.

Handler uses anthropological techniques to explore the complexities of ethnic identification. In effect he asks the question 'did people know the dance steps?' His study of Quebecois ethnic identity led him to observe families in face to face situations celebrating weddings and other rites of passage. He also observed local events in small Quebec towns which in one way or another provided evidence of the very nature of French Canadian 'culture'. He was interested in the construc-tion of a Quebecois ethnicity which manifested itself in claims about folk songs and dance, themselves symptomatic of a style of living seen to be essentially French Canadian. Only by observing families holding parties and attending community hall 'get togethers' could he answer the question of the authenticity of the cultural claims. His observation that people danced with uncertainty and had to watch others – with some embarrassment – led him to conclude that the culture referred to had an uncertain hold on those who might be expected to be its principal bearers – small-town Quebecois. It seems to us that this quite minute anthropological observation provides a valuable piece of information about the grounded or constructed nature of the culture which was being claimed as authentically and distinctively Quebecois.

A second question is textual – what does the Ministry of Museums in Quebec say about itself? By examining a decade of organization and re-organization of Ministries in the province – which required minute inspection of bureaucratic documents as a guide to the formal organization of culture in Quebec – Handler was able to show how the public categories which gave an institutional and 'discursive' basis to the project 'Quebec' had manufactured a Quebecois set of claims replacing a French Canadian set of claims. At the same time he demonstrated how the part played by the Catholic church had steeply diminished in the period observed, the 1970s and 1980s.

We suggest that only by using these two methodologies – the one anthropological, the other textual – can we gain comparable insights into what the terms Quebec nationalism and French Canadian ethnicity mean both as symbolic (cultural) systems and as components of life as lived. In particular they address the key problems of the 'authenticity' of the national claim and of the constructed character of Quebecois distinctiveness. Handler's is an enlightened and enlightening account of the politics of culture which makes plausible claims for the centrality of culture as object and method of study. But this does not rule out – as Handler seems to claim – the need for a complementary analysis in terms of class structure and social and economic change. The social changes which have entailed the extenuation of family ties and the weakening of communal rites and social organization in Quebec's small towns are the very changes which led to Handler's townsfolk forgetting 'the dance steps' as an index of the local cultures which are so commonly cited as the 'stuff' of folk/national cultures. As rural and small-town Quebec declined in significance so did urban-industrial Quebec grow, including the growth of a largely Francophone Montreal working class, a majority of whom supported separatism in the 1995 referendum.

The other social classes who have supported nationalist/separatist politics in Quebec are in effect a state-employed middle class, the civil servants, the school teachers, planners and welfare workers – the fonctionnaires of the local state. Some of these are the people whose work produced the cultural constructions of the Quebec government, the employees in education, the museum staffs, the archivists and the cultural experts. Handler's analysis in this instance, if not precisely material and political, is notably 'institutional', placing the construction of nation within the frame of the government institutions which fostered it. A third broad grouping mentioned by Handler are the petite bourgeoisie of Montreal and Quebec city who are artisanal producers and/or purveyors of the very cultural goods, such as paintings and handicrafts, which in a tourist market form some of the 'traditional' representations of Quebec. The production of a politicized culture is also an economic process

All these class groupings, we might expect, will have some estimation of how they might flourish or otherwise were Quebec to separate from Canada – or even remain 'in association' with Canada with a maximal degree of devolved power as an autonomous region. They may calculate that Quebec could well flourish within the North American Free Trade area negotiated in the 1990s between Canada, the USA and Mexico. They can hardly expect to flourish outside it, and therefore will be subject to the same pressures of economic liberalization as Canada itself now faces. A post-Canada Quebec state would be constrained to act in the same way as most other nation-states in a global economy – that is, as the local agents of marketization, privatizing welfare, engendering the flexible labour force, and all the associated measures of economic and financial liberalization. If this meant that the Quebec state had to curtail public spending and reduce the state sector labour force, it might find itself undermining some of the class groupings from whom it drew greatest support.

These are instances of what we have called a 'complementary' analysis in terms of class structure and economic and social change. They are not *final resolutions* of the way in which shifts in class structure and the constraints of a global economy will influence nationalist sentiment in Quebec. But they are enough to show that these constraints are real: Quebec today and as an independent state has to compete in a global economy whose effects on other nation-states we could sketch out. Similarly our brief references to classes in Quebecois society indicate that people at different strategic points of the Quebec economy are likely to develop different meaningful constructions of Quebec's present and future. This is not to argue that there is a simple equation of class interest and nationalist ideology. As Balibar and Wallerstein (1991) point out, in the matter of nationalism there is scarcely a class on whom suspicion has not fallen. But to admit that the relationship of class and class interest to nationalism is complex is not the same as saying it is irrelevant. To look for lines of connection between class, economic change and nationalism is not, as Handler argues, 'to fail to take ideologies seriously as meaningful formulations' (1988: 25). His other objections to class analysis – that classes are analytic constructs and that interests cannot be objectively ascertained – are long-standing debates in the field which we do not wish to address here; but his principal argument is for taking 'meaningful formulations' seriously. In his view any attempt to associate ideology with class objectifies ideologies themselves as 'bounded units of discourse'. He offers as an alternative strategy to class analysis 'an interpretive analysis of texts, conversations, and incidents which are unified, for our purposes, only by my experience (and to the degree that my narrative succeeds, by yours)' (1988: 26).

This last seems to us to be precisely the kind of radical subjectivism which is not a necessary element but has often been an unfortunate by-product of the cultural turn. To recognize that a 'culturized' account is productive and successful, and that economistic accounts are reductive, is not to entail the radical subjectivism of Handler's view of social relations.

Recovering the economic: Madonna as cultural icon

We can observe the same possibilities and dangers in a cultural analysis in a second example, the feminist account of the performer Madonna, which exemplifies the current preoccupations with text, representation and sexuality. Madonna, described by Q magazine in March 1988 as 'the most famous woman in the world', has been widely proclaimed as a postmodern heroine (Brooks, 1997), embodying as she does many of the key preoccupations of feminism after the cultural turn: the fluid nature of identity and sexuality; the performative character of the body; the dominance of consumerism and consumer interests over production; the production of gendered texts; and the view of women as active and powerful cultural subjects.

As an emblem of liberated femininity, Madonna symbolizes 'an erotic politics in which the female body can be refashioned in the flux of identities that speak in plural styles' (Schwichtenberg, quoted in Bordo, 1993: 282). Discussions of the Madonna phenomenon collected in a volume by Schwichtenberg (1993) highlight the ambiguities of sexuality and power in the lyrics and video versions of her songs, and the way she has repeatedly restyled her appearance, re-presented her body and restated her own sexual orientation as a demonstration of 'polymorphous perversity'. There could be no better illustration of the post-structuralist view that gender (along with sex) is not a fixed entity but something that is repeatedly fashioned and refashioned through the daily playing out of gendered performances (Butler, 1990). It is this fluidity and performativity of gendered identities which allows for the possibility of the transformation of gender relations; no wonder that young women embrace Madonna as a symbol of female power and a refutation of the older feminist paradigm which, it is argued, all too often presented women as passive victims of structural forces.

While such cultural 'readings' are instructive in developing a new cultural politics of gender, Madonna is at the same time an economic phenomenon (Tetzlaff, 1993). Thus, a product such as *Sex*, a collection of near-pornographic photos of Madonna in erotic poses alone and with an assortment of men and women, can be read as a statement of liberated, transgressive sexuality which challenges the constraining norms of 'compulsory heterosexuality' (Rich, 1980). But it is also an extremely shrewd piece of marketing. Erotic products like *Sex* and the various videos that accompany Madonna's music help to ensure continued sales of her discs. Madonna has successfully commodified her own sexuality.

Both the sex industries and the entertainment industries are particularly crucial to the development of capitalism in its phase of advanced and individualized consumerism within western societies; we may observe at a macro-level the way production has been 'culturized', in the sense that cultural goods are increasingly important as a source of profit; thus culture can be seen as the basis of a further stage of capital accumulation. Madonna's various outputs, and moreover she herself, are typical products of such processes, whereby a specific cultural 'icon' is the basis of an interlinked package of products: discs, videos, books, clothing and other mementos. Indeed, it can be argued that Madonna takes the commodification of sex to a new peak, in which her individuality and her fame add extra dimensions and value, in contrast to more standard erotic materials which use either unknown women or those famous simply for being porn stars. Where can we go beyond this? Perhaps only to the world of virtual reality portrayed in the novels of William Gibson and Neal Stephenson where the consumer can 'jack in' to a computer to have virtual sex with the video star of his/her choice?

In our analysis we have moved from the local to macro-level. While we can study phenomena like Madonna's *Sex* as specific cultural and economic events, it is important to locate them within the global dynamics of capitalism and gender which form their context. Thus the production of *Sex* has important effects at the macro-level. Culturally, it provides legitimation for young women who want to challenge sexual norms and develop their own forms of transgressive sexual practice. Economically, it stimulates the development of new types of pornographic and erotic products targeted specifically at women, now a major growth industry in many advanced capitalist societies. But as we move to the global level we can also begin to explore the limitations placed by social structures on individual agency, and avoid the slippage into voluntarism which we have already suggested mars too much postmodern cultural analysis. We therefore have to note the continuing skew in the representation of gender in pornographic/erotic materials. It is still in the main women rather than men who are the object of the pornographer's gaze. Thus consumer capitalism works with highly gendered forms of representation to maintain male heterosexual dominance, which can easily reappropriate Madonna's 'transgressive' imagery and present her as just another available female body spread out for male enjoyment. Moreover, as Tetzlaff points out, Madonna's projection of empowered female sexuality is ultimately an illusion for most of us. Power comes down in the end to money: 'the gates to the dream world of the screen open only to the few who are useful to cultural industry's search for maximized profit' (Tetzlaff, 1993: 262).

Chaney makes an important if flawed point about the necessity for cultural analysis: 'If the categories of gender are held to be cultural categories then the study and analysis of culture will be self-evidently fundamental as a resource for deconstructing structures of oppression. The same arguments will hold for studies of other forms of difference such as . . . the representational constructions of racial and ethnic identities' (1994: 33–4). We have suggested that Madonna is a good illustration of a cultural politics that challenges existing categories of sex and gender. But the thrust of our argument in this section has been that gender categories are in fact *both* cultural *and* economic. This is not merely to say that any cultural phenomenon has an economic context and vice versa; but that all social phenomena can be 'read' both culturally and materially. An adequate political strategy to overcome gender – and ethnic – inequalities will therefore have to be based on an understanding of both cultural and economic aspects of difference. Just as Fraser says, gender is 'not only a political-economic but a cultural-valuation difference' (1995: 79). The politics of gender and ethnicity must invoke claims both for redistribution and recognition.

Conclusion: a programme for a more balanced account of the 'social'

We have been arguing, in relation to rather different problematics, that we need to combine cultural and economic analyses for complete understanding of ethnic and gendered phenemona, a both/and not an either/or form of analysis. We have used examples to show that cultural phenomena need to be 'read' in their economic and political context. Inverting this, we also believe that economic and political processes develop within particular frameworks of symbol and meaning. In sum, in concrete situations both the economic and cultural are inevitably implicated in social relations.

We have also highlighted the dangers of a one-sided economic or cultural approach. The discussion of ethnicity has suggested that economic analysis on its own misrepresents aspects of the meaning of social action and identification and is likely to be a poor base for political prediction (witness the failure of Marxism to predict the direction of twentieth century history). On the other hand, in relation to feminist accounts of gender, we believe that cultural analysis alone may give a misleading picture if it minimizes economic constraints and fosters the illusion of unrestrained choices and free-floating identities. While a cultural analysis does not have to slide into voluntarism, we must not fall into the trap of thinking that having overcome a misplaced concreteness, all has vanished into thin air or into the cultural ether.

To conclude, we would like to set out a programme for what we see as the way forward for a more satisfactory approach to the 'social' which would encompass within that broad term aspects both of political economy and of cultural analysis, as follows:

1. One-sided cultural accounts are at least as partial and part-blind as one-sided economic accounts of global structures, or of localized phenomena. They may also be equally abstract, for example in dealing in categories and concepts which are at some distance from the lifeworlds of individuals, collectivities, and communities (as is arguably the case with much current feminist analyses). As the examples offered in this chapter have shown, social events and relationships can be read and interpreted economically and culturally within the same moment. Currently sociological attention focuses particularly on cultural aspects of change and the 'politics of difference', demonstrated, for instance, in the re-assertion of Islamic religion and culture around the world and its enthusiastic adoption by many young British South Asian women. But these phenomena need to be positioned within their socio-economic contexts and cannot be read off from an analysis of texts, discourses and forms of politico-cultural symbolism, important as they are. Thus the rise of Islam around the globe must be understood in terms of the global economic and political hierarchies which portrayed Middle Eastern societies as subordinate and inferior to the West; and to the conditions of economic deprivation and inequality in many Muslim societies, such as Egypt, Turkey and Algeria, which increased the support among the rural and industrial proletariats for Islamic parties. But this is not to call for a return to the old Marxist frameworks which reduced nationalism and religious struggle to a side-effect of class struggles. Cultural and economic dimensions must be viewed as of equal significance and each must be contextualized in terms of the other.

2. We need to reduce our expectations of global sociological theories and look more towards 'theories of the middle range'. By global theories we mean those which claim to say something about the macro-structure of societies at a regional level (e.g. western capitalism, feminization of the labour force) or at a global level (globalization, male dominance), and about the direction of those macro-structures and their 'tendencies' (e.g. towards centralization, towards impoverishment of a class or group of countries, by contrast with other classes or regions, towards dominance of transnational corporations, towards sexual equality). Currently, such theories claim more than they can deliver.

3. At the same time, we need to recognize the necessity of such theories which deal with the question of 'structure' and 'direction' without expecting them to be perfected or to provide us with finally telling accounts either of how systems work or the 'inexorable' path they are following. These types of theory are bound to remain imperfect,

incomplete and forever overtaken by events. On the other hand *without them* we have no context in which to place sociological accounts which focus on a much smaller subset of interactions. Thus, in the examples dealing with the understanding of culture and politics – and the politics of culture – which we offered in the last section, we argued that cultural movements must be seen in the context of global economic develop-ments. Indeed it is these very developments which allow cultural politics to emerge and which will inevitably affect their final outcomes, as we suggested in the case of Quebec ethno-nationalism.

4. Structural theories need not be principally 'political-economic' even though we incline to the view that the prime movers of regional, societal, and global change are economic and political. The work of Roland Robertson (1992) offers a good example of a case for under-standing culture as global and analysing global systems culturally. But the examples we have discussed in this article show that cultural changes are economically and politically contextualized whilst being simultaneously cultural in their formation and definition.

5. If we are to allow the distinction between the economic and the cultural, this does not correspond to a distinction between global and local analyses. Structural theories need to be informed by an under-standing of cultural movement; local studies which are purely or primarily cultural are only partial and may be misleading. To put it another way, cultural change is both local and global; equally, economic tendencies are 'worked out' both on a global stage and in the life-as-lived experiences of people and communities.

6. Reconciling cultural and economic forms of analysis will involve a variety of methodological strategies. Local effects, especially of a cul-tural nature, cannot be read off from a global theorizing or even from statistical materials which are used to indicate trends at the macro-level. Interviews, ethnographic techniques and social anthropological immer-sion, textual, archival or narrative analyses and institutional studies may be used to uncover these local aspects, especially their cultural dimensions. On the other hand, there is a continued need for broad structural indicators such as statistical indices of economic and demo-graphic change. A complete analysis of any social phenomenon should draw on both types of methodological strategy.

7. By such devices, the terms of macro-sociological theory (such as nationalism, impoverishment, bourgeoisification, feminization, racism and sexism) need to be translated into life-as-lived observations. Local observation becomes the 'stuff' out of which structural categories are constructed and revised. Only 'local' studies, for example, can tell us how women, and men in male-dominated community settings, cope with women entering the sphere of work, with new child-care and care-of-the-elderly arrangements. These studies, which are bound to be both 'cultural' and 'economic', inform our understanding of trends which are merely indicated by grand-scale demographic and labour market

participation studies. In the same way important departures in the study of ethnicity and national identity show us how identities are shaped on the 'ground floor' of social life, by means of the socially reproduced discourses of everyday life, as well as being formed by discourses which are national and global in their scope. But, as we have argued elsewhere (Bradley, 1996), structural arrangements delineate and set limits for possibilities of identification.

8. To achieve all this, there needs to be a kind of mutual respect across fields of endeavour, often lacking within the sociological and academic community, which recognizes the value of different methodologies and different foci of interest. This is not just a matter of academic tolerance but a consequence of the fact that, given the doubt cast upon systemic accounts of social structure, we are no longer certain where the next insights are coming from. We need to be open to new ideas, perspectives and techniques of investigation, while at the same time exposing them to dispassionate critical scrutiny.

We are arguing, then, for a more modest and open-minded sociology, which will learn from its own mistakes and incorporate insights and strengths from other disciplines: for us, this would be good sociology. If we can achieve this we might avoid a situation in which our steady gaze at the forest was so little informed about how trees grew that we were unable to keep the forest alive; and simultaneously avoid looking so closely at the trees that we fail to notice that the forest is burning down.

Acknowledgements

We would like to thank Ruth Levitas and Irving Velody for helpful comments and also some of the participants at the Lancaster Seminar where the paper on which this chapter is based was first presented.

Notes

1 For example, Rex states 'analysis in terms of cultural, or for that matter of status, differentiation is subsidiary to and does not replace class analysis' (Rex, 1986: 69).

2 From the point of view of a participant, it is not easy to recognize what Anthias and Yuval-Davis refer to as an 'ethnic studies' school at Bristol in the 1970s.

3 Re-emphasize, because the notion of ethnic groups as interest groups or as part of a constellation of political economy (for example Indians as indentured labourers in the Caribbean) is not completely new (see Rex, 1986).

4 For example, Coward and Ellis in *Language and Materialism* (1977); CCCS (1978) on ideologies of femininity in the media; Juliet Mitchell in *Psychoanalysis and Feminism* (1975) grafting Freud on to Marx and extending the notion of the economic revolution with a call for sexual revolution.

References

Adkins, L. (1995) *Gendered Work*, Milton Keynes: Open University Press.

Anthias, F. and Yuval-Davis, N. (1993) *Racialized Boundaries*, London: Routledge.

Balibar, E. and Wallerstein, I. (1991) *Race, Nation and Class: Ambiguous Identities*, London: Verso.

Ballard, R. (1992) 'New clothes for the emperor: the conceptual nakedness of the race relations industry in Britain', *New Community*, 18 (3): 481–92.

Barrett, M. (1980) *Women's Oppression Today*, London: Verso.

Barrett, M. (1992) 'Words and things: materialism and method in contemporary feminist analysis', in M. Barrett and A. Phillips (eds), *Destabilizing Theory*, London: Polity.

Barrett, M. and Phillips, A. (1992) *Destabilizing Theory*, London: Polity.

Beck, U. (1992) *Risk Society*, London: Sage.

Benhabib, S. (1992) *Situating the Self*, Cambridge: Polity.

Bordo, S. (1993) '"Material girl": the effacements of postmodern culture', in C. Schwichtenberg (ed.), *The Madonna Connection*, San Francisco: Westview Press.

Bradley, H. (1996) *Fractured Identities*, Cambridge: Polity.

Brooks, A. (1997) *Postfeminisms*, London: Routledge.

Butler, J. (1990) *Gender Trouble*, London: Routledge.

Butler, J. (1993) *Bodies that Matter*, London: Routledge.

CCCS (Centre for Contemporary Cultural Studies) (1978) *Women Take Issue*, London: Hutchinson.

Chaney, D. (1994) *The Cultural Turn*, London: Sage.

Clement, W. (1975) *The Canadian Corporate Elite: an Analysis of Economic Power*, Toronto: McClelland and Stewart.

Cockburn, C. (1983) *Brothers*, London: Pluto.

Colley, L. (1992) *Britons: Forging the Nation 1707–1837*, New Haven, CT and London: Yale University Press.

Coward, R. and Ellis, J. (1977) *Language and Materialism*, London: Routledge.

Crompton, R. and Le Feuvre, N. (1992) 'Gender and bureaucracy: women in finance in Britain and France', in A. Witz and M. Savage (eds), *Gender and Bureaucracy*, London: Sage.

De Lauretis, T. (1984) *Alice Doesn't: Feminism, Semiotics, Cinema*, Bloomington: Indiana University Press.

Donald, J. and Rattansi, A. (eds) (1992) *'Race', Culture and Difference*, London: Sage.

Eriksen, T. (1993) *Ethnicity and Nationalism: Anthropological Perspectives*, London: Pluto.

Featherstone, M. (1991) *Consumer Culture and Postmodernism*, London: Sage.

Fenton, S. (1996) 'The subject is ethnicity', in R. Barot (ed.), *The Racism Problematic: Contemporary Sociological Debates on Race and Ethnicity*, Lampeter: Edwin Mellen Press.

Fenton, S. (1999) *Ethnicity: Racism, Class and Culture*, Basingstoke: Macmillan.

Flax, J. (1990) *Psychoanalysis, Feminism and Postmodernism in the Contemporary West*, Berkeley: University of California Press.

Fraser, N. (1995) 'From redistribution to recognition? Dilemmas of justice in a post-socialist age', *New Left Review*, 212: 68–93.

Giddens, A. (1991) *Modernity and Self-Identity*, Cambridge: Polity.

Gherardi, S. (1995) *Gender, Symbolism and Organizational Cultures*, London: Sage.

Glucksmann, M. (1995) 'Why "work"? gender and the total social organization of labour', *Gender, Work and Organization*, 2 (2): 63–75.

Hall, S. (1992) 'New ethnicities', in J. Donald and A. Rattansi (eds), *'Race', Culture and Difference*, London: Sage.

Handler, R. (1988) *Nationalism and the Politics of Culture in Quebec*, University of Wisconsin: Wisconsin University Press.

Haraway, D. (1991) *Simians, Cyborgs and Women: the Reinvention of Nature*, New York: Routledge.

Hartmann, H. (1976) 'Patriarchy, capitalism and job segregation by sex', *Signs*, 1 (3): 137–68.

Iganski, P. and Payne, G. (1996) 'Declining racial disadvantage in the British labour market', *Ethnic and Racial Studies*, 19 (1): 113–34.

Jacobus, M., Keller, E.F. and Shuttleworth, S. (1990) *Body/Politics*, London: Routledge.

Jameson, F. (1991) *Postmodernism or the Cultural Logic of Late Capitalism*, London: Verso.

Lash, S. and Urry, J. (1994) *Economies of Signs and Space*, London: Sage.

McIntosh, M. (1979) 'The welfare state and the needs of the dependent family', in S. Burman (ed.), *Fit Work for Women*, London: Croom Helm.

Miles, R. (1982) *Racism and Migrant Labour*, London: Routledge and Kegan Paul.

Miles, R. (1993) *Racism after Race Relations*, London: Routledge.

Miles, R. and Phizacklea, A. (1984) *White Man's Country: Racism in British Politics*, London: Pluto.

Mitchell, J. (1975) *Psychoanalysis and Feminism*, Harmondsworth: Penguin.

Modood, T. (1992) *Not Easy Being British*, Stoke-on-Trent: Trentham Books.

Modood, T. , Berthoud, R., Lakey, J., Nazroo, J., Smith, P., Virdee, S. and Beishon, S. (1997) *Ethnic Minorities in Britain*, London: Policy Studies Institute.

Mohanty, C. (1995) 'Under western eyes: feminist scholarship and colonial discourses', in B. Ashcroft, G. Griffiths and H. Tiffin (eds), *The Post-Colonial Studies Reader*, London: Routledge.

Oakley, A. (1981) *Subject Women*, Harmondsworth: Penguin.

Pakulski, S. and Waters, M. (1996) *The Death of Class*, London: Sage.

Pollert, A. (1996) 'Gender and class revisited: the poverty of patriarchy', *Sociology*, 30 (4): 639–59.

Porter, J. (1965) *The Vertical Mosaic: an Analysis of Class and Power in Canada*, Toronto: University of Toronto Press.

Pringle, R. (1989) *Secretaries Talk*, London: Verso.

Pringle, R. and Watson, S. (1992) '"Women's interests" and the post-structuralist state', in M. Barrett and A. Phillips (eds), *Destabilizing Theory*, London: Polity.

Rattansi, A. (1995) 'Just framing: ethnicities and racisms in a "postmodern" framework', in L. Nicholson and S. Seidman (eds), *Social Postmodernism*, Cambridge: Cambridge University Press.

Rattansi, A. and Westwood, S. (eds) (1994) *Racism, Modernity and Identity on the Western Front*, Cambridge: Polity.

Reitz, J. and Breton, R. (1994) *The Illusion of Difference: Realities of Ethnicity in Canada and the United States*, Toronto: C.D. Howe Institute.

Rex, J. (1970) *Race Relations in Sociological Theory*, London: Weidenfeld and Nicolson.

Rex, J. (1973) *Race, Colonialism and the City*, London: Routledge and Kegan Paul.

Rex, J. (1986) 'The role of class analysis in the study of race relations: a Weberian perspective', in J. Rex and D. Mason (eds), *Theories of Race and Ethnic Relations*, Cambridge: Cambridge University Press.

Rex, J. and Tomlinson, S. (1979) *Colonial Immigrants in a British City – a Class Analysis*, London: Routledge.

Rich, A. (1980) 'Compulsory heterosexuality and lesbian existence', *Signs*, 5 (4): 631–90.

Riley, D. (1988) *Am I That Name? Feminism and the Category of Women in History*, London: Macmillan.

Robertson, R. (1992) *Globalization: Social Theory and Global Culture*, London: Sage.

Robinson, V. (1990) 'Roots to mobility: the social mobility of Britain's black population 1971–87', *Ethnic and Racial Studies*, 13 (2): 274–86.

Roseneil, S. (1995) 'The coming of age of feminist sociology: some issues of practice and theory for the next twenty years', *British Journal of Sociology*, 46 (2): 191–203.

Sawicki, J. (1991) *Disciplining Foucault*, London: Routledge.

Schwichtenberg, C. (ed.) (1993) *The Madonna Connection*, San Francisco: Westview Press.

Scott, J.W. (1988) *Gender and the Politics of History*, New York: Columbia University Press.

Segal, L. (1994) *Straight Sex*, London: Virago.

Teeple, G. (ed.) (1972) *Capitalism and the National Question in Canada*, Toronto: University of Toronto Press.

Tetzlaff, D. (1993) 'Metatextual girl – patriarchy – postmodernism – power – money – Madonna', in C. Schwichtenberg (ed.), *The Madonna Connection*, San Francisco: Westview Press.

Vallieres, P. (1971) *White Niggers of America*, Toronto: Mclelland and Stewart.

Walby, S. (1986) *Patriarchy at Work*, Cambridge: Polity.

Walby, S. (1997) *Gender Transformations*, London: Routledge.

Waters, M. (1997) 'Inequality after class', in D. Owen (ed.), *Sociology After Postmodernism*, London: Sage.

Wieviorka, M. (1994) 'Racism in Europe: unity and diversity', in A. Rattansi and S. Westwood (eds), *Racism, Modernity and Identity on the Western Front*, Cambridge: Polity.

6

Capitalism's Cultural Turn

Nigel Thrift

Introduction

This chapter is concerned with how we might understand 'capitalism' after the cultural turn which has swept across the social sciences and humanities. That task seems pressing. After all, all around us the adverse effects of what we call 'capitalism' seem to be pressing in, in ways which some commentators argue can only presage more uncertainty and insecurity for everyone.

It is not as if the proponents of the cultural turn do not acknowledge the importance of something called capitalism. They do, usually in one of three ways. First, capitalism can be generalized out to an all-pervasive cultural formation, usually through its migration into the symbolic realm. Second, capitalism can be elevated into something so self-evident that it can be trundled on whenever a connective explanation is called for. Third, capitalism becomes a reading. It can then be made into a transcendental haunting, both everywhere and nowhere.

In other words, the force of capitalism is acknowledged but it is turned into a necessary but empty foil for the cultural turn, included certainly, but allowed no life of its own, because it is always already accounted for (Morris, 1988).

The cultural turn involves, then, acts of homage to the importance of capitalism, which, at the same time, act as a means of forgetting all about it and getting on to more interesting things. The results, at least, are clear. 'Cultural' analysis has become more and more sophisticated but it is mixed in with a level of 'economic' analysis which rarely rises above that of anyone who can read a newspaper (Eagleton, 1995).

How has this situation come about? I think there are three reasons. First, analysis of the 'economic' is passé. For the cohort of researchers in the social sciences and humanities that have come into academe since, say, the mid-1980s it is something of the past. Second, and subsequently, the economic is something worked on by others. It is not what 'we' are about. In other words, the abrogation of the economic is an important part of the cultural turn because it helps to produce a sense of identity. Third, the economic can then be regarded as another, rather tiresome, country. Most especially, the economic is about *work* and work is not where culture happens.

Of course, these are gross exaggerations. To begin with, there are writers from the cultural turn who have paid attention to the economy (e.g. du Gay, 1996). Then, a number of writers – myself included – would like to jettison the distinction between the economic and the cultural on the grounds that it creates false oppositions (Thrift, 1996a). And, last but not least, capitalism seems to be undergoing its own cultural turn, as, increasingly, it is argued that business is about the creation, fostering, and distribution of *knowledge*: 'creativity is now seen as an asset class' (Kurtzman, in the *Financial Times*, 18 November 1996, p. 21). It is this last point I want to concentrate on in this chapter, and for two reasons.

First, because what is clear is that since the 1960s, capitalism – however one defines it – has been undergoing some significant changes as the ability of business to gather information and reflect upon it has become greater. Second, because these changes are not ones upon which the disinterested academic can simply look down from an Olympian height; academics are deeply implicated in the genesis of this 'knowledgeable' capitalism and this knowledgeable capitalism is increasingly impinging on what were once regarded as traditional academic preserves.

Therefore, this chapter is in three main parts. In the first section, I outline the changing division of labour associated with the production and distribution of knowledge which makes the relationship between academia and capitalism more complex and more interconnected than previously, and which makes the putative relationship between the self of the academic and the other of business a more difficult one to sustain. In the second and longest section, I want to look at the process by which the international business community has come to adopt a new kind of discourse about what the economic is about as it increasingly emphasizes the importance of knowledge. I argue that this cultural turn is giving rise to what I call 'soft' or 'knowledgeable' capitalism. Then, in the final section, I draw some brief conclusions.

The groves of business? The business of academe?

The academic study of business increasingly emphasizes the importance of information and knowledge. There are numerous examples of this statement, but four will do to make the case. First, there is the growth of an information economics based on notions of transaction costs, information asymmetries, spillover effects, intangible and non-homogeneous commodities, and the like (see, for example, Stiglitz, 1994). Second, there is the growth of interest in learning-by-doing, that is in harnessing the full potential of the knowledge that is incorporated into the bodies of workers, including the potential to innovate (Nonaka and Takeuchi, 1995). Third, there is the growth of interest in a business history which considers the information infrastructures that typify business organizations (Bud-Frierman, 1994). Then, fourth, there is the growth of work that is based on investigating and elaborating the conventions that underlie the success or failure of particular urban and regional economies. These conventions are, in effect, particular, culturally specific, information infrastructures, which are seen as the keys to economic success.

Why this interest in information and knowledge? Five reasons seem particularly germane. The first is the massive *increase in information*, consisting of an expansion in the volume of data that can be processed and transmitted per unit of time (Perez, 1985). The second is the increasing emphasis on *innovation*. Innovation necessarily involves the generation and deployment of information and knowledge, but the production of this knowledge is highly problematic since it involves 'non convexities' (fixed, sunk costs, increasing returns to scale), the inevitable absence of a complete set of markets (since there cannot exist competitive markets for commodities that have yet to be conceived of, let alone invented), lack of homogeneity (since every piece of information produced must be different from any other piece of information produced, or it is not new knowledge), strong asymmetry (since the buyer cannot know all the information until the information is brought), and the degree to which knowledge resembles a public good (since it is difficult to appropriate all the benefits of a particular piece of information, and therefore difficult to exclude others from enjoying the benefits – indeed, it may be undesirable to do so) (Stiglitz, 1994). The third reason is the renewed emphasis on *fallibility*. The transmission of information and knowledge is usually noisy and incomplete, and decision-making can be organized in different ways which can amplify or diminish effects of this noise and incompleteness. Thus, one of the reasons why non-hierarchical organizations have become more popular in business is because they are more likely to give bad decisions a second chance to be rectified. The fourth reason is the increasing emphasis on *learning* in businesses, and most especially on learning-by-doing, as a means of maximizing an organization's potential. Then there is one final reason, the reason I want to concentrate on in the rest of this section of this chapter. That is the increasing interaction between business and academe (Strathern, 1995a; 1995b; Hill and Turpin, 1995; Readings, 1996). In a sense business has become more academic as academe has become more business oriented. It is no longer possible, if it ever was, to think of academia as an epistemologically privileged sphere. Similarly, it is no longer possible to write off business as though it were the haunt of the epistemologically challenged; business has become more 'intelligent' in a number of ways. To begin with, much of the workforce in many countries, and especially management, has become steadily more qualified. Then, it is possible to see the evolution of an independent intelligence community, produced by the business media (including providers of business information, like market researchers), by research analysts and press commentators, and by the continually expanding framework of various forms of business education, all the way from Harvard Business School to Covey 'University'. Again, business has become more responsive to ideas from outside business, partly as a result of this new educational infrastructure.

There are, then, an increasing number of symmetries between academia and business, of which four are particularly striking. First, academia and business share many of the same concerns; for example, they share the need to transform information, of which there is a surfeit, into new knowledge. Similarly, they share the need to construct supple institutional structures which can react swiftly to change. Second, in both academia and business the increasing commodification of knowledge has only pointed to the value of knowledge which cannot be commodified, and especially to the value of practical knowledge, knowledge that cannot be written down and packaged (Thrift, 1985). Thus words like practice and skill have become an important part of the vocabulary of both communities. Third, both academia and business increasingly share many of the same vocabularies, of which the most prevalent is the notion of 'culture'. Fourth, the spaces of knowledge have become as critical to business as to academia. In a world in which more and more information is increasingly able to circulate and circulate rapidly, information *skills* are still highly concentrated in particular locations, in particular offices, in intra-organizational links and in firm networks.

Of course, these symmetries have disturbed the values and procedures of academia. For example, academics from both the right and the left (Plant, 1996) have argued that, increasingly, the kind of static hierarchy of knowledge that was (apparently) typical of the period up until the 1960s, with academics in universities located at the top of the hierarchy as able to offer the best validated knowledge, is being replaced by a flatter, more diverse and more interconnected set of knowledge communities, which mount a real challenge to the pre-eminence of academia by concentrating on learning by doing, often at-a-distance. As Plant (1996: 207–8) puts it:

> As Foucault writes, the 'University stands for the institutional apparatus through which society ensures its uneventful reproduction, at the least cost to itself'. Today's academy still has its sources in Platonic conceptions of knowledge, teaching and the teacher–student relationship, all of which are based on a model in which learning barely figures at all . . .
> The academy loses its control over intelligence once it is even possible to imagine a situation in which information can be accessed from nets which care for neither old boy status or exam results. . . . Released from its relation to teaching, learning is no longer coded as study and confined to some particular zone, specialised behaviour or compartmentalised period of time.

A lecturer no longer controls the process, ensuring the development of well-rounded individuals one step at a time, serial fashion: those once defined as students learn to learn for themselves.

This situation is uncomfortable. There are four possible responses. One is to flee from it. Some of the cultural turn might be interpreted in this way, as a retreat into the attics as the rest of the house is flooded out (although, ironically, it is increasingly a retreat to the examination of consumer products which are produced by capitalism). Another response is to simply condemn it. This is easy enough but gets us nowhere. The third is to embrace it. Plant's ideas, thoughtful though they undoubtedly are, are closer to the designs of modern business than she might think. The fourth response, the one I want to make in this chapter, is to try to face the dilemmas produced by such thinking by realizing that theoretical developments now routinely leak across the old boundaries between academia and business and, in turn, these developments are helping to produce a new form of capitalism, what I call 'soft capitalism'.

The rise of soft capitalism

In this section, I want to provide an outline of a new managerialist discourse in which knowledge is both the central subject and object. But it is important to be clear about its status. First, the discourse is not just an ideology. Thus:

> While it is undoubtedly true that these discourses and practices of work reform have played, and continue to play, an active part in reproducing hierarchies of power and reward at work, or that they have been consciously deployed at various times to attenuate the power of trade unions and their prerogatives for the reproduction of collective interests and the defence of collective rights, it is especially important to note that they are not simply 'ideological' distortions; in other words, that their claims to 'knowledge' are not 'false', nor do they serve a specific social function and answer to pre-formed economic needs. Certainly these discourses of work reform arise in specific political contexts, and have potential consequences, but they are not merely functional responses to, or legitimations of, already existing economic interests or needs. Rather than simply reflecting a pre-given social world, they themselves actively 'make up' a social reality and create new ways for people to be at work. (du Gay, 1996a: 53)

In other words, the new managerialist discourse must be 'understood primarily as a form of rhetoric . . . spoken by managerial professionals not to mention professors of management – in ways that are not necessarily coterminous with organizational practice itself' (Nohria and Berkley, 1994: 125–6). It describes:

a world that, literally, does 'not exist'. According to those who have developed the term there is no organisation that displays all the characteristics of a 'full' transplantation. The concept of a 'learning organisation' is extremely complex; few would be confident in knowing when they have seen one. 'Network' structures dissolve the boundaries between one organisation and another; with the virtual corporation the disappearing act is complete. (Goffee and Hunt, 1996: 3)

It is no surprise, then, that managers and workers presented with these new discourses, show some considerable ambivalence (Martin, 1994).

Second, the discourse is not a hermetically sealed, unitary, and static order. It is made up of multiple strands of practice, it is contested and it constantly changes as its proponents foster new conventions. But, for all that, increasingly it forms a background to how business is practised. Third, the discourse's reach is necessarily partial, geographically and organizationally. It started out within US firms and still retains its strongest hold there. It therefore bears the stamp of a US-style competitive individualism (Martin, 1994). And it is chiefly preponderant in the larger multinational business organizations which have the resources to institute it. 'Most of the world's working population continue to be employed in small or medium-sized (rather than "global") businesses; they earn their living in an identifiable "place"; they have familiar work routines; someone they identify as a "boss", and so on' (Goffee and Hunt, 1996: 3). Even then, not all parts of the discourse are adopted equally – all kinds of combinations are possible. But the point is that it has become a part of the *background* hum of business around the world, soaking further and further into the practical order and used more and more often both to account for decisions and to bring decisions into being (Thrift, 1996a). It is the goal that becomes the means that becomes the reality.

For the new managerialist discourse, the period after the Second World War and before the demise of the Bretton Woods system and the fall of the Berlin Wall was a period in which striated spaces abounded: the buttoned-down personality of the company man (Whyte, 1957; Sampson, 1995) for one; the enclosed, hierarchical world of the multi-divisional corporation (Chandler, 1962; 1977), with its monolithic goals of achieving ever-greater size and scale by means of a single corporate strategy realized through a relatively static and formal bureaucratic inner core which passed information upwards from an 'external' environment and control slowly downwards from a closed-off headquarters, for another. Then there were the rigidities that resulted from rules of nation states, like fixed exchange rates, high tariff barriers, and so on. And, finally, orchestrating the whole, was the idea of a management 'science' which would be able to produce the cognitive wherewithal to predict and thereby control the world. *At least in the rhetoric of the time*, then, the world was an organized place, made up of carefully closed-off spaces which could be rationally appropriated and controlled. (We might, of course, argue about the accuracy of that rhetoric, since any glance at the history of the time hardly suggests the stable, golden age of capitalism that is so often written about. Indeed, as early as 1965 management theorists like Emery and Trist were already writing about organizations that could deal with permanently turbulent environments.)

But, from the 1960s on, as the Bretton Woods system declined and then, later, the Soviet Union and Eastern Europe split asunder, so the state of permanent turbulence that Emery and Trist wrote about began to look more like a successful prophecy and less like a struggling prescription, and for a series of reasons, including the following. First, there was the floating of exchange rates, the growth of various offshore capital markets, and finally the growth of markets in financial derivatives, which has produced the merry-go-round of monetary transmission, offshore borrowing and lending, and various hedging strategies, flavoured with a dollop of pure speculation, that we take for granted today. Second, there has been the exponential growth of information generated by the intersection of the financial media, information technologies and the growth of economic research, which, in turn, have produced both more complex representations of, and more ambiguity in, the business organization's environment: the expansion of information has produced new solutions *and* new problems. Third, there has been the growth of numerous new players in the international business world, which has upset the old competitive equilibrium: the Japanese and Koreans certainly, but also now overseas Chinese firms, third-world multinationals, firms from Eastern Europe, and so on. Fourth, there has been the growth of a more differentiated production–consumption nexus in which a more differentiated set of demands on mass producers produce more differentiated consumers, and so on, increasing both the range and fickleness of many markets. Fifth, there has been a general speed-up in transportation and communications. This speed-up has had numerous differentiated, multiple, and sometimes contradictory effects which mean that it cannot be bracketed within a general description like 'time–space compression' (Thrift, 1995), but that there have been effects which have been sufficiently extensive to allow commentators to write of a world of flows (e.g. Lash and Urry, 1994) seems less open to debate. Sixth, as a result of these and other reasons, national economies have generally performed in a less coherent way which has made it even more difficult to predict economic outcomes.

For the managers of business organizations, the consequences are clear. First, almost any business organization is vulnerable. 'AEG, Boeing, Degussa, Gulf Oil, Sears Roebuck and many other famous enterprises have seen their market shares seriously eroded. Pan Am and other erstwhile leaders have crashed like giant trees in the forest. Other former leaders have, like the Cheshire cat, disappeared leaving only their names behind. Dunlop is now a Japanese brand and RCA a French one' (Stopford, 1996: 5). Second, managers are expected to react much more swiftly; 'whereas once we might have expected a new CEO to turn round a struggling business in five years we are now expecting that manager to do so in 12 months' (Goffee and Hunt, 1996: 4). Third, large business organizations are, on average, becoming smaller employers, and their attraction is perhaps less than it was in the days of the 'company man'. Managers are now both more likely to switch from organization to organization and more likely to find managing or even starting up a smaller firm an appropriate challenge.

Given the scale of these kinds of change, it is perhaps not a surprise that a new managerialist discourse has been produced which both frames them and forces them. This discourse depends, first of all, on new metaphors which attempt to capture a more turbulent, uncertain and insecure world. At first, the metaphors tended to be ones of excess, overload and saturation. But many of these early metaphors can now be seen as:

> the product of the first hysterical reactions to information technologies. 'Overload' in reference to what? Saturated in reference to whom? The relative, historically contingent nature of these terms is seldom if ever entertained within the discourse, which prefers to present them as timeless. (Collins, 1995: 12)

So, very gradually, new visual and linguistic metaphors started to emerge which began to refigure (or, in the jargon, reframe) the business organization's relationship with the world, and the role of the manager within that organization (Morgan, 1986; 1993; Martin, 1994; Buck-Morss, 1995; Crainer, 1995; Collins, 1995). These metaphors were based on the notion of constant adaptive movement – 'dancing', 'surfing', and the like – and of organizational structures that could facilitate this constant adaptation, both by becoming more open to the changing world and by engaging the hearts and minds of the workforce in such a way that the organizations could exist as more open entities:

> We talked of structures and their systems, of inputs and outputs, of control devices and of managing them, as if the whole was one huge factory. Today the language is not that of engineering but of politics with talk of cultures and networks of teams and coalitions, of influences and power rather than of control, of leadership not management. It is as if we had suddenly woken up to the fact that organisations were made up of people after all, not just 'heads' or 'role occupations'. (Handy, 1989: 71)

What each of these new metaphors has in common, then, is a concern with looser and more agile organizational forms which are better able to 'go with the flow', which are more open to a world which is now figured as complex and ambiguous, and with the production of subjects who can fit these forms (du Gay, 1996).

Amongst the sources of the new international discourse of managerialism can be counted the following. First, the business organization's 'environment' is figured as multiple, complex and fast-moving, and therefore as 'ambiguous', 'fuzzy' or 'plastic'. Of late, most of the inspiration for such a description has come from non-linear systems theory, and especially from the work of authors like Casti, Prigogine, and the like (see *Journal of Management Inquiry*, 1994). Second, the business organization is seen as attempting to form an island of superior adaptability in this fast-moving environment. This it achieves in a number of ways, which, taken together, constitute the international business community's 'linguistic turn'. Most particularly, it attempts to generate suitable *metaphors* which allow it to see itself and others in a distinctive (but always partial) fashion (Morgan, 1986; 1993). It tries, as well, to *embody* these metaphors in its workforce, a goal which it achieves via a number of means, including experiential learning, learning which involves placing the workforce in situations which demand co-operative responses to the uncertain and unknown (Martin, 1994). The organization also pays close attention to the resources of *tacit* (familiar but unarticulated) *knowledge* embodied in its workforce and to the generation of trust, both within its workforce and with other organizations. Work on tacit knowledge has been almost entirely generated from the writings of Michael Polanyi (Botwinick, 1996) (rather than, for example, Heidegger, Merleau-Ponty or Bourdieu) who, in turn, drew on the ideas of gestalt psychology. Polanyi's (1967: 20), most famous saying 'we can know more than we can tell' has become a vital part of business discourse, as a way into the problem of mobilizing the full resources of a workforce. In turn, Polanyi's work has underlined the need to generate *trust* or (as Polanyi often called it) confidence, since 'the overwhelming proportion of our factual beliefs continue . . . to be held at second hand through trusting others' (Polanyi, 1958: 208). Third, the business organization must therefore be framed as a flexible entity, always *in action*, 'on the move, if only stumbling or blundering along' (Boden, 1994: 192), but stumbling or blundering along in ways which will allow it to survive and prosper, most particularly through mobilizing a culture which will produce traditions of learning (collective memories which will act both to keep the organization constantly alert and as a reservoir of innovation (Lundvall, 1992)) and extensive intra- and inter-firm social networks (which will act both as conduits of knowledge and as a means of generating trust). Fourth, the business organization is seen, as has already been made clear, as a cultural entity, which is attempting to generate new traditions, new representations of itself and the world, and increasingly, an ethical stance towards the world because the link between knowledge (as a political economy of information refigured as a culture) and power has been made crystal-clear (Pfeffer and Salancik, 1978; Pfeffer, 1992). In other words, the business organization is increasingly built on 'a refusal to accept established knowledge' (Kestelholn, 1996: 7).

Fifth, the business organization must be made up of willing and willed subjects. Thus Foucault's pastoral mode of discipline makes its way into the business organization as a set of new definitions of what it is to be a person:

> Breathing strange new life into the old artistic ideal of the 'organic' – of 'the cultivated moral personality' and 'life as a work of art' . . . characterises work not as a painful obligation impressed upon individuals, nor as an activity only undertaken by people for instrumental purposes, but as a vital means to self-fulfilment and self-realisation. As Kanter (1990: 281) comments, life in the entrepreneurial corporation has 'a romantic quality'.
>
> By reorganizing work as simply part of that continuum along which 'we' all seek to realise ourselves as particular sets of person-outcomes, self-regulatory, self-fulfilling individual actors – 'enterprise' seeks to 're-enchant' organised work by restoring to it that which bureaucracy is held to have crassly repressed: emotion, personal responsibility, the possibility of pleasure, etc. (du Gay, 1996: 25)

As important, in some ways, as the new managerialist discourse itself has been the growth of the agents responsible for its spread across the globe. Together, they form an emergent and increasingly powerful 'cultural circuit of capital' which has only existed since the 1960s. This circuit, which is now self-organizing, is responsible for the production and distribution of managerial knowledge to managers. As it has grown, so have its appetites. It now has a constant and voracious need for new knowledge. Chief amongst the producers of the managerial discourse which this circuit disseminates are three institutions: business schools, management consultants and management gurus.

Through the 1960s, 1970s and 1980s formal business education, and especially the MBA course, has produced a large number of academics and students who act both to generate and transmit the new knowledge (Alvarez, 1996). In the United States, admittedly the most extreme example, almost one in four students in colleges and Universities now majors in business while the number of business schools has grown five-fold since 1957 (Kogut and Bowman, 1996: 14). In the top business schools, academics compete with one another to teach students *and* to produce new ideas. Some of these leading schools are now run as *de facto* companies. For example, at Wharton, the Dean, Thomas Gerrity, has tried to put business process re-engineering into operation:

> In companies re-engineering makes a big fuss of tearing down what it calls functional chimneys and reallocating staff to teams. Mr Gerrity has divided both his students and his professors into teams of six: each student team

includes at least two non-Americans; each faculty team includes professors from different academic disciplines. Both are evaluated in teams. Mr Gerrity has also torn down the barriers that divide the school from the University and from the business world. Students now offer consultancy to other parts of the University (on how to bring medical technology to market (for example)) and to local businesses. They also study fluffy things like leadership, to the chagrin of many academics but the delight of businesses.

As with other re-engineering exercises, a number of things introduced in its name look like common sense dressed up in fancy language (students are now sent abroad for 'global immersion'). Mr Gerrity has changed the system for granting tenure and awarding annual pay rises in order to shift the emphasis from publishing academic articles (once the only road to success) to teaching and 'leadership'. He has hired a policy firm, Opinion Research, to survey opinion among his constituencies. He has introduced a system of mentoring, so that senior professors can show their juniors how to teach, and quality circles, so that students can tell their teachers what they think of them. (*The Economist*, 13 April 1996: 83)

Another generator and distributor of new knowledge has been management consultancy (Clark, 1995). Management consultancy is, without doubt, a growth industry:

Between 1970 and 1980, the revenue of management consultants registered with the Management Consultants Association doubled; from 1980 to 1987 it increased fivefold. In the UK, over the eleven years 1980–1991 the number of consultants registered with the MCA more than quadrupled to 6963 and their fees increased almost seventeenfold. By the early 1990s there were reported to be 100,000 consultants world-wide. Growth figures in recent years for major players in the global consultancy game confirm the continuing acceleration in business from the late 1980s. Thus the largest company, Andersen Consulting, has been posting 9 per cent growth regularly (and as high as 19 per cent in the recession year of 1992). The second largest player doubled revenue to $1.2 billion between 1987 and 1993. Coopers and Lybrand, third largest (but second in Europe), saw revenue grow 107 per cent over the five years to 1993, and by then had 66,000 staff in 125 countries. (Ramsay, 1996: 166)

Using VAT data Keeble et al. (1994) estimated that in 1990 the UK management consultancy industry comprised 11,777 firms with a combined turnover of a little over £2.5 billion. Management consultancies act as a vital part of the cultural circuit of capital. To begin with they provide ideas. For example, Arthur Andersen

has three research centres and a massive international database, to which all 40,000 consultants are supposed to contribute. The company spent nearly 7% of its budget, or $290 million, on training in 1995, more than any rival. To have a chance of becoming a partner, an Andersenite needs to have put in over 1000 hours of training – some of it at the company's 150-acre campus outside Chicago. (*The Economist*, 4 May 1996: 90)

Then, they are responsible for much of the packaging of management knowledge, usually producing formulas which can be applied over and over again in different situations. Using Latour's by now familiar vocabulary:

> each assignment provides consultants with an opportunity to project their special and distinctive competences to clients by 'bringing home' distant events, places and people. This is achieved by (a) rendering them *mobile* so that they can be brought back; (b) keeping them *stable* so that they can be moved back and forth without additional distortion; and (c) making them *combinable* so that they can be circulated, analgamated and manipulated (Latour, 1987b, p. 223). Legge (1994, p. 3) writes that this is precisely what management consultants do when they make the experience of (distant) firms accessible and combinable through the development of (in Latour's terms) equations or packages – such as McKinsey's decentralisation package, Hay MSL's job evaluation package or even Peters' eight rules of excellence. (Clark, 1995: 56)

In turn, to make these packages credible to exisiting and potential clients requires considerable international work, involving a diverse range of social skills (Clark, 1995). And this work is clearly successful. For example, Ramsay (1996) cites reports that, in an 18 month period stretching over 1994 and 1995, 94 of the top 100 British companies had used management consultants.

Then, there is one other major generator and distributor of new knowledge, the management guru (Huczynski, 1993; Micklethwait and Wooldridge, 1996). Gurus come in many shapes and sizes. Huczynski (1993) distinguishes between academic gurus like Michael Porter, Rosabeth Moss Karter, Theodore Levitt, John Kay, Gareth Morgan and Peter Senge, consultant gurus like James Champy, Peter Drucker, Tom Peters, John Naisbitt, and Kenich Ohmae, and hero-managers like Mark McCormack, Akio Morita, John Harvey-Jones, Donald Trump and Lee Iacocca. Then, there are other gurus who are less easy to classify, for example Benjamin Zander, conductor of the Boston Philharmonic, who provides inspirational lectures on music as a metaphor for management (Griffith, 1996).

These gurus often only run small operations. But, equally, their operations may be substantial. Most impressive of all is the leadership centre run by Stephen Covey in Provo, Utah.

> Having started ten years ago with a staff of two, the Covey leadership centre now employs 700 people and has annual revenues of over $70 million. Mr Covey is building a large campus to house it on the edge of Provo, his home town. But even in its current state, scattered about the town, the centre is a sleek business machine. Its staff are surrounded by enough technology to make a journalist salivate. They have an army of unpaid helpers, thanks to Mr Covey's insistence that the best way to learn his ideas is to teach them.

The centre is divided into three core businesses. The first is management training. Throughout the year high-fliers flock to Provo to spend a week reading 'wisdom literature', climbing mountains, discussing personal and business problems and forming into teams. The second is producing personal organisers. These are meant to help people set priorities – so much time for jogging, so much time for your mother-in-law – as well as organise appointments. The third is spinning out new ideas. The centre has a second best seller, 'Principle Centred Leadership'; and a third in preparation, the 'Seven Habits of Highly Effective Families'. (*The Economist*, 24 February 1996: 106)

There is no strong dividing line between business schools, management consultancies and management gurus. For example, Thomas Gerrity, the Dean of Wharton, was formerly a member of CSC Index, the consultancy which produced the idea of 'business process re-engineering' and which is now retailing notions of 'organizational agility'.

Whatever is the case, it is clear that it is these three institutions that are responsible for producing the bulk of management knowledge. That knowledge chiefly comes in the form of a succession of 'business fads' (Lorenz, 1989), of which there have now been a remarkable number. Between 1950 and 1988, for example, Pascale (1991) noted 26 major fads. Certainly the roll call includes quality circles, the paperless office, the factory of the future, intrapreneurship, brands, strategic alliances, globalization, business process re-engineering (including 'core competences'), employability and more recently, nascent fads and fashions like organizational agility and the accelerating organization (Maira and Scott-Morgan, 1996) complexity theory.

In turn, these ideas have to be distributed. The channels and means of distribution are multiple. First of all, of course, there are the business schools, which teach students the new ideas, the management consultants, constantly presenting clients with new ideas and ways of doing things, and the management gurus, taking fees and retainers, to distribute their insights. Then, second, there is a rapidly growing business media industry which packages and distributes this knowledge. Management knowledge sells, most particularly since the establishment of the non-academic management book in the early 1980s. Yet these kinds of figures are now being surpassed. For example, Stephen Covey's 'Seven Habits of Highly Effective People' has sold more than five million copies world wide since its publication in 1989 (*The Economist*, 24 February 1996: 106) and is currently available in 28 languages in 35 countries (it is doing particularly well in China and South Korea). Hammer and Champy's *Re-engineering the Corporation*, published in 1993, had sold two million copies worldwide by September 1996, and had been translated into 17 languages. Of course, management knowledge is not just diffused via books (and, increasingly tapes and videos). Journals like *Fortune, Business Week*, the *Harvard Business Review* and others also dispense such knowledge, as do myriad trade journals. Most broadsheet newspapers also have management knowledge pages (for example, the *Financial Times*, which can claim to be a global business newspaper, started a 'Management Brief' page in 1994 and also produced a major 26 part series on the current state of management knowledge in 1996) (see Crainer, 1995). There are also now a number of specific television programmes which communicate management knowledge.

Finally, there is one more means of dissemination which is particularly important in the case of management knowledge. This is the management seminar, which is a mixture of drill and, increasingly, religious revivalism. Such seminars are big business across the world. For example, in 1990 Borks and Swet estimated that corporations in the United States spent $30 billion on business training in general. There are many kinds of seminar, of course. There are, to begin with, the modest seminars which import skills, usually offered by training companies or management consultants.

> Their advertising literature about short seminars and courses emphasises personal and interpersonal techniques. Such offerings include seminars such as 'Time Management International', 'Liberating Leadership Team', Leadership Development's, 'Close that Sale', Karrass's 'Effective Negotiating' [named after the management guru Dr Chester Karass] and the one day seminars from Career Track with talks such as 'Management skills for Technical Professionals' and 'How to Set and Achieve Your Goals'. Attendance at these seminars is substantial if the firm's publicitity literature is to be believed. The 'Close that Sale!' seminar claims 59,000 participants from 70 companies. Time Management International claims that 28,000 people participated in its worldwide series of seminars during 1986. Finally, Effective Negotiating claims a world-wide participation rate of 150,000. Such courses are usually of one day's duration. They are offered at a low fee and attract a high attendance, often over one hundred people. They feature a 'high energy' presenter and offer their audiences 'tested techniques' and 'proven skills'. (Huczynski, 1993: 186)

But there are also high-profile series of seminars featuring management gurus, often stretching over two or three days, which communicate knowledge which is not easily standardized. Thus, Byrne (1986) reported on a type of executive seminar called a 'skunk camp'. The similarity between his description of it and a religious retreat is instructive. The 'holy man' leading this event was Tom Peters, the co-author of one of the world's best selling business books. The cost to each participant's company was $4000, and at this particular event the day began with a group jogging session. Following a communal breakfast, the members gathered in the conference room 'waiting for enlightenment'. Byrne reported:

> In walks our rumpled leader. Head down, hands in the pockets of his brown shapeless cords, he paces relentlessly. His voice climbs to the treble clef as he runs through the litany. 'Dehumiliate. . . . Get rid of your executive parking

spots. . . . Get everybody on the same team. . . . There are two ways to get rich: superior customer satisfaction and constant innovation.'

Byrne's description has similarities with one reported by Huczynski (1993) of a Just-in-Time seminar run by Eli Goldratt (co-author of the book, *The Goal*):

> Goldratt appeared promptly at 9.15am, and in contrast to all the delegates who were wearing suits, he wore neither a jacket nor a tie and was wearing a skull-cap and open-toed sandals. He began by saying he had no prepared slides or any notes. The expression 'the cost world' was used to denote the old order and the 'through put world' to denote the new one. Towards the end of the session, Goldratt threw out the question, 'where shall we begin the improvement?'. The audience responded with a chorus of cries of 'Us', 'Ourselves' and other similar expressions. (Huczynski, 1993: 44–5)

Often, seminars will include books or videos in the price, so that a seamless web of production and reinforcement of ideas is produced.

Increasingly, seminars are being produced on an extraordinary scale. For example, in September 1996 Stephen Covey, Tom Peters and Peter Senge combined forces in an interactive 'supergroup' presentation on 'How to make your team unstoppable', broadcast by satellite to 30,000 people in 250 cities in 40 countries around the world (in Britain the venue was Birmingham at a cost of £199 per person).

Then, finally, there are management 'audiences'. How many seminars, and of what type, do they attend? What do they get out of them? What do they read and what sense do they make of their readings? How is the knowledge they gain from seminars and readings inscribed in management practices? It is fair to say that we know remarkably little about this aspect of the capitalist circuit of cultural capital: there are only very small amounts of audience research (but see Engwall, 1992). Instead, we have to infer the character and motivations of audiences from general trends, and the few studies there are. Thus, first, we know that managers are becoming better educated almost every-where. For example, 'as more managers complete MBA-type pro-grammes, they become more sophisticated, and are able to understand and apply more complicated management ideas' (Huczynski, 1993: 48). Second, it is clear that managers do read more books (and listen to tapes and watch videos) than previously. Third, at the same time, through the increased 'packaging' of ideas in seminars and books, management ideas have become more accessible. Fourth, managers clearly want and need new ideas. They need them to make their way in organizations, to solve particular company problems, to act as an internal motivational device, to guard against their competitors' adoption of new ideas, and simply to provide a career enhancer. In the latter case, the new idea demonstrates to others that the manager is creative, up-to-the minute and actively seeing improvements, thereby increasing that individual's visibility in the organization. Equally, the new idea can act as a defence, can provide a quick-fix solution in a difficult period, or can even simply reduce boredom (Huczynski, 1993). Fifth, the management book or seminar can act to raise or boost levels of belief. Thus, attendees at seminars by management gurus may have already read all the ideas in books, but this is not the point:

> Managers may attend Tom Peters' seminars to become immersed in his personality. In fact, if he was not to say what they have already read, they would come away disappointed. . . . One executive at a leading multinational talks of needing his 'Drucker fix' every two years. (Huczynski, 1993: 201)

Again, seminars may retail experiences of such intensity that they change the terms of what it means to be a person, as can happen in experiential seminars. For example, Martin (1994) documents how the initial cynicism of some participants in these kinds of seminar is gradually overtaken by the experience of the seminar. Sixth, and finally, more managers are now women. Some commentators have argued that much of the change in the metaphorical framing of modern capitalism is a result of the feminization of management knowledge which, at least in part, results from the greater presence of women in management and the workforce (Clegg and Palmer, 1996).

To summarize, what seems clear is that managers themselves search for four main qualities from management knowledge (Huczynski, 1993). The first of these is predictability:

> managers want to find ideas that make a constantly changing environment less confusing and threatening; for however brief a period. In order that they do not appear as part of the problem of constant change, management ideas are packaged so that they can be perceived as something already known but able to be reprioritised. The most popular management ideas seem to be those which successfully integrate a number of ideas into a single bite-size whole. The second quality is *empowerment*. Managers want to be told which ideas will achieve what results and which techniques are to be associated with the actions; managers want 'permission' from accredited sources to act. Third, managers want *esteem*. One way of achieving this is to be seen as the champion of a management idea or ideas. In a number of companies, the promotion of the latest management fad by managers has been used to help them gain company-wide visibility in the promotion stakes. Management idea championing can represent a low-risk way of signalling to those with the power to promote that managers are not averse to change, do not mind challenging established views, but that while they are prepared to look critically at the system in which they work, they will not unduly 'rock the organisational boat'.
>
> Further esteem can be gained if the idea is not of the black-box variety, that is it offers (and is seen to offer) the championing managers the scope to make

their own contribution to it. Thus it then gives them greater ownership of the idea in the perception of others. It might be thought that this is a high-risk strategy, since the idea may fail to yield the expected benefits. [But] . . . assessments of success and failure tend to be very vague in this area, and all parties concerned have a vested interest in not admitting to failure. (Huczynski, 1993: 212–13)

Then, finally, managers want self-belief. Thinking about the self has a long history in management. For example, Kurt Lewin (1951) invented the so-called T-group, an early form of the encounter group which encouraged colleagues to expose their true feelings about each other, while Maslow's (1954) 'enpsychian' management and McGregor's (1960) 'Theory Y' all emphasized 'the need as a human to grow spiritually'. In other words, managers, like many other contemporary individuals, have, for some time, been enjoined

to live as if running a *project* of themselves: they are to *work* on their emotional world, their domestic and conjugal arrangements, their relations of employment and the techniques of sexual pleasure, to develop a style of being that will maximise the worth of their existence to themselves. Evidence from the United States, Europe and the United Kingdom suggests that the implantation of such 'identity projects', characteristic of advanced democracies, is constitutively linked to the rise of a breed of new spiritual directors, 'engineers of the human soul'. Although our subjectivity might appear our most intimate sphere of experience, its contemporary intensification as a political and ethical value, is intrinsically correlated with the growth of expert languages, which enable us to render our relations with our selves and others into words and into thought, and with expert techniques, which promise to allow us to transform ourselves in the direction of happiness and fulfilment. (Rose, 1996: 157)

This emphasis on self-belief as a function of personal growth is perhaps best exemplified by the growth of New Age training which attempts to import New Age ideas via techniques like dancing, medicine wheels, and the use of the I Ching (Heelas, 1991a; 1991b; 1992; 1996; Rupert, 1992; Huczynski, 1993; Roberts, 1994; Rifkin, 1996). New Age thinking has become popular in management for a number of reasons. To begin with, its world view, which draws on not only eastern and western spiritual traditions but also quantum physics, cybernetics, cognitive science and chaos theory, chimes with the Genesis discourse. Then, its emphasis on personal development fits with the rise of 'soft skills' like leadership, intuition, vision and the like. In turn, New Age's stress on changing people works in with attempts to change the management (and workforce) subject, particularly because changing oneself or others seems a feasible and certain task compared with many others that management faces.

Most generally, the idea is to transform the values, experiences and to some extent the practices of what it is to *be* at work. The New Age Manager is imbued with new qualities and virtues, new in the sense that they differ from those found in the unenlightened workplace. These have to do with intrinsic wisdom, authentic creativity, self-responsibility, genuine energy, love and so on. Trainings are held to effect this shift. Furthermore, work itself is typically seen to serve as a 'growth environment'. The significance of work is transformed in that it is conceived as providing the opportunity to work on 'oneself'. It becomes a spiritual discipline. (Heelas, 1996: 90)

Whatever the case, New Age training is a big business. For example, the New Age think tank, Global Business Network is underwritten by major companies like AT and T, Volvo, Nissan, and Inland Steel. Some companies like Pacific Bell, Procter and Gamble, Du Pont and IBM, offer, or have offered, their employees 'personal growth experiences' in-house. Thus, IBM provides 'Fit for the Future' seminars which introduce employees to the *I Ching*. It is claimed that this links internal intuitions with external events. IBM's manager of employee development is quoted as saying that 'it helps employees understand themselves better' (Huczynski, 1993: 57). The list goes on:

Other organisations include those run by Tishi (follower of one of Muktunanda's successors, who has recently, and somewhat controversially, brought the 'Values and Vision' training to Harper Collins in Britain), Branton Kenton's Human Technology Consultants, Emerge (which has worked with Virgin Retail), I and O, Transform Ltd (partly inspired by Rudolf Steiner), the Creative Learning Consultants, Potentials Unlimited, The Results Partnership Ltd, Keith Silvester's Dialogue management training services (influenced by Psychosynthesis), Impact Factory (running the 'Money Factor'), Dave Baun's 'Charisma Training', and Anthony Robbins' 'Unleash the Power Within' weekends. The recently opened London Personal Development Centre alone claims to provide '300 courses, workshops, seminars, and lectures', 'designed to bring new creativity and vision to business'. (Heelas, 1996: 64)

In Britain, New Age training therefore also crops up, often in unlikely places. For example, the Bank of England, British Gas, Ernst and Whinney, Mars, and Legal and General have all sent executives to be taught how to do the Whirling Dervish dance, so as to allow their top managers to find inner peace and so increase the business potential. Then again, 'the Scottish Office sent thousands of its employees on "New Age Thinking" courses run by Louis Tice of the Pacific Institute which aimed to train the minds of workers to make them "high performance people" in their work and private lives' (Huczynski, 1993: 56). Meanwhile Decision Development, a British New Age training company, was offering to boost the spiritual, emotional, and creative powers of clients. The company uses the American Indian Medicine Wheel 'to take managers on a journey to discover their spiritual, emotional and creative self. The wheel allegedly enables trainees to access their inner selves by examining their dreams and fantasies' (Huczynski, 1993: 56). Another company uses 'an inward-focussed version of outdoor activities which involves mythical aspects of the "Dungeon and Dragons" variety where managers dress as druids and witches to find a magic elixir to revive a dying child' (Huczynski, 1993: 56–7). Some of these companies are currently using *The Celestine Prophecy* as a focus for training (Redfield, 1994), and this is to ignore the use of *Star Trek* as a managerial primer (Roberts and Ross, 1995).

What, then, is the task of the reinvented manager in this newly figured world? The new managerialism depends on the notion that the world is uncertain, complex, paradoxical, even chaotic (*Journal of Management Inquiry*, 1994). The manager must somehow find the means to steer a course in this fundamentally uncertain world, which she or he does by six main means (for a comprehensive review, see Ghoschal and Bartlett, 1995). First of all, there is an emphasis on the competitive advantage, in a business world that is increasingly constituted by information, that is incurred by knowledge. Whereas managers

> used to think that the most precious resource was capital, and that the prime task of management was to allocate it in the most productive way, now they have become convinced that their most precious resource is knowledge and that the prime task of management is to ensure that their knowledge is generated as widely and used as efficiently as possible. (Wooldridge, 1995: 4)

In Drucker's (1988: 16) famous words, 'Knowledge has become the key economic resource and the dominant, if not the only source of comparative advantage.' Second, the task of the manager is increasingly seen as the harnessing of extant organizational knowledge and the generation of new organizational knowledge, most especially by tapping the existing tacit skills and talents of the workforce, and then enhancing these competencies and by stimulating critical thinking skills which can overcome established prejudices: informally by providing greater communication between workers within the organization so that beneficial practices spread, and formally by instituting means of gaining further qualifications and the institution of strategic conversation (Badaracco, 1991; Leonard-Barton, 1995; Roos and van Krogh, 1996). Third, the manager no longer aims to produce an overall corporate strategy which is then mechanistically instituted in and through a corporate bureaucracy. Rather, the aim is to produce an emergent 'evolutionary' or 'learning' strategy which is 'necessarily incremental and adaptive, but that does not in any way imply that its evolution cannot be, or should not be analysed, managed, and controlled' (Kay, 1993: 359). Such a strategy will be based on what are seen as the particular capabilities of a business organization, which are then amplified via informal methods of control which rely on a much greater grasp of the issues involved, and which also mean that whole layers of bureaucracy, most of whose time was taken up with oversight, can be shrunk or, in the jargon, 'delayered' (Clarke and Newman, 1993). Fourth, in order to achieve evolutionary strategies, and informal control, the manager has to become a kind of charismatic itinerant, a 'cultural diplomat' (Hofstede, 1991), constantly imbuing the business organization's values and goals, constantly on a mission to explain and motivate an increasingly multinational and multicultural workforce in an increasingly global firm. Not surprisingly, such a task of producing affective effects is not easy. In an earlier study, Mintzberg (1973) found that managers spent between a half and three quarters of their time simply talking to people. Stewart (1976: 92) for example, found that 'Management is a verbal world whose people are usually instructed by personal contact rather than on paper'. Much of the rest of the time, they spent travelling, spending as much as three out of every four weeks on business trips as they personally try to weave the culture of their organization together. In other words, the example of these studies shows that the chief business of business organizations is talk, talk and then more talk in order to achieve some measure of agreement (Boden, 1994); 'conversations are the backbone of business' (Roos and van Krogh, 1995: 3). Or to put it another way,

> most of what managers do is discourse: it consists of discussion, ordering, synthesizing, presenting, reporting – all activities that take place through the media of various texts and representations of immediate co-presence. Management mostly concerns words that do things, presented in many various arenas, sometimes personally, sometimes impersonally, sometimes in role, sometimes unscripted and unwarranted by the roles that exist already, the narratives already written. Management, above all, is a performative activity: it does what it says and it says what it does: its utterances and its actions are so frequently fused, so politically meshed. (Clegg and Palmer, 1996: 2)

Fifth, the manager must not only weave the organization together but must also ensure that, through dedicated networking, she or he can produce and sustain external relationships of trust with other firms, which become vital conduits of information and future business. Through her or his interpersonal skills and cultural sensitivity, the manager not only builds an internal but also an external relational 'architecture' (Kay, 1993). Thus, and sixth, management is no longer seen as a science. Rather, it becomes an art form dedicated to 'the proposition that a political economy of information is in fact coextensive with a theory of culture' (Boisot, 1995: 7). In other words, the manager sets out to re-enchant the world (du Gay, 1996).

Thus, as writers as different as Sampson (1995) and Buck-Morss (1995) have noted, the rational company man of the 1950s and 1960s, skilled in the highways and byways of bureaucracy, becomes the corporate social persona of the 1990s, skilled in the arts of social presentation and 'change management'. And the giant multidivisional corporation of the 1950s and

1960s now becomes a 'leaner', 'networked', 'post-bureaucratic', 'virtual' or even 'post-structuralist' organization, a looser form of business which can act like a net floating on an ocean, able to ride the swell and still go forward. (Drucker, 1988; Eccles and Nohria, 1990; Heckscher and Donnellon, 1994).

The managerial discourse is undoubtedly an exaggeration that, in turn, exaggerates its own importance (Knights and Murray, 1994). For a start, it reflects 'cultural variations' which are not just variations but root and branch differences. The Japanese firm, with its cultural emphasis on informal reciprocity, is quite clearly a different animal from the US firm, with its emphasis on formal contract (Kay, 1995). And both types of firm are different from Overseas Chinese or European firms (Thrift and Olds, 1996). Then again, it overstates the degree to which it has been adopted: many business organizations remain bureaucratic, monolithic, and decidedly non-consensual.

But, what seems clear is that this 'new managerialism' is becoming the hegemonic account, both of what the post-Bretton Woods business world is like, and of how best to exercise corporate power within it, across the world:

It has contributed to some changes in management practice (however unevenly) and forms of organisational transformation. It has also provided a new and distinctive language of management which has played a significant role in legitimating claims to both organisational and social leadership. (Clarke and Newman, 1993: 438)

Most importantly of all, perhaps, the new managerialist discourse has empowered its managerial subjects by presenting them with an expanded opportunity to dream 'global dreams' (Barnet and Cavanagh, 1995). New forms of managerial subject are being produced through the application of an odd mixture of the 'psy disciplines' (Rose, 1996), New Age, and the like. Most particularly, these subjects are being taught to internalize the world as theirs in which to operate with self-esteem and self-confidence (French and Grey, 1996). As Strathern (1995a: 179–80, my emphases) puts it, appropriating actor-network theory:

How large, Latour asks, is IBM? An actor of great size, mobilising hundreds of thousands of people, it is always encountered via a small handful. . . . We never in this sense leave the local. The local is not just the people you talk to at IBM or BP but the desks, the paperwork, the connections distributed through the system, that is, the instruments that create a global field. From this point of view it makes no sense to go along with the literalism, that 'global' is bigger than 'local'. It is simply where one is at. But if one never leaves the local where is the global? It has to be the infinitely recurring *possibility* of measurement – not the scales but *the capacity to imagine them*.

As part of their ability to act, pressed into operation as design or intention, people's sense of scale produces a reflexive sense of context or locale. That is, it is a capacity which prompts comparisons, whether of commensurate things (along one scale) or of things not reducible to a common scale at all. Either way, we can imagine that it enlarges the world. . . . If so, we may take such scaling as a technique for knowing oneself to be effective (have relational effects: Law, 1994, pp. 102–3) regardless of agency. . . . Anthropologists will never understand the power of those who think the world is their market . . . unless they appreciate *the energising effect of such expanded horizons*. The expanded horizon, like the world view, is *how things are made effective locally*.

Conclusions: the hard edge of soft capitalism

The near-hegemony of this new managerialist discourse has three main consequences, each of them uncomfortable. The first is that it has what used to be called 'material consequences', effects that can be measured out in terms of pain, heartbreak, and shattered lives. Business organizations that take the managerialist discourse on board often become involved in programmes of direct 'downsizing', cutting back on the workforce with all the human misery this brings, made more of a shock, perhaps, because so many 'redundant' middle management 'layers' have been stripped out, as well as the jobs at the bottom of the occupational hierarchy which are always targeted and forfeited. Business organizations have also been involved in considerable indirect 'downsizing'; for example, through programmes that lay off significant numbers of subcontractors so as to produce a core network of closely allied firms. Then, not to be taken lightly, organizational change has brought with it other forms of stress and strain, from the 50 year old executive who is being shunted into a part-time consultancy to the new graduate who must downsize their expectations of a corporate career. In other words, this new form of the exercise of corporate power is not necessarily any 'nicer' than what has gone before; for all the caring rhetoric, lean can just as easily be mean, and learning can mean stomach-churning. The sword of management is, as always, two-edged: economic success is, now as then, brought at the cost of the workforce, as much as to its benefit. Most of the angst in the new managerialist discourse is produced by and for the middle class; not the working class.

Then there is a second consequence of this discourse. That is that, for all the commitment to an open-ended view of subjecthood, *in practice* the conception of the person (and the model of action) that is presumed is, more often than not, a narrow one which involves super-exploitation of both managers (who are expected to commit their whole being to the organization) and workers (who are now expected to commit their embodied knowledge to the organization's epistemological resources as well). In other words, the net effect may well be to reduce the different conceptions and comportments of the person which are to hand and, worse, to transfer these reduced conceptions and comportments to other spheres of life (du Gay, 1996).

There is a further consequence of this new managerialist discourse which returns me to the point from which the chapter started. It becomes even clearer (if this ever needed saying) that there is no intellectual community which can be separated off from other communities, in which the intellectual community has the power to decode the world, whilst all the other communities just slope ignorantly about. As Bauman (1987) has pointed out, the intellectual community has now moved from a position as legislator of the world to simply one of a number of interpretative communities. In the case of the relationship between the international intellectual and international business community this tendency has been strengthened by increased traffic between the two communities (for example, as a result of the growth of management education, and the increasing use of intellectual ideas in management), by the growth of an independent intelligence and analytical capacity within international business, and by the growth of the media as a powerful disseminator of and trader in ideas between the two communities: the cultural turn in the social sciences and humanities now has a direct line into, and indeed is a part of, the cultural turn in capitalism.

Acknowledgement

This chapter is a version of 'The rise of soft capitalism', published in *Cultural Values*, 1: 21–57, and is reproduced here with permission of Blackwell Publishers.

References

Alvarez, J.L. (1996) 'The international popularisation of entreprenerial ideas', in S. Clegg and G. Palmer (eds), *The Politics of Management Knowledge*, London: Sage.

Badaracco, J.L. (1991) *The Knowledge Link*, Cambridge, MA: Harvard Business School Press.

Badaracco, J. and Webb, A. (1995) 'Business ethics: the view from the trenches', *California Management Review*, 37 (2): 28–36.

Barnet, R.J. and Cavanagh, J. (1995) *Global Dreams: Imperial Corporations and the New Order*. New York: Simon & Schuster.

Bauman, Z. (1987) *Legislators and Interpreters*, Cambridge: Polity.

Boden, D. (1994) *The Business of Talk*, Cambridge: Polity.

Boisot, M.H. (1995) *Information Space: a Framework of Learning in Organisations, Institutions and Culture*, London: Routledge.

Botwinick, A. (1996) *Participation and Tacit Knowledge in Plato, Machiavelli and Hobbes*, Lanham: University Press of America.

Buck-Morss, S. (1995) 'Envisioning capital: political economy on display', in L. Cooke and P. Wollen (eds), *Visual Display: Culture Beyond Appearances*, Seattle: Bay Press, pp. 110–41.

Bud-Frierman, L. (ed.) (1994) *Information Acumen: the Understanding and Use of Knowledge in Modern Business*, London: Routledge.

Byrne, P. (1986) 'Business fads', *Business Week*, 20 January: 40–7.

Chandler, A. (1962) *Strategy and Structure*, Cambridge, MA: MIT Press.

Chandler, A. (1977) *The Visible Hand*, Cambridge, MA: Belknap Press.

Clark, J. (1995) *Managing Consultants: Consultancy as the Management of Impressions*, Buckingham: Open University Press.

Clarke, J. and Newman, J. (1993) 'The right to manage: a second managerial revolution?', *Cultural Studies*, 7: 427–41.

Clegg, S. and Palmer, G. (eds) (1996) *The Politics of Management Knowledge*, London: Sage.

Cohen, M.D. and Sproull, L.S. (eds) (1995) *Organisational Learning*, London: Sage.

Collins, H.M. (1990) *Artificial Experts: Social Knowledge and Intelligent Machines*, Cambridge, MA: MIT Press.

Collins, J. (1995) *Architectures of Excess: Cultural Life in the Information Age*, London: Routledge.

Crainer, S. (ed.) (1995) *The Financial Times Handbook of Management*, London: Pitman.

Drucker, P. (1988) 'The coming of the new organisation', *Harvard Business Review*, 88: 45–53.

Du Gay, P. (1996) *Consumption and Identity at Work*, London: Sage.

Eagleton, T. (1995) 'Review of Derrida's Spectres of Marx', *Radical Philosophy*, 73: 35–7.

Eccles, R. and Nohria, N. (1990) 'The post-structuralist organisation', *Harvard Business School Working Paper*, 92–1003.

Economist (1995) 'Trust in me', *The Economist*, 16 December 1983.

Emery, F. and Trist, E. (1965) 'The causal texture of organisational environments', *Human Relations*, 18: 21–32.

Engwall, L. (1992) *Mercury meets Minerva*, Oxford: Pergamon.

French, R. and Grey, C. (eds) (1996) *Rethinking Management Education*, London: Sage.

Ghoschal, S. and Bartlett, C.A. (1995) 'Changing the role of top management: beyond structure to process', *Harvard Business Review*, 73: 86–96.

Goffee, R. and Hunt, J.W. (1996) 'The end of management? Classroom versus boardroom', *Financial Times*, 22 March: 3–4.

Griffith, V. (1996) 'Creating virtuality', *Financial Times*, 22 November: 14.

Hammer, M. and Champy, J. (1993) *Re-engineering the Corporation: a Manifesto for Business Success*, London: Michael Brealey.

Handy, C. (1989) *The Age of Unreason*, London: Arrow.

Heckscher, C. and Donnellon, A. (eds) (1994) *The Post-Bureaucratic Organisation: New Perspectives on Organisational Change*, Thousand Oaks, CA: Sage.

Heelas, P. (1991a) 'Cuts for capitalism: self-religions, magic and the empowerment of business', in P. Gee and J. Fulton (eds), *Religion and Power: Decline and Growth*, London: British Sociological Association, pp. 27–41.

Heelas, P. (1991b) 'Reforming the self: enterprise and the character of Thatcherism', in R. Keat and N. Abercrombie (eds), *Enterprise Culture*, London: Routledge, pp. 72–90.

Heelas, P. (1992) 'The sacralisation of the self and New Age capitalism', in N. Abercrombie and A. Warde (eds), *Social Change in Contemporary Britain*, Cambridge: Polity, pp. 139–66.

Heelas, P. (1996) *The New Age Movement: the Celebration of the Self and the Sacralisation of Modernity*, Oxford: Blackwell.

Hill, S. and Turpin, T. (1995) 'Cultures in collision: the emergence of a new localism in academic research', in M. Strathern (ed.), *Shifting Contexts: Transformations of Anthropological Knowledge*, London: Routledge, pp. 131–52.

Hofstede, G. (1991) *Cultures and Organisations*, New York: McGraw-Hill.
Huczynski, A. (1993) *Management Gurus: What Makes Them and How to Become One*, London: Routledge.
Journal of Management Inquiry (1994) Special issue on chaos and complexity, *Journal of Management Inquiry*, 3 (4).
Kanter, R.M. (1990) *When Giants Learn to Dance*, New York: Routledge.
Kay, J. (1993) *Foundations of Corporate Success*, Oxford: Oxford University Press.
Kay, J. (1995) 'The foundations of national competitive advantage', *Fifth ESRC Annual Lecture*, London.
Kay, J. (1996) *Why Firms Succeed*, Oxford: Oxford University Press.
Keeble, D., Bryson, J. and Wood, P.A. (1994) *Pathfinders of Enterprise*, Milton Keynes: School of Management, Open University.
Kestelholn, W. (1996) 'Toolboxes are out; thinking is in', *Financial Times*, 22, March: 7–8.
Knights, D. and Murray, F. (1994) *Managers Divided: Organisation, Politics and Information Technology Management*, Chichester: Wiley.
Kogut, B. and Bowman, E.H. (1996) 'Redesigning for the 21st century', *Financial Times*, 22 March: 13–14.
Lash, S. and Urry, J. (1994) *Economies of Signs and Space*, London: Sage.
Latour, B. (1987a) 'The enlightenment without the critique: a word on Michel Serres' philosophy', in A.P. Griffiths (ed.), *Contemporary French Philosophy*, Cambridge: Cambridge University Press, pp. 83–97.
Latour, B. (1987b) *Science in Action: How to Follow Scientists and Engineers through Society*, Cambridge, MA: Harvard University Press.
Latour, B. (1993) *We Have Never Been Modern*, Brighton: Harvester Wheatsheaf.
Law, J. (1994) *Organising Modernity*, Oxford: Blackwell.
Legge, K. (1994) 'On knowledge, business consultants, and the selling of TQM', unpublished paper.
Leonard-Barton, D. (1995) *Wellsprings of Knowledge: Building and Sustaining the Sources of Innovation*, New Canaan, CT: Harvard Business School Press.
Lewin, K. (1951) *Field Theory in Social Science*. New York: HarperCollins.
Lorenz, C. (1989) 'The rise and fall of business fads', *Financial Times*, 24 June: 24.
Lundvall, B.A. (ed.) (1992) *National Systems of Innovation: Towards a Theory of Innovation and Interactive Learning*, London: Pinter.
McGregor, D. (1960) *The Human Side of Enterprise*, New York: McGraw-Hill.
Maira, A. and Scott-Morgan, P. (1996) *Accelerating Organisation*, New York: McGraw-Hill.
Martin, E. (1992) 'The end of the body?', *American Ethnologist*, 19: 121–40.
Martin, E. (1994) *Flexible Bodies: the Role of Immunity in American Culture from the Days of Polio to the Age of Aids*, Boston: Beacon Press.
Maslow, A.H. (1954) *Motivation and Personality*, New York: Harper.
Micklethwait, J. and Wooldridge, A. (1996) *The Witch Doctors: Making Sense of the Management Gurus*, London: Times Books.
Mintzberg, H. (1973) *The Nature of Managerial Work*, New York: Harper & Row.
Morgan, G. (1986) *Images of Organisation*, London: Sage.
Morgan, G. (1993) *Imaginisation: the Art of Creative Management*, London: Sage.
Morris, M. (1988) 'Banality in cultural studies', *Discourse X*, 10: 2–29.
Nohria, N. and Berkley, J.D. (1994) 'The virtual organisation: bureacracy, technology and the implosion of control', in C. Hecksher and A. Donnellon (eds), *The Post-Bureaucratic Organisation: New Perspectives on Organisational Change*, Thousand Oaks, CA: Sage, pp. 108–28.
Nonaka, I. and Takeuchi, N. (1995) *The Knowledge-Creating Company: How Japanese Companies Create the Dynamics of Innovation*, Oxford: Oxford University Press.
Pascale, T. (1991) *Managing on the Edge*, Harmondsworth: Penguin.

Perez, C. (1985) 'Microelectronics, long waves, and world structural change', *World Development*, 13: 441–63.

Peters T. (1989) *Thriving on Chaos*, London: Pan.

Pfeffer, J. (1992) *After Power*, New Canaan, CT: Harvard Business School Press.

Pfeffer, J. and Salancik, G.R. (1978) *The External Control of Organisations*, New York: Harper & Row.

Plant, S. (1996) 'The virtual complexity of culture', in G. Robertson, M. Mash, L. Tickner, J. Bird, B. Curtis and T. Putman (eds), *Futurenatural: Nature/Science/Culture*, London: Routledge, pp. 203–17.

Polanyi, M. (1958) *Personal Knowledge: Towards a Post Critical Philosophy*, London: Routledge and Kegan Paul.

Polanyi, M. (1967) *The Tacit Dimension*, London: Routledge and Kegan Paul.

Pollin, R. (1995) 'Financial structures and egalitarian economic policy', *New Left Review*, 214: 26–61.

Porter, M. (1990) *The Competitive Advantage of Nations*, New York: Macmillan.

Porter, T. (1994) 'Information, power and the view from nowhere', in L. Bud-Frierman (ed.), *Information Acumen: the Understanding and Use of Knowledge in Modern Business*, London: Routledge, pp. 217–30.

Ramsay, H. (1996) 'Managing sceptically: a critique of organization fashion', in S. Clegg and G. Palmer (eds), *The Politics of Management Knowledges*. London: Sage, pp. 155–72.

Readings, B. (1996) *The University of Ruins*, Cambridge, MA: Harvard University Press.

Redfield, J. (1994) *The Celestine Prophecy*, London: Bantam.

Rifkin, G. (1996) 'Finding meaning at work', *Strategy and Business*, 5.

Roberts, R. (1994) 'Power and empowerment: New Age managers and the dialectics of modernity/postmodernity', *Religion Today*, 9. 3–13.

Roberts, W. and Ross, B. (1995) *Make it So: Leadership Lessons from Star Trek, The Next Generation*, New York: Simon and Schuster.

Roos, J. and van Krogh, G. (1995) *Organisational Epistemology*, London: Macmillan.

Roos, J. and van Krogh, G. (1996) *Managing Knowledge: Perspectives on Cooperation and Competition*, London: Sage.

Rose, N. (1996) *Inventing Our Selves: Psychology, Power and Personhood*, Cambridge: Cambridge University Press.

Rupert, G. (1992) 'Employing the New Age: training seminars', in J. Lewis and J.G. Melton (eds), *Perspectives on the New Age*, Albany: State University Press of New York Press, pp. 127–35.

Sampson, A. (1995) *Company Man: the Rise and Fall of Corporate Life*, London: HarperCollins.

Stewart, R. (1976) *Contrasts in Management*, Maidenhead: McGraw-Hill.

Stiglitz, J.E. (1994) *Whither Socialism?*, Cambridge, MA: MIT Press.

Stopford, J. (1996) 'Managing in turbulent times', *Financial Times*, 22 March: 5–6.

Strathern, M. (1995a) 'Foreword', in M. Strathern (ed.), *Shifting Contexts: Transformations in Anthropological Knowledge*, London: Routledge, pp. 1–11.

Strathern, M. (1995b) 'Afterword', in M. Strathern (ed.), *Shifting Contexts: Transformations in Anthropological Knowledge*, London: Routledge, pp. 177–85.

Strathern, M. (1996) 'The new modernities', in J. Wassman and V. Keck (eds), *Common Worlds and Single Lives: Constituting Knowledge in Pacific Societies*, Cambridge: Cambridge University Press.

Thrift, N.J. (1985) 'Flies and germs: a geography of knowledge', in D. Gregory and J. Urry (eds), *Social Relations and Spatial Structures*, London: Macmillan, pp. 366–403.

Thrift, N.J. (1991) 'For a new regional geography 2', *Progress in Human Geography*, 15: 456–66.

Thrift, N.J. (1995) 'A hyperactive world?', in R.J. Johnston, P.J. Taylor and M. Watts (eds), *Geographies of Global Change*, Oxford: Blackwell, pp. 18–35.

Thrift, N.J. (1996a) *Spatial Formations*, London: Sage.

Thrift, N.J. (1996b) 'Shut up and dance, or, is the world economy knowable?', in P.W. Daniels and W. Lever (eds), *The Global Economy in Transition*, London: Longman, pp. 11–23.

Thrift, N.J. and Olds, K. (1996) 'Refiguring "the economic" in economic geography', *Progress in Human Geography*, 20: 736–54.

Whyte, W.H. (1957) *The Organisation Man*, New York: Basic Books.

Wooldridge, A. (1995) 'Big is back: a survey of multinationals', *The Economist*, 24–30 June: 1–22.

7

Changing the People: Social Engineering in the Contemporary Workplace

Paul Thompson and Patricia Findlay

It is virtually impossible to manoeuvre your way around a large manufacturing or service organization without hearing managers and even workers talking about 'the culture' and why it is or isn't being changed. Not since the heyday of motivation theory has an academic concept penetrated workplace life so deeply. And for all its popular usage, culture or the 'cultural turn' is indeed an intellectual product. For more than a decade now managerialists and social scientists alike have been making 'academic talk' of a paradigm shift from technical or bureaucratic modes of workplace regulation to culture and the management of meaning; from treating employees in a regimented and calculative manner, to winning their hearts and minds. This chapter has a very simple purpose – to analyse the nature of this contemporary form of social engineering and to evaluate the extent to which those who run organizations intend to and are effective in 'changing the people'.

It is tempting to dismiss outright the idea of a cultural *turn* when applied to work organizations. For much that goes on inside of modern (or, if you prefer, postmodern) organizations bears little resemblance to the management of meaning, unless we embrace the foolish and self-defeating notion that culture is everything. As we approach the end of the century, the experience of organizational life for most employees, including many professionals and managers, is characterized by tougher times in their work and employment. Within the labour process, there is expanded monitoring of tasks and work intensification; new technical and behavioural rules; extensive use of financial targets and controls, audits and assessments; structured systems, standardized packages and design procedures. The employment relationship is increasingly characterized by continual restructuring, downsizing, outsourcing and temporary contracts.

Some of this is new, at least in the form it takes, much of it shows considerable continuity with the past – that realm of 'traditional' organization when management was driven by command and control, not vision and values. Yes, it *is* tempting, if only to remove some academic heads from whatever cloud or sandpit they reside in. But it would be a mistake.

The culture club – something is going on

Culture 'talk' indicates that *something* is going on, even if it is not the replacement of traditional forms of regulation and restructuring. The term was brought into the public arena primarily through its association with a number of companies who proclaimed their distinctive corporate 'ways'. Though something like the HP Way was linked mainly to a value-driven approach, often drawn in some mystical manner from the life and sayings of Dave and Bill, Hewlett Packard's founders, it was always clear that these brand leaders reinforced the message through a distinctive set of recruitment, reward and control practices. These created and sustained highly individualistic employment relationships that were aimed at undercutting alternative and collective value systems whether built on occupational, professional or trade union bases. In other words 'strong cultures' were also highly instrumental and calculative in character. They did, however, also engage directly with aspects of people's sense of self, creating 'an exchange that is more than economic' (Kunda, 1992: 209). This management of the self works both ways. Employees are acted on, but they also have to pick up the cultural cues and construct an organizational self. Anyone who reads the best of the literature, such as Kunda's account of life at 'Tech', can see convincing evidence of how notions of culture begin to permeate the everyday perceptions and language of employees.

As the popularity of the approach spread, many more large companies joined the culture club. But very few had an agenda as sophisticated or practices that were as integrated as Hewlett Packard and IBM. The most common development was the attempt by large companies to undertake generalized change programmes, wrapped up in 'changing the culture' rhetoric. In substance, what they tended to be doing was to underpin corporate restructuring with a legitimacy-oriented value-driven message, or facilitating a change of business direction, for example from public to private utility. Such approaches have been seen as ways of breaking down older attachments to unions or conceptions of public service, as well as traditional functional divides.

Moving away from the all-purpose change process, culture has been associated with more specific initiatives such as customer care programmes in the service sector. The meaning of corporate culture in this context is primarily the provision of normative and behavioural scripts for new initiatives with customers or clients, again requiring some level of management of self and mobilization of emotional labour (Sosteric, 1996; du Gay, 1996). On a related terrain, 'TQM [total quality management] and other quality initiatives were often soaked in a rhetoric of cultural transformation' (Reed, 1996: 145). The rhetoric was aimed at both triggering and scripting new work practices and responsibilities. In turn it overlapped with human resources management (HRM) ideas in that the emphasis on mobilization of commitment was perceived to require internalization of values generated by the new corporate cultures (Legge, 1989; 1995; Guest, 1990).

This internalized commitment has been expected to happen in a variety of inter-related ways. Values are seen to cascade through the organization via mission statements, other documentation and meetings, generating a 'trickle-down' effect. This may be backed up by more-formal training programmes, for example in the case of teamworking or customer care, as well as specific, cross-functional project groups with responsibility for defining and disseminating the new values (Hope and Hendry, 1995; Marks et al., 1997a). Or the emphasis may be on a combination of value statements and transfer of responsibility, self-regulation providing the 'learning' mechanism. It is certainly the case that there are few large organizations now without mission statements, and many companies have invested time and resources in varieties of 'soft skills' training or 'normative re-education' (Rosenthal et al., 1997). Consultants are now adept at offering culture change workshops where employees are given the opportunity to 'question their old beliefs and experience the positive aspects of the culture being encouraged' (Ogbonna, 1992: 5).

The issue, therefore, is not so much whether anything is going on under the culture banner, but how to understand it. This is not merely a question of academic definitions. In all this activity there is considerable confusion over what changing the culture actually means. One aspect of this confusion has special significance for our argument in this chapter. In our own research on change programmes (Marks et al., 1997b), we noted the deployment of two rhetorics. In the first, culture signified creating a vision or set of shared values that would guide the change process generally. On the other hand, culture was also used to signify an inherited tradition or set of practices, normally identified as in need of transformation. Here, culture is grafted on as the term for the 'way we do things round here'. The important thing about this latter usage is that it can and often does exist independently of any explicit attempt to shape and change values. This differentiation of culture as practices and values overlaps with the oft-noted distinction between 'soft' and 'hard' notions of TQM or HRM (Legge, 1989; Wilkinson et al., 1992). What we are saying here is that despite its ideological provenance, culture talk may have little to do with the values and vision thing. This is worth keeping in mind for the subsequent discussion.

Retracing the steps

Having outlined very broadly what we think might be going on under the culture banner in organizations, this section aims to briefly re-trace the steps of how culture talk developed in the academic domain: first by looking at managerialist, then social science literatures.

Learning to love the company

Some sociologists and anthropologists have long been interested in organizational cultures, but have largely proceeded from the bottom-up, concerned to reveal the mosaic of subcultural meanings and practices beneath the formal. Management academics occasionally paid some attention to the more top-down dimension, but efforts such as Handy's (1976) distinction between role, task and person cultures were sporadic and had relatively limited impact. Pettigrew's (1979) article in *Administrative Science Quarterly* was more influential, but the big impact came in 1980 when Business Week led on its cover with a piece about corporate culture, and within a few years the bandwagon had truly begun to roll (Kennedy, 1996: 159–62).

The four key books of this period – Ouchi (1981), Pascale and Athos (1982), Peters and Waterman (1982) and Deal and Kennedy (1982) – brought 'organization man' out of the cold and back into fashion. Employees had to learn to love the company and companies had to give them good reasons for doing so. The promotion of culture as corporate glue and source of increased productivity was tied to a combination of a reading of the existing practices of US firms and that of the large Japanese corporations. The latter was particularly important, for as Dahler-Larsen (1994: 4) notes, 'The cross-national character of the problems of competitiveness has motivated a focus on *cultural* [emphasis in original] factors in this search for determinants of relative competitive advantages.' But looking through the Japanese lens alone could never have been acceptable. By developing a parallel reading through the experience of dynamic, high tech and service companies, corporate culture could be positioned as an integral feature of a new form of competitiveness, a vision which also resonated with the growth of entrepreneurial ideologies under New Right administrations in the US and UK (Silver, 1987; du Gay, 1991).

Thus the management writers engaged in a spot of retrospective product making, discovering the existence of 'strong cultures', allied to the formulas for reproducing them. In a very useful overview of the career of a concept, Parker argues that culture was constructed as a form of forgetting. Noting the extensive history of writings on what became labelled as 'culture' in management and sociology, he observes that, 'When Peters and Waterman, Deal and Kennedy, Ouchi and others began to write about organizational or corporate culture in the late

1970s and early 1980s it was if the idea had sprung from nowhere' (1998: 2). The extent to which corporate culture was indeed a product can be seen in the fact that all except Ouchi were connected to the leading consultancy firm, McKinsey. For those organizations that then embraced the idea that culture was a source of competitive advantage, to be initiated and managed, it becomes more a case of effect than cause. There is considerable dispute about how effective such a turn was, even among managerialists, but the culture club had many join its ranks, if for no other reason than that noted by Alvesson (1990: 38): 'On a corporate level having a distinctive "culture" of its own appears to have a symbolic value for corporations eager to appear progressive, modern and having a good public image.'

As the practice extended, at least on the surface, and an ever-growing number of consultants and HR practitioners fed at the honey pot (Thackray, 1986), so did the tentacles of the argument. An organizational idea increases its purchase when it can be packaged as part of a more general paradigm shift. From the mid-1980s managerialists began to intensify 'new economy' arguments characterized by a qualitative shift from bureaucratic, command and control organizations to high-trust relations and high-skill, empowered employees. Of necessity, culture became the perceived currency of the new arrangements because (alongside information technology) it facilitated the replacement of rules, hierarchies and centralized power. This was reinforced by the emphasis on knowledge as the key commodity in the post-industrial economy. The co-ordination of knowledge work and workers could not be vertical, but horizontal, collegiate and cultural (see Warhurst and Thompson, 1998). At the same time management writers promoted the idea that, as companies become more transnational, culture is the glue that binds the increasingly diverse activities and units together (Bartlett and Goshal, 1990).

The cultural turn in the workplace was therefore a heady and complex brew. But at its heart, both practically and theoretically was the link to commitment. By the end of the 1980s, commitment had replaced motivation as the new holy grail of management. It performs substantially the same functions for managers, who now agonize over whether employees have 'really bought in' to the message in the same way as talk of whether they were 'really motivated' used to dominate the interface between ideas and practices.

Learning to love the concept

A remarkably similar trajectory can be traced in social science writing on corporate culture. Just as employees were enjoined to love the company, many academics have gradually persuaded themselves to love the concept. It was not always like this. As charted elsewhere (Willmott, 1993; Thompson and Ackroyd, 1995), academics spent the first phase of

reaction demolishing it. This was not difficult given the limited conceptualization and superficial ways of gathering information via corporate
stories and slogans (see Thompson and McHugh, 1995: 209–12). A more
important and positive point was being made here, that a top-down
conception of culture was an impoverished one and violated everything
that serious research told us about the depth and plurality of cultures
and organizational symbolism. Cultures could neither be invoked,
created, changed nor even managed by corporate dictat (Smircich, 1983;
van Maanen and Barley, 1985; Meek, 1988; Anthony, 1990; Ackroyd and
Crowdy, 1990).

But not all critics followed the same path. If culture *could* be managed,
even partially, then it needed to be analysed as part of management's
armoury of controls. This favourite theme of radical commentators was
developed in a highly influential article by Ray (1986). Fusing together a
radical interpretation of Durkheim as progenitor of the enterprise as
sacred community, with use of labour process theory (LPT), she was able
to demonstrate that existing forms of bureaucratic and humanistic
regulation left control externalized and unable to generate sentiment or
emotion. In contrast, 'control by corporate culture views people as
emotional, symbol-loving, and needing to belong to a superior entity or
collectivity' (1986: 295).

Within this framework were the seeds of the cultural turn among
radical critics. For culture was not just another 'strategy', it could be the
ultimate form of control, the one that reached parts others could not. But
re-reading the piece now reminds us how circumspect Ray was. She
made clear that all this was *potential*. It may not work, it may not be
generalizable outside the USA, it was riven with contradictions, existed
alongside other controls, and workers could well resist it. Such qualifications were soon to be swept aside. For those who took up and
extended the 'ultimate' control argument saw corporate culture as part
of a much wider transformation of society and how we should view it.
In other words, the 'cultural turn' in the workplace perspective passed
into the hands of post-structuralists and postmodernists.

Not surprisingly given the emphasis on 'post', such theorists have
their own radical version of a paradigm shift, but, like the managerialists, culture is presented as the main currency of the new social relations.
For culture facilitates the shift from rule-based, bureaucratic forms, to the
new fluid flexibility of contemporary patterns of accumulation and post-
bureaucratic organization where employees follow values rather than
rules (see Willmott, 1993: 519; Garsten and Grey, 1997: 214). Nor is this
confined to organizational governance. The shift is a hegemonic political
project conjoining culture in the enterprise with the enterprise culture,
'In effect, its concerns are very much those of the Thatcherite project:
economic and moral revival through a programme of "cultural change".
Like Thatcherism, the "search for excellence" requires a veritable "cultural revolution", one in which organizations learn to "thrive on chaos"

(in the decentred global free market economy) and to renew continually their enterprising spirit' (du Gay and Salaman, 1990: 15).

Whether as workers or citizens, the shift is held to be effective on exactly the terms developed by managerial writers – its capacity to reach deeper and transform what and how people think and feel. Admittedly it is in a different and often Foucauldian language, the key phrase of which is the 'engineering of the soul'. This term, much repeated elsewhere, is particularly associated with the writings of Rose (1990). He argues that the twentieth century has seen the progressive infiltration of subjectivity by power. Organizations in workplace and society have, with the help of psychologists and other experts, increasingly produced the employee and citizen as a knowable person whose subjectivity is publicly constructed, observed and recorded, then internalized as self-discipline. As these interventions developed, 'The minutiae of the human soul – human interactions, feelings, and thoughts, the psychological relations of the individual to the group – had emerged as a new domain for management' (1990: 72). This may seem a long way from a 'cultural turn', but the 1980s are seen as marking a qualitative leap forward in revamping the 'psycho-technology of the workplace' (1990: 103) and fashioning the 'optimized autonomous subjectivity of the worker' (1990: 105).

In this context the rise of corporate culture is moved centre stage given that the theory and practice often have an explicit concern with emotional and social engineering. The best known exposition of the cultural power of corporations is made by Willmott (1993). In order to do so he must first persuade us to set aside the first generation of academic critics – now dubbed 'culture purists'. Willmott makes a powerful critique of such programmes as nascently totalitarian monocultures in which alternative values and sources of resistance are marginalized or squeezed out. But in doing so he affirms their effectiveness, not least because such mechanisms are not simply top-down, but are self-disciplinary, working in part through tying individual identity to the positive attraction of participation in practices which provide a sense of belonging. Like other theorists (Alvesson, 1991; Deetz, 1992; Casey, 1995), Willmott seeks to replace the language of control and coercion by that of *seduction*. In this brave new world, companies produce what Casey calls 'designer employees', through a process of discursive colonization of their selves at work and often at home. The seduction arises from the security of belonging to simulated communities. Echoing themes from Ray, Casey argues that in relation to her case study organization 'The new Hephaestus employee becomes somebody in his association with the reified company and through performance of his team-family work role' (1995: 189).

Casey's mention of teamworking reminds us that culture turn arguments are not confined to general corporate programmes. The themes of managerial intervention into the employees' soul and the construction of self-disciplining, productive subjects, have been taken up and turned into a critique of contemporary management control methods by a number of writers in a labour process tradition. We are presented with the familiar themes of panopticons, peer pressure, internalized surveillance and TQM as total management control (Sewell and Wilkinson, 1992a). What is produced technically by the electronic panopticon can also be produced socially from within the team in a process which 'operates directly on the subjectivity of individual members' (Sewell and Wilkinson, 1992b: 108). Drawing on their case study of cultural change and teamworking in Phoneco, McKinlay and Taylor extend this argument to its logical conclusion by arguing that the company had initiated a 'new cultural politics of production' and that the mobilization of commitment beyond consent is the 'definitive corporate agenda of late capitalism' (1998: 13–14).

From culture to subjectivity

We can see that the role of identity in the negotiation of cultural boundaries is a recurring theme. For some it is the main plot device. Reflecting perhaps a peculiarly British dimension to contemporary debates, Knights, Willmott and their associates have for a decade conducted a relentless campaign to insert the 'missing subject' into discussion of the labour process. This takes its cue from Braverman's well-known and misguided decision to exclude consideration of employees' subjective inputs or responses to the transformation of work. It may appear that this is tangential to the main purposes of this chapter, but it is not. Whereas the first part of our discussion has focused on the ways in which companies 'act on' people, what is at stake in the second key element in discussions of contemporary change processes is the other side of the equation – how do employees experience and respond to the cultural projects of management?

The core of this influential body of work (see Knights and Willmott, 1989 for the best summary, and O'Doherty and Willmott, 1998 for evidence of splits in the ranks) is a notion of *identity work* carried out by individuals. Bringing together influences that include Giddens and Foucault, it is argued that, in modern society, identity becomes a major preoccupation because the subject is constituted as both 'autonomous' and divided from others. Therefore there is a tension between the attempt to secure a stable identity and the particular conditions of modern life. In turn this renders them vulnerable to the expectations and demands of power.

An emphasis on the construction and crafting of a variety of selves within power–knowledge discourses means that identity is never fixed, but the *search* for secure and stable identity is presented as a constant, a 'pervasive existential project uniting quite differentiated subjectivities' (Collinson, 1992: 29). This attempt to create a sense of the ambiguity of human agency therefore appears, and to an extent is, a free floating, existential perspective. Moreover, it is frequently counterpoised to the standard, supposedly economistic concerns of orthodox labour process theory and industrial sociology. For a younger generation of researchers, control and resistance and the effort bargain are old hat to be replaced by concerns with 'the management of identity and security, and the subjugation and constitution of individuals through panopticism and cultural managerial discourse' (O'Doherty, 1994: 2). Nevertheless, the workplace remains in the picture because it is a key terrain for identity work, and this eternal struggle to realize self-identity helps to explain the interdependent relationships between capital and labour and employee identification with the goals of the enterprise. In terms of the debates in this chapter, the seduction circle is complete because the cultural intent of management meets employee desire in a mutually beneficial though, for radicals, destructive relationship.

Critique

This is a very large territory and we cannot respond to or cover everything in the rest of this chapter – for example, the arguments concerning culture as the 'glue' of corporate internationalization (but see Thompson et al., 1998). Suffice to say, we find the cosy convergence between managerialist and radical theorists to be based on very shaky foundations. We aim to show that the cultural turn in the workplace, though important, is not as novel, significant or effective as proponents believe.

Social engineering – more of a detour than a turn

Designer culture is being presented to us, to borrow Chandler's well-known formulation, as the new 'visible hand' of corporate life. The problem is that even the most cursory historical glance demonstrates a recurring interest in workplace social engineering. As Jacques (1996) has recently demonstrated, capital has always attempted in different ways to 'manufacture the employee', for example in the 1920s through 'welfare work' programmes in the USA. Indeed attempts to engender integration and loyalty through selected non-job benefits, company unions and workplace social communities were part of a move towards a welfare capitalist model (Edwards, 1979).

Britain had long had a tradition of corporate paternalism which reflected the interweaving of work and community life (Joyce, 1980). It has tended to be associated with small-scale family firms or socially conscious businesses such as Lever Brothers, and the Quaker-based Cadbury and Rowntree empires who believed in some kind of moral purpose and obligation. But as Ackers and Black (1991) convincingly demonstrate, a more sophisticated and widespread form of paternalism developed in the inter-war years that moved beyond 'traditional' forms of authority and small-scale family ownership. The important point is that these were culture strategies by any feasible definition and clearly aimed at employee's hearts and minds. They also manifested many of the feted characteristics of contemporary 'strong culture' companies in the support mechanisms such as internal labour markets and employment security.

This did not require or manifest an equivalent historical turn to cultural control mechanisms. The firms most concerned with social engineering in the USA and UK were often also the most innovative in the development of what was seen as other forms of 'scientific management', combining the 'cultural' with bureaucratic and technical controls. Like today, social engineering came in a variety of packages. US firms were more likely to pursue a unitarist agenda, while those in the UK were much quicker to accommodate to trade unionism.

Of course, as now, not everyone was in the culture club. But it was not a marginal phenomenon. Indeed the relatively stable period of economic expansion after 1945 facilitated a consolidation of the trend. Many large firms, even if not in strictly defined industrial towns or occupational communities, were embedded in their localities and drew on family networks and continuity of labour supply (see Thompson and McHugh, 1995: 207–9). Factories were often social regimes with mutual obligations and a network of personal relations and management styles. Interestingly, many such large firms in the UK evolved into a form of pluralist or bargained paternalism: strong, but not unitarist cultures which co-existed with trade unions and the management of other interests and identities (Ackers and Black, 1991: 48).

By the middle of the 1960s a number of factors were combining to undermine the conditions which sustained paternalistic pluralism. Long-term social and economic changes were beginning to displace the existing inter-relations between work, community and family. Firms were finding it more difficult to maintain traditional forms of management and co-ordination as their operations became more complex, large scale and dispersed over wider boundaries. In Britain a period of intense restructuring and rationalization took place encouraged by a modernizing Labour Government – manifested by greater concentration of capital, take-overs and mergers. Paternalistic pluralism was often a casualty of changes in forms of ownership and management. These changes coincided with a more general move towards 'hard systems' and formalistic, procedural processes in the organization of the labour process, industrial relations and decision-making.

So where does the re-birth of corporate culture described earlier come into the picture? While the 'discovery' was, as we have seen, filtered through the lens of Japan and new global competition, the adoption of culture strategies by many large organizations in the 1980s and beyond should also be seen as attempts to 'repair' the costs of a shift towards more explicitly calculative and instrumental relationships. Of course there were differences of context and characteristics of the managerial discourse. Influenced by the perceived 'best practice' of Japanese and US high-tech firms, the orientation was much more unitarist and hostile to rival cultures. In addition the rhetoric of commitment and human capital had largely replaced that of loyalty. But the fact remains that the 1980s developments were not so much a turn as a return to familiar themes in new languages. The period of systems-driven restructuring was the detour not the norm.

It is not difficult to imagine the objections from new paradigm theorists, whether from the managerialist or radical camp. Old-style corporate cultures, it might be objected, were built primarily on a passive ingredient – loyalty. The new regimes are based on something active and internalizable to values and feelings – commitment. One can see a conceptual difference, but it is not as simple as that. Firstly, loyalty is based on the mobilization of emotions and the capacity to coalesce company and subcultural identities. Secondly, as the corporate culture literature largely accepts, loyalty underpins commitment. Rhetorics of team and family, reported by Casey and Kunda, would be just that if unsupported by material mechanisms to tie employee interests to the firm. In this context, the mobile nature of capital and the tendency towards continual restructuring would appear to militate against sustaining cultural identifications. We will return to these themes later in the context of an examination of the character and context of contemporary change programmes.

Strong claims – weak evidence

The idea that current managerial initiatives and organizational change processes are producing a 'productive subject' is unsustainable on the evidence presented, though we are aware that for those who see no distinction between representation and reality, this may be a non-issue

There are a number of aspects to this. Too many claims are made of a top-down nature with little or no direct evidence. Frequently the problem is that assumptions about employees are read off from managerial subjectivity. The stated goals of senior management, or corporate discourses are too often *the* evidence. This tendency is revealed most starkly in Rose's *Governing the Soul*, which we discussed earlier. He presents us with an often fascinating and certainly wide-ranging account of the incorporation of the human sciences into managerial discourses in the workplace and at various levels and functions of the state. The overall theme is 'the development of new languages for speaking about subjectivity and new techniques for inscribing it, measuring, and acting upon it' (1990: x). But the discussion never moves beyond those languages.

Throughout the book it is difficult if not impossible to find any examples of whether or how any of these discourses were operationalized outside the text, or whether any concrete effects were observable on employee subjectivities or souls. As no difference between discourse and any other form of practice is acknowledged, Rose is able to state blithely that 'There is no longer any barrier between the economic, the psychological and the social' (1990: 118). The substantive invisibility of labour as an active subject runs alongside endless expositions of the activities of experts and their technologies of subjectivity. But even here there is a problem, for the decentring of the subject means that it is hard to locate agency. For example, Rose is keen to tell us that it is no longer necessary to talk of actual agencies or mechanisms of the state, but merely to refer to broader processes of governmentality (1990: 5). These are presented in typically excessive terms in which a conspiracy of connections substitutes for real people and practices: 'Networks of power were formed that brought every individual into the view of the public authorities and their field of action' (1990: 63).

Nor is Rose alone in simply inferring effects on subjectivity from processes of organizational restructuring. The labour process-oriented writing, mentioned previously, with its emphasis on surveillance and electronic panopticons, is also problematic. Even if we accept the notion of increasing personal and collective surveillance as part of contemporary organizational restructuring, it is a much bigger leap to sustain claims that the panoptic gaze 'operates directly on the subjectivity of individual members'. For example, in Sewell and Wilkinson's (1992b) case study of Kay Electronics, though words such as consent are bandied about, there is no direct evidence concerning the subjective experience of employees. We are merely told that workers put up little opposition to or did not dissent from the operations of disciplinary mechanisms.[1]

The second problem of weak evidence is that even where qualitative material is collected in case studies, it is often simply attributed to respondents' concerns with identity, concerns which are seen as distinct and discontinuous with traditional terrains of work and management. For example Grey deals with the process and effects of the annual 'cull' of employees in accountancy firms. This apparently involves the 'frenetic, surveillance of self and others for evidence of respective standing within the firm' (1994a: 8). In other words salary, job assignment and job ratings. All fairly conventional materialist stuff you might think. But no. Uncertainty about one's fate is intimately linked to an identity-driven project of the self (1994a: 15–16). There are no actual quotes or other primary material about employees against which these attributions of identity concerns are evaluated. McCabe and Knights (1995) give an account of the development of TQM in a large insurance company. The quotes from employees reveal how they cope with attempts to tighten control over time and effort. There is not the slightest indication of effects of new or old control techniques on their identity/ subjectivity. Yet in the aptly named following section, the authors go 'In Search of Subjectivity'. As always they find it, but only through theoretical attribution: 'the case of Inco indicates a complex web between staff subjectivity and staff responses to quality initiatives' (1995: 36); 'Staff will, of course, respond differently to these dialectical forces, their responses being bound-up with their sense of themselves and particular identities to which they are attached' (1995: 40).

The effects of gaps between strong claims and weak evidence, and the failure to acknowledge the difficulties in moving from discourse to practice, combine to reinforce the illusion of a high level of 'knowability' about employee subjectivity. Despite continued references to the need for a 'full theory' of the missing subject, it is, unfortunately, highly exclusive in character.[2] For all the references to unstable and precarious identities, we have been presented with an image of subjectivity as a very specific, identifiable phenomenon. Subjectivity is essentially about identity work; or more precisely, about the search for a secure identity within power relations. In this sense, the core analysis comes perilously close to essentialism or a notion of an essential project of the self. Yet this is a project that is largely attributed to the behaviour it describes, a theoretical construction about security with very insecure analytical and empirical foundations.

Rediscovering labour as a self-active subject

In the cultural turn and the search for subjectivity *labour* as a subject has gone missing. Management has become the central actor, the author of new initiatives and disciplinary practices which labour is subject *to*, or subjects *itself* to. There is, in other words, far too much emphasis on discourses or practice which operate *on* the subjectivity of labour, without labour as an alternative voice, with its own distinctive 'themes', 'accents' and meanings being centred (McNally, 1995: 18). Too often the language of Foucauldian-influenced researchers is of the 'good' or docile worker who adjusts to the techniques propounded by those who would engineer our souls (for example, see Rose, 1990: 11).

These problems are part of the explanation for the absence of any substantial recognition of resistance in applications of Foucauldian ideas to the labour process. Despite its formal place in the understanding of power relations, the role of resistance is under-theorized and seems to exist mainly as a reaction to and stimulation of power (Dews, 1986). No matter what the employee does at work as individual or collectivity, labour remains trapped in a seemingly self-defeating struggle against normalizing disciplines or by the search for ontological security (see Willmott, 1995: 22–3). Employees' own cultural resources in terms of their 'traditional' craft, occupational or class identities or forms of informal self-organization are seen as marginalized or destroyed by the onward march of new managerial discourses and the post-industrial self (see Casey, 1995: 179–97).

We don't have to go far to recover some notion of labour as a self-active subject. Indeed the search for subjectivity may not be quite as necessary as its proponents claim, in that attempts to construct a labour process orthodoxy that denied the importance of subjectivity are highly misleading. During the second wave of LPT the subject was (re)inserted in three main ways. First as a source of *opposition* to capital; hence the creation of the famed 'control-resistance paradigm'. Despite Braverman's (1974) underestimation of the role of worker resistance, the work of Edwards (1979), Friedman (1977), Edwards and Scullion (1982) and many others suggested that alternative forms of managerial control were reciprocally related to a variety of forms of worker resistance.

The second insertion was as a source of *creativity*, without which capital could not successfully transform labour power into profitable labour. Cressey and MacInnes (1980) clearly documented the limitations of the concept of the real subordination of labour, linking the central problem of the indeterminacy of labour power to labour's two-fold character. They note that capital employs labour primarily for its subjectivity, for that part of it which can never be defined or substituted, although they acknowledge that labour's subjectivity will not always be directed towards resistance. Similarly, Friedman's account of responsible autonomy acknowledges capital's reliance, to varying extents (depending on both competitive and labour market pressures), on the tacit skills and creative involvement of shop floor workers.

Third, labour as a subject was introduced as a source of *consent*. Burawoy's (1979) influential analysis focused on workers' participation in production games and routines, as well as its co-operation and interest in specific structural mechanisms, such as internal labour markets and internal states. On the surface, Burawoy gives a Marxist twist to the process of making out, with workers deriving relative satisfactions from games (such as pride and social prestige, reduction of fatigue and boredom, and a sense of power in relation to machinery), and, as a consequence of participation, actively contributing to the reproduction of social relations at work. But he broke genuinely new ground in moving from consent purely as a 'state of mind' and ideological subordination, to the *organization* of consent involving labour as an active subject, as well as the integrative effects of new developments in factory regimes. Though he overestimated the extent to which participation in games automatically generated acceptance of rules, Burawoy's work is important in recognizing the role of everyday workplace practices in 'constituting workers as individuals rather than members of a class' (1979: 30).

Adding in labour as active agency or subject in this phase can in one sense be seen as a classic case of bending the stick back in the dialectic between action and structure, though clearly within the specific parameters of the wage–effort bargain and employment relationship. But notwithstanding the range of well-known criticisms of the overall contribution of these authors, their importance lay in the emphasis on the decisive role of various aspects of worker subjectivity on capital's basic problem of the indeterminacy of labour as an obstacle to the securing of surplus value.

We fully accept, however, that this is only part of the picture. Given its Marxian and radical Weberian lineage, LPT lacks the conceptual tools to focus on and understand some aspects of the shaping of subjectivity. For example, as Fineman and Sturdy note, in LPT, issues of consent or resistance are seldom represented in terms of how those involved experience or feel. Researching these issues, at the interface of emotion theory and labour process theory, extends and develops both bodies of knowledge: politicizing the former, emotionalizing the latter (1997: 32). We also recognize the significance of the identity work of individuals and collectivities, and the value of post-structuralist research which illuminates how different selves are crafted in a workplace context (for example, Kondo, 1990).

But we are concerned to avoid the negative consequences of assuming any *a priori* judgement of what 'motivates' identity work. Instead, our starting point is simply that we can observe that workplace actors as knowledgeable agents draw on *symbolic resources* in their relations of contestation and co-operation. They may do so for a variety of reasons, including: to assert their own identities or shape others within struggles over power and resources, to legitimate their own actions or de-legitimate others; or as a means of surviving and developing satisfactions from particular conditions of work and employment. Taken together with the above restatement of labour as active agency, we believe that the notion of symbolic resources can go some way to enabling us to understand the experience of culture change in the workplace.

We have argued that on empirical, theoretical and methodological grounds, there is considerable doubt that contemporary cultural change processes can either create or sustain the goal of internalized commitment. We will now explore these issues in a more concrete and detailed way through an analysis of current workplace developments.

Culture wars at work

The depth and intensity of contemporary social engineering varies enormously. Certainly no-one should get carried away with the idea that very many organizations have well-designed and fully operationalized culture strategies. The majority find it difficult to govern their routine operations let alone their employee's souls. But what is the evidence of the effectiveness of culture change initiatives among employees?

We have already noted a number of high-profile cases of apparent corporate colonization. Even if one were prepared to ignore any theoretical predispositions, it is noteworthy that much of the evidence is taken from high-tech firms, often in the USA, or foreign transplants in non-union environments, with homogeneous, often largely professional workforces. It is interesting that Kunda (1992) is careful to show that Tech's normative exchange does not extend beyond the core engineering employees to the army of secretarial, clerical and temporary staff. Too often the specificities of organizations and sectors are underplayed or ignored. McKinlay and Taylor's Foucauldian-influenced study of the US microelectronics firm Phoneco's strong culture strategy on a greenfield site in Scotland is unusual in showing an awareness of both context and constraints: 'There could be no more favourable setting for corporate ideology to colonize the psyche of their workforce. And yet, advanced HR practices have not enabled management to "govern the soul" of its employees' (1998: 13–14).

The main body of case study and survey evidence is equally sceptical (e.g. Kunda, 1992; Guest, 1992; Ogbonna, 1992; Scott, 1994; O'Donnell, 1996; Wilkinson et al., 1997; Jones, 1997). Though it records a diversity and unevenness of responses, the prominent themes are distancing behaviour, cynicism, deep acting, and resigned behavioural compliance rather than value internalization. While such negative responses may be seen as limited by some commentators, compared with the reistance which could or should be shown the important issue is that they are *not* internalization or colonization. In some respect we are taken back to the older critique of the sheer difficulty of shifting the 'deep fabric' of organizational cultures.

There are some studies that show that a systematic exposure to particular change discourses can have a significant impact on attitudes and perceptions: for example, Rosenthal et al.'s (1997) account of an HRM and quality initiative in a leading supermarket. But not only did they make clear that this was not management hegemony or total control, they demonstrated how staff used the rhetoric to bring management into line with their expectations and the espoused values of the programme. It is striking how much of the evidence indicates an employee awareness of management motives and of the rhetoric–reality gap. Totalizing discourses seem to be pretty thin on the ground. Indeed some of the most persuasive evidence comes from companies themselves, who are finding that their own employee attitude surveys are revealing high levels of distrust and dissatisfaction (Summers, 1993; Marks et al., 1997b).

Explanations for the general lack of 'progress' often focus on contextual factors. Evaluating the broader evidence, Coopey notes that 'It seems clear for our review of various initiatives that no attitudinal transformation has been achieved. Instead, in the 1980s, employee behaviour has been reshaped under the pressure of various concrete measures such as plant closures, redundancies, delayering and closer monitoring' (1995: 70). Another recent overview backed up by their own case study is equally sceptical. Hope and Hendry observe that 'recent research into imposed cultural change programmes in the late 1980s raises doubts about their effectiveness as change mechanisms, as management control devices and as contributors to business performance' (1995: 61). They too argue that the objectives of the programmes may be incompatible with the new business climate in which organizations are under intense pressure to become leaner through 'delayering' and 'downsizing'. The same studies are, however, equally likely to pick up on the more processual or internal issues; citing the attenuation of the message through the usual suspects – managerial resistance, inadequate support or support systems, functional divides, slow and hierarchical decision-making.

Taking this weight of evidence into account, it seems an odd time for critical social theorists to be reinforcing the management illusion that corporate success has to be driven by culture change, or that internalization is feasible. In an apparent paradox it may be that by overplaying the likelihood of such change, they and their managerialist counterparts have underestimated the extent of movement 'on the ground'. Hope and Hendry (1995: 70) hit this particular nail on the head when they observe that 'It was clear from the research conducted within Healthco that the change initiatives that have concentrated on behaviour have been far more successful than the initiatives concerned with inculcating shared values', and quote one manager as saying that 'to be honest with you the value side of things I think is very wishy washy' (1995: 70, 69). This is entirely consistent with our own research into the Scottish Spirits industry (Marks et al., 1997b), where the culture segment of the change programme had been felt to have made least progress. Such slipperiness is rooted in the dual rhetorics about culture as changing values and practices that we identified earlier. Whereas management may be reluctant to separate these dimensions, social scientists should have fewer worries.

There is another sense in which the focus on internalization may be distorting an understanding of the relationships between change programmes and subjectivity. If we return to the broader conceptualization of the subjectivity of labour outlined earlier, it could be argued that many contemporary initiatives are geared towards or have the effect of engaging the creativity and consent of employees, rather than their internalized commitment. This can be illustrated with respect to teamworking. The shift to teamwork as a means of restructuring the technical division of labour is precisely premised on engaging what Friedman called the 'positive aspects of labour power' that are marginalized in more traditional forms of organization of the labour process. For teams to work, members must be prepared to be creative, to solve problems, to use their knowledge and skills in continuous improvement. That does not mean that the normative dimension is absent. Though the primary goal of teamworking is technical/instrumental, the initiatives are more likely to be effective if 'team players' are nurtured who can promote the cohesiveness of the group, accept collective and personal responsibility, be willing to initiate and communicate, etc. But even this is not *dependent* on the internalization of values and a process of self-disciplining power.[3] Like other initiatives, it can work if there is a combination of localized consent to the specific change process and support mechanisms in the sphere of reward systems, decision-making and industrial relations which promote and reward 'appropriate' behaviour.[4] To expect more is to evince considerable naiveté, not just about management but workers, or more precisely their work, too. For as Warhurst and Thompson observe, 'When management asks workers to be "really" committed and emotionally engaged, it is likely to be asking for impossible outcomes from those whose conditions of labour lack the necessary characteristics of autonomy and trust that would lead to making those "investments"' (1998: 12). This insight allows a useful comparison to the relationship between cultural change and the work of managers and professionals.

Managers, professionals and the culture burden

It may be that internalized commitment to work, and to the objectives of change programmes, are more likely to be associated with managers and professional employees. Arguably, other employees need not invest emotionally in change initiatives in order to survive or succeed. Managers, however, are explicitly charged with delivering change programmes, and with monitoring and reporting on employees in this regard (Mulholland, 1998). Thus, not only are there greater pressures on managers to internalize cultural change, there are also more rigorous checks on their suitability, for example, through assessment centres. As Hope and Hendry note, 'the new managerial behaviour requires an investment of "self" rather than dogged mimicry of behaviour or values set down in a corporate handbook. If the self is not engaged then the power is reduced, for the required behaviour is distanced from the person itself' (1995: 63). This may be somewhat overdoing it, as anyone who has observed cynical but effective managerial operators can testify. However, it remains the case that managers, particularly at senior level, have to carry the culture burden. They have to sell the message to the troops and explain why it's not working to the board, however sceptical she/he may be. In this sense, it is probably more realistic to identify managers as the strata that is 'motivated' by change programmes.

In addition, the conditions of managerial work may make internalized commitment more likely for managers, and for non-managerial employees with similar discretionary content in their work. In Oliver and Lowe's study, senior managers had difficulty in explaining why they were 'besotted with the company' and worked long hours voluntarily, denying the effects of peer or boss pressure, and suggesting that it was 'difficult to distinguish between work per se and the way you are as a person' (1991: 443, 447). The authors themselves, whilst sensitive to the difficulties in researching individual behaviours in the workplace, explain the responses partly in terms of high-discretion jobs. Further, the greater likelihood of managers to endorse culture change may be simply explained with reference to who is more likely to benefit from change. Ownership of successful change initiatives brings with it not only material rewards, but also the power to drive the initiative in appropriate directions. As Mulholland notes, 'the appropriation and ownership of change initiatives becomes the prize to be competed for' (1998: 192).

Lastly, change programmes themselves may be an important vehicle through which managers establish the legitimacy of their own positions. Popular management theory is now the central symbolic resource available to those designing and implementing change programmes (Thompson and O'Connell Davidson, 1994): a 'vocabulary of motive', according to Webb (1996), which justifies actions and seeks to influence others and oneself. As Watson (1994) contends, 'flavours of the month' are a resource for organizational control and for making sense of their own identities and work activities, offering managers a new language and a new 'art' of governing organizational life (du Gay, 1993).

So far so good for cultural change amongst managers; yet we must be careful not to overstate the differences between managerial and non-managerial employees, nor to suggest that such change programmes are unequivocally positive for managers. Managers, possibly more so than other workers, may bear the cost of any previous association with 'bad' cultures, and any failure to deliver 'newer' and 'better' cultures. Furthermore, many of the supporting conditions of work previously referred to are under widespread attack, as managers become subject to greater monitoring, appraisal and pressures for accountability and accreditation. Increasing personal insecurity amongst managers at all levels may well be striking at one side of the commitment/security bargain which arguably governed managerial work in the past, and corporate management appear to have conceded that the price of continued managerial loyalty is too high. Mulholland makes this point well: 'If review and appraisal is introduced with the intention of reducing the managerial scope for misbehaviour, then trust and loyalty in return for career and secure employment no longer forms the basis of the relationship between subordinate managerial layers and corporate management in the privatized utilities' (1998: 201). What, then, forms the basis of managers' employment relationship? For Herriot and Pemberton (1998), it is mutual instrumentality and a more straightfor-ward effort–reward bargain. The emerging portfolio career is hardly a solid foundation for shared values and trust.

We should also be mindful of divisions within management. If we accept the likely existence of a link between ownership and endorsement, we may wish to distinguish between the experience of those managers directly responsible for culture change, such as personnel/human resource management, and others. Not only are senior personnel figures often centrally involved in cultural initiatives, they are in prime positions both to recruit and to promote 'culturally appropriate' managers to key positions in the organization, thus further disseminating the message. Yet according to Anthony, the producers of culture are the group most likely both to be encaptured by cultural change programmes and to be alienated in the process. He is sceptical of the extent to which beliefs and values are transmitted from culture managers, and suggests that the failure to transmit shared meanings leads to the 'isolation of the managers of organizational culture, locked into deeper commitment to values that are not shared' (1990: 3).

The conditions of work of professionals are also more conducive to commitment. In addition, these conditions are often accompanied by a professional ethic, or an ethic of public service, resulting in health or education professionals working well beyond what any reasonable interpretation of the employment contract might suggest (Anthony, 1990). The key component here is shared values rather than management efforts to impose norms, giving professional cultures or ethics their almost indefatigable character. However, it could be argued that what most distinctively defines these groups is not ethics, but their technical competence or expertise in providing a service the quality of which the client or employer may not be expected to be able to judge (Crompton, 1990), thus taking us back more firmly to discussions of conditions of work. Their situation is clearly not static. In recent years, many professional/expert groups (for example, academics, social workers, health care workers) have, like managers, found themselves increasingly under pressure, not only in terms of time and effort, but also in relation to the degree of autonomy they have in their work. This has been felt particularly, although not exclusively, by those in the public sector given moves towards quasi-markets, 'quality' audits, and other forms of bureaucratic regulation.

It is hardly surprising that greater pressure, routinization and monitoring of professional/expert work has led to a range of negative consequences. Yet again, there is good reason to suspect that the bargain struck with employers has been altered: greater questioning of the autonomy and status of professional/expert workers has led to a greater questioning by such employees of the basis of their commitment, resulting in a more explicitly instrumental or calculative approach. This is most readily evident in the apparent shift of emphasis in appraisal systems away from issues of professional career development, and towards more explicit measuring and monitoring. As a consequence, the focus of appraisees shifts to those aspects of work which are most explicitly measured, and, by implication, are most valued by the organization (Townley, 1993). *A priori*, this may represent an acceptance amongst professionals/experts of the 'new' cultural values, and, indeed, some of those values, such as higher quality, better client service and accountability, may not conflict, in principle, with occupational values. Yet definitions of quality, service and accountability remain hugely contested in many organizations, and any emphasis on their achievement in the context of scarce and often diminishing resources exacerbates the inevitable tension between the interests of clients/customers and the interests of workers. This takes us back to the behavioural compliance referred to earlier. While some accounts have explained the actions of professional/expert employees in terms of endorsed values (such as Grey's discussion of accountants), the same behaviour is easily read in a more conventionally materialist way, with behavioural compliance (and some deep acting) as the route to sustaining organizational membership and rewards.

Of greater concern, however, is the possibility that such initiatives actually result in unintended consequences and produce a no-win situation for all, by destroying the elements of professional/expert work which managers were attracted to in the first place. Arguably, the self-policing undertaken by professional/expert workers in the past was less driven by fears of explicit sanction for under-performance or inappropriate behaviour, and more by concerns relating to personal development, colleague support and client/customer expectations. Yet the result of cultural change initiatives has often been to tie employee performance more explicitly to a managerialist agenda, and thus both the definition of and the costs associated with misbehaviour alters. Striking at the conditions which supported loyalty and self-discipline in high-discretion jobs risks removing a source of restraint on behaviour and replacing it with practices and values which are far less effective in influencing employee actions. Thus, attempts to re-cast the configuration of trust and loyalty within an organization may involve considerable risk for managers.

Conclusion

A concern with culture and its management is, on the evidence in this chapter, a significant part of contemporary organizational life. Yet it has also been burdened with vastly inflated expectations in often ludicrously overdone language. If any seduction has been going on, it has been academically self-induced. There is now a massive gap between the corporate restructuring of the 1990s with its attendant downsizing, delayering, work intensification and more calculative, contractual employment relationships, and the warm, fuzzy culture/HRM rhetoric of the 1980s that still functions as the dominant organizational discourse (Littler et al., 1994). Without some level of employment security, career paths and internal labour markets, it is difficult to see what exactly are the sinews of 'strong' cultures. Many employees are experiencing the breaking down of the old psychological contract, without the provision of a new one.

This message is not lost on employees. It is less of a question of an economy dominated by 'sign value' as it is of employees reading the signs. Organizations cannot be 'value-led' if the values are not effectively supported and sustained. If mission statements and the vision thing ever held any purchase, it is likely to be of diminishing influence. Furthermore, if these processes do accelerate, it is probable that we will see a shift in the nature of controls in the labour process and employment relationship towards the bureaucratic and calculative.

While culture will be increasingly revealed as instrumentalized for economic purposes, it does not mean that its management will disappear from the workplace. Cultural differences between organizations still matter, and senior management will still pursue specific 'culture strategies'. More importantly culture will remain as the primary language of change, both general and specific, central to the management of meaning. Curiously it will survive in part because of its confused character, in particular the conflation of changing values and practices discussed at the start of this chapter. Because culture has become something of a 'catch-all' in which the instrumental, the economic and the behavioural are subsumed, it can absorb the loss of vision in an emphasis on the language of changing 'the way we do things round here'. Employees may not have bought into the message, but they have learned to live in and with it, to become culturally literate in a way that management cannot always control.

It would, therefore, be wiser if academics avoided the grand claims that a new cultural politics of the workplace has become *the* defining feature of late capitalism or early postmodernity. Similarly, while issues of subjectivity are important, what is needed is a broadening of the current narrow concerns with identity, to have a capacity to move identity work beyond a purely discourse-based framework; and to re-emphasize labour as knowledgeable agency or agencies acting to transform their conditions of existence.[5] Whether the subject is 'missing' or not, the specific context of the capitalist labour process and political economy often is. Empirical and theoretical work should be located less in the abstract concerns for existential identity and more in how organizational actors are attempting to reconstruct the reciprocal but contested nature of the psychological contract in contemporary social, economic and political conditions.

We want to end on a note of caution about this whole enterprise. It has been one of the themes of this chapter that neither managers nor social scientists actually know much about employee subjectivity, at least in the sense of values, internalized or otherwise. Given that the number of in-depth ethnographies of the quality of Kunda's (1992) account of life at 'Tech' is likely to be small, we need more imaginative ways of exploring the relationships between behaviour and values, including the ways in which employees draw on the symbolic resources generated from new management initiatives. But no amount of use of more qualitative methodologies can escape the fact that there are natural limits to how far we can get 'inside people's heads' – constraints theorists need to be sensitive to this before making the next sweeping statement about culture and identity.

Notes

1 Such 'new control' theories do not necessarily make claims, inflated or otherwise, about subjectivity. For example, while we might be sceptical about Delbridge, Turnbull and Wilkinson's argument that JIT/TQM practices have eliminated worker counter-controls, the article is a description of a factory regime and its effects on work intensification rather than subjectivity.

2 Knights and Willmott also have a tendency to filter a variety of other theoretical and empirical work through their own narrow reading of subjectivity, often repackaging contending workplace analyses as if their real intent or effect has been identical to Knights and Willmott's own. See Thompson and Findlay (1996) for examples.

3 We don't want to be dogmatic here. It *may* be underpinned in this way, as Barker's (1993) case study appeared to show. But teamworking as heavy social engineering is not typical of the evidence of current initiatives (Marks et al., 1997b).

4 This is consistent with evidence from Beer et al. (1990) that emergent and organic behaviour-led change was more successful than imposed, top-down culture programmes.

5 The extent to which a notion of agency is retained by those concerned with theorizing subjectivity as identity varies. Collinson attempts some integration of the concept (see 1992: 29–30, 45).

References

Ackers, P. and Black, J. (1991) 'Paternalist capitalism: an organization in transition', in M. Cross and G. Payne (eds), *Work and the Enterprise Culture*, London: Falmer Press.

Ackroyd, S. and Crowdy, P.A. (1990) 'Can culture be managed? Working with the "raw material": the case of the English slaughtermen', *Personnel Review*, 19 (5): 12–18.

Alvesson, M. (1990) 'On the popularity of organisational culture', *Acta Sociologica*, 331 (1): 31–49.

Alvesson, M. (1991) 'Corporate culture and corporatism at company level: a case study', *Economic and Industrial Democracy*, 12: 73–102.

Anthony, P.D. (1990) 'The paradox of the management of culture: or, he who leads is lost', *Personnel Review*, 19 (4): 3–8.

Barker, J.R. (1993) 'Tightening the iron cage: concertive control in self-managing teams', *Administrative Science Quarterly*, 38: 408–37.

Bartlett, C. and Goshal, S. (1990) 'The multinational corporation as an international network', *Academy of Management Review*, 4: 27–39.

Beer, M. et al. (1990) 'Why change programmes don't produce change', *Harvard Business Review*, (Nov–Dec): 158–66.

Braverman, H. (1974) *Labour and Monopoly Capital*, New York: Monthly Review.

Burawoy, M. (1979) *Manufacturing Consent: Changes in the Labour Process under Monopoly Capitalism*, Chicago: Chicago University Press.

Casey, C. (1995) *Work, Self and Society*, London: Routledge.

Collinson, D. (1992) *Managing the Shopfloor: Subjectivity, Masculinity and Workplace Culture*, Berlin: De Gruyter.

Coopey, J. (1995) 'Managerial culture and the stillbirth of organisational commitment', *Human Resource Management Journal*, 5 (3): 56–76.

Cressey, P. and MacInnes, J. (1980) 'Industrial democracy and the control of labour', *Capital and Class*, 11: 5–33.

Crompton, R. (1990) 'Professions in the current context', *Work, Employment and Society*, Special Issue, May: 147–66.

Dahler-Larsen, P. (1994) 'Corporate culture and morality: Durkheim-inspired reflections on the limits of corporate culture', *Journal of Management Studies*, 31 (1) 1–18.

Dawson, P. and Webb, J. (1989) 'New production arrangements: the totally flexible cage?', *Work, Employment and Society*, 3 (2): 221–38.

Deal, T. and Kennedy, A. (1982) *Corporate Cultures: the Rites and Rituals of Everyday Life*, Reading, MA: Addison-Wesley.

Deetz, S. (1992) 'Disciplinary power in the modern corporation', in M. Alvesson and H. Willmott (eds), *Critical Management Studies*, London: Sage.

Delbridge, R. and Lowe, J. (1996) 'The social relations of supervision', paper for the International Labour Process Conference, Aston University, Birmingham, March.

Delbridge, R., Turnbull, P. and Wilkinson, B. (1992) 'Pushing back the frontiers: management control and work intensification under JIT/TQM factory regimes', *New Technology, Work and Employment*, 7: 97–106.

Dews, P. (1986) 'Power and subjectivity in Foucault', *New Left Review*, (March–April): 72–95.

du Gay, P. (1991) 'Enterprise culture and and the ideology of excellence', *New Formations*, 14: 45–61.

du Gay, P. (1993) 'Entrepreneurial management in the public sector', *Work, Employment and Society*, 7 (4): 45–61.

du Gay, P. (1996) *Consumption and Identity at Work*, London: Sage.

du Gay, P. and Salaman, G. (1990) 'New times and old hat: enterprise culture and the search or excellence', Employment Relations in the Enterprise Culture Conference, Cardiff Business School, September.

Edwards, P.K. and Scullion, H. (1982) *The Social Organisation of Industrial Conflict: Control and Resistance in the Workplace*, Oxford: Blackwell.

Edwards, R. (1979) *Contested Terrain: the Transformation of Industry in the Twentieth Century*, London: Heinemann.

Fineman, S. and Sturdy, A. (1997) 'Struggles for the control of affect', International Labour Process Conference, Edinburgh, March.

Friedman, A. (1977) *Industry and Labour: Class Struggle at Work and Monopoly Capitalism*, London: Macmillan.

Garsten, C. and Grey, C. (1997) 'How to become oneself: discourses of subjectivity in post-bureaucratic organizations', *Organization*, 4 (2): 211–28.

Grey, C. (1994a) 'Organisational Calvinism: insecurity and labour power in a professional labour process', paper to the 12th International Labour Process Conference, Aston University, Birmingham.

Grey, C. (1994b) 'Career as a project of the self and labour process discipline', *Sociology*, 28 (2): 479–97.

Guest, D. (1990) 'Human resource management and the American dream', *Journal of Management Studies*, 27 (4): 377–97.

Guest, D. (1992) 'Employee commitment and control', in J.F. Hartley and G.M. Stephenson (eds), *Employment Relations*, Oxford: Blackwell.

Handy, C. (1976) *Understanding Organisations*, Harmondsworth: Penguin.

Heriot, P. and Pemberton, C. (1998) *New Deals*, Chichester: Wiley.

Hope, V. and Hendry, J. (1995) 'Corporate culture – is it relevant for the organisations of the 1990s', *Human Resource Management Journal*, 5 (4): 61–73.

Ingersoll Engineers (1996) *The Way We Work*, London.

Jacques, R. (1996) *Manufacturing the Employee: Management Knowledge from the 19th to the 21st Centuries*, London: Sage.

Jones, O. (1997) 'Changing the balance? Taylorism, TQM and work organisation', *New Technology, Work and Employment*, 12 (1): 13–24.

Joyce, P. (1980) *Work, Society and Politics*, London: Methuen.

Kennedy, C. (1996) *Managing with the Gurus*, New York: Century Books.

Kerfoot, D. and Knights, D. (1994) 'Empowering the "quality worker": the seduction and contradiction of the total quality phenomenon', in A. Wilkinson and H. Willmott (eds), *Making Quality Critical*, London: Routledge.

Knights, D. (1995) 'Hanging out the dirty washing: labour process theory in the age of deconstruction', paper to 13th International Labour Process Conference, Blackpool, April.

Knights, D. and Willmott, H. (1989) 'Power and subjectivity at work: from degradation to subjugation in social relations', *Sociology*, 23 (4): 535–58.

Kondo, G. (1990) *Crafting Selves*, Chicago: University of Chicago Press.

Kunda, G. (1992) *Engineering Culture: Control and Commitment in a High Tech Corporation*, Philadelphia: Temple University Press.

Legge, K. (1989) 'Human resource management: a critical analysis', in J. Storey (ed.), *New Perspectives in Human Resource Management*, London: Routledge.

Legge, K. (1995) *Human Resource Management: Rhetorics and Realities*, London: Macmillan.

Littler, C., Bramble, T. and McDonald, J. (1994) 'Organisational restructuring: downsizing, delayering and managing change at work', *Industrial Relations Research Series*, 15 (December).

Lyon, D. (1994) *The Electronic Eye*, Oxford: Polity.

McCabe, D. and Knights, D. (1995) 'TQM: reaches the subjectivity that other management initiatives cannot', paper to 13th International Labour Process Conference, Blackpool, April.

McKinlay, A. and Taylor, P. (1998) 'Through the looking glass: Foucault and the politics of production', in A. McKinlay and K. Starkey (eds), *Foucault, Management and Organisation*, London: Sage.

McNally, D. (1995) 'Language, history and class struggle', *Monthly Review*, 47 (3): 13–31.

Marks, A., Findlay, P., Hine, J., McKinlay, A. and Thompson, P. (1997a) 'In search of perfect people: teamwork and team players in the Scottish spirits industry', paper to International Workshop on Teamworking, University of Nottingham, September.

Marks, A. Findlay, P., Hine, J., McKinlay, A. and Thompson, P. (1997b) 'Handmaid's tale or midwives of change? HR managers and organisational innovation', *Journal of Strategic Change*, 6: 469–80.

Meek, V.L. (1988) 'Organisational culture: origins and weakneses', *Organisation Studies*, 9 (4): 453–73.

Milkman, R. (1998) 'The new American workplace: high road or low road?', in P. Thompson and C. Warhurst (eds), *Workplaces of the Future*, London: Macmillan.

Mulholland, K. (1998) '"Survivors" versus "movers and shakers": the reconstitution of management and careers in the privatised utilities', in P. Thompson and C. Warhurst (eds), *Workplaces of the Future*, London: Macmillan.

Munro, R. (1994) 'Governing the new province of quality: autonomy, accounting and the dissemination of accountability', in A. Wilkinson and H. Willmott (eds), *Making Quality Critical: New Perspectives on Organizational Change*, London: Routledge.

Newton, T. (1994) 'Resocialising the subject: a re-reading of the Grey's career as a project of the self', Working Paper Series No. 94/16, Department of Business Studies, University of Edinburgh.

O'Doherty, D. (1994) 'Institutional withdrawal? Anxiety and conflict in the emerging banking labour process', paper to 12th International Labour Process Conference, Aston University, Birmingham.

O'Doherty, D. and Willmott, H. (1998) 'Recent contributions to the development of labour process analysis', paper to the International Labour Process Conference, UMIST, April.

O'Donnell, M. (1996) 'Into the mystic: cultural change and TQM teams in the NSW public sector', *Journal of Industrial Relations* (Australia), 38 (2): 241–63.

Ogbonna, E. (1992) 'Managing organizational culture: fantasy or reality?', *Human Resource Management*, 3 (2): 1–12.

Ogbonna, E. and Wilkinson, B. (1990) 'Corporate strategy and corporate structure: the view from the checkout', *Personnel Review*, 19 (4): 9–15.

Oliver, N. and Lowe, J. (1991) 'The high commitment workplace: two cases from a high-tech industry', *Work, Employment and Society*, 5 (2): 437–50.

Ouchi, W.G. (1981) *Theory Z*, Reading, MA: Addison-Wesley.

Parker, M. (1998) 'Organisational culture and the disciplines of organisation: the career of a concept', paper to 16th International Labour Process Conference, UMIST, Manchester, April.

Pascale, R.T. and Athos, A.G. (1982) *The Art of Japanese Management*, Harmondsworth: Penguin.

Peters, T.J. and Waterman, R.H. (1982) *In Search of Excellence: Lessons of America's Best-Run Companies*, New York: Harper & Row.

Pettigrew, A. (1979) 'On studying organisational cultures', *Administrative Science Quarterly*, 24: 570–81.

Ray, C.A. (1986) 'Corporate culture: the last frontier of control?', *Journal of Managment Studies*, 23 (3): 287–97.

Reed, M. (1996) 'Re-discovering Hegel: the "new historicism" in organisation and management studies', *Journal of Management Studies*, 33 (2): 139–58.

Rose, N. (1990) *Governing the Soul: the Shaping of the Private Self*, London: Routledge.

Rosenthal, P., Hill, S. and Peccei, R. (1997) 'Checking out service: evaluating excellence, HRM and TQM in retailing', *Work, Employment and Society*, 11 (3): 481–503.

Scott, A. (1994) *Willing Slaves? British Workers Under Human Resource Management*, Cambridge: Cambridge University Press.

Sewell, G. and Wilkinson, B. (1992a) 'Someone to watch over me: surveillance, discipline and the just-in-time labour process', *Sociology*, 26 (2): 271–89.

Sewell, G. and Wilkinson, B. (1992b) 'Empowerment or emasculation? Shopfloor surveillance in a total quality organisation', in P. Blyton and P. Turnbull (eds), *Re-Assessing Human Resource Management*, London: Sage.

Silver, J. (1987) 'The ideology of excellence: management and neo-conservatism', *Studies in Political Economy*, 24: 105–29.

Smircich, L. (1983) 'Concepts of culture and organisational analaysis', *Administrative Quarterly*, 28: 339–58.

Smith, S. and Wilkinson, B. (1995) '"No doors, no offices, no secrets, we are our own policemen!" – capitalism without conflict?', in S. Linstead, R. Grafton-Small and P. Jeffcutt (eds), *Understanding Management*, London: Sage.

Sosteric, M. (1996) 'Subjectivity and the labour process: a case study in the restaurant industry', *Work, Employment and Society*, 10 (2): 297–318.

Summers, D. (1993) 'Management – the right attitude: staff surveys are popular, but can be fraught with problems', *Financial Times*, 14 June.

Taylor, S. (1998) 'Emotional labour and the new workplace', in P. Thompson and C. Warhurst (eds), *Workplaces of the Future*, London: Macmillan.

Thackray, J. (1986) 'The corporate culture rage', *Management Today*, (Feb.): 67–70.

Thompson, P. (1989) *The Nature of Work*, 2nd edn, London: Macmillan.

Thompson, P. (1990) 'Crawling from the wreckage: the labour process and the politics of production', in D. Knights and H. Willmott (eds), *Labour Process Theory*, London: Macmillan.

Thompson, P. and Ackroyd, S. (1995) 'All quiet on the workplace front: a critique of recent trends in British industrial sociology', *Sociology*, 29 (4): 619–33.

Thompson, P. and Findlay, P. (1996) 'The Mystery of the missing subject', paper to the 14th International Labour Process Conference, University of Aston, Birmingham.

Thompson, P. and McHugh, D. (1995) *Work Organizations*, 2nd edn, London: Macmillan.

Thompson, P. and O'Connell Davidson, J. (1994) 'The continuity of discontinuity: managerial rhetoric in turbulent times', *Personnel Review*, 24 (4): 17–33.

Thompson, P., Jones, C., Nickson, D. and Wallace, T. (1998) 'Internationalisation and integration: a comparison of manufacturing and service firms', *Competition and Change, The Journal of Global Business*, 3, 387–415.

Townley, B. (1993) 'Performance appraisal and the emergence of management', *Journal of Management Studies*, 30 (2): 27–44.

Van Maanen, J. and Barley, S. (1985) 'Occupational communities, culture and control in organisations', in B.M. Staw and L.L. Cummings (eds), *Research in Organisational Behaviour*, vol. 11, Greenwich, CT: JAI Press.

Warhurst, C. and Thompson, P. (1998) 'Hands, hearts and minds: changing work and workers at the end of the century', in P. Thompson and C. Warhurst (eds), *Workplaces of the Future*, London: Macmillan.

Watson, J. (1994) 'Management "flavours of the month": their role in managers' lives', *The International Journal of Human Resource Management*, 5 (4): 893–905.

Webb, J. (1996) 'Vocabularies of motive and the "new" management', *Work, Employment and Society*, 10 (2): 251–71.

Webster, F. and Robbins, K. (1989) 'Plan and control: towards a cultural history of the information society', *Theory and Society*, 18 (2).

Webster, F. and Robbins, K. (1993) 'I'll be watching you: comment on Sewell and Wilkinson', *Sociology*, 27 (2): 243–52.

Wilkinson, A., Marchington, M., Ackers, P. and Goodman, J. (1992) 'Total quality management and employee involvement', *Human Resource Management Journal*, 6 (4): 849–71.

Wilkinson, A., Godfrey, G. and Marchington, M. (1997) 'Bouquets, brickbats and blinkers: total quality management and employee involvement in practice', *Organisation Studies*, 18 (5): 799–820.

Willmott, H. (1993) 'Strength is ignorance, slavery is freedom: managing culture in modern organisations', *Journal of Management Studies*, 30 (4): 515–52.

Willmott, H. (1995) 'From Braverman to schizophrenia: the diseased condition of subjectivity in labour process theory', paper to 13th International Labour Process Conference, Blackpool, April.

8

Social Differentiation, Transgression and the Politics of Irony

Larry Ray

This discussion aims to place debates about culture, economy and politics in the context of sociological theories of social differentiation.[1] I argue that some adherents to the culturalization thesis, along with some postmodernists, in effect suggest that contemporary societies are undergoing a process of de-differentiation. However, this claim requires close examination. I will suggest that modern societies operate with relatively stable boundaries between discrete subsystems which are defined according to specific criteria of relevance. However, these are open to transgressions, that constitute major fault lines in contemporary societies. Many social movements are concerned either to challenge existing boundaries or to defend them, and the act of transgression can write new scripts for political identity and action that can be deeply subversive. However, the transgression of boundaries is not the same as their collapse, nor logically, can it be. This point is illustrated by counter-hegemonic movements in Poland (and elsewhere in Eastern Europe) in the final years of the Communist system. I argue that unlike more established forms of political protest, innovative kinds of political action were developed in the late 1980s for which no readily available interpretative script existed. Their theatrical stance effaced traditional boundaries between the 'political' and 'cultural' and was deeply de-legitimating in the context of severe systemic crisis. However, their longer-term impact was always likely to be limited, and the politics of the post-communist settlement returned to more familiar patterns.

The 'cultural turn' and social differentiation

Along with postmodernist theory, and often intertwined with it, the 'cultural turn' is a diffuse position in the social sciences, which views social life as a process of inscribing order (and circumscribing disorder) in which we can understand ourselves as the creators or bricolators of meaning. The processes of everyday life are constructed through 'culture', thus reversing or abolishing the dichotomy between an economic 'base' and cultural 'superstructure'. Instead, in social science, carnivalesque voices explore problematics of representation to subvert the 'canonised voices in social studies with polyphonic diversity' (Jeffcutt, 1994: 39) generating a 'post-culture of semiotic promiscuity and preference for pastiche and parody' (Crook et al., 1992: 35). Further, for Crook et al. (1992: 47ff) economic material 'reality' has collapsed into culture, which is gaining the effectivity once ascribed to material relations. They write of 'culture hyper-differentiation' in which the pattern of social differentiation characteristic of modernity generates a multiplication of boundaries (goes 'hyper') to the point where this implodes into new forms of fluidity and chaos. For Lash (1988) and Lash and Urry (1994: 272) modernity is characterized by vertical and horizontal differentiation, organized capitalism and the development of separate institutional, normative and aesthetic spheres, each with their specific conventions and modes of evaluation. There are multiple separations of high and low culture, science and life, auratic art and popular pleasures. Postmodernity by contrast involves de-differentiation, disorganized capitalism, and a breakdown of both the distinctiveness of each sphere, and of the criteria which legislate within each vertical dimension. Following Baudrillard, representation and reality dissolve into systems of floating signifiers, which for Lash and Urry (1994: 276) is illustrated by new consumption patterns, reflecting a transition from mass (Fordist) consumption to more individualized (post-Fordist) consumption. Here 'cool' consumers respond to the global array of available images and experiences with ironic detachment.

To some extent, this is yet another debate with Marx's ghost, in that culturalization draws attention to a shift from class-based politics to new social identities, 'communities of affect' (Hebdige, 1989) and expressive rather than instrumental concerns. Indeed, for over a century cultural and material constructions of the social have been batted back and forth in sociology, and a central motif of Max Weber's work was to effect their reconciliation. This was tellingly illustrated by his closing remark in the Protestant Ethic thesis that 'it is not my intention to substitute for a one-sided materialistic view of history an equally one-sided idealistic view: both are equally possible' (Weber, 1976: 183). However, culturalization aims to transcend this dichotomy, suggesting that it is no longer possible to speak of separate orders of economy and culture at all. For Jameson late capitalism operates in an environment where nature has gone, so nothing exists outside culture, which itself has become 'second nature'. He writes of the 'photorealist cityscape' of late capitalism as an 'hallucinatory exhilaration' combined with depthlessness – the world threatens to become 'a glossy skin, a rush of filmic images without density' (1991: 6). This attests to the 'mutation of the sphere of culture' which, having lost its earlier 'semi-autonomy', has exploded in a 'prodigious expansion of culture throughout the social realm' such that 'everything . . . can be said to have become "cultural" in some . . . sense' (1991: 51). Consumption, further, is no longer merely an adjunct to but the essence of capitalist functioning, leading to an 'aestheticization of reality' (1991: 48). Such claims about culturalization challenge classical formulations of the problem which presupposed culture and economy as mutually interacting but separate.

The cultural turn encompasses most social sciences, such that in 'practically every corner of international political economy the same phenomenon can be recognized: an increased emphasis on the discursive constitution of economic life' (Leyson and Thrift, 1997: 190). Focusing on language and stressing the instability of meaning in language undermines the effort to dissolve communication into a 'real' of action or into a universal definition (Poster, 1995: 75). This emphasis on cultural construction coincided with increased spatial awareness, linking both of these with globalization – another (sometime) companion of postmodernism. Thus the definition of 'culture' as a discrete and enclosed space is suspect, and spatial metaphors (albeit still being formed) might replace such a definition (Leyson and Thrift, 1997: 192). Lash and Urry (1994: 142–3) claim that 'social life today is increasingly culture-laden; . . . being replaced by a "culture society" [which] . . . is more than an aestheticization of life. It is a *Vergesellschaftung* (societalization) of culture . . .' in which culture becomes inscribed into society via information-intensive industrial production.[2]

These claims clearly invite charges of exaggeration, of swinging the pendulum too far, and so forth. They further invite rhetorical, materialist responses, of which there have been plenty (e.g. Eagleton, 1996).[3] But I would like to suggest a different approach to these claims, which examines what they assume about the nature of the social, in particular about the processes of differentiation and de-differentiation. The cultural turn is premised on a theory of deep social de-differentiation, which Lash (1988) makes explicit. Modernist forms, he says, depended on differentiation – of the cultural from the social, aesthetic from theoretical, sacred from secular and science from religion, whereas in postmodernism, cultural value spheres of science, morality and art lose their autonomy, culture is no longer separate from the social, so culture and commerce interfuse and feed on one another in simulacra, chaos and instability.

This is a claim which, if true, has far-reaching implications. In macrosociological theories, from Spencer and Durkheim through to Parsons, Luhmann and Habermas, social differentiation was being regarded as a crucial feature of contemporary social systems. This can be illustrated briefly. Talcott Parsons's AGIL schema is a theory of social differentiation which specifies functional dimensions of adaptation (e.g. the economy), goal-attainment (e.g. the polity), integration (e.g. societal community) and latency (e.g. cultural legitimation) (Parsons, 1971). The L-subsystem was particularly important in providing continuity of cultural meaning and stored memories of how to manage interactions across boundaries. Further, in complex societies there was increasing social distance both within and between subsystems as AGIL was replicated within each – thus for example the economy divides into capitalization (A), production (G), organization (I) and human relations (L). In these terms, differentiation of the economy and polity, concerned with material survival, from culture and community, concerned with social integration, was an evolutionary achievement that would not be easily reversed.

Complex, impersonal interactions are co-ordinated through 'steering media' such as money and power, which reduce complexity by developing highly abstract codes through which the system distinguishes itself from its environment (Luhmann, 1993: 78). In the economy, money acts as a symbolic token, a medium of exchange that can be passed around, thus bracketing time-space by 'coupling insubstantiality and deferral, presence and absence' (Giddens, 1990). Money is the paradigm case since it enables value to circulate in abstract form, commodifying social relations previously mediated by reciprocity, obligation, patronage and indenture. That is, abstract media of communication are loosened from particular cultural moorings and projected into a global dimension creating possibilities for highly complex impersonal communications. Differentiation involves the fragmentation of social life into increasingly discrete spheres, and in particular the separation of the polity and economy, public and private, society and personality, along with cultural pluralism and previously unprecedented levels of organizational complexity.[4]

Social differentiation enables subsystems to maintain sufficient internal complexity to respond to problems generated in their environments (Luhmann, 1982: 230). For example, the economy has more internal complexity (division of labour, separation between work and household, networks of distribution, etc.) than politics, so it has greater opportunity to store and transfer reduced complexity. Consequently, with the evolution of modern societies, the economic system has taken over many risks from politics, since conversion of risks into monetary terms enables them to be digitalized and depoliticized (Luhmann, 1993: 184). Differentiation establishes time delays in which systems can respond to environmental pressures in their own ways, processing information to respond to outside impulses and selecting courses of action (1982: 145). In the political system, political codes are repertoires that schematize and simplify political discourse (such as progressive/conservative, government/opposition, state/society, public/private interests) and short-circuit debate by compacting otherwise complex nuances into easily recognizable oppositions. Thus Richard Münch (1990: 463) has argued that social differentiation is the 'only possible answer' to the problem of social order under modern conditions.

Now, one does not have to accept theories of functional differentiation in their entirety to acknowledge that if there is *any* validity in this line of argument then there may be some problems with the culturalization thesis. If a key feature of modernity is increasing complexity, which presupposes increasing differentiation among institutional orders of society, culture and personality, then the kind of radical de-differentiation implied by advocates of the cultural turn begins to look implausible. Three further points are worth noting here.

First, since social differentiation is a response to increasing complexity, no one social site can assume responsibility for steering the system as a whole. If this is so, then it seems prima facie unlikely that culture could become so dilated as to take over functions of economy, polity and community, or if it did, various functional sites would appear latently, within the cultural subsystem. Secondly, de-differentiation, where it occurs, may not involve the actual collapse of subsystems. During the Thatcher period in Britain for example, higher education was increasingly reoriented towards the managerial/market logic of the economy. Thus values of cognitive rationality, specific to higher education, were weakened by the abolition of tenure, adoption of managerial forms of 'quality control', 'market-relevant' courses, etc., but this did not abolish the distinction between educational and economic subsystems (Mouzelis, 1999). One subsystem may encroach on another but the boundaries between them remain, thus an increasing cultural inflection of economic or political life would not necessarily involve the collapse of one into the other.[5] Indeed, such a collapse would open the social system to the chaos of unmediated complexity. Thirdly, social differentiation describes organizational tendencies of longue durée that pre-date 'modernity' by hundreds, if not thousands, of years. Social differentiation was not specific to modernity, but was also a feature of traditional societies and emerged as economic contacts grew between communities that did not share a common value system (Schuluchter, 1985). So, if culturalization entails de-differentiation, it needs to be shown that modern societies experience a collapse of differentiated cultural value spheres and a blurring of the institutional order of society, culture and personality. Not only would such an argument be difficult to sustain, but advocates of culturalization do not always maintain this themselves. Lash for example claims that there is an 'elective affinity' between cultural post-modernism and 'disorganized capitalism', which as Kumar (1995: 139ff.) notes, undermines the claim that economy has collapsed into culture. Further, Lash and Urry (1988; 1994) themselves refer to what are in effect new kinds of social differentiation in postmodern society, such as new consumption cultures, niche markets and ironic role distanciation.

Social differentiation into institutional orders of culture, economy and polity may be relatively stable features of contemporary societies, but this does not mean that transgression of these boundaries is impossible. Indeed, social systems are created and sustained by action, which has an inherent capacity to innovate and disregard conventional forms of life. To act, said Hannah Arendt, 'means to take initiative, to begin . . . which we are free to do' (1959: 157). Indeed, one of the problems with culturalization theories is that for all their talk of fluidity and instability, they generally give little attention to action, which gets marginalized by preoccupation with discourses and texts. This was a problem too for classical theories of social differentiation. Social action was supposedly central to Parsonian theory but was actually reduced to patterned systematic activity constituted by roles defined by the AGIL schema. Moreover, Parsons translated Weber's *das Handeln* as 'action', thereby losing its double meaning of performance and commercial transaction, that is, its dramatic and material connotations (Nichols, 1977). The dramatic connotation was restored by subsequent inter-actionist theories, such as Goffman's (1959) stress on the centrality of performance and presentation in everyday life. In a rather different way, Habermas's theory of communicative action restores the dual meaning of action as instrumental and as meaningful-communicative, corresponding to the perlocutionary and illocutionary types of speech, respectively (e.g. Habermas, 1991: 235ff.). Action thus entails the acceptance or not of conventional institutional orders and displays capacities for communicative-symbolic and material-instrumental goals.

Now, if we combine a dual concept of action with the theory of social differentiation, then the institutional orders of polity, economy and culture are the context within which action and speech oriented to audiences and publics is performed. According to this view, 'culture versus materiality' is too static a way of viewing a dynamic process that is constituted through action which has both symbolic and material dimensions and, most important here, the capacity for transgression. The transgression of stable boundaries and forms of action can in itself be subversive, one example of which is feminist mobilization around the idea of 'the personal as political'. This involves politicization and reconstitution of the previously 'apolitical' realm of gender relations, though in the process the notion of 'the political' changes too. Con-versely, the defence of boundaries between symbolic and instrumental areas may be a potent source of social movement mobilization, as in the case of resistance to commodification which defends areas of social life concerned with cultural reproduction, values and mutual understand-ing (Habermas, 1989: 267). Any transgression of previously established frontiers nonetheless presupposes the existence of boundaries that can be effaced. The next section will explore this idea further.

Transgression and Harlequinade

The cultural turn in sociology has been regarded, then, as inverting the economy–culture relation to give priority to the latter, or as absorbing what were previously regarded as material or 'real' relations into cultural ones. In opposition to these claims, I have suggested that contemporary societies are inevitably socially differentiated into multiple institutional orders through action and communication. In these terms, I will now suggest that it is perhaps more fruitful to examine the potentially subversive effects of transgression of boundaries, through social movement practice that I will call the 'Harlequinade'.

Rebellion is by its nature transgression. But it also entails dramatization, operating both in and out of a culture by means of public deeds (the original Greek meaning of 'drama') by contrast with 'theatre' and its connotations of contemplative *theoria* (Nichols, 1977). Through drama-rebellion, theatre leaves the confines of 'culture' and enters the realm of the mundane, which includes of course the everyday worlds of power and privilege. I do not have in mind here political theatre so much as theatrical politics that spills out of socially circumscribed spaces, to deploy dramatic arts (such as frivolity, pathos, comedy and irony) in settings where they were previously inappropriate. Kolakowski suggested that there is an antagonism between two philosophies – one that perpetuates the absolute and one that questions absolutes – a dichotomy symbolized in the antagonism between the priest, as guardian of the absolute, and the jester who moves in good society with impertinence. In 'every era the jester's philosophy exposes as doubtful what seems most unshakeable . . . derides common sense and reads sense into the absurd' (Kolakowski, 1969: 33–4). But as Raymond Nichols (1977) argues, Kolakowski's metaphor can be taken further, since the jester divides into two – the Fool and the Harlequin. The Fool, as in the medieval figure of the Lord of Misrule, parodies established customs and institutions (such as awesome mysteries of the mass) but only in order to release social tensions and hence reintegrate the social order. These were integrative transgressions that nonetheless had the potential to threaten the powers that be – hence the periodic banning of Fools' festivals. The Harlequin, however, is an altogether more complex and subversive figure who redirects attention and reverses the established order of things, such as poverty and wealth, freedom and slavery.

Originating from the sixteenth century *Commedia dell' Arte*, the Harlequin marked the appearance of popular theatre performed at fairs and festivals which made frequent allusions to local authorities and traditions. Alongside Renaissance high theatre there developed studies of provisional dialects and the lives of peasants, while plays became simpler in theme and broader in treatment. Miscellaneous material mingled and combined like pieces of glass in a kaleidoscope in a new form of entertainment, Improvized Comedy (Beaumont, 1976: 27). In these, the Harlequin would interrupt a scene in progress, perhaps by demonstration of astonishment or fright, or by humorous extravagances alien to the matter in hand (Beaumont, 1976: 30). The Harlequin was often obscene, but always mocking, clownish, insolent, feigning naiveté and stupidity.

These arguments are in similar vein to Mikhail Bakhtin's famous study of Rabelais (1984) where laughter, in the Renaissance carnival, builds its own world in opposition to the official world of church and state. The carnival, and the Harlequin in particular, acted on the borderline between life and art (Bakhtin 1984: 88). Indeed, ambivalence is at the core of the carnival, in which appearances are neither true nor false, the actor is also a spectator, and death is often also rebirth. In opposition to high culture, the carnival is a celebration of 'lowness', degradation, debasement, defecation, urination and copulation. Yet this is not a simple contrast of 'popular' against 'refined' pleasures, but signifies impending crisis in the old order – the mask of the Harlequin 'is related to transition, metamorphosis, the violation of natural boundaries' (1984: 40). The Harlequin's somersaults are topographical – oriented to heaven and earth, the underworld, top and bottom, interplay of the face by the buttocks. At the same time the hierarchical physical and social world of the Middle Ages was crumbling in the wake of a new world based on horizontal lines and real space. In developing a new conception of the world, Rabelais used folklore to make the top and bottom change places, since the greatest treasures are hidden underground (1984: 403).

Popular theatre in general and the Harlequinade in particular were regarded with disdain by classical theatre but also often by the authorities – troupes were suppressed where they appeared too subversive, and Sir Robert Walpole (British PM 1721–42) physically attacked a Harlequin who mocked his Excise Act (Nichols, 1977). But the Harlequinade was not merely satire, since the actor had to understand and use the alternative resources of cultural traditions of society, while innovating and appearing at least spontaneous. The Harlequin always appeared in public, and touched public authority, but the audience was not invited to identify with the actor, whose mask and costume indicated disassociation from the ongoing scene, but to recognize that the familiar world had become strange and alien (Nichols, 1977). 'I am as impudent as the devil' says the Harlequin in *Arlequin Chevalier du Soleil*, and the mask was derived from demonic lore and legend (Beaumont, 1976: 78). The Harlequin was only partly present in the scene, the rest was in dim communion with Unknown Powers. Indeed the Harlequin has its origin in diabolical ambivalence – its grotesque manner and costume was a challenge to conventional demands of the sublime. Yet the parody of official culture presupposed knowledge of it. To enjoy Paul Scarron's parody of Virgil (*Virgile Travesti*, 1653) for example, it was necessary to be familiar with the *Aeneid* (Bakhtin, 1984: 305).

The Harlequin became a symbol of transgression and rebellion – action that is innovative and directed to a public, capturing drama and theatre. The mask conveyed a mixture of devilry, mockery, sensuality, artfulness and mystery (Beaumont, 1976: 48). This kind of comedy can be dangerous, as theatre and politics play off against each other generating an infinite series of reflecting mirrors. The Harlequin derided common sense and read sense into the absurd, provoking unnerving visions of customary ways. One can see in this social form, perhaps, the epitome of culturalized politics.

Orange Alternative and the politics of irony

The potential (and limitations) of this kind of transgression of the cultural and political will be illustrated with reference to the decay of communist rule in Poland in the 1980s[6] and specifically to 'Orange Alternative', an activist group based in Wroclaw. The role of social movements in the fall of communism in Eastern Europe varied in different places, and in some cases the system imploded with relatively little pressure from mass protests, which appeared only briefly.[7] Protest and alienation from the system often took 'apolitical' forms of withdrawal, privatism, alcoholism, and dealing *na leva*, 'on the side', in extensive informal economy and society (Bugajski and Pollack, 1989: 187ff; Hankiss, 1991; Ray, 1996: 125ff.). Poland, however, was exceptional in that the PUWP faced the mass opposition of Solidarity, which continued to organize underground after it was banned in 1982. Poland was the weakest link in the Soviet bloc, having witnessed periodic mass opposition since 1956 (Misztal and Jenkins, 1995)[8] and the advent of Solidarity perhaps signalled more generally that the system as a whole was doomed.

The nature and development of dissident politics in Poland differed from protest movements in western countries and reflected the particular conditions of state socialism. An 'over-extended administered public sphere' (Habermas, 1989: 384) blocked pluralistic channels of political activity while (paradoxically) politicizing everyday life to an extent unparalleled in western democracies. One upshot of this was that the rule of the Party provided a visible focus for almost all disputes (especially economic ones), which therefore always became 'political' (Bunce, 1983; Ost, 1991; Ray, 1996). In an attempt to depoliticize (and thereby further differentiate) everyday life, some anti-Communist social movements claimed to be reclaiming 'civil society' and the rights of autonomous activity independent of the state. The anti-Communist movements were described as 'self-limiting revolutions' that eschewed central control of power or any *pouvoir constituant*, and opposed radical revolution (Arato, 1991). Their organization was diffuse, they offered no utopian vision of the future, and at times claimed to develop an 'anti-political politics' (Havel, 1988). However, despite the different context from that of the West, some writers see in these strands of anti-Communist social movement a similarity with a 'postmodern politics' of 'unrestrained recycling of archaic and unorthodox concepts within pluralist frameworks' (Ost, 1990: 16–17). Crook et al. (1994: 158) claim that the politics of the post-Stalinist generation did not fit with the conventional framework of bureaucratization, but rather were expressed in new movements with symbols, icons and repertoires disseminated by television, thus heralding the advent of a new politics.

According to this view, anti-Communist politics shared with western postmodernism concerns with identity, lifestyle, youth culture, and playful ironic parody. This resonates too with recent theories of social movements, characterizing them as addressing questions of 'the grammar of forms of life', that is, equal rights, self-realization and participation, rather than the 'old politics' of wages, housing, redistribution and trade union rights (Habermas, 1989: 375). In similar vein, Melucci (1989: 203) writes of social movements as 'nomads of the present', that 'operate as signs' through which expressive rather than instrumental ends are pursued.

Now, the backcloth for this kind of activism in Poland was the Praetorian rule of General Jaruzelski, during which time Solidarity was illegal, although it continued to operate through underground networks. Underground Solidarity was amorphous, with few regularized procedures, although it did organize strikes and demonstrations in the later 1980s, as dialogue between the Government and the union was resumed. However, martial law prompted the formation of 'new wave' protest, many participants in which had still been at school or college during the initial Solidarity period (1980–1). Too young to make decisions, they were given tasks like pasting up posters and perhaps held minor positions in various organizations. On 13 December 1981 the military coup came as a shock to people who had placed hopes in the more traditional forms of political and trade union organization in Solidarity.[9] These younger activists mostly avoided prison, becoming key players in the underground opposition, recreating destroyed organizations, forming and running groups and quasi parties. After 1982 a network of underground committees was formed, and by 1983 these published over 500 illicit newspapers (Ramet, 1991: 68). The younger members organized underground printing, distributing leaflets and became the core of demonstrations against martial law, although the activists were generally unknown, by contrast with the opposition stars such as Walesa, Kuron and Moczulski. Soon, though, they too were being arrested, interrogated, shot at, whilst harbouring a sense of the failure of traditional forms of political organization (Tadeusz Korab, *Politbuda* 1 October 1988, Gdansk).[10]

The 'new wave' shared an 'anti-political' philosophy in the sense that they eschewed ideological battles or labels whilst redefining the nature of 'the political' in more cultural and dramaturgical ways. In the process a new (in that context) form of political action emerged which one could describe as a 'Harlequinade' in that it was about dramatic transgression of prevailing conceptions, in order to make the system appear alien and absurd. There were many such groups, which had no formal organization yet but which were able to establish 'nomadic' connections, not only within Poland, but also with western and other eastern European social movements. One of these was *Wolnosc i Pokoj* ('Freedom and Peace', WiP) which organized around issues of disarmament and conscription, making links with western peace and ecology groups. WiP embodied a pastiche of ideas, including pacifism, anarchism, Catholicism, Solidarity, punk and ecology. 'As a movement' they claimed, 'we have no ideology, no uniform, no hairstyle . . . . What unites us is our opposition to omnipresent force' (*WiP West Bulletin* 1, Spring 1988). An important strategy of their campaigns was to push the authorities into public contradiction. One example of this was to make Otto Schimek a 'patron saint' of WiP. Schimek was an Austrian conscript in the Wehrmacht who had been shot in Poland for disobeying orders in 1944. Because the PUWP Government could not acknowledge the right of conscientious objection, they were forced into the position of justifying the sentence passed on Schimek, thereby undermining their links with West German peace movements, for whom Schimek was also a potent symbol of protest (Jacek Czaputowicz, *Biuletyn WiP* 2, Warsaw).

An underlying philosophy of the new wave was 'happy are the despots who are hated – woe to them when they are ignored'. The police truncheon is effective as long as it is taken seriously by those against whom it is used – who respond themselves by throwing stones or petrol bombs (Boreyko, 1989). The force used against protesters must be minimally legitimate to the extent that those who carry out the orders regard them as issued by a proper authority, but the truncheon looses its effectiveness when it is laughed at. In students' cartoons Jaruzelski, Urban (a Government spokesperson) and the police were no longer portrayed as the thugs of previous years, but looked instead like gaping idiots (Wojciech Maziarsk, *Kultura*, June 1988). Despite military law, the beatings and general repression, the regime was failing to instil fear because it was entering a profound legitimation crisis, which the politics of irony helped intensify.

One movement that aptly encapsulates this style of politics was Orange Alternative, organized by an activist, Wlademar Fydrych (alias 'the Major') who arranged 'happenings' that attempted to depart from the standard script for political protest. Fydrych's responses when interviewed for *Uncensored Polish News Bulletin* for example, illustrate his desire to subvert the established attributions of reasons and objectives (Ramet, 1991: 85):

Question: What does 'happening' mean?
Answer: Happening is just what happens to happen.
Question: Do you set up happenings in order to expose the totalitarianism of the system under which we live?
Answer: I do them because I do them.
Question: But one does things because of some reason, or for something.

> *Answer*: Well, yes. When I was preparing for the gnome happening, I
> assumed that we would have a good time, with sweets and streamers.

Orange Alternative described its politics as 'socialist surrealism', or
'how to be curious orange', on the basis that in a repressive system, any
collective non-conformist action, such as everyone wearing orange,
would threaten the state. The Major's aim was to 'treat the communist
system of Poland as a work of art' (Ramet, 1991: 86), that could be
decoded and approached with irony and parody. Orange Alternative
aimed to offer a distorting mirror to everyday life in Poland, and
claimed merely to lay bare the absurdity of the system, by reducing to
absurdity the actions of the authorities. 'Socialist surrealism' claimed to
be 'realistic' in that it represented the reality of life in Poland perhaps in
the sense of slogans of Paris 1968, 'Le rêve est réalité!' and 'Soyez
réalistes, démandez l'impossible!' (Besançon, 1968).

Banners and slogans are the sustenance of political mobilization and
operate as political codes – reducing complexity into binary oppositions
of friend and foe. This usual script of political discourse operated both
for the PUWP and for Solidarity who shared an epic, heroic conception
of political struggle in terms of 'liberation' and 'social justice' which
were contested within a public domain. But Orange Alternative's
'banners' parodied this script with ironic play on the slogans of the
regime, its competition with the West and administrative failures, such
as chronic shortages:

> More People's Councils – fewer hospitals!
> The Warsaw Pact – an Avant-Garde of Peace!
> Let's make our town outdo Los Angeles – dress colourfully!
> Toilet paper R.I.P. – We can also wipe the government's!
> Molotov, yes! Ribbentrop, no!

An example of their operations was the 'Eve of the October Revolution' (a parody of Christmas Eve) which was advertised through
leaflets in bombastic text:

> ΠΡΑΒΔΑ will set us free. Comrades it is time to shake off the indifference of
> the popular masses! Let us begin to celebrate the Eve of the October
> Revolution!

At 4:00 p.m. on 6 November 1988, several groups gathered on Swidnick
Street in the centre of Wroclaw, with an eight-metre long cardboard
model of the cruiser Aurora, while another procession carried a
similar model of the battleship Potemkin. Others had pointed paper
caps on their heads, marching along emulating a column of Bolshevik
General Budienny's cavalry. Another group, dressed as Red Army
soldiers, carried wooden rifles and demanded the rehabilitation of

Trotsky, prompting a German reporter to cite this as the largest demonstration of Trotskyists in Eastern Europe! They were joined by hundreds of passers-by wearing red clothing (as requested on the leaflets) and demanding (with double irony) that the working day of militiamen and the secret service be limited to eight hours.[11] None the less, the militia broke up the demonstration, breaking under batons hallowed symbols of communism such as the Potemkin and Aurora, and General Budienny's 'cavalry' were arrested (*Nasze Wiadomosci*, 42, 28 February 1989). Orange Alternative happenings usually ended in arrests, and at a similar 'Bolshevik demonstration' staged by Warsaw students, a participant, Rafel Szymczyk, became the first Pole since 1945 to be arrested for carrying a portrait of Lenin in public!

That the puns and irony would be readily understood by audiences illustrates how this was a politics of Harlequinade. Such was the case during the *Dzien Krasnali* festival, which has the double meaning of 'Day of Elves' and 'Day of the Reds', where demonstrators wore pointed elf's hats, which became the cartoon symbol of the Major, drawn on walls around Wroclaw. Likewise the summertime *U-paly* (Heatwaves) event punned the word *pala* (club) which could be taken to mean 'Beneath the Club (weapon)'. These were combined with the 'Who's scared of toilet paper?' action in which this sought-after commodity was freely distributed. At the pre-Christmas parade of Father Christmases a march set off from Wroclaw University towards Swidnicha Street, led by the Major, dressed as a devil blowing a trumpet. A banner at the head of the parade read 'Father Christmas is the only hope for reform'. When the ZOMO (riot police) went in to arrest the Father Christmases, whom they found roped together, they were showered with sweets and Christmas decorations.

When in Spring 1989 over three thousand demonstrators in Wroclaw carried effigies with dark sunglasses (General Jaruzelski's favourite fashion) they were attacked with tear gas. The 'Major' was prosecuted but, at his trial, demonstrators appeared dressed in orange, witnesses appeared in orange, one woman claiming to be the Major's fiancée, with punk hair and wheeling a velveteen lion. Outside the crown shouted slogans 'Pershing Missiles No! Sanitary towels yes!'. Meanwhile in the courtroom another witness (male, this time) also claimed to be the Major's fiancée. In the face of this carnival of parody, which undermined the legitimacy of the court, militia witnesses faltered and stammered, and after six hours the 'Major' was acquitted (Boreyko, 1989).

This politics of irony extended to their treatment of Solidarity too. In response to the PUWP's referendum on reforms, in November 1987, Solidarity called for a boycott, on the grounds that participation would lend legitimacy to the Government. But Orange Alternative called on people to vote *twice*, 'making Wroclaw the city of a 200% turn-out!' thus parodying both the faked election results of the (earlier) communist period and the glorification of over-fulfilled planning targets. Thus

Orange Alternative were not simply challenging the regime but the nature of political discourse. Solidarity and the PUWP, after all, inhabited the binary opposition of 'civil society/state', a political code in which both laid claim to the rhetorical fiction, the 'sovereign people' as a collective subject. Thus Bauman (1994: 18) comments that two apparent adversaries, Adam Michnik and General Jaruzelski, were 'integral (though mutually opposite) partners of the same historical discourse', and only together could they dismantle communism.[12] By contrast, Orange Alternative illustrated politics as a Harlequinade which used its knowledge of culture to parody and delegitimate authority via a public that participated in the street theatre of the absurd. Playing with cultural icons of the communist system, mimicking and parodying the proceedings, while always playing to the public, they offered no romantic or heroic alternative to the existing system, no grand vision of the future. On the other hand the revelry did not admit tragic despair either – since its very playfulness presupposed that action could have effects, that transgression of the established boundaries was worthwhile.

Repairing the rupture?

According to Crook et al. (1994: 35), with culturalized new politics, 'action is divorced from underlying material constraints . . . and enters the voluntaristic realm of taste, choice and preference'. They view this as a permanent reconfiguration of the political, despite the 'inevitable normalization' that is likely to follow (1994: 164). To what extent is the emergence of new politics illustrated by the anti-Communist politics of irony? It would be superficial to suppose that there is a simple answer to this. It is true that new social movement politics, evident in feminist, eco-political and sexual identity groups, has become a stable (if small) part of the post-communist scene (Hausner et al., 1994; Kurczewska and Bojar, 1995).[13] However, the Harlequinade is an episode that disturbs the narrative plot, then closes. Similarly, satire, parody and irony it seems, were effective weapons of opposition groups but after the fall of communism there was a period of normalization and depoliticization. Alongside the Major's antics in 1989, the Round Table talks had been in progress, working towards an agreed transfer of power from the PUWP to a democratically elected parliament. Not all Solidarity factions had been conformable with this, particularly not Solidarnosc Walczaca (Fighting Solidarity), based in Wroclaw, to which some Orange Alternative activists had belonged. However, the talks resulted in the semi-free elections of June 1989, in which Solidarity won 99 of the 100 seats in the Senate (Upper House) although 65 per cent of the seats in the Sejm (Lower House) were reserved for the PUWP. This was followed by Presidential elections in November–December 1990, won by Lech Walesa, and in October 1991 by genuinely competitive elections which resulted in a succession of centre-right coalition governments. This was reversed in September 1993, when the Democratic Left Alliance and the Polish Peasant Party, both with roots in the PUWP, formed a new government.

This stabilization of parliamentary politics was accompanied by what many commentators viewed with concern as a 'depoliticization' of Polish society. Only 43 per cent voted in the October 1991 elections (Kramer, 1995), and according to Bauman (1994: 28), in 1991 90 per cent of Poles had not attended a single political meeting nor belonged to any political party. Yet this may be less a cause for concern so much as an indication that with the implosion of the sovereign power of the Party, Poland, like other central-east European countries, was undergoing a differentiation of civil and political life, in which the polity became a more narrowly circumscribed sphere of activity. The familiar scripts of political exchange began to take shape, condensing complex issues into binary codes such as government/opposition, church/state, Catholic/secular. In this context depoliticization perhaps reflected new boundaries emerging between the civil, political, economic and private.

Post-communist societies moreover, faced urgent systemic problems that accentuated redistributive questions even if these were culturally inflected (as will be seen below). These problems included:

- the historical pattern of industrial concentration in large plants, with whole regions dependent on a single enterprise for employment welfare;
- a dearth of domestic capital or savings and highly selective foreign buyers, mainly interested in hiving off those parts of industries with growth potential;
- an obsolete industrial structure which is highly polluting and geared to capital goods and military production;
- the consequent political choice between asset liquidation, mass unemployment and social destabilization on the one hand, and continued subsidy and protection of state enterprises on the other;
- a diminishing revenue base which leaves few domestic resources to tackle problems of environmental destruction and crumbling infrastructure, which in turn impede economic internationalization;
- the need to develop strategies for privatization and marketization and choices between 'shock therapy' and gradual transformation, while attempting to control the unregulated transfer of assets from the state sector into the hands of the former nomenklatura;
- hyper-inflation and economic collapse, accompanied by a rise in poverty especially among workers. See Table 8.1, which shows increasing rates of poverty in Poland during the first three years of post-communism.[14]

Before closing this discussion, it is worth noting two developments that took shape in the context of these challenges – the revival (or reinvention)

TABLE 8.1 *Social costs of the transition from communism in Poland* (percentages living below subsistence level in each group)

	1989		1991	
	Total	Children	Total	Children[3]
Workers	15.8	19.1	38.1	57.9
Mixed[1]	7.9	10.3	21.2	30.4
Farmers	17.2	20.3	39.4	50.9
Pensioners[2]	36.2	na	33.0	na

Source: Branko Milanovic, *Social Costs of the Transition to Capitalism: Poland 1989–91* (unpublished)

[1] Households of both industrial and rural workers.
[2] Negligible numbers of children living with pensioners.
[3] Percentages of children is higher than total number of households because poverty affects families with 4–5 children more than smaller families.

of redistributive politics and difficulties of stabilizing political discourse within new boundaries, which illustrates a more negative aspect of culturalization. The latter issue relates to problems of overload of complexity mentioned earlier.

Redistributive politics

The post-communist settlement has seen a reappearance of redistributive politics, the resolution of which is, for some, crucial to the future of democratization (Ost, 1995). Now, one may argue that 'real socialism' was a terminal form of redistributive politics, the eclipse of which opens the way for new and diverse politics of recognition and identity. Yet real socialism did away with the problem of redistribution by politicizing and therefore cancelling out all economic agency (Mokrzycki, 1995). It is thus in post-communist society, with the reappearance of the market that redistribution becomes a fundamental social and political problem, prompted in part by the rapid increase in relative poverty following the 1989 Balcerowicz Plan. While Solidarity initially supported Balcerowicz's 'shock therapy',[15] by 1994 Marian Kraklewski (leader of the remnant of the union) proposed a new economic order based on self-management and social welfare. This was partly a response to the challenge posed by the revitalized former communist trade union, the OPZZ,[16] but was also a response to government austerity measures, such as the *popiwck* tax on wage increases, introduced in 1990 to stem inflation (Kramer, 1995). The new interest-based politics of redistributive conflict, however, presupposes the market as the principal means of resource distribution, the operations of which it aims to regulate and adjust in favour of industrial workers (Mokrzycki, 1995). It thus signals the beginning of increased differentiation between the economy and polity as discrete spheres of activity.

Culture and boundaries

One may go further and suggest that a culturalized politics does not in any way contribute to the formation of complex interdependent structures. The process of subsystem differentiation is a risky and uncertain process, especially during the transformation of a highly politicized society to one in which power is self-limited and dispersed within procedural thresholds. In the face of complex and difficult problems there may be a tendency for action to regress towards culturally available solutions that do not permit the formation of fluid and adaptive systems. In this sense, 'culturalized' forms of politics may persist that are both regressive and inadequate to deal with a complex and multi-layered social order. When millionaire Stanislaw Tyminski contested the 1990 presidential election under the banner 'Party X', the empty meaning of the signifyer 'X' captured the inchoate character of political discourse. Civic identities, in which cultural and religious values were separated from a formal-rational polity have been slow to develop in post-communist societies. This is partly because of the persistence of an irredentist and essentialist notion of 'the national community' which was often understood as an organic, undifferentiated and spiritual entity, in opposition to an oppressive (and foreign) state.[17] In Poland this is evident in the often bitter disputes over the post-communist constitution which illustrated the difficulties of forming stable separations between formal-rational and religious-cultural procedures.

Rather than a celebration of hyper-differentiated dissolution of boundaries, the constitution debate illustrated how (in some contexts) the failure to separate culture and politics can hinder the emergence of public-rights-based discourse. A Constitutional Tribunal drafted a new constitution for debate by the National Assembly (Senate and Sejm) prior to being put to a referendum. A critical issue was the role of the Church, in particular whether agreement could be reached with the Sejm over a proposed Concordat with Rome that was to give the Church special constitutional status in the 'Polish State of the Catholic Nation'. Between 1993 and 1997 this was resisted by the largely secular, left-of-centre Sejm. In addition to the constitutional role of the Church was the question of abortion rights, which were greatly curtailed by 1990 legislation (Fuszara, 1993). Parliament's attempt to pass new legislation in 1993 that would have restored the relatively liberal legislation of 1956, was vetoed by the President, claiming moral and populist rather than constitutional authority. The Church, Solidarity Labour Union and Lech Walesa intimated that, failing an agreement on the Concordat and the inclusion of a clause protecting 'human life from the moment of conception', they would urge rejection of the new constitution (EECR, 1995 4, 1: 18–20).

This they did, when the constitution (that rather fudged these issues) was finally put to a referendum in May 1997, although it was accepted by a narrow margin of 53 to 46 per cent. The institutionalization of rights-based active public spheres then, may be dependent on the formation of boundaries between cultural and political spheres of competence.

Conclusions

This discussion has attempted to re-cast the culturalization debate within the framework of social differentiation. Whilst it would be fool-ish to deny the ways in which cultural and economic life are mutually inflected, I believe that a more productive way of approaching these questions is through an understanding of the creation, maintenance and permeability of boundaries, necessary to prevent pollution or distortion of one sphere by the standards of another, especially the moral by the instrumental. The appearance of new wave politics in Poland did reconfigure 'the political' in innovative and dramaturgical ways, contri-buting to an ongoing decomposition of communist authority. However, it did so in a particular historical context in which martial law had closed off many avenues of political articulation, leaving open an ironic play with the regime's own symbolic system while avoiding the requirement to set out programmes and policies. Against the narrative play of the Round Table negotiations, the new wave was an interlude, a Harlequinade of insolent and challenging mockery. But in the face of problems of systemic reconstruction after 1989, the political terrain became inhabited by familiar figures of interest-based and redistributive politics combined with attempts to separate cultural from formal values of political conduct.

However, I am not suggesting that the lesson to be learned here is that the 'material' always returns in the last instance. Rather, I am suggesting that in complex differentiated societies action is both self-limited within discrete spheres, and can transgress these – sometimes with potent effects. The 'culture turn' aims to overcome the play of the symbolic vs non-symbolic systems but in the process slips into a pre-sociological mode of reasoning. Sociology should surely move beyond the actor/effect, symbolic/real dichotomies with reference to social systems that have no originating point and within which all events and institutions are symbolically mediated. All social action deploys sym-bolic and meaningful systems through which it becomes inter-subjectively shared. However, complex societies (indeed virtually *all* societies) require differentiated institutional orders to manage chaos and complexity by framing action within rules of relevance and appro-priateness. Much of the socialization process involves learning to live within these orders to the extent that they become latent, which to a large extent they do. However, societies are characterized by fault lines

– boundary disputes where power, resources and symbolic systems are mobilized to redefine the limits of institutional orders. Transgressions may readjust boundaries but not eliminate them as such, while social stabilization is likely to re-establish concerns defined by subsystems.

Notes

1 'Culture', as Raymond Williams said, 'is one of the two or three most complicated words in the English language' (1983: 87). In sociological terms it can refer to 'historically constructed meanings and social scripts' (Smelser and Swedberg, 1994: 19); the 'order corresponding to meaningful action' expressed in for example, 'religious ritual, socialization and education to dramaturgical innovation' (Alexander, 1990: 1–2). It can refer to symbolic systems, social meanings and values (which are not identical to each other), and since these mediate the lives of all individuals, all social action is culturally inflected. However, to conclude from this that everything is culture would be as trite as the converse – reasoning that since all social action has resource implications, everything is economic. This discussion proceeds on this basis.

2 This is a slightly curious version of the culturalization thesis since it insists on offering a material (productive) basis for the dominance of culture. Can one detect here a recycling of the old Althusserian notions of relative autonomy and structures in dominance?

3 'Culturalism is an occupational hazard of literary intellectuals and has slotted marvellously well into a certain reading of the current political situation of the West' (Eagleton, 1996: 123). The latter, he says, is one of emphatic defeat of the left to which one response has been the denial of both materiality and totality.

4 This does not mean that mediatized interactions are freed from cultural embedding – on the contrary, money depends on trust and confidence (L-system) and power on legitimacy (I-system).

5 Economic activity is understood here as utilitarian criteria of resource maximization guided by interests, while culture refers to values and morals guided by a logic of recognition. This contrast is developed by Honneth (1995). Conflicts over the extension of market-like mechanisms into higher education are motivated in part by the sense of injured feeling arising from the violation of deeply-rooted expectations regarding recognition.

6 The actual name of the ruling party from 1948 to 1989 was the Polish United Workers Party (PUWP).

7 They were perhaps what Weber called 'communities of fate' (*Schicksalsgemeinschaften*) retaining little cohesion once their common enemy was vanquished.

8 Poland was unusual in other ways too – for example, agriculture had not been collectivized and by 1986, 70 per cent of food production came from private plots (Lovenduski and Woodall, 1987: 87).

9 Solidarity was initially willing to work within the existing constitution, and its role was (briefly) institutionalized by the Gdansk Agreement (1981) which provided for the separation of state and trade unions, the right to strike, and end of censorship and workers' self-management. Whether Solidarity would have entered a power-sharing pact with the government in 1980–1 is not clear, but Walesa (1988: 152) writes as though this was a possibility, when he refers to 'the favourable climate that . . . developed during the strike negotiations. If our

movement was to become the driving force of change . . . we needed the government's support in the sharing of power.'

10 Another aspect of the new wave was the appearance of punk bands as a vehicle of political despair, with names like *SS-20, Pathology of Pregnancy, Shortage, Crisis* and *Trybuna Brudu* ('Dirt Tribune', rhyming with *Trybuna Ludu*, the Party newspaper). But my main concern here is with culturalized politics rather than politicized culture.

11 Orange Alternative liked to 'celebrate' the police. On Policeman's Day they took a six-metre 'flower' to police HQ and festooned patrol cars with flowers.

12 With the decline of ideological commitment among the PUWP, the appearance of technocratic values diminished policy differences between the two contenders. In his 1982 May Day speech ('The Philosophy of Revolution') Bronislaw Lagowski argued that, under Solidarity, collective control of individuals would prove more penetrating than ever, whereas democracy was premised on limitation of the state. In 1986 Prime Minister, Prof. Zbignieu Messner ('Thesis Concerning the Second Stage of Reform') argued that the market economy, independent banking and the profit motive were central to social development.

13 It should be noted that Kurczewska and Bojar discuss new social movement activity in Poland, but with evident disapproval, since it does not in their view take account of Poland's cultural specificity, although they do not say what this is.

14 I discuss these issues and their ramifications in post-communist politics at more length in Ray (1996). See also Hausner et al. (1995) and Holmes (1997).

15 'Shock therapy', associated with the former Polish Minister of Finance, Leszek Balcerowicz, is a strategy for rapid privatization and marketization in which prices free float, enterprise subsidies are withdrawn, firms thus face market clearing prices, foreign competition. According to this view, the worse the resulting economic situation, the more effective will be the 'cold turkey' strategy (Balcerowicz, 1993).

16 *Ogolnopolski Porozumienie Zwiakow Zawodowych*, All Polish Federation of Trade Unions. By mid-1991 Solidarity's membership had fallen from its 1981 level of 10 million to 1.6 million.

17 The first post-communist Prime Minister Tadeusz Mazowiecki, for example, regarded interest-based politics as an undesirable legacy of the communist past (Ost, 1995).

References

Alexander, J. (1990) 'Analytic debates', Introduction to J. Alexander and S. Seidman (eds) *Culture and Society: Contemporary Debates*, Cambridge: Cambridge University Press.

Arato, A. (1991) 'Revolution, civil society, and democracy', in Rau (ed.) *The Reemergence of Civil Society in Eastern Europe and the Soviet Union*, Oxford: Westview Press, pp. 161–82.

Arendt, H. (1959) *The Human Condition*, New York: Doubleday Anchor.

Bakhtin, M. (1984) *Rabelais and His World*, Bloomington: Indiana University Press.

Balcerowicz, L. (1993) *Common Fallacies in the Debate on the Economic Transition in Central and Eastern Europe*, London: EBRD working paper 11.

Bauman, Z. (1994) 'After the patronage state: a model in search of class interests', in C. Bryant and E. Mokrzycki (eds) *The New Great Transformation*, London: Routledge, pp. 14–35.

Beaumont, C. (1976) *The History of the Harlequin*, reprint of 1926 edn, New York: Arno Press.

Besançon, J. (ed.) (1968) *Les Murs ont la parole, Journal Mural, Mai 1968*, Paris.

Boreyko, R. (1989) 'Major's socialist surrealism', *The Bloc, Voice of Central and Eastern Europe*, (152–3): 44–6.

Bugajski, J. and Pollack, M. (1989) *Eastern European Fault Lines*, Boulder, CO: Westview.

Bunce, V. (1983) 'The political economy of the Brezhnev era: the rise and fall of corporatism', *British Journal of Political Science*, 13: 129–58.

Crook, S., Pakulski, J. and Waters, M. (1992) *Postmodernization: Change in Advanced Societies*, London: Sage.

Eagleton, T. (1996) *The Illusions of Postmodernism*, Oxford: Blackwell.

Fuszara, M. (1993) 'Abortion and the formation of the public sphere in Poland', in N. Funk and M. Mueller (eds) *Gender Politics and Post-Communism*, London: Routledge, pp. 241–52.

Giddens, A. (1990) *The Consequences of Modernity*, Cambridge: Polity.

Goffman, I. (1959) *Interaction Ritual*, New York: Anchor Books.

Habermas, J. (1989) *The Theory of Communicative Action, Lifeworld and System: a Critique of Functionalist Reason*, vol. 2, Cambridge: Polity.

Habermas, J. (1991) 'A reply', in A. Honneth and H. Joas (eds) *Communicative Action – Essays on Jurgen Habermas's 'The Theory of Communicative Action'*, trans. J. Gaines and D.L. Jones, Oxford: Polity, pp. 214–64.

Hankiss, E. (1991) 'The "second society": is there an alternative social model emerging in contemporary Hungary?', in F. Fehér and A. Arato *The Crisis in Eastern Europe*, New Brunswick: Transaction Books.

Hausner, J., Jessop, B. and Nielsen, K. (1995) *Strategic Choice and Path-dependency in Post-Socialism*, Cheltenham: Edward Elgar.

Havel, V. (1988) 'Anti-political politics', in J. Keane (ed.) *Civil Society: New European Perspectives*, London: Verso, pp. 381–98.

Hebdige, D. (1989) 'After the masses', in S. Hall and M. Jaques (eds) *New Times*, London: Lawrence and Wishart.

Holmes, L. (1997) *Post-Communism, an Introduction*, Cambridge: Polity.

Honneth, A. (1995) *Struggle for Recognition – the Moral Grammar of Social Conflicts*, Cambridge: Polity.

Jameson, F. (1991) *Postmodernism – or the Cultural Logic of Late Capitalism*, London: Verso.

Jeffcutt, P. (1994) 'From interpretation to representation', in M. Parker and J. Hassard (eds) *Postmodernism and Organizations*, London: Sage, pp. 1–24.

Kolakowski, L. (1969) *Towards a Marxist Humanism*, New York: Grove Press.

Kramer, M. (1995) 'Polish workers and the post-communist transition 1983–93', *Europe–Asia Studies*, 47 (4): 669–712.

Kumar, K. (1995) *From Post-Industrial to Post-Modern Society*, Oxford: Blackwell.

Kurczewska, J. and Bojar, H. (1995) 'A new society? Reflections on democracy and pluralism in Poland', in C. Bryant and E. Mokrzycki (eds) *Democracy, Civil Society and Pluralism*, Warsaw: IFiS Publishers, pp. 143–204.

Lash, S. (1988) 'Discourse or figure? Postmodernism as a regime of signification', *Theory Culture & Society*, 5 (2–3): 311–36.

Lash, S. and Urry, J. (1994) *Economies of Signs and Space*, London: Sage.

Leyson, A. and Thrift, N. (1997) *Money/Space*, London: Routledge.

Lovenduski, J. and Woodall, J. (1987) *Politics and Society in Eastern Europe*, London: Macmillan.

Luhmann, N. (1982) *The Differentiation of Society*, New York: Colombia University Press.

Luhmann, N. (1993) *Risk – a Sociological Theory*, Berlin: de Gruyter.

Melucci, A. (1989) *Nomads of the Present*, London: Radius.

Misztal, B. and Jenkins, J.C. (1995) 'Starting from scratch is not always the same', in J.C. Jenkins and B. Klandermans (eds) *The Politics of Social Protest*, London: UCL Press, pp. 324–64.

Mokrzycki, E. (1995) 'Class interests, redistribution and corporatism', in C. Bryant and E. Mokrzycki (eds) *Democracy, Civil Society and Pluralism*, Warsaw: IFiS Publishers, pp. 205–18.

Mouzelis, N. (1999) 'Modernity: a non-European conceptualization', *BJS* 50 (1): 141–59.

Münch, R. (1990) 'Differentiation, rationalization, interpretation: the emergence of modern society', in J. Alexander and P. Colomy (eds) *Differentiation Theory and Social Change*, New York: Columbia University Press, pp. 441–64.

Nichols, R. (1977) 'Rebels, beginners and buffoons: politics as action', in T. Ball (ed.) *Political Theory and Praxis: New Perspectives*, Minneapolis: University of Minnesota Press.

Ost, D. (1990) *Solidarity and the Politics of Antipolitics: Opposition and Reform in Poland since 1968*, Philadelphia: Temple University Press.

Ost, D. (1991) 'The crisis of liberalism in Poland', *Telos*, 89: 85–95.

Ost, D. (1995) 'Labor, class and democracy: shaping political antagonisms in post-communist society', in B. Crawford (ed.) *Markets, States, Democracy: the Political Economy of Post-Communist Transformation*, Boulder, CO: Westview, pp. 177–203.

Parsons, T. (1971) *The System of Modern Societies*, Englewood Cliffs, NJ: Prentice-Hall.

Poster, M. (1995) *The Second Media Age*, Cambridge: Polity.

Ramet, S.P. (1991) *Social Currents in Eastern Europe – the Sources and Making of the Great Transformation*, London: Duke University Press.

Ray, L.J. (1996) *Social Theory and the Crisis of State Socialism*, Cheltenham: Edward Elgar.

Schuluchter, W. (1985) *The Rise of Western Rationalism: Max Weber's Developmental History*, Berkeley: University of California Press.

Smelser, N.J. and Swedberg, R. (eds) (1994) *The Handbook of Economic Sociology*, Princeton, NJ: Princeton University Press.

Walesa, L. (1988) *Path of Hope – an Autobiography*, London: Pan.

Weber, M. (1976) *Protestant Ethic and the Spirit of Capitalism*, trans. A. Giddens, London: Allen & Unwin.

Williams, R. (1983) *Keywords*, London: Fontana.

9

Performing Politics: The Dramatics of Environmental Protest

Bronislaw Szerszynski

In this chapter I want to take up and develop some questions about the relationship between politics and culture that Larry Ray and Andrew Sayer raise in their introduction to the present volume. That I will do this in relation to contemporary environmental protest is not to imply that there is something about the politics of the environment *per se* that marks it out as needing a different theoretical approach, but simply because in recent decades the environment as an issue domain has – and not without good reason – served as the channel for much of the inventiveness of contemporary cultural energy. Radical environmental protest, I will suggest, can provide us with rich materials for an exploration of the more general relation between politics and culture. In particular, environmental protest actions often exhibit what might be called a 'semiotic excess', an excess of meaning beyond any narrow notion of political effectiveness, and it is the question of how we *understand* this excess which will be the starting point for the reflections which follow.[1]

But radical environmental protest is also of interest because, while being a highly culturalized form of politics, it cannot easily be categorized under many of the theoretical labels used to understand such politics. Firstly, it cannot without distortion be simply seen as another example of the 'stylization of life', as a simple instrumental display of cultural capital by one group in order to mark themselves out as superior to another (Bourdieu, 1984). To do so would be to ignore the deep critique of contemporary society carried by such groups, or at least to regard this critique as nothing but another mark of distinction – as just another emblem of cultural membership, and as a weapon of *ressentiment* in the war for cultural superiority over others. Such a reduction, as I will argue below, would be a *theoretical* loss, in that it would diminish our capacity to discriminate between different kinds of social collectivity and action, reducing all to the dynamics of the style subculture. But it would also be an *ethico-political* loss, in that it would be implying that any forms of human action which seem to be normatively motivated, whether one agrees with them or not, are simply disguised forms of instrumentality and competition (see Chapter 2).

Secondly, neither does radical environmental politics clearly belong to the category of 'identity politics', whereby a specific social grouping defends its rights to be recognized as a distinct subculture (Taylor 1992; Fraser 1995). Political activists such as those protesting against the construction of roads or runways do not simply want to be left alone to follow their way of life unhindered, or to have that way of life culturally valued and validated. Indeed, they go out of their way to put themselves in the way of society-as-usual, disrupting major construction projects and everyday traffic flow in order to communicate their message to society – and a message not on behalf of themselves as a group but on behalf of nature. This is a cultural politics which operates not simply by marking and performing the boundary of its own form of life. It does so in such a way that beckons those outside its boundary, hailing them with a moral claim that one *should* be on the *inside*. 'Where are *you* in the Eco-War?', asks a cover of the movement magazine *Pod*. This is the kind of moral call characteristic of a distinction that seeks to universalize and thus eradicate itself.

Thirdly, although following an alternative lifestyle is an integral feature of contemporary direct action, integral to the protest lifestyle is a purposive orientation, which also marks it out from – or at least marks it as a distinctive variant of – the politics of self-realization and life decisions termed 'life politics' by Anthony Giddens (1991: 214–26). Individual self-realization and the more communal pursuit of the good life are indeed features of radical environmental protest, but this is a self-realization which is achieved through political effectiveness, and a good life which is always on the edge of being instrumentalized by the protest culture as simply a means to the higher end of the defence of nature. Constant self-monitoring in the name of individual responsibility is also characteristic of the protest subculture, but this is not simply felt as the demand to respond reflexively and responsibly to the choices that life lays before us, but as a call actively to pursue a project of societal transformation (Castells, 1997: 356–8; Szerszynski, 1997: 41–4).

But apart from testing the adequacy of existing categories of contemporary politics, what light can radical environmental protest shed on the relation between culture and politics? In order to explore this question, let us use the helpful first approximation of the relationship between cultural, economic and political forms of action given by Ray and Sayer in their introduction. Firstly, they point out that, whereas cultural forms of action are focused on their *meaningfulness*, economic forms of action are oriented towards *effects*. Secondly, they argue that cultural forms of action are 'primarily' oriented towards internal goods, while economic forms are instrumental, and oriented to external goals. Thirdly, they then allow that all economic activities have a cultural dimension, although 'the converse does not apply', so that economic activities can be seen as a subset of the larger class of all human activities which have a cultural dimension (pp. 5–9).

Regarding politics and ethics, Ray and Sayer describe ethics as properly belonging to that class of human activities which are cultural, but not economic, since ethics is primarily concerned with the pursuit of internal, rather than external, goods. Secondly, however, the story of mainstream politics in the last half century has been one of a declining interest in notions of the good life, which formed the framework for post-war debate about economic redistribution, and an increasing tendency to see economic matters as a purely technical matter of good management. Thirdly, however, more culturalized versions of politics have emerged, partly in reaction to this narrowing of mainstream politics – sometimes with an emphasis on aesthetic cultural values, and sometimes, as with social movements such as environmentalism, on moral values. However, Ray and Sayer defend the enduring relevance of the distinction between different forms of human activity, such as those of culture, politics and economy, against those arguing for their progressive de-differentiation (e.g. Lash and Urry, 1987; 1994; Crook et al., 1992).

While I share many of the worries expressed by Ray and Sayer about the theoretical and political adequacy of positions that see culture and politics as collapsing in on each other, this is not, however, because I share their confidence in the salience of this distinction. One thing that their account highlights is the difficulty in treating cultural forms of action as a distinct subsection of human activities, whose relationship with other kinds of action such as politics and economics may or may not be changing. As Ray and Sayer at times hint, instrumental forms of orientation such as those found in economic behaviour are no less cultural, no less saturated and underpinned with cultural meanings, than orientations to intrinsic value, such as those of ethical action. The 'dis-embedding' brought about in the post-war period by the erosion of solidarities should thus be understood not as the evacuation of meaning, the stripping away of culture and thus as the laying bare of sheer, meaningless economic instrumentality, but as the growth and imposition of different, alienating meanings (cf. Szerszynski et al., 1996: 13).

Similarly, I want to suggest, politics is also always cultural. Dominant notions of political and civic life are no less performative than the dramatic protests described in Chapter 8, or below in my own; they simply operate according to different cultural logics. These differences have to be understood not just in terms of values, beliefs and goals, but in terms of different models or dramaturgies of human action, and of different models of the semiosis or meaning-bearing quality of human action. However, direct action politics does appear to be more cultural and symbolic than institutional politics, and this for two distinct reasons. Firstly, unfamiliar cultures characteristically do appear more 'cultural' than well-known ones, the familiarity of the meanings of which makes them appear more banal. Secondly, the culture of dramatic protest is itself one which is in a sense reflexive, in that it folds back on and ironizes itself, bringing its own cultural-ness more to the foreground (Seery, 1990).

It is these features of radical protest actions, I want to suggest, that make the study of such actions useful for sensitizing us to the performative nature of politics more generally. In the next section I want to set out some of the background for this claim, by sketching the history of the recent wave of environmental direct action, and drawing attention to ways in which it lends itself to analysis in terms of cultural meanings. I will then go on to do this in more depth with one specific form of environmental direct action – the use of the Street Party by the movement Reclaim the Streets – analysing it in terms of dramaturgical form. I then explore how this kind of event might fit into a spectrum of performance genres, in order to show how seeing political protest in terms of performance often – but unnecessarily – involves an implied reduction of the social movement to the style subculture. Finally, I return to the claim that all politics should be viewed as performative in character, making some suggestions about how changes in the character of environmental protest might be symptomatic of wider changes in conceptions of political and civic identity.

Protest as tactic / protest as meaning

The 1990s have seen an upsurge in direct action movements concerned with the environment. In 1991 the first British groups modelled on the US environmental direct action network Earth First! (EF!) were founded, with the same characteristically anarchistic 'structure' as the American movement. A splinter group, the Earth Liberation Front, separated in 1992, concentrating on the 'monkeywrenching' (ecological sabotage) made famous by EF! in the USA, while Earth First! itself concentrated on more visible and collective forms of non-violent direct action. Nineteen ninety-two also saw the beginning of the recent wave of protest activities against the British road-building programme, firstly at Twyford Down and later at dozens of rural and urban sites across the country. Protesters at these events are typically drawn from two distinct social groupings – local residents, often quite 'establishment' in background and outlook, and young, unemployed and geographically mobile 'eco-warriors', living in 'squats' or in on-site protest camps (Doherty, 1996; McKay, 1996; Seel, 1996).[2]

At about the same time the closely related protest movement Reclaim the Streets (RTS) emerged in London. From the beginning RTS also focused on opposition to the car, but less as a destroyer of rural habitats and more as a 'condensing symbol' for the general inhuman priorities of consumer capitalism. First formed in 1991, RTS in its earlier years carried out a number of protest actions drawing on protest repertoires not dissimilar to those employed by older organizations such as Greenpeace and Friends of the Earth (FoE) – the ritual smashing of cars in public places, and the painting of bicycle lanes on London streets, for example. After a two-year lacuna resulting from RTS's absorption into the wider direct action protests against the building of the M11 in East London, RTS re-emerged in 1995. As well as other RTS protests, 1995 saw the birth of the RTS 'Street Party', where motorized traffic in urban streets is halted, and the resultant spaces 'reclaimed' temporarily by crowds enjoying sound systems, jugglers and street theatre. Two such Street Parties took place in that year, followed by the extraordinary M41 Street Party of July 1996, involving eight thousand people, sound systems and food stalls, which stopped motorway traffic for eight hours (Anonymous, 1997).

There are a number of features of the Street Party that will be of particular interest in the analysis that follows. Firstly, in contrast with many earlier forms of protest, it is marked by a high level of festivity, as the 'business as usual' of consumer capitalism being suspended in favour of a convivial, celebratory anarchy. Secondly, RTS and many of the overlapping direct action movements mentioned above are more like 'disorganizations' than organizations, with a high degree of autonomy both for individual participants and for RTS cells in different cities. The idea of the 'Street Party of Street Parties' serves not only as a utopian vision of a universal rejection of capitalism and consumerism, but also as a description of how different RTS groups federate together, a network of networks without a centre (Anonymous, 1997: 5–6). Thirdly, the space for the Street Party is both created by and is the occasion for highly aesthetic and symbolic forms of direct action.

In all of these dimensions of RTS actions there is an apparent fusion between the pragmatic and the expressive. The creation of a festival is at once a calculated, political tactic to help bring about a different society in the future, and a realization of desire in the present. The disorganized, acephalic nature of RTS is at once an enactment of deeply held political values and a means of evading policing. Similarly, the specific forms that direct action takes in the Street Party seem to be at once expressive, symbolic acts and highly effective tactical techniques.

Let me expand on this last point. Brian Doherty has identified four particular tactical innovations of recent actions against roads and traffic – lock-ons, walkways, tunnels and tripods (Doherty, 1997: 8–9). *Lock-ons* – originally, involving protesters inserting an arm into a tube and handcuffing themselves to a concreted bar at the other end – first achieved prominence during the M11 evictions, but have undergone a fairly constant process of refinement in later protests. *Walkways*, created by suspending ropes between trees or houses, have been frequently used in road protests, particularly in the case of the impending eviction of more settled 'camps'. *Tunnels,* which protesters constructed to enable locking-on underground, were first used at Fairmile to delay the use of heavy plant during the construction of the new route for the A30, and rose to further public prominence in 1997 during the protests against the third runway at Manchester Airport. Finally, the *tripod,* where a protester is suspended from a tripod of three ten-foot scaffolding poles, was first used to stop traffic in 1995 in Greenwich by RTS, and tripods have since been used at both urban and rural protests (Doherty, 1997: 8–9). All of these tactical innovations have been highly effective in disrupting the construction of new roads and runways, in halting the flow of traffic on existing roads, in extending the life of protest events, and in helping ensure widespread media coverage (cf. Road Alert!, 1997: 111–17).

However, in another way, these forms of action are clearly more than simply technical innovations, simple means-to-an-end. These actions are clearly at least as significant – both for the protesters and for their fascinated, attentive public – for their cultural meanings as for their political effectiveness. In the terms of my introduction above, they exhibit a semiotic excess. How are we to understand this excess? Later in this chapter, I want to point out some problems with understanding it solely in terms of the need to mark the boundaries of the protest subculture. If, as Alberto Melucci has argued, political conflicts are nowadays to a large extent played out at the level of the symbolic codes with which society understands itself and the world, then the most important question may not be how the performance of highly com-mitted actions signifies to others amongst the committed (although this process clearly has a role), but how they signify to *society as a whole* (1989: 60; 1996: 357–60). In order to advance this claim, it may first be useful to explore some of the dramatic features of the RTS Street Party. If the movement and its actions have to be analysed in terms of meanings, not just instrumental effectiveness, how are these meanings performed?

Protest as drama

When analysed as a performance, the RTS event can be seen to possess a number of distinctive features, attention to which can help us locate it in relation to other instances of ritual, theatrical, political and festive performance.

1. The RTS performance takes place in the 'found' space of the public street, rather than in the specially dedicated arena in which most theatre occurs in modern society. As such, it echoes the integration of theatre and ritual with everyday life that is found in small-scale

societies (Schechner, 1988: 61), and in the political street theatre of recent decades (Kershaw, 1992), for both of which dramatic events are not necessarily assigned to specific, segregated spaces. It is also in this way consistent with some of the uses of space in more conventional dramaturgies of civic action, based around social meeting places rather than segregated auditoriums (Habermas, 1989). But if it is *found* space, it is also *seized* space, taken and used on the terms of the protesters (Kershaw, 1997: 263).

2. The temporality of the Street Party differs from that of officially authorized marches. Like Hakim Bey's Temporary Autonomous Zone (TAZ), the beginning of the event is set in secrecy by the protesters themselves, and the end is imposed by the 'authorities', when they succeed in dispersing the Party (Bey, 1991). Unlike the classic CND march to Trafalgar Square of the 1950s and 1960s, the event has no natural, internally generated close of its own. If the opening has to be set by the protesters, the close is usually imposed by the authorities – and yet comes not as a failure of the event, but as its final dramatic moment (Schechner, 1988: 6–8).

3. Whereas at certain kinds of performance – such as weddings and opening nights – at least some of the audience are in some way *integral* to the event itself (Schechner, 1988: 193–6), those at the Street Party are *accidental*. This accidental audience takes two forms – the pedestrians who happen to be passing down the street in question, and the motorists who try to; but also the wider audience constituted through mass media coverage.

4. Like many more recent protest events, and unlike the more traditional marches of earlier decades, the RTS dramaturgy employs predominantly *polysemic* modes of signification, without clear demands, programmes or enemies. Unlike more didactic political theatre, this kind of performance 'is not "about" something' in any clear sense (Schechner, 1993: 89). The oft-cited economic arguments against road building, for example (e.g. Evans, 1997), often seem more like symbolic weapons than the real 'point' of the protests. Slogans, where they are used, are more 'aphoristic and punning', and the images used are heteroglossic and connotative, rather than narrowly denotative, of 'desired ideals and utopias' (Kershaw, 1997: 274). As Kershaw puts it, such protest dramaturgies function predominantly less through factual truth claims or normative prescription, but by placing the imaginary and the real in new relationships for the spectator, disrupting and thus exposing the performance of 'politics as usual' (1997: 263, 257).

But if the protest actions such as the RTS Street Party are to be seen as performances in this way, above and beyond their direct material and political consequences, who are these performances for? I want to explore this question in relation to analyses of protest actions influenced by the work of the French sociologist Michel Maffesoli. According to Maffesoli, contemporary sociality is marked by a shift away from the classic modern individual, gathering together with others in 'banal associations' in order to pursue common goals (cf. Mellor and Shilling, 1997), and towards a 'neo-tribal' culture structured into new affectual collectivities oriented to the sheer warmth or 'puissance' of fellow-feeling (Maffesoli, 1996). His analysis of contemporary collectivities is in effect a Durkheimian variation on the 'stylization of life' thesis, seeing them as dominated by the logic of style subcultures, with no goals beyond the performance and maintenance of their own boundaries.

Sociologists and political scientists influenced by Maffesoli, such as Kevin Hetherington (1998) and Brian Doherty (1997), have applied this kind of theoretical approach to the 'semiotic excess' of protest movements, analysing it in terms of the performance of subcultural identities. While acknowledging the important contribution made by such analyses, in the next section I want to use the concept of 'performance genre' in order to point out the limitations of this approach. I will suggest that this way of understanding the emblematic symbols and gestures of contemporary protest remains at the – admittedly important, but nevertheless secondary – level of exploring their role in marking out membership and strengthening affectual bonds within protest subcultures, rather than their role in wider political culture.

Protest as play/protest as game/protest as ritual

If protest action is a performance, what kind of performance is it? Who are the intended audience(s)? While I share with Maffesoli and Hetherington an emphasis on the performative nature of such protests, I want to part company with them on the question of what *kind* of performance it should be understood as. A useful starting place for an exploration of this question is the 'performance chart' used by Richard Schechner in order to suggest some of the differences between play, games, sport, theatre and ritual. Crucially, according to Schechner, in play the rules are subjective, provided by the player his or herself. Play is 'free activity'. In games, sport and theatre, by contrast, the rules are intersubjectively agreed by the participants. In ritual, by contrast again, the rules are experienced not as chosen by the individual or the group, but as grounded in an ultimate reality (Schechner, 1988: 12–16).

Schechner's descriptions of these categories does raise certain problems, as does his tendency to treat them as overly distinct. Nevertheless, we can use his distinction between three broad categories of performance – play, games and ritual – as a starting point for a consideration of environmental protest in terms of performance genres. I will consider the appropriateness of each of these three in turn as interpretative categories in which to place the RTS Street Party. Firstly, I want to look at the limitations of regarding the Street Party as predominantly a rule-breaking activity – as a carnivalesque suspension of everyday conventions to allow the free play of individual creativity. Secondly, I want to explore the implications of regarding whether it should better be understood as more akin to a game or sport – as an expression of collective identity through the adoption of certain 'rules' of performance. Thirdly, I will consider the possibility of examining it as a form of civil religion – as the public performance of prophetic counter-rituals which challenge society's representation of itself and its priorities. As I hope will become clear, this exercise can help us better understand the cultural logic of contemporary protest.

Carnival and play

Since the Paris of May 1968 it has become almost a commonplace to compare protest events with the Carnival of early modern Europe.[3] This festive celebration, culminating on Shrove Tuesday, was a time of misrule, when established mores and customs of behaviour were overturned in favour of licence and pleasure, and figures of authority were subjected to mimicry and mockery (Bristol, 1985). But Baz Kershaw has argued against using Carnival as a useful point of reference for understanding contemporary protests, on the basis that to do so is to endorse a cathartic model of festivity. For Kershaw, Richard Schechner's equation of protest events with Carnival 'prevent[s] him from discriminating sufficiently between events which change and those which reinforce existing social orders' (Kershaw, 1997: 266).

It is certainly true that theories of Carnival have tended to regard it as a 'safety valve' – as an officially sanctioned and self-contained vehicle for the release of anti-social sentiments amongst the public – and thus as functioning to help stabilize the social order. According to this view, then, inasfar as Carnival is understood as free play, it is ultimately conservative in its effects. For Roger Callois, for example, the festival is a collective binge which brings about greater social conformity not so much through catharsis but more through the sheer exhaustion brought about through excess (Callois, 1959; cf. Bristol, 1985: 34). Other theoretical approaches to Carnival also view it as having a conservative role. For example, the 'archaic survival' theory of Carnival saw it as a re-enactment of an ancient, forgotten sacrificial ritual from an earlier, agrarian society. This, too, in effect, understands Carnival as a form of social control but, as Michael Bristol puts it, not by the people's rulers but by their ancestors (1985: 28–9). Durkheim (1915) combined both this and the cathartic theory of festivity in his analysis of ritual as functioning to enhance social cohesion.

Bristol points out that both the cathartic and the survivalist understanding of Carnival impute a lack of reflexivity and social learning to Carnival behaviour (1985: 27). If calling it 'ritual' would seem to emphasize the recapitulation of older scripts, calling it 'play' would seem to emphasize behaviour unconstrained either by custom or by any instrumental purpose. But later theorists of Carnival have explored it not just as an escape valve for social tensions but also as a vehicle for the playful exploration of social alternatives. The anthropologist Arnold van Gennep, like Durkheim, saw the carnivalesque suspension of business-as-usual as ultimately reconciliatory in nature, as finding its completion in the subsequent return to conventional social mores. But in his ambiguous and transitory liminal stage, he allowed for the satisfaction and exploration of wishes normally forbidden (1960). Building on van Gennep's work, Victor Turner distinguished between the *liminal* – unreflective and recapitulatory – and the *liminoid* – self-consciously mimetic, and sometimes subversive (1977). The latter may include aspects of play, but is also serious symbolic work.

Early modern Carnival can itself be seen to have had a purposefulness that is obscured by labels such as festivity and licence. Drawing on the work of Natalie Zemon Davies, Bristol argues that festivity and licence were relatively unimportant features of the Carnival. He argues that Carnival principally functioned to reinforce communally-accepted codes of behaviour amongst community members, to expose and criticize departures from accepted patterns of governance amongst elites, and to perform and express utopian fantasies of peace and plenty (Bristol, 1985: 52).

I will want to suggest that, in as far as contemporary environmental protest does partake of the Carnival, it does so in terms closer to these, rather than in those of the licence and freedom implied by the cathartic model. Below I will want to suggest that these features of this kind of protest can best be understood in terms of public ritual. However, it has to be acknowledged that, insofar as ritual is understood as the recapitulation of timeless and immutable gestures grounded in a transcendent reality, and as binding the social as a whole, then protest performances do not look like ritual. So in the next section I want briefly to consider another, mid-range set of performance genres – that embracing games, sport and theatre – within which rules of performance extend beyond the free play of individual creativity, but not beyond the playing community in question. A Maffesolian analysis of protest performances, I want to suggest, absorbs them into this kind of performance genre, with the consequent loss both of the possibility of discriminating between the public performance of protest and the more general performance of cultural memberships, and also of the capacity to acknowledge the full social and political significance of contemporary protests.

Games and subcultures

By 'game' I am following Schechner's usage that distinguishes this kind of performance from the free play of individuals by the way that games

– such as chess, or football – rely on the following of shared, negotiated meanings and values. It is at this mid-range of performance, I would suggest, that the analyses developed by Maffesoli and Hetherington rest. Hetherington, for example, treats protest actions as an instance of the more general performance of identity by members of the protest subculture, to other members, within their own closed argot. They are 'performances . . . recognisable to others who share a particular identi-fication' (1998: 142).

Showing one's 'moral credentials' to other protesters is clearly an important part of the practice of political protest (Szerszynski, 1997), but in Hetherington's analysis the performance of highly visible transgres-sive protest actions to others becomes little more than a badge of membership as a 'moral elect':

> In the occasion, therefore, political action and the performance of identity are inextricably intertwined. The symbolism and the performance are what hold the two together. The political actions as well as the alternative ways of living . . . are occasions in which identities are performed. (1998: 146)

Any seemingly normative action with the goal of affecting the wider world is thus reduced to the emblematic performance of group mem-bership. The consequences of protest action are simply side-effects of the performance of signs of subcultural membership, which loop back and function to reinforce the group (Maffesoli, 1996: 17) – by provoking policing reactions, and thereby strengthening the group identity as being marginal and different (cf. Douglas and Wildavsky, 1982).

The power of protest actions to convey meaning to non-members of the movement is clearly underplayed in this kind of analysis. Following Hetherington, Doherty describes the road protest camp as:

> a heterotopic space in which it becomes possible to express a new way of life. (Doherty, 1997: 13)

But if such emblematic protest actions were *only* performances of the symbols of membership to other movement members, then their *real* audience would be the 'integral' one of the movement itself, not the 'accidental' one of the wider public. However, RTS, by its performance in central public space, presents perhaps the hardest case for this interpretation, taking place as it does not in the marginal spaces of squats and protest camps but in the key public space of modern society – the urban high street. In Hakim Bey's terminology, the Street Party is not a Tong – a secret society formed for the subcultural pursuit of illicit practices – but a TAZ – a Temporary Autonomous Zone, an overt, deliberate and visible re-coding of public space (1991; n.d.).

To follow Hetherington's analysis, insofar as protest actions are regarded as performance, it is as the performance of a 'we–they' boundary, between those inside and outside the protest community. Performing to the wider public is merely a roundabout way of performing one's membership to other members of the protest subculture. (Indeed, the very focus on the term 'identity' seems to suggest such an analysis, drawing attention away from the intrinsic relationality of the performative aspects of personhood – the way that the significatory aspects of human action go *beyond* the self.) I want to suggest that we should treat emblematic protest actions as also involving the performance of an 'I–you' dialogue (Singer, 1984: 92), that tries to draw in, involve and challenge the public observer as interpretant of the symbolic actions.[4] To do this, I want to consider protest as ritual, as a form of civil religion.

Ritual: protest as civil religion

With its roots in the political philosophy of Jean-Jacques Rousseau and the sociology of Emile Durkheim, 'civil religion' as a term is usually used to refer to public ceremonials such as Presidential inaugurations which are supposed to bind national societies together as a unified whole (Rouner, 1968). There are many characteristics of contemporary environmental protest which might make it seem a strange candidate for such a category. Firstly, the Street Party, with its inventiveness, individuality and spontaneity, seems far away from the easily recognizable repetitions of civic ceremony – of coronation, inauguration and election, for example. Secondly, of course, the RTS event is transgressive, challenging rather than reinforcing the smooth performance of civic order. Finally, its symbols, in their non-linearity and polysemy, seem incapable of strengthening social solidarity in the way that civic ritual is meant to, since their connotations and interpretations seem to encourage divergence and multiple interpretation.

Although Schechner accentuates the given-ness of ritual, when compared with more theatrical or ludic forms of performance, other writers have drawn attention to the way that rituals can be invented and created. Ronald Grimes points to the work of the Polish theatre director Grotowski as an example of the way that inventive performance can transcend entertainment and become psychically efficacious (Grimes, 1982: 177). For Grimes, such created rituals can transcend the private and individual in their realm of meaningfulness, but are more effective at the mid-range of creative subcultures than at the societal-scale of sacred or civic ritual As such, Grimes would seem to be in accord with Hetherington in locating such secular rituals in our middle category of 'game', as the performance of a 'restricted code' of emblematic gestures that can only signify for 'insiders'. Can there not be meaningful public rituals that signify *beyond* the members of a shared subculture, but which at the same time are not simply the familiar civic rituals of consensus and *status quo*?

In a discussion of acts of flag desecration, Welch and Bryan (1997) describe the ferocity with which those who have symbolically degraded or defaced the American flag have been treated in history. Implicit in their account is the assumption that, whereas flag *veneration* is clearly a form of civil religion, flag *desecration* is not – indeed, they treat it as a form of opposition to civil religion, a protest against its unthinking, ritualized qualities. But what Welch and Bryan overlook is the way that the flag desecrators *themselves* have to be seen as engaging in civic ritual, although of a very different kind – and this is an answer to my second question, about the assumption that civil religion is by definition reactionary. Civic ritual *can* be otherwise – indeed, American political life can itself be seen as having an important strand of civil religion within it that is more prophetic than priestly, more radical than conservative, shaped more by Quaker than by Puritan theology (Kent and Spickard, 1994). As Andrew Shanks has argued, civic commemoration, however rarely might actually be the case at present, *can* be critical and repentant as well as triumphalist. Much protest action has to be seen in this light – as a calling to remembrance of past evils, or of present blindness, as a challenge to forgetfulness and concealment. At its best it can be a dramatization of the truth through liturgy, a performative recognition of our own 'solidarity in sin' (Shanks, 1995).

But if the RTS Street Party *is* civil religion, what are its specific features? What is it trying to tell us about who we are? What would we enact ourselves into being by performing, or being otherwise drawn in by, its liturgy? Firstly, what is striking about the forms of contemporary direct action is their emphasis on what might be called a 'politics of vulnerability'. Barricades have long been used in protest actions in order to delay the operations of the authorities. However, while in earlier protests they also served the function of protecting the protesters, today's barricades – or their equivalent, in the form of lock-ons, walkways, tunnels and tripods – are more likely to function by putting protesters at *greater* risk. Indeed, tactical innovation in the roads protests, as Doherty emphasizes, has largely taken the form of heightening and further dramatizing the risk to the protesters (1997: 9).

This dramatization seems to echo a more general emerging emphasis on vulnerability and flaw in notions of moral and political agency, as also exemplified in the growth of self-help groups (Back and Taylor, 1976) and of radical disability politics (Hughes and Paterson, 1997). This emphasis contrasts markedly with the Hobbesian tradition of politics underlying modern liberal democracy, with its notion of political agency predicated on a reputation for *in*vulnerability.[5] But in other ways it coheres with many developments in moral and political theory. Ethical theorists as different as Levinas and Habermas share a recognition that ethics and politics starts from vulnerability, from the acknowledgement that our very self-identity and subjectivity depends on our inter-subjective openness to the Other (Vetlesen, 1997). The polysemy of contemporary protest also seems rooted in an at least unconscious recognition of the vulnerability of signification that public political action brings in the age of the mass media. That our essence, in Shakespeare's words, is 'glassy' means that our being is open-ended, is only completed (and then only temporarily) by those that observe us (Singer, 1984). That protest actions *signify* means that they cannot simply be autonomous, self-contained acts of virtue (Szerszynski, 1997: 46). But that they signify as polysemic *symbols*, not as signs indicating a single message, means that that signification is inherently unstable. The intelligibility of the protesters' actions are 'given over to others', both helping to constitute the viewing public as a moral community, and at the same time thematizing a radical incompleteness at the heart of human personhood (Matzko, 1993: 29).

Secondly, the dramatics of the Street Party serve in a complex way to expose the coercive power of the state. The 'soft' forms of domination characteristic of liberal democracies are very difficult to make visible, but the RTS Street Party manages to do this, often quite deliberately, through symbolic challenge, and this in a number of ways. One is by staging a carnivalesque 'time-out' from the conventional rhythms of consumerism, which attempts to demonstrate their non-inevitability by joyfully casting them aside with apparent ease. But another is by provoking the state to go to ever more elaborate – and often violent – forms of repression in subduing the protest (Doherty, 1997: 9).

Thirdly, the Street Party can also be seen as operating powerfully at the level of what might be called the 'semiotics of the everyday', reclaiming public space from the 'system' in the name of the 'lifeworld'. According to this more situationist reading of the Street Party, it operates principally not simply as a carnivalesque catharsis but as a ritual, a performative declaration which dares, through simple acts of renaming, to 'reclaim' familiar spaces for different, more convivial and human-scaled kinds of performance, and thus challenges the symbolic codes of capitalism, consumption and economic growth. The constant conscious and unconscious play in RTS actions and literature on the contrasting connotations of the words 'Road' – as thoroughfare for traffic – and 'Street' – as meeting place, as dwelling – provides powerful resources for this symbolic challenge, drawing in the observer through meta-phorical challenges to dominant codes (Anonymous, 1997: 4). This is a politics of prefiguration, anticipating in the here-and-now a different and better world, through utopian moments which stand not as program-matic signposts but as symbolizations, as partial glimpses of another way of being (Kershaw, 1997: 264–5).

Conclusion: performing politics otherwise?

In many ways the analysis presented above is consistent with the position developed by Ray and Sayer in the introduction to this volume.

Like them I am unconvinced by the historical claim that there has been a progressive de-differentiation of societal spheres, whereby a cultural sphere and a political sphere were once, but are now no longer, distinct from one another. Furthermore, I agree that this 'culturalization thesis', claiming as it does that it is becoming progressively difficult to distinguish forms of human action as operating according to different logics, has ethical and political implications that are sufficiently worrying as to justify our being perhaps more than usually exacting in our demands for supporting argument. Nevertheless, I do not find it useful to treat 'culture' as applying to a separate subclass of activity – as if some forms of human action are intrinsically less cultural, less inscribed with meaning, than others. And I *do* entertain the notion that the particular cultural logic of political and civic action may be undergoing a process of pluralization and change, as evidenced perhaps most starkly in the changing dramaturgies of political protest.

However, it might be objected that, of *all* the different kinds of political action that I might have talked about in terms of 'performance', to speak of radical environmental politics in this way seems particularly counterintuitive. The notion of 'performance' seems to imply a distancing of the 'real' self from one's actions, the playing of a role that is determined at least partly by factors outside oneself. The politics of environmental direct action, by contrast, seems more like a translation into political form of the kind of moral style described in Charles Taylor's book *The Ethics of Authenticity*, one that valorizes the realization and expression of one's true, inner self (Taylor, 1991). In radical protest groups, there is no 'party line' to which one can sign up, no pre-defined roles into which one can step – each action and avowal must come from the individual's heart (Szerszynski, 1997).

Richard Sennett described the emergence of this understanding of the self in his *Fall of Public Man* (1986: 259–68). For our purposes, it is interesting that he saw it as marking the diminishing of the possibility of public life, in a way that in a sense parallels the analysis of Maffesoli. He argued:

- that public life depends on an impersonal code of comportment, expression and display, according to formulaic codes of dress and speech entered into by all, and disconnected from their private identities;
- that the contemporary demand to 'be yourself' in all situations collapses the distinction between private and public selves, and makes public display too linked to particular concrete individuals to constitute a genuine public sphere; and
- that political life under such conditions is characterized by a lack of playfulness; it becomes too ardent and dogmatic, as people's identities are too tightly caught up in their public avowals to permit more open exploration.

What we are seeing in contemporary environmental protest, I would argue, is a new mode of performing the public sphere which might escape Sennett's strictures. Although the Puritan mode of performing civic life has suffered a diminution, we may be witnessing the emergence of a new form of public ritual, one that is more plural and contestatory in its demands, and polysemic in its imagery and speech – one that weds authentic personal display with playfulness and irony (Seery, 1990). The cultural power of contemporary protests, I would suggest, lies at least partly in the polysemic and unstable nature of its symbolism, which draws us in as subjects and citizens in new and challenging ways, inviting society to redefine itself, its aspirations and priorities. As such, it perhaps hints at a way of performing politics otherwise.

Notes

An earlier version of this chapter was presented as 'Action's Glassy Essence: The Dramatics of Environmental Protest', at the annual conference of the RGS/IBG, Kingston University, 5–8 January 1998. I would like to thank Brian Doherty, Baz Kershaw, Andrew Hindley, Ian Ball, Graeme Chesters, Tom Cahill and Nick Hunt, conversations with all of whom have greatly helped the writing of this chapter.

1 I am grateful to Ted Benton for suggesting this way of describing the questions explored here.
2 Elsewhere I have referred to this form of environmental action as a 'sectarian' ecological piety (Szerszynski, 1997).
3 Although in fact the role of festivity in French radical politics clearly goes back to the Revolution (Ozouf, 1988), and beyond (Le Roy Ladurie, 1981).
4 Though such attempts to draw in outsiders are admittedly often vitiated by the more 'restricted' cultural codes – such as those of music, dress and modes of speech – of protest subcultures.
5 I am indebted to Alan Holland and John O'Neill for giving me this contrast.

References

Anonymous (1997) 'Reclaim the streets!', *Do or Die*, 6: 1–6.
Back, Kurt W. and Taylor, Rebecca C. (1976) 'Self-help groups: tool or symbol?', *Journal of Applied Behavioral Science*, 12 (3): 295–309.
Bey, Hakim (1991) *T.A.Z.: The Temporary Autonomous Zone, Ontological Anarchy, Poetic Terrorism*, New York: Autonomedia.
Bey, Hakim (n.d.) 'Tong aesthetics', *http://www.hermetic.com/bey/tong.html*.
Bourdieu, Pierre (1984) *Distinction: a Social Critique of the Judgement of Taste*, trans. Richard Nice, London: Routledge and Kegan Paul.
Bristol, Michael D. (1985) *Carnival and Theatre: Plebeian Culture and the Structure of Authority in Renaissance England*, New York: Methuen.
Callois, Roger (1959) *Man and the Sacred*, trans. Meyer Barash, Glencoe, IL: Free Press.
Castells, Manuel (1997) *Power of Identity*, Malden, MD: Blackwell.

Crook, Stephen, Pakulski, Jan and Waters, Malcolm (1992) *Postmodernization: Change in Advanced Society*, London: Sage.

Doherty, Brian (1996) 'Paving the way: the rise of direct action against road-building and the changing character of British environmentalism', paper presented to the conference *Alternative Futures and Popular Protest II*, Manchester Metropolitan University, 26–28 March.

Doherty, Brian (1997) 'Tactical innovation and the protest repertoire in the radical ecology movement in Britain', paper presented to the European Sociological Association Conference, Essex University, 27–30 August.

Douglas, Mary and Wildavsky, Aaron (1982) *Risk and Culture: an Essay on the Selection of Technical and Environmental Dangers*, Berkeley: University of California Press.

Durkheim, Emile (1915) *The Elementary Forms of the Religious Life*, trans. J. Swain, London: George Allen & Unwin.

Evans, Paul (1997) 'Dark side of the roads', *The Guardian*, 15 January, 'Society' section, pp. 4–5.

Fraser, Nancy (1995) 'From redistribution to recognition? Dilemmas of justice in a "post-socialist" age', *New Left Review*, 212: 68–93.

Giddens, Anthony (1991) *Modernity and Self-Identity: Self and Society in the Late Modern Age*, Cambridge: Polity.

Grimes, Ronald L. (1982) *Beginnings in Ritual Studies*, Lanham, MD: University Press of America.

Habermas, Jürgen (1989) *The Structural Transformation of the Public Sphere: an Inquiry into a Category of Bourgeois Society*, Oxford: Polity.

Hetherington, Kevin (1998) *Expressions of Identity: Space, Performance and the Politics of Identity*, London: Sage.

Hughes, Bill and Paterson, Kevin (1997) 'The social model of disability and the disappearing body: towards a sociology of impairment', *Disability and Society*, 12 (3): 325–40.

Kent, Stephen A. and Spickard, James V. (1994) 'The "other" civil religion and the tradition of radical Quaker politics', *Journal of Church and State*, 6 (4): 373–87.

Kershaw, Baz (1992) *The Politics of Performance: Radical Theatre as Cultural Intervention*, London: Routledge.

Kershaw, Baz (1997) 'Fighting in the streets: dramaturgies of popular protest, 1968–1989', *New Theatre Quarterly*, 13 (51): 255–76.

Lash, Scott and Urry, John (1987) *The End of Organized Capitalism*, Cambridge: Polity.

Lash, Scott and Urry, John (1994) *Economies of Signs and Space*, London: Sage.

Le Roy Ladurie, Emmanuel (1981) *Carnival in Romans: a People's Uprising at Romans 1579–1580*, trans. Mary Feeney, Harmondsworth: Penguin.

Maffesoli, Michel (1996) *The Time of the Tribes: the Decline of Individualism in Mass Society*, London: Sage.

Matzko, David Matthew (1993) 'Postmodernism, saints and scoundrels', *Modern Theology*, 9 (1): 19–36.

McKay, George (1996) *Senseless Acts of Beauty: Cultures of Resistance Since the Sixties*, London: Verso.

Mellor, Philip A. and Shilling, Chris (1997) *Re-forming the Body: Religion, Community and Modernity*, London: Sage/TCS.

Melucci, Alberto (1989) *Nomads of the Present: Social Movements and Individual Needs in Contemporary Society*, London: Hutchinson Radius.

Melucci, Alberto (1996) *Challenging Codes: Collective Action in the Information Age*, Cambridge: Cambridge University Press.

Ozouf, Mona (1988) *Festivals and the French Revolution*, trans. Alan Sheridan, Cambridge, MA: Harvard University Press.

Road Alert! (1997) *Road Raging: Top Tips for Wrecking Roadbuilding*, Newbury: Road Alert!

Rouner, Leroy S. (ed.) (1968) *Civil Religion and Political Theology*, Notre Dame: University of Notre Dame Press.

Schechner, Richard (1988) *Performance Theory*, New York: Routledge.

Schechner, Richard (1993) *The Future of Ritual: Writings on Culture and Performance*, London: Routledge.

Seel, Ben (1996) 'Frontline eco-wars! The Pollok Free State road protest community: counter hegemonic intentions, pluralistic effects', paper presented to the conference *Alternative Futures and Popular Protest II*, Manchester Metropolitan University, 26–28 March.

Seery, John Evan (1990) *Political Returns: Irony in Politics and Theory from Plato to the Antinuclear Movement*, Boulder, CO: Westview.

Sennett, Richard (1986) *The Fall of Public Man*, London: Faber & Faber.

Shanks, Andrew (1995) *Civil Society, Civil Religion*, Oxford: Blackwell.

Singer, Milton (1984) *Man's Glassy Essence: Explorations in Semiotic Anthropology*, Bloomington: Indiana University Press.

Szerszynski, Bronislaw (1997) 'The varieties of ecological piety', *Worldviews: Environment, Culture, Religion*, 1 (1): 37–55.

Szerszynski, Bronislaw, Lash, Scott and Wynne, Brian (1996) 'Introduction: ecology, realism and the social sciences', in Scott Lash, Bronislaw Szerszynski and Brian Wynne (eds), *Risk, Environment and Modernity: Towards a New Ecology*, London: Sage, pp. 1–26.

Taylor, Charles (1991) *The Ethics of Authenticity*, Cambridge, MA: Harvard University Press.

Taylor, Charles (1992) *Multiculturalism and 'The Politics of Recognition'*, Princeton, NJ: Princeton University Press.

Turner, Victor (1977) 'Variations on a theme of liminality', in Sally F. Moore and Barbara G. Myerhoff (eds), *Secular Ritual*, Amsterdam: Van Gorcum, pp. 35–57.

van Gennep, Arnold (1960) *The Rites of Passage*, trans. Monika Vizedom and Gebrielle Caffee, Chicago: University of Chicago Press.

Vetlesen, Arne Johan (1997) 'Worlds Apart? Habermas and Levinas', *Philosophy and Social Criticism*, 23 (1): 1–20.

Welch, Michael and Bryan, Jennifer (1997) 'Flag desecration in American culture: offences against civil religion and a consecrated symbol of nationalism', *Crime, Law and Social Change*, 26 (1): 77–93.

10

The Culture Did It: Comments on the 1997 British General Election

Mary Evans

In May 1997, the British Labour Party won a massive electoral victory over the Conservative Party. After eighteen years of Conservative rule, a period which many commentators saw as bringing about the transformation of British political culture, the apparent hegemony of Thatcherism was overthrown. To some observers of British politics the 1997 General Election was very specifically about issues such as the level of funding of state education and the National Health Service; to others, what was involved were more complex questions about the relationship between culture and politics, and in particular the cultural form (and specifically the cultural form of masculinity) which the Conservative Party had come to represent. This reading of the link between political event and cultural change coincided with the re-emergence in feminist debate of discussions about the material and the cultural. Nancy Fraser (1998) and Judith Butler (1998) took up issues which had been raised in the 1970s about the origin of women's subordination. In that decade writers such as Heidi Hartmann had attempted to 'marry' (for such was the term used by Hartmann (1979)) Marxism and feminism and had argued that the needs of capitalism were such as to demand a separation of home and workplace, a separation which brought with it the exclusion of women from paid work.

This account of the origin of women's exclusion from paid work (and with it the public and political world) was questioned by authors who argued that although an effect of capitalism had been the separation of home and workplace (and the relegation of women to the home) this was not inevitable. As Michelle Barrett (1979) wrote:

> although the general tendency towards the separation of home and workplace has proved oppressive to women, this is because the problem so starkly posed – who was to be primarily responsible for childcare? – was resolved, according to an ideology of gender that pre-dated capitalism, in the interests of men.

In this suggestion that ideological, rather than natural or biological, factors played their part in the construction of the gendered boundaries of the social world lay the basis from which subsequent feminist work went on to demonstrate the social construction of gender difference. Veronica Beechey and others showed how the assumed personal characteristics of women were inter-linked with the gendered labour market (Beechey, 1977; Phillips and Taylor, 1986); at the same time access to child care became (with the right to abortion and the control of fertility) the cornerstone of feminist demands.

In these debates (and campaigns) lay assumptions which were formed before Margaret Thatcher became Prime Minister and before the full impact of the rediscovery and rereading of Freud contributed to a rethinking of the relationship between the symbolic and the material. A central intervention in this re-consideration came from Stuart Hall, who argued, following Gramsci, that culture (constructed in terms of the themes of identity, cultural products and shared cultural experiences) is a crucial element in power. Hall's *Culture, Media, Language* (published in 1980 as a shared project with Dorothy Hobson, Andrew Lowe and Paul Willis) set out an agenda which was to dominate the study of British social life for the following decades. Essentially, what Hall (and his co-authors) did was to show ways of including the understanding of culture in material and structural conditions. To be 'in power' following Hall, came to be understood as to be in command not just of a particular structure but also of a particular discourse. As Hall was to point out, the policies of Margaret Thatcher were powerful because they were coherently organized around a particular fusion of cultural themes, a triumphalist reading of British history combined with an ideology of apparent individual emancipation.

The impact of Hall's work on the study of culture is acknowledged to have been extremely significant. Not least, it alerted the left to the centrality of culture in formal politics and contributed to the emergence of 'New Labour'. Throughout the 1980s, and much more so in the 1990s as the economic limitations of Thatcherism became apparent, the British Labour Party was reconstructed as a party which could offer a cultural engagement with Thatcherism. In this project the Labour Party claimed an identity with the nation as close as anything the Conservatives could identify and began a renegotiation with the language and appearance (quite as much as the content) of British politics. Central to this project was a reconceptualization of gender and politics: the Labour Party recognized both the massive increase in the number of women in paid work and the impact of feminism on younger women. Part of this recognition was the realization that women increasingly only supported male politicians who appeared to integrate the specific needs and understanding of women in both their politics and their behaviour. Whether or not women actively accepted and identified with feminism was irrelevant: what became clear was that masculinity no longer signified authority. For all her commitment to convention and tradition, Mrs Thatcher's gender had undermined expectations about the gender of power. Feminism, in common with the left generally, began to rethink the relationship between culture and politics.

In doing so, feminism in the 1980s and 1990s became increasingly preoccupied with the analysis of the symbolic and all forms of representation. Although campaigns around issues such as equal pay and abortion continued, the energy (particularly the academic energy) of feminism in the Thatcher years was devoted to the understanding of texts and texts as a discourse. It was acknowledged that the majority of the poor were women, and that in material terms the majority of women remained locked into low-paid, service sector jobs, but the explanation of this situation was seen to lie clearly in the gendered domestic division of labour. Women did the caring work (most specifically of children) and therefore women did not enter the labour market on the same terms as men. New Labour took up this analysis and its implicit agenda and committed itself to shifting, through action by the State, the impact of child care on Labour market participation. It was an agenda which clearly had great appeal, since women (and especially younger women) voted for Blair and his party in large numbers.

The result of the last British General Election has been described as a 'political earthquake' on the same scale as Asquith's 1906 Liberal victory or the 1945 Labour landslide. We can now collect the various descriptions of the event – even whilst we can also note that many of these descriptions use images of the natural world. Thus David Mellor spoke of a 'tidal wave' and Professor Anthony King of 'an asteroid hitting the earth and destroying practically all life'.[1] These accounts of 1 May suggest an understanding of social life which is roughly on a par with accounts of the anger of the Gods, and in King's case indicate something of an inability to conceptualize social and political life without Conservative party politicians. Sociologists hope to do better than this, and to be able to offer an understanding of Blair's electoral triumph which does not – metaphorically – throw up its hands and turn to the forces of Nature for explanation. Although natural – in the sense of biological – differences will not be absent from this chapter, what I propose to do is to use the case of the last General Election to make some comments about the relationship between gender and politics.

Inevitably, given post-Enlightenment dichotomies of Culture and Nature, it is to science – and to the social science of psephology in particular – that many commentators turn first for their explanation of what happened. This information tells us that the most significant factors about 1 May were that the Conservative vote collapsed to its lowest level since 1832, turnout fell by 5% and the swing to Labour was highest in London and in seats outside those 57 marginals which Labour needed to win. Leaving aside the first point, on the grounds that comparison of the Conservative vote in 1832 with that of 1997 is highly questionable, we then need to ask further questions about both the apparent increase in non-voting and the apparent overall enthusiasm of the British population for the Labour Party. In the case of the latter point, we now know, from the work of John Curtice and Michael Steed in the Nuffield study of the 1997 British General Election, that only 31% of the electorate actually felt enthusiastic enough about the Labour party to vote for it.

No one who has observed British politics in the 1990s could fail to identify dissatisfaction with the Conservatives as a major reason for Labour's victory. Given the record of corruption, hypocrisy and incompetence of the Conservative governments of Margaret Thatcher and John Major it was hardly surprising that many people would either vote against the Conservatives (rather than for Labour) or refuse to vote for the Conservatives despite longstanding loyalties and associations. (As Geddes and Tonge (1997: 32) put it, 'Constitutional issues were of less importance than sleaze, unity and image'.) But the sheer size and scale of the Labour victory suggests that something else was at work besides a contrast between a history of what became known as sleaze and the expectation of managerial competence. That 'something', that massive gap between the performance of the parties, could have been the difference in cultural styles of the parties and the way in which that of the Labour Party seemed to bear some resemblance to that of the majority of the electorate. The case of the Cabinet Minister Michael Portillo illustrates particularly sharply the contrast: every time he spoke in public he seemed both defensive and aggressive; a sorry spectacle of that anxious masculinity which Alex Guinness and John Cleese have made such successful careers of representing. Sympathetic therapists might identify unresolved problems of masculine identity but few could avoid noticing both the subtext of terrified masculinity as well as the actual text of bluster and xenophobia. When he spoke at the penultimate Conservative Party conference and abused all aspects of the Social Chapter, he represented the kind of figure who is now well known throughout current popular culture as the man who is frightened of women, foreigners, gays and any human or abstract phenomenon that does not come packaged in a tight collar and a formal sentence structure. The endlessly replayed moment at which Portillo realized that he had lost his parliamentary seat to his Labour opponent Stephen Twigg encapsulated not just a victory of Labour over Conservative, but a victory for an identifiably different set of both political and cultural expectations. As critics remarked in reviews of the film *Titanic*, the 'Brits' – in the shape of Portillo clones – are a popular and frequent target of contemporary popular culture. In part, antagonism towards aspects of conventional British masculinity is derived from changing expectations of the public presentation of self, but it is also derived from a recognition of the part which conventional constructions of masculinity played in maintaining material as well as cultural domination over subject people in the British overseas Empire.[2]

Portillo is, of course, the outsider to English culture who over-identified with what he saw as the ruling class, and more importantly, the ruling culture. That 'national culture' (the subject of discussion, and debate, between Perry Anderson and E.P. Thompson, and others) was represented in the formal values of national institutions such as the monarchy and the Church of England.[3] At no time was that aspect of British culture the single cultural form of British society: as critics pointed out, dissent, diversity and difference were always part of British cultural life.[4] Indeed, at certain key periods in British history (most notably the Second World War) a specifically popular (and populist) working-class culture assumed a much greater social and political recognition (Calder, 1971). Thus Portillo's identification with a specific aspect (and practice) of British culture was a clear commitment to a culture which was hierarchical, deferential, homophobic and committed to the view that a particular kind of the formal presentation of self represented – in itself – moral authority. In the 1960s this view was already becoming anachronistic, but by the 1980s it had become something of a museum piece. Mrs Thatcher could hold the cultural ground for the Conservatives in part because she was a woman but also because she effectively mined a rich vein of English culture in which the assumption of a shared common sense, the refusal of conventionally constructed authority (of the Harold Macmillan / Alex Douglas-Home tradition) and xenophobic philistinism could be effectively located within a radical politics of the right. As Raphael Samuel has pointed out – from a political position far from that of Mrs Thatcher – history 'offers us images – "hyper realities" – in which the old is faked up to be more palpable than the here-and-now' (Samuel, 1994).

After Mrs Thatcher, male Conservativism (for it was literally that) had little with which to identify that was in any way generally popular, or part of many people's experience. There was apparently hope of arousing anti-European feeling, but to generations brought up both working and taking holidays in Europe it was a bizarre expectation. Equally, the attack on single mothers and the assertion of the absolute moral authority and legitimacy of the so-called traditional nuclear family was a wild miscalculation in a society in which almost everyone had some experience – whether direct of not – of other family and personal circumstances. As Angela McRobbie wrote in 1994, just after the James Bulger case:

> Most people in their everyday lives now understand the reality of single parenthood, either directly or by close observation. Women of all ages, all social and ethnic backgrounds, know what unhappy marriage can mean, and they are not going to endorse a return to traditional family values, with the misery and the violence that these have so often entailed. It is extraordinary that the Tories do not realise the depths of opposition to this idea from the ranks of women, and that even now they have not taken into account the centrality of women and their opinions in political culture today.

Equally insulting to the electorate was the way in which some senior figures in the Conservative Party treated the women with whom they had personal, rather than general, relationships: as either powerless in public terms or as endlessly long-suffering wives or disposable mistresses in private. Obviously this reflected on the understanding and practice of the sexual politics of these figures, but it did something more: it sent out a message of adherence to increasingly redundant moral and sexual categories, in which women were virgins and whores and men the hapless victims of their own sexual desires. Thus when the Conservative MP David Mellor expected sympathetic collusion for his behaviour, what he found was a public which saw it only as in some sense both infantile and old fashioned. What had clearly entirely escaped Mellor was a sexual culture in which there was no longer any absolute social imperative to be what is known as 'a family man', but that there is an expectation that this particular personal choice – like any other – carries with it assumptions about moral codes.

In the (many) moral failings of the Conservative government of the last eighteen years there is one consistent aspect which separates it from much of the electorate: the belief that the public and the private worlds can be kept separate and that those in power should be able to live private lives which are above public scrutiny. Every Conservative politician forced to resign because of his own conduct blamed the press: it was, we were asked to believe, in some sense our fault for wanting to know about them that led to their downfall. Nobody seemed to have told the Conservative Party either about Caesar's wife or about those increasingly well-known ideas of denial, projection, and emotional literacy. To generations brought up on the endless emotional analyses and discussion of soap operas and the popularization of therapy the behaviour and the explanations for the behaviour of this group of men had little resonance with an increasingly educated public.

The glue which had held together the dead (or dying) world of the Conservative Party was a glue which was made up of the fear (of outsiders), social deference and respect for traditional authority. The Royal Family contributed to this reversal of deference by its own behaviour and by its almost comic refusal of emotional reality. Traditional authority was closely associated with deference but it was also closely linked with patriarchal authority, a form of authority which had been consistently resisted both culturally and socially throughout the 1970s and the 1980s. The social and personal expectations which provided support for the Conservatives were therefore increasingly disappearing throughout the 1980s and 1990s. At the same time, the cultural gap between governed and governing was growing wider. There was – by 1990 – more plurality and diversity in British society, but to the mind set of the Conservatives it was impossible to recognize or come to terms with it. John Major's vision of village cricket and warm beer was embedded not just in the past but in a masculine version of the past.

The men who identified with that vision might have appeared reliable Conservative voters to John Major, but to many women and many men that vision was saturated with formality. Typically, the only woman in John Major's picture of England (the spinster on her bicycle) was separate from the main game and biking away from it. In electoral terms, of course, that is precisely what happened on 1 May: the electorate, once advised by the Tory peer Norman Tebbitt to 'get on its bike' did precisely that. The problem, for the Conservative Party, is that many people biked off in the wrong direction.

As constituent images of late twentieth century Britain, bicycles and cricket are less than absolutely representative of the culture or the society as a whole. My argument then, is that the Conservatives lost, as overwhelmingly as they did on 1 May, not just because voters wanted more money spent on education and health but because they could no longer identify with the understanding and experience with which the Conservative Party was associated. With characteristic frankness, the one-time Conservative Minister Edwina Currie said on the night of the General Election that unless the Conservative Party radically rethought both its politics and its presentation then very shortly 'only old men would be voting for it'. Now, so far, what the above suggests is that I am advancing a fairly orthodox argument about cultural shifts and changes as explanations for changes in electoral politics. Precisely the kind of change, in fact, which associates the 1945 Labour victory with the 'mood' of the British people after the end of the Second World War (Morgan and Evans, 1993: 109–34). We do know that in 1997 more women voted Labour than voted Conservative and that the evidence once produced by political scientists of the generation of Jean Blondel (1963) and Robert McKenzie (1963) to demonstrate the essential conservatism and support for the Conservative Party of women no longer holds true. There is now a considerable literature on the 'gender gap' in voting throughout liberal democracies (e.g. Randall and Waylen, 1998). Women, especially younger women, vote for political parties which seem to offer a greater commitment to the public provision of education, health and welfare. The absence of male incomes in households – for whatever reasons – makes it inevitable that women will demand from the state what is unlikely to be provided privately. Thus cultural and political change coincide. The changed expectations, and aspirations and experiences of many women about family and personal life (derived from greater experience of education and paid employment as much as shifts in moral and sexual ideologies) have resulted in a diminution of the traditional distinctions between the private, household world of women and the public, political world of men. A conceptual model which once assumed that men would meet the material needs of women and children has been disrupted by both the inability of men to provide and the refusal of women to be provided for, given the context in which provision was assumed to occur.

It is in this context of changing expectations that we have to note that moral campaigns to re-invent the traditional family also have a firm economic agenda: more private provision could reduce welfare spending. For the right, 'private' provision means the re-establishment of male breadwinner families; for the left, it involves women-into-work programmes. Given the expectations which many women now have about combining motherhood and paid work – thus avoiding the possibility of direct male *economic* control – it is inevitable that women will support political parties which construct policies that enable this aspiration. Hence women, in diverse ways, have very clear interests in supporting political parties which promise generous levels of welfare provision. Indeed, an equation has emerged in many western societies in which changes in the organization of the family now dictate public policy. The case of British government policy over single mothers illustrates this situation particularly clearly: the government is attempting to reverse longstanding assumptions about the unsuitability of attempts to combine motherhood and paid work in order to ensure that public spending is not tied to an understanding of child support in which the state takes over the role of male providers. It is a policy which may be both unacceptable and unworkable for a number of reasons, not the least of which is the assumption that women (indeed people) responsible for the care of young children are able – let alone willing – to be in paid work. But without discussing this particular case (which involves complex and diverse issues) I want to suggest that it illustrates the breakdown of those boundaries of the private and the public which once lay at the root of our political culture but are now beginning to transform it. Central to that transformation is the changing relationship of women, in both a symbolic and a literal sense, to politics. It is the nature of that transformation which I now wish to try and assess.

The general euphoria of 1 May and the welcome to Blair's government inevitably suggested a new era in British politics. That sense of a new consciousness has subsequently been linked to what commentators described at the time of the death of Princess Diana as the 'feminization' of British culture. That – deeply contentious – view has been attacked by Elizabeth Wilson (amongst others) and described, variously, as essentialist, undemocratic, mystifying (in both the Marxist and more general sense) and socially reactionary. Elizabeth Wilson (1997), in particular, identified in the praise for Diana, a profoundly conservative enthusiasm for private charity rather than public provision. The politics of the death of Diana are (at least to some of us) fascinating, not least because they offer such an immediate litmus test of individual attitudes. But, of the general pattern of attitudes which have emerged, I would like to make two points. The first is that the social reaction to Diana's death, and more particularly to accounts of her life, seem to suggest what I would describe as an attempt to personalize the social world. The second – and as equally linked to the 1 May election result – is the construction of the social world less through the denial of the private than through the increasing valorization and prioritization of the private. As Hannah Arendt (1959: 194) acutely observed, totalitarianism can just as much be constructed through excessive personalization as through its negation. Thus when individuals wrote of their dissent from mourning for Diana, they often wrote of the 'fascism' of the event and the 'bullying' of the Royal Family to mourn. At the same time, it has to be observed that whatever the dissent from the collective mourning for Diana, there was considerable, publicly expressed grief at her death. That grief revived memories of the public euphoria at the time of the coronation of Elizabeth II, euphoria described by Edward Shils and Michael Young (1953):

> In a great national communion like the Coronation, people become more aware of their dependence upon each other, and they sensed some connection between this and their relationship to the Queen. Thereby they became more sensitive to the values which bound them all together.

The Shils and Young article about the coronation (which begins with the sentence – of which Princess Diana might have been proud – 'The heart has its reasons which the mind does not suspect') was challenged at the time by Norman Birnbaum (1955), who argued that the Coronation demonstrated the absence rather than the presence of shared values. Amongst the people who apparently did not share the public grief at Diana's death were members of the Royal Family themselves: their public sorrow at the loss of the Royal Yacht Britannia was visibly greater than their sorrow at Diana's funeral. Nevertheless, defenders of the rights of the Royal Family to express (or fail to express) themselves in whatever way they felt suitable did touch on concerns which many share about the supposed moral superiority of grief and emotionalism. But if our political and social culture is being feminized as some writers suggest, we need to ask questions about the implications of this and the status – if any – of feminization as both an actual and possible agent of social transformation. First, we need to note that feminization has been identified in other historical contexts; indeed, a reading of the history of Britain and the United States in the last two hundred years suggests that there was always a tension between masculine and feminine cultures. John Brewer in the *The Pleasures of the Imagination* (1997: 115–22) quotes extensively from Mary Wollstonecraft and other women writers of the eighteenth century who protested both at the exclusive identification of women with feeling and at the idea that culture should become more feminine. Jane Austen's *Sense and Sensibility* is an extended essay against emotionalism; Eleanor Dashwood's unspoken thought that a particularly crass man did not deserve 'rational opposition' speaks legions about women's claim both to rationality and to non-participation in conventional masculinity (Austen, 1969: 255). In another country and almost another century Ann Douglas, in *The Feminisation of American Culture* (1996) identifies the development in the United States of a culture of romance and subjectivity derived from a literature specifically written for women. Most importantly, however, Douglas does not present this feminization of cultural life in the United States in positive terms; the feminization of which she speaks is, in her view, socially reactionary and opposed to the interests of both women and men. What she describes as a 'defeat within victory' became a pattern of emancipation for women in the United States: victory because women were allowed formal emancipation, but defeat because full participation in public office was denied (Douglas, 1996: 76).

All these authors – writers of fiction as much as professional academics – are concerned with the post-Enlightenment impact of the rise of science and rationality and the increasing institutional separation of public and private, culture and nature. Feminist writers have now thoroughly documented the impact of these dichotomies, but in looking forward, and at the present, we need to look again perhaps at the way in which gender is linked to political agency and the implications of this for our political systems. Women, in liberal democracies, now constitute a significant proportion of the work force, even if women's participation in paid work is still largely located in part-time, low-status work. Conventional expectations now include higher education for women and a toleration of women in public politics. It is equally widely expected, if not practised, that there should be greater toleration in men of the feminine – although the reverse is not so fully endorsed. All these factors about our own society, and others, could lead us to suppose that political life, and political discourses, are being affected by what Giddens (1992) has described as a 'transformation of intimacy'.

However, I would like to suggest an alternative – if less conclusive – interpretation. The structural changes in gender and work in the twentieth century are relatively uncontroversial. My concern is less with these changes themselves than with the impact of these changes in association with the cultural shifts in the West since the 1960s. In summary, those women in generations born after the Second World War have discovered and identified the perilous and fragile relationship between the feminine and late modernity. It is often assumed that what we call postmodernity, or late modernity, or what we could equally well call the late twentieth century, offers women more in the sense of personal choice and autonomy because its expectations are plural and diverse. So what is assumed is a continuity between the early modernity of the first decade of the twentieth century – what Virginia Woolf defined as the 'crowded dance of modern life' – and the late twentieth century. However, what has become equally clear in the twentieth century is the domination of our culture by what I would describe as 'modernity as project' – an orientation to the world of purposive, rational control through which the secular and individualistic societies in which we live can be organized and controlled. This project (which dates from the beginning of the nineteenth century) entails the construction of models of the management of the market economy and is largely derived from male experience. The gendered agenda of modernity was, however, largely hidden or refused. As Giddens (1994: 63) has suggested:

> what is Weber's discussion of the Protestant ethic if not an analysis of the obsessional nature of modernity? The emotional travails of women, of course, have no place in Weber's study – nor do the private or sexual lives of the purveyors of the entrepreneurial spirit.

Women's relationship to, and ability to participate in, this project have always been problematic; Jane Austen and Mary Wollstonecraft were the first to notice that a more radical, and feminist approach to cultural change was not to feminize the public but to integrate men into the private. However, what modernity did establish was a discourse about civil rights, and from the earliest years of the nineteenth century it is possible to identify women – and men – concerned with the extension of rights to numerous categories of people hitherto excluded from the emergent identity of citizen. But this focus on the public, essential as it was to the emancipation of women, established a compensatory dynamic in the social organization of gender relations in which men's experience became the normative basis for that of women. The nineteenth century campaigns, in both Britain and the United States, for women's suffrage, higher education and financial and sexual autonomy were generally grounded in a comparison with the rights allowed to men. Modernity thus allowed the participation of women in civil society, but the allowance was based on a model of formal participation which entirely excluded a discussion of difference or the relationship between the public and the private. In the second part of the twentieth century 'gender of modernity' has been discovered in contexts such as assumptions about morality (see, for example, the work of Carol Gilligan, 1993), discourses about the relationship of the state and the citizen (for example, Carole Pateman, 1988) and the place of sexual ambiguity in the cultural avant-garde (Pateman, 1988; Gilligan, 1993). It is not, therefore, that modernity is masculine, but that the project of modernity is gendered in complex ways which refuse straightforward emancipatory explanations.

It is at this point that I wish to re-introduce the issue of gender in the context of the British General Election of 1997 and to return to that claim, at the beginning of this chapter, that women's engagement with the Labour Party was an important factor in the Labour victory. My argument is that this engagement was both literal – in the sense that we can test and empirically know how many more women voted Labour than did men – but more important, symbolic. That is, that the public perception of the relationship of the Labour Party to the world was generally perceived as more feminine; less rigid, less socially hierarchical and more rooted in 'ordinary' experience. What the Labour Party did not project was the redundant, imperial masculinity which was literally embodied in the persons of such senior Conservative politicians as Michael Heseltine and Michael Portillo. The form of masculinity which the Labour Party projected was one in which either the collective presence of senior Labour Party figures included women or individual male figures who attempted to communicate a form of authority which was both less authoritarian (and by association patriarchal) and more inclusive of 'everyday' (that is, female) experience. Thus a public language evolved in which emphasis on schools, health and transport encoded, and included, specifically female concerns. These concerns very specifically related to the caring functions which women (either voluntary or not undertake). Writing about the Labour victory, the journalist Polly Toynbee said:

> For the times really have changed. Labour won because they represented the modern world and not John Major's imagining world of spinsters on bikes and warm beer. The greatest social change that Labour embodies has been among women, their lives and expectations. That was the symbolism of getting so many women into parliament. (Toynbee, 1998)

But, and it is a very considerable but, popular expectations about the Labour Party – located in the modern wish for both defined project and the integration of experience – could well founder on the questions of women and the family. The issue of the relationship of women to the social world immediately became, for the Labour government, problematic. The party came to power with a record number of women MPs – people clearly organized around the idea of a project – and immediately attempted to impose the same assumptions about project and autonomy on non-working women who are dependent on state benefits. This group – with every reason to suppose a supportive government – suddenly found itself confronted by an entirely unsupportive one, and one apparently anxious to resist symbolic and potent ideas about motherhood and the ties of infancy. The very drama of motherhood and its place as the definitive signifier of female sexuality were translated into a negative absence from paid work.

Given the present rate of divorce in families with children in Britain it is likely that the numbers of women attempting to support children without significant male assistance will not decrease. The link between changes in the family and poverty still remains little appreciated: it is widely known that single mothers are poor, but it is less widely said that amongst the causes of single motherhood is both a refusal of traditional masculinity by women and a flight from it – as Barbara Ehrenreich (1983) pointed out over twenty years ago – by men. We do not, I would argue, often reflect on this aspect of contemporary society, because the questions it raises are too problematic for public discussion. Yet in this change in family relations lies what should be a central concern of the late twentieth century: the issue of the extent to which society is prepared to accept the new complexities of gender relations or will refuse them – with potentially even further consequences of social disruption – in favour of the endless self-monitoring of experience and behaviour. In attempting to deny the personal and subjective implications of motherhood with policies which emphasize capitalist imperatives, the government increases those existing tensions around gender which have already had destabilizing effects in terms of the organization of the household but are also likely to increase the demands and the expectations on the welfare state. It is ironical that just as post-Soviet Eastern Europe has dismantled its system of state-subsidized child care, so Blair's Britain is busily engaged in establishing the state-supported child care system which was the basis of women's participation in paid work in state socialist societies (Einhorn, 1995).

So the policy towards single mothers occupies a paradoxical place within a culture in which – as suggested above – women literally and women symbolically produced cultural and political change. It is a policy which is in accord with the rationalizing and managerial impetus of the contemporary state, but it is equally a policy which in its attack on a powerful symbol undermines both the coherence of the culture and the more specific instance of the loyalty of women to a particular political party. Equally, it also poses ideological problems for that political party (or indeed for any other) since to be against women in the sense of undermining the most symbolically effective aspect of womanhood inevitably suggests a party, or a group, which is for men, and masculinity. To many feminists – whose reading of modernity and capitalism is not gender blind – this hardly comes as a great surprise. But in the 1990s, when the political embrace of femininity is both marked and deliberate, politicians find themselves in the difficult situation of wishing to appeal to women, but at the same time denying the subjectivity which contributes to women's experience. It is thus that a political culture which seemed to endorse the feminine was utilized for political advantage, yet at the same time it is apparent that the age-old resistance of women to explicitly patriarchal interests may continue to have a more marked, and more complex, effect on political life than was ever supposed in manifestos about policies for women.

The Labour Party's victory in 1997 was one which was achieved through the sophisticated analysis and management of cultural change in contemporary Britain. Changing perceptions about masculinity and femininity were integrated into an understanding of both shifts and continuities in the experiences of women and men. But post-electoral policy clearly differs from pre-electoral rhetoric, in that a Government, rather than a political party involved in electoral politics, has to engage with economic and social issues which are seldom specifically cultural in their origin. Late modernity, we might remember, does not take place outside a material context, and however much we may wish to assume modernity, and the modern world, to be culture, it is a narrative which has very clear, defining limits. Amongst those limits is the relationship between poverty and absence from paid work. In trying to break this relationship for women the government appears to be engaged in the kind of emancipatory programme which would have been endorsed by Engels: the problem, however, is the late twentieth century has now recognized the value of unpaid work (indeed it is included in the GNP) and governments cannot both recognize its contribution to social well-being (or in a less coded form, stable capitalism) and undermine it.[5] The problem of culture, for capitalism as for any other form of government, remains as crucial, and potentially disruptive, as ever. But in tracing the relationship of women to one specific, limited period in British politics, we can perhaps begin to examine more fully the part that gender plays in politics and cultural change and through this increase the likelihood of theorization which does not either refuse gender as significant in social theory or describe the social world in terms only of its patterns of consumption and fantasy. As the feminine becomes more transparently part of the aesthetic of modernity – a part forecast by critics as diverse as Simmel and Virginia Woolf – so we have to ask how far the symbolic feminine can be used and integrated into those societies of late modernity which are also inevitably committed (through liberal arguments about the extension of citizenship quite as much as through the imperatives of the capitalist economy) to diminishing gender difference.

It is through the discussion of this aspect of social life in the late twentieth century that it may be possible to make gender as active a participant in social change as class. We know, from the work of feminist sociologists such as Sylvia Walby (1986) and Annie Phizacklea (1990), that gender plays a crucial part in determining participation in the labour market. If we also allow that symbolic constructions of femininity are as crucial in determining the political culture as is class, then we can begin to integrate the material and the culture which allows an understanding of both objective situation and individual subjectivity. It is apparent from those recent debates between Nancy Fraser and Judith Butler referred to at the beginning of this chapter that feminists have begun to review the debate over the material and the culture. In this newly revived debate Judith Butler (1998: 42) has remarked that:

> The economic, tied to the reproductive, is necessarily linked to the repro-
> duction of heterosexuality. It is not that non-heterosexual forms of sexuality
> are simply left out, but that their suppression is essential to the operation of
> that prior normativity. This is not simply a question of certain people

suffering a lack of cultural recognition by others but, rather, a specific mode of sexual production and exchange that works to maintain the stability of gender, the heterosexuality of desire, and the naturalisation of the family.

What Judith Butler is doing here is taking issue with feminist writers – and in this case most particularly Nancy Fraser – who argue that the cultural politics of capitalism are independent of it. To Nancy Fraser, there is no reason *per se* why capitalism should care about the politics of sexual identity or the gender of those who care for children.

This position is unacceptable to Judith Butler, since to her the oppression of gays and lesbians is directly linked to the stability of capitalism. To Butler, Nancy Fraser is a 'neo-conservative Marxist' and intent upon dismissing prejudice against dissenters from heterosexuality as 'merely cultural' and insignificant when compared with economic exploitation. The debate recalls those differences within feminism in the 1970s, particularly in the re-assertion by Nancy Fraser (1998: 147) of the argument that capitalism has no implicit need for a specific form of gender relations:

> Empirically, therefore, contemporary capitalism seems not to require heterosexism. With its gaps between the economic order and the kinship order, and between the family and personal life, capitalist society now permits significant numbers of individuals to live through wage labour outside of heterosexual families. It could permit many more to do so – provided the relations of recognition were changed!

In terms of the specific case of the British General Election of 1997 (and the debates and discussions which preceded it) it would appear that very few people, outside the Conservative Party, assumed (with Judith Butler) that heterosexuality and the reproduction of the family were essential components of either capitalism (which was hardly challenged by anyone in the 1997 Election campaign) or the efficient working of the market economy. What was assumed was that the ability to participate in paid labour was an essential condition of citizenship. Attempts by the Conservative Party to re-establish the normative ascendancy of the heterosexual nuclear family had led not to their electoral success but the their electoral failure. The impact of changes in the family (and most specifically women's refusal to continue to accept male authority in exchange for male economic support) was such as to produce a social and political culture which endorsed the facilitation of participation in paid work. In this sense, therefore, changes in family and personal relations are clearly associated with the expectation that capitalism will be gender blind: whatever the expectations of the past, it became apparent in May 1997 that there was no longer a place for distinctions against women (or sexual minorities) in the market economy of the late twentieth century.

Acknowledgements

This chapter is based on a paper to a seminar in the Department of Sociology at the University of Lancaster in February 1998. I am very grateful to Jackie Stacey for inviting me to that seminar and to those present (especially Andrew Sayer and Larry Ray) for their helpful comments.

Notes

1 Quoted in Andrew Geddes and Jon Tonge (1997).

2 Those constructions of masculinity are discussed and developed by Anne McClintock (1995).

3 The debate between Perry Anderson and E.P. Thompson began in 1965. Primarily it was concerned with Thompson's assertion of the theoretical radicalism of English empiricism; in contrast Anderson argued that English culture was deeply conservative and a-theoretical.

4 Richard Hoggart and Raymond Williams, most importantly, had stressed the diverse cultures of Britain. See Hoggart's *The Uses of Literacy* (first published in 1957) and Raymond Williams's *Culture and Society* and *The Long Revolution* (published in 1958 and 1961, respectively).

5 Engels envisioned state responsibility for child care; see Marx and Engels (1985: 107).

References

Arendt, Hannah (1959) *The Human Condition*, New York: Doubleday.

Austen, Jane (1969) *Sense and Sensibility*, Harmondsworth: Penguin.

Barrett, Michelle (1979) *Women's Oppression Today*, London: Verso, p. 165.

Beechey, Veronica (1977) 'Some notes on female wage labour in capitalist production', *Capital and Class*, 3: 45–66.

Birnbaum, Norman (1955) 'Monarchs and sociologists: a reply to Professor Shils and Mr Young', *Sociological Review*, 3: 5–23.

Blondel, Jean (1963) 'Towards a general theory of change in voting behaviour', *Political Studies*, 13: 93–5.

Brewer, John (1997) *The Pleasures of the Imagination*, London: HarperCollins.

Butler, Judith (1998) 'Marxism and the merely cultural', *New Left Review*, 227: 33–44.

Calder, Angus (1971) *The People's War*, London: Panther.

Curtice, John and Steed, Michael (1997) *The British General Election of 1997*, London: Macmillan.

Douglas, Ann (1996) *The Feminisation of American Culture*, London: Papermac.

Ehrenreich, Barbara (1983) *The Hearts of Men: American Dreams and the Flight from Commitment*, London: Pluto.

Einhorn, Barbara (1995) 'Ironies of history: citizenship issues in the new market economies of Eastern Europe', in Barbara Einhorn and Eileen Yeo (eds), *Women and Market Societies*, Aldershot: Edward Elgar, pp. 217–33.

Fraser, Nancy (1998) 'Heterosexism, misrecognition and capitalism: a response to Judith Butler', *New Left Review*, 228: 140–9.

Geddes, Andrew and Tonge, Jon (1997) 'Labour's landslide? The British General Election 1997', *ECPR News*, 8 (3): 31.

Giddens, Anthony (1992) *The Transformation of Intimacy*, Cambridge: Polity.

Giddens, Anthony (1994) 'Living in a post-traditional society', in Ulrich Beck, Anthony Giddens and Scott Lash (eds), *Reflexive Modernization*, Cambridge: Polity.

Gilligan, Carol (1993) *In a Different Voice*, Cambridge, MA: Harvard University Press.

Hall, Stuart, Hobson, Dorothy, Lowe, Andrew and Willis, Paul (eds) (1980) *Culture, Media, Language*, London: Hutchinson.

Hartmann, Heidi (1979) 'The unhappy marriage of Marxism and feminism: towards a more progressive union', *Capital and Class*, 8: 1–33.

McClintock, Anne (1995) *Imperial Leather: Race, Gender and Sexuality in the Colonial Context*, London: Routledge.

McKenzie, R.T. (1963) *British Political Parties*, London: Mercury.

McRobbie, Angela (1994) 'Folk devils fight back', *New Left Review*, 203: 107–16.

Marx, Karl and Engels, Friedrich (1985) *The Origin of the Family, Private Property and the State*, Harmondsworth: Penguin.

Morgan, David and Evans, Mary (1993) *Battle for Britain*, London: Routledge.

Pateman, Carole (1988) *The Sexual Contract*, Cambridge: Polity.

Phillips, Anne and Taylor, Barbara (1986) 'Sex and skill', in Feminist Review (ed.), *Waged Work: A Reader*, London: Virago, pp. 54–66.

Phizacklea, Annie (1990) *Unpacking the Fashion Industry*, London: Routledge.

Randall, Vicky and Waylen, Georgina (1998) *Gender, Politics and the State*, London: Routledge.

Samuel, Raphael (1994) 'Living history', in his *Theatres of Memory*, London: Verso, pp. 169–202.

Shils, Edward and Young, Michael (1953) 'The meaning of the coronation', *Sociological Review*, 1: 63–81.

Toynbee, Polly (1998) 'Women to blame again', *The Guardian*, 4 March.

Walby, Sylvia (1986) *Patriarchy at Work: Patriarchal and Capitalist Relations in Employment*, Cambridge: Polity.

Wilson, Elizabeth (1997) 'Saint Diana', *New Left Review*, 226: 136–45.

11

New Labour: Culture and Economy

Stephen Driver and Luke Martell

Under Tony Blair, New Labour modernizers have made much of the moral rather than economic arguments for socialism. Values, like community and responsibility, they argue, are what really defines socialism or the centre-left, not technical means or instruments such as public ownership, tax-and-spend or state-welfare (see, for example, Blair, 1995c; Wright, 1997). New Labour has defined itself in ethical terms. In matters concerning human behaviour, whether in parenting or in the classroom, on welfare or on the streets, New Labour has set out a communitarian moral agenda about duties in the community and the rights and responsibilities of individuals. Both the Thatcherite 'get what you can' individualism and rights-claiming social democracy, it is argued, left a moral vacuum in society which needs to be filled (Blair, 1995a). But does New Labour's moralism amount to a 'cultural turn'? Or to put it another way, is New Labour an instance of the culturalization of politics?

Culturalization theses

There is no single culturalization thesis. Among the issues discussed in this book are a variety of theses about the culturalization of society and politics. We do not wish to dwell on these, as they are outlined more fully in the introduction and other chapters of this volume. But five culturalization theses can be identified which seem most relevant to politics and to changes in the ideas and policies of the British Labour Party.

One thesis is that there has been a shift in interest, among political agents, from inequality to difference; from the political economy of resource distribution to the politics of identity and cultural recognition. Political actors are less concerned with economic inequality and more with cultural difference as a positive value. The economic dimensions of inequality have become less focused on than cultural considerations, and difference has shifted from being a problem to something of value (see, for example, Fraser, 1995).

A second thesis is that there has been a shift from economic to cultural explanations of the economy. The economy is not just a matter of economic instruments and technical processes. It is increasingly seen to be significantly marked by cultural and moral underpinnings. Different forms of economy have different cultural bases which affect their shape and success. Analyses of economic difference and success focus less and less on technical economic processes and more on cultural differences.[1]

A third thesis is that politics is decreasingly concerned with economics and more with moral concerns. Political actors perceive that they have a decreasing amount of control over the economy, largely because of processes such as globalization. Therefore they attempt instead to pursue changes in culture or morality. Or they perceive that we live in a post-material world where people with higher standards of living than in the past are more concerned with moral than economic issues. Politicians are more interested in moral or missionary government than economic intervention (Demos, 1995).

A fourth thesis is that there is a shift away from critiques of commodification and consumerism to their celebration. Consumption in the market is seen as a source of fulfilment rather than alienation. This goes hand in hand with a shift from economic to cultural emphases: analyses from a culturalist perspective see as positive for the consumer what analyses from economic perspectives saw as problematic for the producer (Ray and Sayer, this volume).

A fifth thesis is that politics has become increasingly culturalized not only in content but also in style. The stylization of politics and the importance of its form have reached new heights in the hands of spin doctors and media manipulators (Jones, 1995; 1997). The mediatization of politics and aesthetic considerations have become so important as to displace substance from politics.

New Labour and the cultural turn

At first glance, New Labour seems to fit these culturalization theses quite well. There has been a shift away from ideas of equality as economic redistribution towards equality of opportunity and individual potential, in New Labour ideas and policies. Labour's political economy is concerned with the cultural bases of capitalist success: there has been much debate on the centre-left about the contribution of cultures in other countries to their economic success and about the extent to which elements from successful cultures of capitalism can be learnt from in Britain. Labour has explicitly argued that globalization ties its hands economically. Moral exhortation, guidance and legislation have been big parts of its agenda, on parenting, teaching methods and welfare, alcohol, smoking and hunting, to mention just a few. Some of the first signs of turbulence to hit Blair's Labour government were accusations of bossiness and over-zealous moralism. Labour modernizers have also switched concern from producer to consumer interests. And much has been made of the meticulous care, co-ordination and manipulation that has gone into the presentation of Labour's image to the public. Spin-doctoring, it is thought, has been taken to new heights by the media managers of the modern Labour Party. In all these respects New Labour would seem to be a prime candidate for support for the thesis that politics has been culturalized.

But what is New Labour all about? What do its economics and social policy amount to? What is the communitarianism Blair espouses which would seem to be central to Labour's moralism?[2] Do Labour's economics, social policy and communitarianism show an example of a 'cultural turn' in contemporary politics?

New Labour, new times: economy, welfare and social justice

Labour's changing ideas and policies are based on the idea that we live in 'new times'. New times became a familiar analytical device, as well as slogan, in *Marxism Today* in the 1980s. Stuart Hall and Martin Jacques (1989: 11) suggested that: 'The world has changed, not just incrementally but qualitatively'. For many on the left, new times brought together ideas about how modern (and to some, *post*modern) societies were being transformed by new economic, social and cultural forces like post-Fordism and globalization; how the old class structures and political allegiances were disappearing; how society had become less bound by tradition, deference and patriarchal relationships; how civil society had become more differentiated, pluralistic and individualistic; and how the individual subject was becoming reflexive and fragmented in terms of its identity. In the economy, new times meant mass production giving way to flexible specialization; in society, they had led to the fragmentation of social relations and cultural identities. Where, for much of the twentieth century, society had been marked by social uniformity and the unified subject, new times were bringing about a social diversification and the 'de-centred' subject.

For Hall and Jacques, the political consequence of new times was that the left must move with them and found a politics 'beyond Thatcherism'. For the Labour Party, this meant shedding its 'Labourist' trade union roots and embracing the more culturally inflected politics of the new social movements (see also Laclau and Mouffe, 1985). Tony Blair shares this 'post-Thatcherite' reading of contemporary politics. Or at least, he shares a *version* of it, one which focuses on the political economy of late twentieth-century market economies. As a response to new times, New Labour has embraced the flexibility (and efficiency) of the market; but leading Labour modernizers like Blair and Jack Straw are far less comfortable with the social fragmentation that new times has brought, seeing it less as a basis for new political alliances and more as a problem of social order.

On the economy and welfare state, Labour modernizers have made it clear that there is no going back to the political economy of state socialism or social democracy. The free market reforms of Thatcherism, in particular privatization and the deregulation of the labour market, are to be retained. Blair has carried the radical modernizer message that the reforms of eighteen years of Conservative government are not to be undone by the new Labour government. Indeed, in the case of the welfare state, it is Labour not the Conservatives who are now making the case for radical reform involving a considerable extension of the principle of individual responsibility. The rewriting by Blair of the old Clause Four, which committed the party to common ownership of property, was symbolic of New Labour's break with the past. The appropriateness of public and private is now seen by Labour as a matter of practical rather than ideological concern (Blair, 1997). Furthermore, Labour modernizers have shifted away from a concern with producer interests to those of the consumer. Blair has explicitly said that a Labour government will not be dictated to by producer interests; and that trade unions can assume 'fairness but not favours' (Blair, 1994a). In opposition, Labour developed plans to tighten up on the regulation of financial services and the privatized utilities; and to tougher competition policy – all, at least in part, in the interests of giving consumers a better deal. The education and health reforms of the Labour government are in large part about delivering better standards to the users of these services: 'producers' such as teachers and health workers can expect a harder ride in the push to drive out incompetence, inefficiency or waste in the interests of pupils and patients.

This 'post-Thatcherite' strategy, Blair argues, is necessary because new times require new means for achieving old socialist values (Blair, 1995c). Globalization, for example, is perceived to have undermined national Keynesian strategies of demand management: capital is internationally mobile, and demand cannot be manipulated by national governments to create full employment. Rather, governments have a more limited role in helping to create the stable low-inflation macroeconomic conditions and skilled labour markets which attract capital investment and bring job opportunities (Brown, 1994). New economic times for New Labour are also post-industrial in character. Labour modernizers have made great play of the importance of information and communication technologies and the cultural industries to advanced market economies. These sectors have been singled out by Labour as worthy of special promotion: for example, Labour's attempt to pursue public–private partnerships to network schools; and Blair's courting of entertainers and designers. New Labour has embraced the idea that the shift from Fordism to post-Fordism has brought with it a far greater need for flexibility on the part of companies to adapt to global markets and rapid technological change. Similarly workers have to be flexible to take on new skills and face greater insecurities in the labour market.

Social policy in such conditions is conceived less as a means to redistribute incomes and wealth, or to act as a band-aid for capitalism, and rather as a means of increasing individual opportunities by creating labour market flexibility in a global economy *and* expanding the non-inflationary growth rate of the British economy. In New Labour-speak, welfare should offer 'a hand-up, not a hand-out'. Governments should help individuals get on in an uncertain world, not lock them into dependency and social exclusion. In terms of delivery, New Labour reject what they perceive was the statist approach of post-war social democracy. Labour modernizers advocate the devolution of responsi-bilities from the state to a variety of agencies: individual self-help or the private sector, for example, as in private pensions, university education and health. Devolution of powers, to schools and GPs for instance, is to be maintained and to some extent modified, not reversed. Welfare and educational rights are seen as requiring greater responsibilities in return: responsibilities of parents on attendance, punctuality and home-work, for example, and of welfare recipients to take up jobs and join welfare-to-work schemes. Much of this breaks with the universal and comprehensive ideas of uniform state welfare and with pre-Blair social democracy's emphasis on rights to education and welfare (Blair, 1995b; 1996c; Labour Party, 1995a and b; 1996a and b).

Labour's post-Thatcherite – and post-communist – political economy has relied in part on the 'models of capitalism' debates. In this literature (see, for example, Albert, 1993; Hutton, 1995) it is perceived that the major global conflicts are no longer political, between capitalism and socialism: capitalism has won that battle. Now global competition is economic, between different forms of capitalism.[3] What distinguishes the different forms of capitalism are, among other things, their different cultural bases. Japanese and German capitalisms, for example, while very different from each other, are seen to share interventionist and collaborative institutional networks and cultures. Relationships are less market-based and more long-term. Britain and the USA are more indi-vidualistic and laissez-faire, with relationships conducted more through the market, at arms length and with shorter-term objectives.

In Singapore in 1996, Blair advocated greater stakeholding in cor-porate affairs: making companies more accountable to a greater variety of stakeholders than just shareholders. This, many believed, would lead to a more long-term constructive engagement in companies rather than short-term, dividend-oriented, arms-length relations (Blair, 1996a; see also Kelly et al., 1997). Subsequently, such a corporate model of stakeholding has been eclipsed in New Labour thinking by an individual version of stakeholding. This sees society (not specifically the corporation) as an entity in which all individuals should have a stake. Certain groups, the young and long-term unemployed, single parents and people locked into welfare dependency are, it is said, currently excluded from society and from the opportunities others have. They need to be brought back into society and given a stake in it through job opportunities. Hence the welfare-to-work programme, the Social Exclusion Unit, the minimum wage and the ambition to reform the tax and benefit system to provide incentives for the unemployed to take paid work.

New Labour's embrace of the market economy and of welfare reform forms the basis for a new policy consensus with the Conservatives in Britain. There are, to be sure, differences. The Labour government is more activist in the labour market: on welfare-to-work, the minimum wage and the Social Chapter. But on the broad sweep of fiscal and monetary policy, as well as the principles of welfare reform – namely, greater individual responsibility to match welfare rights – New Labour has moved onto the political and policy territory mapped out by the Conservatives in the 1980s. Indeed, in opposition, it was Labour's claim that it, not the Tories, had the competence in government to deliver stable, low-inflationary growth and welfare reform, among other things.

Where does all this leave Labour's idea of social justice? Despite the financing of the welfare-to-work programme (from a 'windfall tax' on the privatized utilities), the Labour government came to power with a commitment to not raising income tax levels and to sticking with the previous Tory government's public spending plans. This may in part have been a shrewd political move to avoid damaging accusations that New Labour was the devil in disguise – and that a Labour government would revert to old Labour habits of tax-and-spend. But this is to underestimate the scale of the Blair revolution in the Labour party. The Commission on Social Justice (1994) paved the way for Labour modernizers in the 1990s to explicitly reject redistributional economic and social policies as the basis for social justice. Social justice for New Labour is now about greater equality of opportunity: it is about 'social inclusion' and 'fairness' (in terms of tax rates, for example). Gordon Brown, for one, is on record arguing that Labour's key aim is greater equality of opportunity in a lifelong sense rather than more equal outcomes (Brown, 1994; 1997a; 1997b). There is certainly a redistributional element to the windfall tax; but the egalitarian effects of welfare-to-work are likely to be minor if there are any at all.

Economic and social policy: the culturalization thesis considered

So where do these shifts in economics, social policy and social justice leave us in relation to the culturalization theses? On the surface the policy changes under Blair seem to lend some support to the idea that politics, at least in the case of the Labour Party, has become more cultural in the terms of the theses we set out above. First, there has been a shift away from economic and social egalitarianism to ideas of equality of individual opportunity and social inclusion; secondly, observations about the cultural bases of different forms of capitalism have fed into New Labour's economic reforms; and thirdly, New Labour has embraced the market economy, distanced itself from producer interests and thrown its lot behind the consumer. In all these three areas, however, we wish to argue that these shifts in ideology and policy are not as much instances of culturalization as they may at first appear to be.

First, the shift away from egalitarianism is more about opportunities than difference; and as much about a shift away from socialist to a narrower liberal conception of equality as it is a cultural turn. New Labour's emphasis on individual opportunity and the fulfilment of individual potential is not especially linked to a celebration of difference. Insofar as individuals are seen as important, New Labour focus on their *opportunities* to participate in society, in particular, access to the labour market. This is not the same as emphasizing their *difference*; and it certainly does not amount to a celebration of cultural diversity or the fragmentation of cultural identity thought to be a central feature of contemporary culture and society. Having equal opportunities could lead to the pursuit of activities which are different, or individuals could conform with social mores: difference is not really the point here. Similarly, where Labour modernizers emphasize the importance of individuals fulfilling their potential, the emphasis is on individuals fulfilling what they are capable of, whether this involves conformity to general norms or greater difference. If anything, Labour are much more concerned with individuals fulfilling duties and obligations to society and of individuals sharing in common values and moral norms. Indeed, social fragmentation is seen as undermining individual opportunity.

There is little distinctively *cultural* about New Labour's shift away from egalitarian notions of social justice to one focused on individual opportunity. The distinctive feature of New Labour is less the valuing of cultural diversity and more a straightforward move from left rightwards in terms of political economy: from the left's traditional concern with redistributive justice to the right's concern with just deserts. Indeed, Labour modernizers justify the shift from egalitarianism to equality of opportunity on the basis that inequality is needed to provide incentives, and is often deserved and desirable, and that redistributive equality is unattainable because of limits on increases in income taxation. Moreover, equal opportunities are conceptualized in a very economic way. For New Labour it is mainly about individuals gaining a stake in society through employment. A great deal rests, in Labour's one-nation stakeholding, on *economic* inclusion.[4] In this way, New Labour's 'new times' are fundamentally economic in character, concerned less with cultural diversity and more with economic flexibility. Where New Labour does address the nature of contemporary cultural identity, as we shall see shortly, there is a concern that social fragmentation is undermining social cohesion.

Secondly, New Labour's economics may be culturally conscious; but the central feature of the Labour government's economic policy is the rejection of the political economies of state socialism (in particular, state ownership and planning) and social democracy (in particular, Keynesian demand mangement) in favour of liberal free markets and anti-inflationary fiscal and monetary policies. On closer inspection, New Labour's economics are best understood in terms of a left–right shift as much as in terms of an economic–cultural one. Despite the interest shown by Labour modernizers in foreign models of capitalism, it is this shift from one set of economic models to another set (in large part, models which break on left–right lines) which defines New Labour. The focus of the new Labour government's economic policies is quite traditional, concerned with the regulation of the labour market, levels of taxation and public expenditure and interest rates; there is little interest in the cultural bases of economic life; and certainly little interest in doing anything about the culture of British capitalism in the manner advocated by Will Hutton or David Marquand (see Marquand, 1988; Hutton, 1995). Indeed, Labour modernizers may find attractive different features of capitalisms the world over – and under Blair, New Labour has found the Anglo-Saxon model, with its flexible Labour markets, far more attractive than the more heavily regulated Continental model – but they have also been keen to impress that cultures of capitalism cannot be transplanted onto British soil; that Britain has its own cultural traditions which a Labour government has to work within; and that economic policy should be based on the indigenous culture (Blair, 1995b; Darling, 1997). Such a view certainly demonstrates a sensitivity to culture, but it is accommodating rather than transformatory; or at least it is in the case of Britain: Blair and Brown are prone to lecture Continental European policy-makers that they should adopt the British model of flexible labour markets to reduce dole queues – and so, by implication, to work against their own cultural heritage. Furthermore, Labour modernizers' penchant for design, information technologies and the cultural industries – 'cool Britannia' – hardly amounts to a cultural turn by Labour's leaders. Conran, computers and Britpop certainly help *New* Labour to project an image of *New* Britain; but it is their perceived contribution to economic growth and to British exports which lie at the root of Labour's love of culture.

Thirdly, New Labour's shift away from producer to consumer interests does not amount to a celebration of the culture of consumption: 'I shop therefore I am' is unlikely to make it into any Blair speech! Indeed, there is a certain unease among Labour modernizers with the idea that meaning and value in modern society are based on individual choice in the market place. On family policy, for example, Labour modernizers single out the 'terrible price for the application of choice-based individualism to the business of being a parent' (Wright, 1997: 109). On the specific question of the consumer, New Labour is more concerned whether consumers get a fair deal – and that public service providers, especially local government, put consumer interests first – than with the cultural joys of consumption. And there is of course the political imperative for New Labour to distance itself from links with the trade union producer groups which helped both to define and to sustain Old Labour. Labour is certainly concerned that consumers should have adequate rights and choices, whether as parents or patients in education and health, or as users of financial services, for example. But this is a reaction against the disempowerment of users under paternalistic Old Labour and free-market Thatcherism. It is as much about the poor treatment of consumers in the past at the hands of a distant state or narrow-mindedly profiteering businesses than any positive celebration of consumerism. And as we shall turn to now, much of Labour's communitarianism involves a critique of the 'I, me, mine' economic egoism of Thatcherism, which Labour modernizers argue has destroyed the moral bonds of society (Blair, 1995a).

Labour's communitarianisms and the cultural turn

If there are fewer signs of a cultural turn in Labour's economic and social policies than there might at first sight appear to be, is there anything in its communitarianism which might support a culturalization thesis?[5] It is certainly true that New Labour, with one eye on the traditionally Tory voters of middle England, and in part also driven by a genuine ethical zeal, is keen to emphasize moral values. New Labour's communitarian arguments are at one and the same time a political response to the Conservative Party's grip on power *and* a cultural critique of modern society – its values and institutions.

Labour's communitarianisms operate at three levels.[6] At a *sociological* level communitarianism offers Labour a retort to the neoliberal view that there is no such thing as society, only individuals and their families. For Blair, individuals do not become what they are outside of the community of which they are members. They are constituted through the social relations in which they are embedded. At an *ethical* level, Labour is communitarian because it believes community is a good thing. New Labour offers community as better than a society in which everyone runs around pursuing their own self-interest or simply claiming rights. Politically, Labour argues that the community can do things which individuals by themselves cannot. Furthermore, as we shall see, Labour has particular ideas of what *sort* of community is a good one. On a *meta-ethical* level (concerning the justifications for ethical prescriptions), Labour avoids the relativism of some communitarian thinking, claiming instead that there is a moral agenda which they believe that the one-nation community of Britain, at least, should follow.[7]

There is, then, in New Labour thinking a sociological and ethical communitarianism which provides the modernizers with a framework for public policy-making which in certain areas has a strongly moral flavour concerned with the good life in the community. In terms of the culturalization thesis, we shall argue that New Labour's communitarianism is: first, a *political* response to the New Right and to Old Labour which involves a cultural critique of neoliberal individualism and rights-claiming social democracy; and secondly, a *conservative* cultural turn which marks it off from progressive left politics.

Beyond neoliberalism and social democracy

New Labour's communitarian arguments have two principal objectives. First, to provide an alternative to conservative neoliberalism. Second, to distance the party from its social democratic past. Communitarianism offers Labour modernizers a political vocabulary which eschews market individualism, but not capitalism; and which embraces collective action, but not class or the state.[8]

Labour's communitarianism challenges the neoliberal market model in two ways. First, it denies that successful economies live by competitive individualism alone: community values like co-operation and collaboration are just as vital to a successful market system. Public–private partnerships, for example, and a role for the state in provision of education and training are essential for economic success. Second, communitarians challenge the neoliberal belief that welfare is best left to the free play of private enterprise. There is a greater role for government and public agencies in ensuring that those who are outside of the labour market can be incorporated back into society. Laissez-faire has contributed to social fragmentation: a dangerous cocktail of poverty and anomie. Social cohesion is in part to be rebuilt through welfare-to-work.

Against social democracy, Labour's communitarians challenge what they see as a statist approach to welfare. This, they argue, has fostered dependency and been too universalistic. It has not allowed sufficient space for devolved management, local initiative or individual choice. It has placed a large fiscal burden on society and contributed to moral decay. The welfare state has undermined the capacity of individuals to help themselves by getting off benefits into work or, where appropriate, by financing their own health, education or pensions. Labour's communitarians challenge the post-war rights-claiming culture which ignored duties and responsibilities. Rights were claimed without reciprocal duties to seek work, or to fulfil parental obligations regarding their children's education, for example.

New Labour's right cultural turn

Labour's interest in communitarianism is a response, then, to perceptions of both neo-liberal individualism and of statist and rights-claiming
liberal social democracy. In respect of both, Labour modernizers have
deployed cultural arguments concerning the values of modern society
and the way people live and conceive their lives. As Blair argued in his
1995 Spectator Lecture: 'we do not live by economics alone . . . a society
which is fragmented and divided, where people feel no sense of shared
purpose, is unlikely to produce well-adjusted and responsible citizens'
(Blair, 1995a; see also Rentoul, 1995, for a biography of Blair which
shows the development of this aspect of the Labour leader's thinking).
Blair went on to attack what he saw as the 'do your own thing' social
individualism of social democracy and the 'get what you can' message
of Conservative neoliberalism. But if New Labour's embrace of 'community' is a cultural turn – a turn away from the essentially socio-
economic arguments which defined Old Labour – then it is a *conservative* one which shares little in common with the cultural politics of the
progressive left. Indeed, closer affinities may be found between New
Labour and the Conservative right (see Gray, 1995; Scruton, 1996). We
shall identify dimensions of New Labour's communitarian politics
which show the conservative inflection of its cultural turn.

First, Labour is torn between pluralist and conformist communitarianisms. On the one hand, Labour is attracted by the idea of greater
pluralism in social and constitutional policy. This is part of its attempt
to break with the statism of paternalistic social democracy and with the
authoritarian aspects of Thatcherism. The Labour government is pursuing welfare reforms which maintain or extend the decentralization of
social administration (in education and health, for example); and which
place greater emphasis on the diversity of provision and on greater
individual responsibility (in the funding of pensions and higher education, for example). The Labour Party also came to power in 1997 with
major plans for a politically more pluralistic Britain with devolution to
Scotland and Wales and reform of English local government.

Alongside these plans for greater devolution, on the other hand, is a
far less pluralist political discourse, not always clearly defined, which
emphasizes the 'strong community'. This discourse has sought to create
the ethical foundations for public policy: as the leading modernizer
Tony Wright puts it: 'If there is no agreement on what a good society is,
or a rejection even of the concept of a good society, then it is scarcely
surpising that we have trouble in making progress towards it. Unless
we believe in community, as a cohesive and inclusive network of
mutual obligations and shared responsibilities, we shall never build
such a community' (Wright, 1997: 108). In New Labour thinking on
social policy, there is an attempt to establish what those 'mutual obligations' and 'shared responsibilities' are in terms of the family, schools

and behaviour in public and private spaces – all of which we shall return to shortly. In New Labour's 'strong community', greater emphasis is placed on the individual's conformity to social norms than on the devolution of powers.

A second dimension is between less and more conditional forms of communitarianism. As an alternative to competitive individualism, New Labour emphasizes its commitment to government intervention to help the poor and excluded: a communitarianism where the community cares about its worse off members. New Labour talk about a stakeholder one-nation society in which government will help the long-term and youth unemployed and lone parents, for example, and ensure they have a stake and individual opportunities in society (e.g. Blair, 1996a). But this more traditionally socialist or social democratic sort of communitarianism has been joined by a more conditional communitarianism where community help increasingly requires greater reciprocal obligations. So, for example, welfare rights should be conditional on recipients fulfilling certain duties, like accepting a training place when offered; or individuals should be partly responsible for contributing to the fees for their university degree; parents should fulfil obligations on attendance, homework and such like in return for the right to state education. So while there is a strong and clear intention to help the disadvantaged and excluded, this communitarianism is not merely one-way. Helping others becomes conditional on reciprocity: a shift from a less to a more conditional communitarianism.

On a third dimension, Labour's communitarianism is increasingly conservative and less progressive in the content of the values it supports. To be sure, individual Labour politicians are more or less liberal and progressive on many issues, as they have been in the past. However, in New Labour thinking as a whole, conservative values have come to the fore. The conservative character of Labour's communitarianism can be seen in three policy areas: education, family policy and law and order. In each case, progressive values (and progressive public policy approaches) are being marginalized. Labour modernizers have explicitly rejected many of the liberal and progressive policy positions which were both a feature of the Labour Party since the 1960s and of the left more generally. On education, David Blunkett has led the attack on 'progressive' teaching and learning methods, insisting that schools should place a greater emphasis on traditional methods, such as whole class teaching, and on the 3Rs to raise education standards. Indeed, in government, Labour has moved to introduce more teaching of the basics (English and mathematics) in primary schools; and even to establish Education Action Zones within which the National Curriculum can be suspended to make more room for the 3Rs. On law and order, Home Secretary Jack Straw has continued to make New Labour as much tough on crime as it is tough on the causes of crime. New Labour's approach to the criminal justice system turns its back on the party's liberal approach, especially regarding young offenders, established in the 1960s. There is a far greater emphasis on the individual's responsibility for their crimes – rather than on the socio-economic conditions which might 'cause' crime which was the feature of Labour in the past. There is too in New Labour thinking on crime a much greater prominence given to the family as a factor in shaping an individual's propensity to criminality; and there is greater support for the two-parent family as the basic moral unit of society. New Labour has also embraced 'zero tolerance' of petty crime and 'anti-social behaviour' rather than using social policy to deal with the causes of minor deviance. New Labour is unstinting in its support for the rule of law, even when it applies to striking trade unions, environmental pressure groups and the 'socially excluded' like 'squeegee merchants' and the homeless. New Labour's education, family and law and order policies are indicative of how uncomfortable many (although not all) Labour modernizers are with the 'expressive revolution' and the progressive and libertarian social policies which were a feature of the 1960s and 1970s.[9]

Along a fourth dimension, Labour's communitarianism appears to be increasingly prescriptive rather than voluntary. 'The only way to rebuild social order and stability', Blair wrote, 'is through strong values, socially shared, inculcated through individuals, family, government and the institutions of civil society.' The Labour leader added that this should not be recipe for 'a lurch into authoritarianism or attempt to impose a regressive morality' (Blair, 1996e: 8). Yet in two senses – one to do with moral values and the other with institutional agency – Labour's communitarianism is prescriptive. First, Labour modernizers propose a value-led politics as a means of securing social cohesion: New Labour seem to be saying the moral glue which holds society together has been weakened by too much rights-claiming and too much individualism; and that a Labour government might restore the bonds of social cohesion through an appeal to greater individual responsibility and to shared values and institutions. Such an appeal to shared moral values is at the expense of more socio-economic appeals to redistributive justice and universal welfare provision as the basis of citizenship and social cohesion. While Labour's welfare-to-work programme seeks to bring about social inclusion via the labour market, the reasons for social exclusion are in part seen to be to do with the values and attitudes individuals hold. Moreover, the emphasis on individual responsibility for welfare in New Labour thinking has taken the party away from the idea that citizenship and social cohesion is rooted in socio-economic measures such as a universal welfare state and redistribution.

Secondly, at the level of agency, New Labour's communitarianism is prescriptive because, in the absence perhaps of any alternative, the party's moral agenda is being enacted by central government and by statute. New Labour talks a lot about how the community can do things individuals themselves cannot, but they often fall short of identifying exactly who or what the community is. Blair argues that '"Community" cannot simply be another word for "state" or "government"' (Blair, 1996b). But when Gordon Brown and others talk about using the 'power of the community' to pursue Labour's aims it is not clear who the community can be other than the state (Brown, 1994). While we doubt that New Labour could accurately be described as 'authoritarian', it *is* prescriptive: Labour modernizers demonstrate a willingness as public policy-makers to define and legislate the moral boundaries of the community. In the case of the Labour government's education and law and order policies, it is quite clear that it is central government which is establishing what 'the community' should do: in these social policy areas, dirigisme is still the order of the day.

By contrast, in the economy and regarding business, the Labour government has tamed such prescriptiveness, preferring voluntary agreements to legal sanctions to change corporate behaviour (Blair, 1996a; Darling 1997). This brings us to our final dimension, one which stretches from communitarianism applied to individuals to communitarianism applied to corporations. Here the moral communitarianism of personal responsibilities which go with citizenship rights has not been matched in strength by the economic communitarianism of corporate obligations which go with property rights. Corporate stakeholding, which embodies the latter, has faded away relative to the personal conservative communitarianism of the former. Stakeholding is used less in the stronger sense of obligations of companies to stakeholders other than shareholders. This was one aspect Blair proposed in his speech to the Singapore business community when he set out stakeholding as New Labour's big idea, and it is what figures such as Will Hutton continue to advocate (Hutton, 1995; Blair, 1996a; see also Kelly et al., 1997). However, stakeholding in New Labour thinking has come more to mean helping *individuals* gain a stake in society, a leg-up into the economy through its welfare-to-work programme. This is less about corporate accountability and more about individual economic opportunities. So the communitarian discourse on individual responsibility in return for rights has continued while that on corporate responsibilities has waned.

Labour's communitarianisms and the culturalization of politics?

So Labour is torn between conformist and pluralist communitarianisms and increasingly advocates conditional, morally prescriptive, conservative and individual communitarianisms at the expense of less conditional, redistributional, socio-economic, progressive and corporate communitarianisms. The result is that New Labour is more 'cultural' if that is taken to mean that it is interested in the values, meanings and identities of modern society – at the expense of the socio-economics of capitalism in any socialist or social democratic sense. As Labour has moved to accept the policy terrain left by the Conservatives in the 1990s, the politics of New Labour have taken a 'cultural turn'. The new Labour government is interested in the way people live their lives, in families, as neighbours, in the classroom, on the street; it is concerned with the values of modern British society and the extent to which those values bind the nation together: 'one nation, one community', as Blair puts it (Blair, 1996b).

However, the character of the communitarianism which New Labour has embraced inflects its cultural turn in a conservative direction, away from the cultural politics of the progressive left. It is ill at ease with the process of social, cultural and individual fragmentation, preferring to grasp onto traditional values and institutions as offering the foundations of social order. New Labour's post-Thatcherite politics – its rejection of social democracy and Thatcherite neoliberalism – is cultural in the sense that the ethics and institutions of both social democracy and Thatcherite neoliberalism are seen as having adverse behavioural and social impacts: social democracy created a rights-claiming dependency culture; and Thatcherism promoted a society of egoists. But where the cultural politics of the progressive left have sought to celebrate the 'expressive revolution' and the multiple identities of (post)modern civil society, and even in some cases the culture of the market (if not perhaps its dynamics), many leading Labour modernizers have viewed the individualism inherent in such processes with unease since they believe that it leads to the erosion of the institutions and values which provide the bedrock for social cohesion. And in the face of such processes, New Labour has embraced a cultural politics which appeals to institutions (the nation, the family, the community) and values (obligation, duty) which might re-impose order out of such perceived social and moral chaos.

But if New Labour's communitarianism is a cultural turn, albeit a conservative rather than progressive one, the idea that New Labour represents a culturalization of politics needs to be qualified in two senses. First, at the level of *explanation*, Labour's communitarianism makes as much sense seen as a *political* response to the New Right and social democracy as it does as an instance of the *culturalization* of politics. As we have outlined, Labour's communitarianism is in part a reaction to the perceived paternalistic statism and rights-claiming of post-war social democracy and the individualism and authoritarianism of Thatcherism. It may also be partly to do with perceived economic processes such as globalization which are seen to limit government economic powers; social changes such as the growth of the middle class which are seen to require changes to Labour's electoral message; and electoral limitations on socio-economic solutions such as tax-and-spend, redistribution and corporate stakeholding. It might be that, faced with limited manoeuvrability on economic egalitarianism, the party has moved to a more cultural politics where it feels it *can* have some impact.

Secondly, the cultural conservatism of New Labour's communitarianism is mirrored by a decisive rejection by Labour modernizers of the political economy of socialism and social democracy, as we saw in the first part of this chapter. The cultural critique of the welfare state – that it had adverse behavioural consequences – is interweaved in New Labour thinking with a turn away from the forms of economic management and planning associated with post-war social democracy, and which can be interpreted as a shift politically from left to right as much as from economy to culture. As with the New Right, cultural and economic arguments operate in tandem. New Labour are economically more liberal and culturally more conservative: the latter has not displaced the former.

Taken together, this combination of liberal economics and social conservatism decisively marks New Labour off from the cultural politics of identity, consumerism and difference identified in the culturalization theses we have referred to above. The liberal economics are concerned not with the celebration of the act of consumption in the market place, but with securing investment, stability and economic growth. Labour's embrace of the market is not especially desired because of an attachment to a celebration of consumption. Blair, as we have seen, has condemned the acquisitive materialism and greed cultivated by Mrs Thatcher (Blair 1996b). And the conservatism of Labour's moralism is at odds with the difference and identity politics posited as evidence of culturalization in the theses outlined at the beginning of this chapter. Influenced by postmodernism, these celebrate diversity and difference rather than uniformity and conformity. And they see fulfilment of potential coming through identity politics, whereas New Labour's emphasis, as we have seen, is on economic opportunities in the labour market. Insofar as the individual is important to New Labour it is their opportunities to gain a stake in society, their choice in the face of a pluralism of provision of public and private services, and the responsibilities they owe in return for rights that are of concern: identity is not the crucial issue here.

The stylization of politics

The last of the five culturalization theses we outlined at the start of this chapter is less about the substance of New Labour ideas, which has been our focus so far, and more about the style in which Labour has been presented. According to this thesis, the development of a mass media has resulted in politics becoming increasingly a matter of image and presentation. The political process and political culture has become caught up in the postmodern world of self-referential signs: a culture composed of constructed images without foundation where meaning is relative. In such a world, New Labour is just one soundbite rapidly rebutting another: what 'message' there is, is a concoted candy floss of words and images in search of votes. This view sees the modernization of the Labour Party as little more than an image make-over to win over an electorate concerned more with presentation than with policies.

Contemporary party politics is, certainly, as much concerned with image and appearance as it is with the substance of political programmes (Jones, 1995; 1997). The modern Labour Party has taken political communications *in Britain* to new heights – much of what New Labour did on the campaign trail had been learnt from Clinton and the New Democrats in the USA (see Rentoul, 1995, ch. 13; Jones, 1995; 1997; Butler and Kavanagh, 1997). Under the direction of Peter Mandelson (who became Labour's communication director in 1985) and Philip Gould (who had been on the campaign trail with the Democrats in the 1992 US Presidential elections), the Labour Party's political communications were thoroughly modernized. Under Mandelson, a 24-hour campaign and media centre was established at Millbank Tower on the Thames in London close to Westminster. This centre worked to the party leadership and was single-minded in keeping the party 'on message' as the election approached: 'Conservative media specialists watched in admiration as Labour politicians repeated their soundbites on the main evening news programmes' (Butler and Kavanagh, 1997: 58). Labour's 'spin-doctors', led by Blair's press secretary Alistair Campbell (former Political Editor of the Daily Mirror) and Gordon Brown's Charlie Whelan, successfully put across Labour's interpretation of events to the media, albeit bringing accusations of both bullying and flattery. Under Gould's constant prompting, campaigning techniques were brought over from the USA, most famously the Rapid Rebuttal Unit, a computerized database of information for countering the Tory message (it was used, for example, to respond quickly in November 1996 to Conservative costings of Labour's draft manifesto). Under Campbell, Labour courted the tabloid press, in particular *The Sun* and *Daily Mail*. Hopeful that the Tory tabloids would give Labour an easier ride than they did in 1992, Campbell's strategy proved an even greater success: on the opening day of the election campaign, *The Sun* came out for Blair. Across the country, Labour gathered and collated information in computer databases on individual voters in key marginal constituencies; and target voters – 'soft Conservatives' and those showing a willingness to switch to Labour – were polled by telephone before and during the election campaign; other computerized marketing techniques like target mailing were used extensively. Labour also commissioned considerable amounts of market research, including small focus groups, to test the party's message. During the heat of the election battle, Labour candidates were faxed a 'Daily Brief' at 1am to coordinate 'the message'; senior Labour figures including Mandelson, Gould, Campbell and Brown met at Millbank at 7am in preparation for an 8.30am press conference. Meeting throughout the rest of the day, the Millbank 'war room' reviewed the campaign in the light of market research and other feedback (Bulter and Kavanagh, 1997). The 'message' Labour sold at the

1997 election was also much influenced by Clinton's New Democrats: the youthfulness and dynamism of Blair and *New* Labour; the idea of 'time for a change'; and of *partnership* between government and the people. The soundbites, as Butler and Kavanagh point out in their review of the campaign, 'were relentlessly repeated': Labour's were 'Two tier health service', 'Britain deserves better' and 'Enough is enough'. And in this battle of the soundbite, Labour won (Butler and Kavanagh, 1997: 235).

Whether voters responded more to New Labour's style is difficult to judge. Blair himself proved a thoroughly charismatic leader, able to communicate with the electorate directly in much the same way as he appealed to individual Labour Party members over the heads of sectional groups. His appeal to 'one nation' (and after the election, to a 'patriotic alliance') allowed Blair to distance New from Old Labour and to project the party as a potential government which would unify the country after eighteen years of individualism. Blair's ability to strike a chord with popular sentiments has served Labour well. As news broke of the death of Diana, Princess of Wales, in 1997, Blair spoke with apparent emotion, *prefiguring* widespread displays of public grief. He called her 'the People's Princess' and negotiated a public funeral incorporating members of the charities she represented. Blair's own 'compassionate agenda' and concern 'for the many not the few' seemed in tune with a public mood which responded to the Princess's perceived like-minded humanitarianism and popular touch. And in his first Labour conference speech as Prime Minister weeks after Diana's death, Blair claimed that New Labour was expressing a more 'giving age'.

But Blair's 'popular touch', his ability to appeal to the hearts rather than the minds of voters, is not the central point. Whatever happened on the 1997 stump – and politicians since the Great Reform Act have had to present their ideas and policies to the people in bite-sized pieces – New Labour are not reducible to a marketing and media monster created by the party's very own Dr Frankenstein, Peter Mandelson. Beneath the soundbites and the ever more careful packaging *is* something substantial. Many on the left may feel uneasy about New Labour's policies, but policies there are in plenty. The first mistake, then, of a cultural view of New Labour's style is that there is nothing real behind that style. Opinion polls suggest that under Blair's leadership, Labour came to be a party trusted on issues where previously they had been thought of as soft, especially by middle-class voters: in particular, the management of the economy and law and order. The presentation of the party may have helped Labour get elected; but in the end what voters found attractive was Blair's policy reforms: on the economy, welfare reform and law and order, which were, in any case, the *substantive* base of the party's soundbites during the election campaign. According to Butler and Kavanagh: 'Surveys do not suggest that many voters decide how to vote on the basis of the skill with which a party's campaign is presented. In

1987 and 1992 Labour was widely judged to have fought at least as good a campaign as the Conservatives but lost both elections decisively' (Butler and Kavanagh, 1997: 237). The messenger could only deliver a message because there was a message to deliver. Indeed, it was the leading Labour modernizer Giles Radice who argued before John Smith's death in 1994 that the message not just the messenger had to change: style alone would not bring the party the 'southern comfort' it needed to win over middle-class middle England (Radice and Pollard, 1994).

A second problem with a cultural interpretation of New Labour's political style is that if there is a cultural turn in political communications, it happened some time ago. Political scientists have various names for this process: the 'Americanization', 'personalization', 'presidentialization' or 'modernization' of politics (see Norris, 1997). These names reflect the perceived influence of American campaigning techniques and media coverage on British electoral politics. Rather than being a recent vintage, politics in Britain has taken an 'American turn' since the 1950s, dating to the spread of television and polling (see Rosenbaum, 1996). It was in this period that politics was turned into a horse-race: the media treating elections as races between parties, with opinion polls giving a constant up-date on the position of the runners and riders; and the party managers responding by putting more and more attention into grooming the politicians in the media and public eye. This, then, brought accusations of the trivialization of politics – that it had been turned into a race like any other – and that politics was being personalized. The policy consensus in Britain in the 1950s contributed to this ever-growing focus on elections as races between personalities. And so the return of a political consensus in the 1990s has seen a return of politics as a horse-race – and so again to bring forth accusations of its trivialization. The 1997 election campaign did focus on the characters and personalities of the party leaders. Indeed, the party managers organized their campaigns on the relative merits of their man. 'Campaign reporting', argue Butler and Kavanagh, 'focused to an overwhelming degree on the utterances and the carefully orchestrated activities of the three main party leaders.' They add for perspective that there was also some indignation from the main parties that the media was failing to report what they were saying; and that the broadcast media in particular were relying on what their commentators said rather than the politicians themselves (Butler and Kavanagh, 1997: 90, 237; tables 8.4 and 9.4).

But even if contemporary British politics is becoming more American – more like the race for the White House than a sober consideration of party policy – does it mark a culturalization of politics? Again, it is worth emphasizing that beneath the spin-doctoring and the media circus of the last election were hard political choices. Some of these concerned policies – devolution and welfare-to-work, for example. Others concerned the competency and even propriety of those who sought to make public policy. In our view, this hardly makes for a postmodern politics of self-referential signs: beneath the soundbites there is something real.

There clearly has been a massive increase through the 1980s and 1990s in the degree of stylization of Labour politics. A party which previously abhored slick PR has learned to excel at it. But we would argue that at least as important as style in winning over public opinion have been changes in the *content* of Labour ideas and policies. The basis for Labour being able to present itself in an attractive way to electors was that there was in substance itself something more presentable to the electorate. Key obstacles to Labour's election in the past had been its inability to re-orient itself towards the desires and attitudes of the electorate. Labour's unilateral nuclear disarmament policy was not accepted by many; its links with the unions led many to fear union domination of a Labour government. People feared that left-wing 'extremism' may dominate a future Labour government and Labour's identification with public ownership was off-putting for many who saw nationalization as an ideological article of faith unconvincing. Middle-class people especially feared income tax rises. It is no coincidence that Conservative election strategy focused on cultivating negative images of Labour in all these areas throughout the 1980s and 1990s. And it is also no coincidence that Labour modernization under Neil Kinnock and Tony Blair focused on jetissoning policies in these areas. The key to Labour's electability in 1997 was only in part, we would argue, the carefully stylized presentation of the party. Rather than overriding substance, the key to Labour's credibility of presentation was that it was able to correspond to quite dramatic changes in the substance of party policy. Culturalization, perhaps, but on the basis of, rather than at the expense of, content.

Conclusions: New Labour and the culturalization thesis

So there is much in the changing ideology of New Labour to support the idea of a culturalization of politics. Labour is conscious of the cultural underpinnings of the economy. It has a strong ethical dimension to its politics. Its politics have been much stylized. But beyond this, Labour fits the culturalization theses we have outlined less neatly.

First, culturalization of the economy. New Labour's economics are conscious of culture. Labour has looked at other cultures of capitalism and aspire to achieve some of their strengths. But they argue that cultures and institutions cannot be transplanted. This shows a sensitivity to the cultural underpinnings of the economy. But it does not see cultural change as the basis of economic success. Labour's economic policy is mostly about the economics and social policy needed to secure economic growth rather than culture. The emphasis is still very much on technical economic solutions in economic policy – macro-orthodoxy and micro-supply-side measures. Labour's economics are a different economics. But they are still economic and not much culturalized.

The real shift is from traditional social democracy to acceptance of the main parameters set down in the economic approach of their Conservative predecessors: from one sort of economics to another and from left to right, rather than from an economic approach to a cultural one. The shift from producer to consumer interests, meanwhile, does not quite amount to a celebration of the culture of commodification. In fact, New Labour has some distaste for such a culture. They are more concerned with consumer choice and rights and as much with the political problems of identification with producer interests as with the cultural joys of consumption.

Secondly, there is social policy and the politics of redistribution. Does New Labour's neglect of the politics of redistribution demonstrate a shift to a more culturalist concern with the politics of recognition and difference? Labour have redefined social justice from economic equality to equality of opportunity. But the move away from egalitarianism has more to do with perceived economic and political limits than a culturalization of politics. And the replacement of egalitarianism with individual potential is more about opportunities than difference and as much about a shift from the left in a rightwards direction as about one from the economic to the cultural.

Thirdly, Labour's communitarianism is as much a response to political and socio-economic factors as a symptom of a process of culturalization in politics. It is also as well explained as a shift from left rightwards. To see Labour's communitarianism only as a 'cultural turn' misses out these more political explanations. Furthermore the right neoliberal and conservative substance of Labour's communitarianism marks it off from the cultural politics of identity, consumerism and difference identified in the culturalization theses we referred to above.

Fourth and finally, the stylization of politics. Labour has certainly become more style-conscious in their politics. The image has become more important relative to content. But the key to Labour's presentation of itself as a credible political force has been changes in substance. It is changes in unpopular policies, substantive changes in the organization, ideas and policies of the party and the competence and dynamism of its leadership that have enabled media management rather than been subsumed by it. Image has not superseded substance in Labour's politics but has, rather, relied on it.

Notes

1 See for example, Hutton (1995) and Albert's (1993) discussions of different models of capitalism, based to a significant extent on the different cultural configurations underlying those models. Also Harrison (1992).

2 For a fuller analysis of New Labour see Driver and Martell (1998). We shall focus on Labour's economics, social policy and communitarianism in this chapter. For reasons of time and space and because it is less directly relevant to the culture and economy issues we are dealing with here, we shall leave aside Labour's approach to political and consitutional reform – these are dealt with in our book mentioned above.

3 Although other commentators suggest they are between religious fundamentalism and liberalism, or North and South, among other possibilities.

4 Ruth Levitas (1996) argues in relation to other proposals for inclusion – from Will Hutton, the EU and the Social Justice Commission (a forerunner to Labour's proposals) – that such approaches are *too* economically focused on employment and labour market participation.

5 We have discussed Labour's communitarianisms more fully in Driver and Martell (1997).

6 We are borrowing here from Simon Caney's (1992) identification of three levels of communitarian argument.

7 These levels of Labour's communitarianisms are evident in a number of places. See, for example, Blair (1995a) and Blair (1996b)

8 Labour's communitarianisms set out as a reaction to old social democracy and neoliberalism can be found in many places. See, for example, Blair (1994b; 1995a; 1995c), and many other Blair speeches and statements collected in Blair (1996d). Also Brown (1994).

9 See Blair (1996d), Labour Party (1995b; 1996c; 1996d), Richards (1996), Downes and Morgan (1997), Straw (1996a; 1996b).

References

Albert, M. (1993) *Capitalism against Capitalism*, London: Whurr.

Blair, T. (1994a) Speech to the Unions '94 Conference, London, 19 November.

Blair, T. (1994b) *Socialism*, Fabian pamphlet 565, London: Fabian Society.

Blair, T. (1995a) 'The rights we enjoy reflect the duties we owe', The Spectator Lecture, London, 22 March.

Blair, T. (1995b) The Mais Lecture, City University, London, 22 May.

Blair, T. (1995c) *Let Us Face the Future: the 1945 Anniversary Lecture*, Fabian pamphlet 572, London: Fabian Society.

Blair, T. (1996a) Speech to the Singapore business community, 8 January.

Blair, T. (1996b) 'Faith in the city – ten years on', speech at Southwark Cathedral, London, 29 January.

Blair, T. (1996c) 'New industrial world', in T. Blair, *New Britain*, op. cit.

Blair, T. (1996d) *New Britain: My Vision of a Young Country*, London: Fourth Estate.

Blair T. (1996e) 'Introduction: my vision for Britain', in G. Radice (ed.), *What Needs to Change: New Visions for Britain*, London: HarperCollins.

Blair, T. (1997) 'Britain can and must do better', introduction to Labour Party *New Labour: Because Britain Deserves Better*, 1997 election manifesto, London: Labour Party.

Brown, G. (1994) *Fair is Efficient: a Socialist Agenda for Fairness*, Fabian pamphlet 563, London: Fabian Society.

Brown, G. (1997a) The Anthony Crosland Memorial Lecture, 13 February.

Brown, G. (1997b) 'Why Labour is still loyal to the poor', *The Guardian*, 2 August.

Butler, D. and Kavanagh, D. (1997) *The British General Election of 1997*, Basingstoke: Macmillan.

Caney, S. (1992) 'Liberalism and communitarianism: a misconceived debate', *Political Studies*, XL: 273–90.

Commission on Social Justice (1994) *Social Justice: Strategies for National Renewal*, London: Vintage.

Darling, A. (1997) 'A political perspective', in G. Kelly et al. (eds), *Stakeholder Capitalism*, op. cit.

Demos (1995) 'Missionary government', *Demos Quarterly*, 7.

Downes, D. and Morgan, R. (1997) 'Dumping the hostages to fortune? The politics of law and order in post-war Britain', in M. Maguire, R. Morgan and R. Reiner (eds), *The Oxford Handbook of Criminology*, Oxford: Clarendon Press.

Driver, S. and Martell, L. (1997) 'New Labour's communitarianisms', *Critical Social Policy*, 52: 27–46.

Driver, S. and Martell, L. (1998) *New Labour: Politics after Thatcherism*, Cambridge: Polity.

The Economist, 'Cultural explanations', 9 November.

Fraser, N. (1995) 'From redistribution to recognition? Dilemmas of a "post-socialist age"', *New Left Review*, 212: 69–83.

Gray, J. (1995) *Enlightenment's Wake: Politics and Culture at the Close of the Modern Age*, London: Routledge.

Hall, S. and Jacques, M. (1989) *New Times: the Changing Face of Politics in the 1990s*, London: Lawrence & Wishart.

Harrison, L.E. (1992) *Who Prospers? How Cultural Values Shape Economic and Political Success*, New York: Basic Books.

Hutton, W. (1995) *The State We're In*, London: Jonathan Cape.

Jones, N. (1995) *Soundbites and Spindoctors*, London: Cassell.

Jones, N. (1997) *Campaign 1997: How the General Election was Won and Lost*, London: Indigo.

Kelly, G., Kelly, D. and Gamble A. (eds) (1997) *Stakeholder Capitalism*, Basingstoke: Macmillan.

Labour Party (1995a) *A New Economic Future for Britain*, London: Labour Party.

Labour Party (1995b) *Excellence for Everyone*, London: Labour Party.

Labour Party (1996a) *Vision for Growth*, London: Labour Party.

Labour Party (1996b) *Getting Welfare to Work*, London: Labour Party.

Labour Party (1996c) *Tackling the Causes of Crime*, London: Labour Party.

Labour Party (1996d) *Protecting our Communities: Labour's Plans for Tackling Criminal, Anti-social Behaviour in Neighbourhoods*, London: Labour Party.

Laclau, E. and Mouffe, C. (1985) *Hegemony and Socialist Strategy: Towards a Radical Democratic Politics*, London: Verso.

Levitas, R., (1996) 'The concept of social exclusion and the new Durkheimian hegemony', *Critical Social Policy*, 16 (1): 5–20.

Marquand, D. (1988) *The Unprincipled Society: New Demands and Old Politics*, London: Fontana.

Norris, P. (1997) 'Political communications', in P. Dunleavy, A. Gamble, I. Holliday and G. Peele (eds), *Developments in British Politics 5*, Basingstoke: Macmillan.

Radice, G. and Pollard, S. (1994) *Any Southern Comfort?*, Fabian pamphlet 568, London: Fabian Society.

Ray, L. and Sayer, A. (1999) 'Introduction', this volume.

Rentoul, J. (1995) *Tony Blair*, London: Little Brown.

Richards, S. (1996), 'Three Rs guaranteed' (interview with David Blunkett), *New Statesman and Society*, 31 May.

Rosenbaum, M. (1996) *From Soapbox to Soundbite: Party Political Campaigning in Britain since 1945*, Basingstoke: Macmillan.

Scruton, R. (1996) *The Conservative Idea of Community*, London: Conservative 2000 Foundation.

Straw, J. (1996a) 'I have a dream – and I don't want it mugged', *The Guardian*, 8 June.

Straw, J. (1996b), 'We'll see juveniles in court', *The Times*, 3 October.

Wright, T. (1997) *Why Vote Labour?*, Harmondsworth: Penguin.

Index

Note: The letter n following a page number indicates a reference in the notes.